TORNADO OVER THE TIGRIS

TORNADO OVER THE TIGRIS

RECOLLECTIONS OF A FAST JET PILOT

MICHAEL NAPIER

Pen & Sword
AVIATION

First published in 2015 by
Pen and Sword Aviation

An imprint of
Pen & Sword Books Ltd
47 Church Street
Barnsley
South Yorkshire
S70 2AS

Copyright MICHAEL JOHN WILLIAM NAPIER © 2015

ISBN 978 1 47383 413 2

Design and artwork by Nigel Pell

Printed and bound in England
By CPI Group (UK) Ltd, Croydon, CR0 4YY

Pen & Sword Books Ltd incorporates the Imprints of Pen & Sword Aviation,
Pen & Sword Family History, Pen & Sword Maritime, Pen & Sword Military,
Pen & Sword Discovery, Pen and Sword Fiction, Pen and Sword History,
Wharncliffe Local History, Wharncliffe True Crime, Wharncliffe Transport,
Pen & Sword Select, Pen & Sword Military Classics, Leo Cooper,
The Praetorian Press, Seaforth Publishing and Frontline Publishing

For a complete list of Pen & Sword titles please contact
PEN & SWORD BOOKS LIMITED
47 Church Street, Barnsley, South Yorkshire, S70 2AS, England
E-mail: enquiries@pen-and-sword.co.uk
Website: www.pen-and-sword.co.uk

Contents

FOREWORD

by
Air Marshal G. J. Bagwell
CB CBE

The day after Mike asked me to write this foreword we met by chance in Heathrow Terminal 5. The casual observer would have seen two old friends who had not met for a while; had they had the privileged insight from reading this book they would have seen two Cold War warriors who had lived through some extraordinary times and enjoyed a life and career that for many can only be realized in their dreams.

I had the privilege and pleasure to know Mike throughout most of the period covered in these pages, and I also served alongside him during many of his exploits, including spending time on the Goldstars in the late 1980s. His story transports us back to an era when the Royal Air Force was much (about three times) larger than today. It was a time when young men and some women (the fairer sex had yet to fully-establish themselves as the equal of their male colleagues – as they have today) joined a Service that was more active overseas than back in the UK, and facing off against a Warsaw Pact, where only the fear of a nuclear exchange maintained a fragile status quo.

But we were under no illusion that the threat of a nuclear escalation would be sufficient to keep the Cold War below boiling point. And so we trained and played hard; we strived to be better than any potential adversary – and sometimes that training and preparation cost the lives of our friends and comrades in arms. But this made us stronger, and all of us carried a sense of youthful invincibility with us wherever we went and whatever we did. We were the front line of defence, and woe-betide anyone who dared to challenge our supremacy.

After the Cold War thawed those same men and women came to be tested in real combat, rather than just the cauldron of major exercises such as the fabled and legendary Exercise *Red Flag* in Nevada. The very first post-Cold War combat took place in 1991, during the liberation of Kuwait in the Gulf War; here, the RAF, and the Tornado in particular had to learn, (sometimes the hard way), that previous tactics had to adapt to meet new threats and imperatives. Since that event, the Tornado has endured twenty-four years of unbroken operational employment in Iraq, Afghanistan, Kosovo and Libya. And as I write, Tornado squadrons are flying combat missions over Nigeria, Afghanistan and Iraq. Although it is now forty years since its first flight, the venerable Tornado and her crews provide some of the most valued and feared capabilities in the air. New sensors, software, weapons and tactics, are melded together by crews who have over twenty years of operational knowledge and experience – she may not be the most modern combat aircraft but there are many on the ground who owe their lives to its presence and intervention.

Of course the RAF today is much smaller than hitherto; in the 1980s and 1990s we had more Tornado squadrons at RAF Brüggen, and more fast jet combat squadrons in Germany than we do now in the entire RAF. But things are very different today and 'peace dividends' from the belief that state-on-state warfare is a distant prospect and 'the economy-stupid' have combined to mean that defence gets far less of the budget than previously; it is a situation compounded by the slightly dubious concept of defence inflation, where we seem to get less and less for our money every year. But despite this we have never been more active and more tested by new threats and enemies who seek to outsmart and outthink us. Rightly, warfare today is a tightly controlled affair, where we play by the rules even when the enemy doesn't understand the concept of the rule of law or chivalry. We are different, and long may that be the case; this book explains how.

There are three fundamental loyalties that inspire and define combat pilots: their mates, their unit and their aircraft. Mike has brilliantly captured the importance of all three in his story and the bonds that once formed last forever. His RAF journey is very typical of many aircrew and he provides a candid insight to what it means to live and work in that environment.

Mike was always a true gentleman, but since this book focusses on his airborne exploits, it is his prowess in the air that comes out loud and clear. But Mike was much more than just a great pilot and operator, he was a comrade and friend to many and it is fitting that he took the time to write this book. Mike, those who flew alongside you salute you and thank you for telling our story alongside yours.

Greg Bagwell

Dedication

Nothing lasts forever. However, from the cosy family atmosphere of the bar in the Officers' Mess at Brüggen in 1985, those of us privileged enough to be part of Royal Air Force Germany at that time probably believed that the Cold War would do just that. In the event it was all over just five years later and now, thirty years on, the Cold War has receded in the public memory to become another semi-forgotten blemish on the course of European history. Today it is difficult to conceive the massive military infrastructure that once existed in Germany and which in its day seemed so permanent. RAF Germany no longer exists and its squadrons have long gone; only the concrete bunkers on its disused airfields remain, like mediaeval castles, as monuments to the military prowess of a bygone age – and a war that was never fought.

But a war it certainly was, by the measure of the human cost alone: the ten years that I spent flying fast jets in the Royal Air Force incurred a significant loss rate. I count myself as being exceptionally lucky firstly, to have achieved my boyhood ambition to be a front-line RAF pilot and secondly, to have survived that unforgettable experience to tell the tale. I count myself as being exceptionally lucky, too, to be able to meet my friends at occasional reunions and reminisce about the 'good old days.' For although all of us who once served together are now scattered across the world, we still see each other from time to time; and when we do, the talk soon turns to RAF days. After a few beers we imagine that we're back there in the mess bar at Brüggen, young men again fresh from a Tornado cockpit. In our imaginations we stand clutching cool beer glasses against sweaty flying suits, the faint mark of an oxygen mask ringing our faces, while we swap stories or trade good-humoured insults. Meanwhile the ghosts of others, less lucky than we were, drift through our thoughts and conversations. And it is to their memory – the friends and acquaintances I knew well, but who were not as fortunate as I was - that I dedicate this book:

Flight Lieutenant Bob Bailey	killed in a flying accident 1984
Flight Lieutenant Guy Ward	killed in a flying accident 1985
Flight Lieutenant Dave Sunderland	killed in a flying accident 1987
Flight Lieutenant Ewan Murdoch	killed in a flying accident 1987
Flight Lieutenant Paul Adams	killed in a flying accident 1988
Flight Lieutenant Steve Wright	killed in a flying accident 1988
Flight Lieutenant Mike Smith	killed in a flying accident 1989
Flight Lieutenant Alan Grieve	killed in a flying accident 1989
Flight Lieutenant Jon Marsden	killed in a flying accident 1990
Flight Lieutenant Kieran Duffy	killed in a flying accident 1991
Flight Lieutenant Norman Dent	killed in a flying accident 1991
Flight Lieutenant Max Collier	killed in action over Iraq, 1991
Flight Lieutenant Graham Southard	killed in a flying accident 1993
Flight Lieutenant Bob Bailey	killed in a flying accident 1994
Flight Lieutenant Simon Burgess	killed in a flying accident 1996
Flight Lieutenant Justin Reeves	killed in a parachute accident 1996
Flight Lieutenant Greg Hurst	killed in a flying accident 1999
Squadron Leader Mike Andrews	killed in a flying accident 1999
Squadron Leader Wez Wesley	died in an accident 1999
Squadron Leader C.J. Donovan	died 2000
Squadron Leader (ret'd) Guy Bancroft-Wilson	killed in a flying accident 2001
Flight Lieutenant Bill Auckland	died 2003
Flight Lieutenant (ret'd) Bob Brownlow	died 2004
Squadron Leader (ret'd) Mike Harland	killed in a flying accident 2007
Wing Commander (ret'd) Hylton Price	killed in a flying accident 2009
Squadron Leader (ret'd) Trevor Roche	killed in a flying accident 2012
Flight Lieutenant Ken McCredie	died 2014

Author's Note and Acknowledgements

The reminiscences in this book are completely accurate – or so my memory tells me. But the human memory is prone to error, so I have done my best to ensure that I have got things right. The manuscript is a blend of notes and diaries that I wrote at the time and articles which I wrote afterwards while events were still fresh in my mind; where I can I have also cross-checked details with my flying logbook. However, it is still entirely possible that others might remember things differently and if so, I hope that they will forgive me if their own memories tell the same story in a slightly different way.

I have tried to write the story in plain English, but despite my best efforts I have been unable to avoid entirely the abbreviations and acronyms that litter the aircrew vernacular. I've minimized their use and I have provided a glossary at the back of this book to explain the terms that I have used. I have only referred to people and military units by nicknames; if you cannot identify them, you probably do not need to know the details. However, I must apologize to the handful of individuals who may recognize themselves under unfamiliar *nommes-de-guerre*: I'm afraid that there were simply too many Douglases, Christophers and Stephens and I only wanted to use one of each!

Of course I am tremendously proud of my achievement to have made the grade and to have enjoyed a successful career as a fast-jet pilot, but I could never have done either of those things without the incredible help and support of a number of fantastic people. Although it seems unfair to name just a few of the many of them that is all I have space for, and I need to record my public thanks to:

Les Hakin, former reconnaissance pilot and flying instructor who inspired me as a young teenager and Andrew Thompson at Ellesmere who helped me so much in preparing for my second visit to Biggin Hill. Paul Smith, Andy Vodden, Geoff Linaker who started making the dream come true by teaching me to fly at Sywell. My coursemates through RAF flying training without whose support and friendship I would never have made it – Andy Jeremy, Trevor Burbidge, Julian Bourne, John Carr, Martyn Cole, Tim Ellison, Norton Hatfield and Neil Rogers. The squadron commanders who trusted in me, who gave me the opportunities to flourish and who forgave my transgressions – Joe Whitfield (to whom perhaps I owe more than most), Pete Dunlop, Jerry Witts, Andy Cairncross, Frank Turner and Tom Boyle. Finally; the three long-suffering, good-humoured and exceptionally competent navigators who

RAF Bruggen, 1994: Squadron Leader Michael Napier.

accompanied me for the large majority of my Tornado flying: Nige Cookson, Steve Lloyd and C.J. Donovan.

I am deeply indebted to Air Marshal Greg Bagwell for writing a foreword to this book. My contemporary on the Goldstars, Greg was, even then, a charismatic and inspiring leader, who was, beyond doubt, the most gifted and capable Tornado pilot of our generation.

Thank you to Mike Lumb, Marcus Cook, Tim Ellison, J.J. Burrows, Andy Jeremy and John Butler for allowing me to use some of their excellent photographs and to Dougie Roxburgh who not only provided me with photographs but also helped me sort through my own collection. Crown Copyright photographs are reproduced with the permission of the Controller of Her Majesty's Stationery Office. I should add here that 'The views and opinions expressed in this book are those of the author alone and should not be taken to represent those of HMG, MoD, the RAF or any other Government Agency.'

I'm grateful to my wonderful godfather, the late John Taylor, who was able to point me in the right direction to look for a publisher for my manuscript, to Brigadier Henry Wilson at Pen & Sword who encouraged me and to Laura Hirst who finally gave the project the green light twelve years later. My sincere thanks go to my editor Jasper Spencer-Smith for his tremendous enthusiasm and practical help.

It is a great truth that you can choose your friends but you cannot choose your family, but even with a completely free vote I would still choose the same one! I'm incredibly grateful to my parents John and Shirley for their love and for their encouragement to pursue my ambition; I'm just pleased that my father was able to read an early draft of this manuscript before he passed away. I must also record that throughout my life my 'little brother' Bob, now a hulking-great army colonel, has been the finest wingman that a fighter pilot could have wished for. And finally I am grateful beyond words to my own family, Shani, Tom and Sophie for their love and support and the interest they have taken both in this book and in the life that I had before them, 'when I had hair.' And thank you, Tom, for providing the inspiration for the book cover.

Michael Napier

Khormakhsar beach, 1966: a 6 year-old me drawing a remarkably accurate image of an English Electric Lightning in the sand.

EPIPHANY
KHORMAKSAR, ADEN, 1966

The road shimmers lazily in the heat, as it flows like a grey river through the sandy dust. On either bank, set back a little and separated from each other by a few yards of sand, the flat-roofed houses, sit whitewashed, brightly reflecting the sunlight. The greenery of their small gardens forms a string of oases on each side. There are no cars to be seen: the only traffic is a 6-year-old boy who is slowly dragging a large cardboard box between the houses along the edge of the road. Dressed only in a pair of shorts and 'chukka' boots, his back has been bronzed by the same sun that has bleached his hair.

Aden is an exciting place when you're 6 years-old; barbed wire and curfews and real soldiers with real guns only add to the adventure. Don't pick up anything you see in the street – it might be a bomb! Of course it is perfectly natural to go to primary school in the back of an army three-tonner, complete with armed escort. And here the sun is always shining and the sea is always warm. It doesn't get much better than that when you're six, especially when you have just become the owner of a large cardboard box. The boy doesn't know yet what his box will become when he reaches his friend's house just along the road – his tiny brow is furrowed as he considers the exciting possibilities. Perhaps it will be a den or even a spaceship.

Then comes a life-changing moment: A rumble like thunder reverberates between the houses. A gathering roar resonates through the air and rolls along the road. It stops the boy and he squints upwards, instinctively shading his eyes against the brightness with small hands. Then he sees them: a pair of Hawker Hunter jet fighters, black silhouettes against the azure-blue sky, like two swifts arcing across the heavens. As he watches open-mouthed, they curve away and disappear into the distance with effortless grace. Their sound follows them, fading to a low hum – and then into silence. At that instant all thoughts of dens or spaceships are banished from his mind: when he reaches his friend's house the box will become a fighter jet. And from that moment the boy knows that one day he will be a fighter pilot.

Over the sea at sunset: a BAe Hawk from RAF Valley. (Tim Ellison)

one

FLEDGELING DAYS

You don't forget your first trip in a fast jet. The moment when we punched through the cloud is indelibly etched on my mind, the feeling of sheer speed as the brilliant white sheet of stratus fell away behind and we hurtled upwards into the blue. Then, just minutes after we had left the runway, we were levelling off at 15,000ft. Up there, time suddenly seemed to stand still: there was hardly any sense of movement and we might have been hovering serenely in the quiet sky. The instructor gave me control and I gently moved the stick. The BAe Hawk quivered, obediently, answering to the slightest pressure from my hand. This aircraft, I realized, was a true thoroughbred, a far cry from the mule-like BAC Jet Provost T5 I'd spent the last year flying. And from here, on an August day at 15,000ft over Snowdonia, I could, for the first time, truly visualize the path which might eventually lead me to a front-line cockpit. And for the first time I could let myself believe that I might actually make it to the end. For the first time, too, I could look back along the route that had taken me up to my present vantage point. It had been a narrow, tortuous track, which wound its way across chasms and under deadfalls, sometimes looping back on itself and frequently passing more inviting false turnings. But I'd made it thus far.

The track had started gently enough: small, easy steps – just like any addiction. First a few drawings, then a whole book full and by the time I was 9 years-old I was clinically obsessed with aircraft. At school, while others had filled their 'Interest Books' with pictures of cars, trains, cats, dogs and furry rabbits, I had filled mine entirely with aircraft.

'Why don't you try cats and dogs in this book,' suggested the teacher as she handed me a new exercise book.

'But I'm interested in aircraft, Miss,' I protested.

'Yes, but you've just filled a whole book with aircraft, so why don't you do something different this time,' she persisted.

'But I'm interested in aircraft, Miss,' I replied yielding no ground.

'Alright then, I suppose you could *start* with aircraft...' conceded an exasperated teacher, probably in the full knowledge that the second book, too, would contain nothing else. And while my classmates read voraciously through the *Famous Five* books, I worked my way through Guy Gibson's *Enemy Coast Ahead* and Paul Richey's *Fighter Pilot*.

Books, films, Airfix models and daydreams of aircrafts kept me happy for the next few years. At my next school, in the wilds of rural Shropshire I joined the Combined Cadet Force (CCF), which seemed a first step towards fulfilling my ambition and gave me the chance to fly. Dressed in uncomfortable 'hairy Mary' trousers, with a parachute nearly as big as me dangling under my buttocks, I was loaded into the back of an ancient De Havilland Chipmunk. In the front seat, an equally ancient pilot was poised ready to fly me around the sky for twenty minutes of 'Air Experience.' I could barely see out of the back of that rattling old kite, which bore itself with none of the grace and elegance that I'd imagined of flight. In fact, the twenty minutes seemed more like a test of endurance: the combined effects of the sun's heat magnified through the canopy, the discomfort of the battledress trousers, and the nauseating odour of oil and rubber, all competed to try to persuade me to empty the contents of my stomach into the blue bag clutched tightly in my left hand!

Not long after that, I fell at the first hurdle. At the age of 16, I reported to the grandly named Officers' and Aircrew Selection Centre at RAF Biggin Hill, naively confident that I was about to be awarded an RAF sixth form scholarship. The next day, after taking the flying aptitude tests, my name was called out and I was instructed to report to the second door on the left. This was not good news – the doors on the left meant failure.

'I'm afraid that I have to tell you that you have failed the aptitude tests for pilot,' a grave-faced Wing Commander informed me, adding that I was now free to leave.

'But I'd like to carry on with the rest of the tests, sir,' I pleaded, explaining that I needed to know what else I had to sort out before I re-applied. He was dubious at first but I argued my point. Intrigued perhaps by my single-mindedness, he arranged for me to complete the rest of the tests. Two days later I sat opposite the wing commander once more.

'The board has been favourably impressed,' he told me and went on to explain what I must do before I ever came back. I must apply for a gliding course, I must spend time looking at technical drawings to learn how machines work; I must apply for a flying scholarship.

A few months later I learnt that I had been selected for a two-week gliding course over the school summer holidays. The excitement was almost unbearable as I imagined myself soaring and wheeling amongst the thermals in some sleek sailplane. The reality was rather more hard-edged, of course: the wood and canvas Kirby Cadet gliders used on the course would have looked at home on a First World War airfield and our flying was to be limited to the confines of the circuit. However, the antiquated gliders flew well enough, and their rugged construction

'Fighter Pilot': me at the controls of a Robin, Sywell, 1977.

saved me more than once from serious damage with my attempts at landing! We were kept busy and I spent the most of the time running around the airfield to retrieve gliders as they landed – the payback for the all-too-brief lessons with my long-suffering instructor. I soon realized that while I was by no means a natural pilot, I could actually do it and I was reassured to discover that I did have some aptitude for my chosen career after all. After two sun-drenched weeks, in that magnificent summer of 1976, I was sent off solo.

A year later, I discovered that the Wing Commander at Biggin Hill had been as good as his word. I had applied for a Flying Scholarship, but had heard nothing further and assumed that I'd been rejected. Then, just before the end of the summer term, a brown OHMS envelope arrived containing an instruction to report to Sywell aerodrome near Northampton. There I would learn to fly a real aircraft. When I got to Sywell, I was delighted to find that these beasts were from an altogether different generation than the venerable gliders of the previous summer. The modern French-built Robin looked to me like a spaceship and its cockpit contained such a bewildering array of instruments that I thought I would never be able to master it. I soon discovered that the whole business of flying a real aircraft was altogether far more complex than a glider. Once again my progress was that of a plodding average student rather than a high-flying natural, but soon enough I was set loose on my own in the skies over Northamptonshire. There is a sense of complete freedom and absolute power that comes from being at the controls of an aircraft in flight: even from just 3,000ft the view is quite unlike anything that a mere earthbound mortal can see. For a 17-year-old boy whose single-minded ambition was to become a pilot, the joyous feeling of achievement was unbelievably thrilling. One glorious day I took a break from practising the manoeuvres I'd been sent up to learn. Instead I spent an hour wandering this way and that, simply enjoying the wonderful experience of flight. It was a typical July day: a flock of small cumulus clouds floated lazily at 4,000ft and the summer haze blurred the distance below the horizon. I pottered about over the Pitsford reservoir and the long-disused airfield at Harrington, bumped by the occasional thermal. Northampton sprawled in the sunshine before me, joined in their turn by Wellingborough and Kettering. Round to the north and west, the gently undulating countryside, mottled with the shadows of the clouds, completed the circle. Four weeks after I started at Sywell, I was the proud owner of a Private Pilot's Licence (PPL).

My second visit to RAF Biggin Hill was rather more successful than the first and I joined the RAF as a university cadet in September 1978. I had fondly thought that I would pass most of my university days in the cockpit, perhaps popping into college for the occasional lecture, but such delusions were soon dashed. As a university cadet, I was told, my priority was to pass my exams – and therefore I couldn't fly each year until I had done so. This shattering news coincided with my discovery that my chosen subject, aeronautical engineering, was about the driest imaginable, so all in all it was a disappointing start to my RAF career! Happily, at the end of the year my enthusiasm was recharged with the annual flying camp, where I learnt to fly all over again. The RAF dressed us in flying suits and helmets, and issued us with thick checklists that were to be committed to memory. It seemed as if we were flying jet fighters rather than little training aircraft and of course we were more than happy to dress up like real pilots! In any case, the Scottish Aviation Bulldog trainer, twice as powerful as the Robin I'd flown at Sywell, seemed to me such a 'hot ship' that it might as well have been a jet fighter.

If the three years with the University Air Squadron (UAS) were a gentle and light-hearted introduction to RAF life and a rather pleasant taster of military flying, my next stop at Initial Officer Training at the RAF College, Cranwell was neither pleasant nor lighthearted. The six months that I spent on that course still seem to me to have been an utterly pointless waste of my time, which served only to turn me from a naively enthusiastic cadet into a deeply cynical, albeit extremely fit, young officer. Even the benefit of thirty years of hindsight does not enlighten me any further as to what the course was trying to achieve. The only disappointment for me on graduation from the course was the discovery that I would remain in the restrictive and suffocating atmosphere of RAF Cranwell for my basic flying training.

Our course convened a week or so later at the School of Aviation Medicine, North Luffenham. We were a mixed bunch, mainly graduates but with a smattering of slightly younger members including Digger and Bill from New Zealand and Tim the Navy who joined us from the Senior Service. From the start we got on well together and in little time, as the course progressed, adversity bonded us tightly together. Perhaps the indication that we pulled together well was that of the fifteen who started the course, only one failed to finish. The going rate for most courses at that time was a 30 or 40 percent failure rate. I still count many on that course amongst my closest friends. Where sympathy was in short supply from the RAF system, we provided it to one-another. Those who were doing well, helped and cajoled those that weren't, and the favours were repaid when the tables turned.

In the week at North Luffenham, we were taught about the physiological effects of flight – the effects that g-forces, lack of oxygen and spatial disorientation would have on our bodies. There were some very convincing practical demonstrations, including an ejection seat which fired up a test rig. It was a rather uncanny experience to strap into the seat, pull the firing handle and then find oneself, just a few milliseconds later, looking down on the tops of everyone else's heads 20ft below with no recollection of how one got there! The course culminated in an exercise in the decompression chamber to demonstrate the effects of a catastrophic loss of pressurisation at high-level and to show us the symptoms of hypoxia. Pointing out that after a decompression there would be a much greater air pressure inside the body than outside it, our friendly doctor advised us lay off the beer and avoid spicy food the night before. Of course we were far too wise to heed the advice of a mere doctor. It was a decision that we came to regret when, one by one, we had to take off our oxygen masks and breath in the heady aroma after fifteen sweaty bottoms had discharged the gaseous remnants of chicken vindaloo and Ruddles beer into the confined space of the chamber. The next week, a somewhat wiser and more cohesive group, we headed back to RAF Cranwell and the start of ground school.

Ground school at Cranwell was chiefly memorable for the allocation of nicknames. One morning we arrived at our classroom to find that one of the senior courses had defaced all our name cards. Many of the graffiti names stuck. I thought it would be best if I did not object too strongly to being called 'Mike the Knife,' as I reckoned if I said nothing it would eventually go away. In this I was correct, although the 'eventually' was about five years longer than I had hoped! Poor old Jules, earnest and scrupulously honest as ever, was foolish enough to let everyone know that he did not like his new name at all, with the result that he became known as 'Fatty' to a generation of RAF aircrew.

The good news when we got onto the flying course was that Cranwell was exclusively equipped with the Jet Provost T5 (JP5), the ultimate mark of this training aircraft. Those lucky enough to complete their training in the comparatively civilized environment of the Vale of York flying training schools had to suffer a gutless earlier version, whose throttle lever varied the noise, but not the thrust, coming from the engine. In comparison our JP5s were powerful and fast, but even so I found the machine to be a complete pig, and I cannot claim to have enjoyed the year that I spent flying it.

Despite the fact that we were now 'proper officers' our status as student pilots meant that everyone else on the station regarded us as the lowest of the low. One particularly irksome manifestation of this snobbery was when the President of

96 Hawk Course, RAF Valley, 1983: Standing l-r: Jules, Tim, Digger, Neil, Me, and Spot; kneeling l-r: ET, Trevor, and AJ.

the Mess Committee (PMC) decided that the car parking spaces nearest to the Officers' Mess should be reserved for instructional staff. Small numbered metal signs were put in front of each space and each instructor was allocated his own numbered slot. This was an injustice too far for JC and me, so we decided to do something about it. That night, in the very early hours, we crept out and removed every single sign. We put them into the boot of JC's car and headed out into darkest rural Lincolnshire. Here we found a suitably deep drainage ditch and flung the signs into it. Our little victory lasted only a few weeks, though: the PMC ordered the numbers to be painted on the tarmac!

JC's car, a magnificent Ford Capri, was our vehicle of choice to get to and from the local pubs of an evening. It took us to some wonderful places but got us into trouble, too. When we came back from the pub one winter evening, JC thought that it would be great fun to perform hand-brake turns in the snow. We drove onto the parade ground at the front of the college and spent a happy ten minutes skidding sideways round it, confident that no one could see us in the darkness. The only obstacles were some small flag posts that someone had carelessly left out on the parade ground. The following morning, standing stiffly to attention in the chief instructor's office, we discovered that the flags were the markers for that morning's initial officer training graduation parade and that the commandant was none too pleased at the random tyre tracks that had appeared across his parade ground overnight! Unfortunately the same tyre tracks had led the RAF police straight to the culprit.

The flying syllabus at Cranwell was virtually identical to that at the UAS, except that the Jet Provost went higher and faster than the Bulldog, so all the speeds, heights and distances were much greater. Even so, it didn't seem any easier and I found the course hard work. RAF flying training is a hard school, with lots of pressure and many opportunities to fail to make the grade. The course required a steep learning curve with frequent 'check rides' to make sure that the student was making sufficiently good progress. It was like a hurdle race with every hurdle to be cleared if you are to pass, and little scope for extra time for those who didn't come up to scratch. For all of us the fear of failing was very real and coloured our entire time at Cranwell: it seemed that a last 'chop ride' was lurking round every corner. My favourite days were the foggy ones where there was no chance to fly and therefore no chance of getting chopped. It was a bit like being on 'Death Row', savouring each day as possibly one's last as a pilot. Somehow though, I managed to plough a steadily average furrow through the course and was selected for fast jets, another step towards the goal of becoming a fighter pilot. The only close call I had was failing my final handling test for, amongst other things, not having clean boots! Mindless trivia was never far from the surface at Cranwell. I was absolutely delighted to see the place in the rear view mirror of my car as, with a sense of liberation, I headed towards the island of Anglesey in North Wales and RAF Valley.

RAF Valley, the home of advanced flying training, was a breath of fresh air both literally and metaphorically. Here the bracing winds blowing off the Irish Sea were mixed with burning kerosene and infused with testosterone to give a thrilling atmosphere of exciting anticipation. We flew the Hawk, a fantastic sports car of an aircraft, which was everything the Jet Provost was not – and more. The feelings of exhilaration, wonderment and power that I'd experienced as a 17 year-old in a light aircraft were as nothing compared to the sensations of flying a real, fast jet. All the enthusiasm that Cranwell had done its best to knock out of me came back with a vengeance. Our Cranwell course had been divided for the smaller Valley course and eight of us started our advanced flying training at the end of the summer. Thanks to a badly-aimed squash ball from my racquet a few weeks later, Trevor joined us from our senior course after spending a month in hospital with a detached retina; so where most courses finished with fewer students than they had started with, we actually gained one. Once again we were a very close-knit team and on the advice of Spot, our politically-aware ex-air traffic controller, we decided early on to go out of our way to make sure that the instructors noticed us. Our opening gambit was to upstage our senior course at their solo party. As junior course our job was merely to be the waiters at the event: we were to remain quiet and subservient in the presence of our betters. It was a reminder to us that we were right at the bottom of the pecking order. However, we didn't see it that way. With borrowed costumes and make-up from the station theatre we made a grand entrance dressed as the 'Black & White Minstrels'. Like most fun things, it was very politically incorrect, but it worked and we made our mark.

Flying the Hawk gave a true sense of power and freedom, and it was never more so than on the really dismal winter days. While the 'ground pounders' and civilians had nothing to look forward to but a miserably dank day, we could escape to frolic in a world of unlimited sunshine. It was a fantastic experience to get airborne from grey drizzle-soaked RAF Valley, climb up through several thousand feet of cloud and then punch out into an explosion of azure blue.

On such a day we would cruise over a shimmering carpet of white toward Snowdonia, with the sun smiling down on us. The Hawk has a comfortable cockpit: cosy, rather than small, with the controls easily to hand and an excellent view out. And most of my attention would be outside. My head would be moving constantly as I searched the sky for other aircraft. Occasionally my eyes would dart to the instrument panel to check the engine or fuel gauges, and then back outside as soon as I could. Inland, beyond Snowdonia, the cloud would inevitably break up leaving a clear piece of sky which was ideal for general-handling practice. Mostly I'd start off with some stalling and steep turns and then practise my aerobatic sequence. I was neither an adventurous nor accomplished aerobatic pilot and I usually started my sequence with a loop. It was not the most imaginative way to impress an instructor, but for me the simple uncomplicated loop contained all the sensations of moving at will in three dimensions and I didn't feel the need to do anything more. I often used Lake Bala as landmark to help keep me orientated as I looped and rolled and the 3-mile strip of water made a perfect 'line feature' to help me make sure I kept my aerobatics in a straight line. As we approached, I would run through the checks quickly to make sure that the aircraft was performing properly and all the switches were in the right place, and then have a good look around to make sure no one else was using the same bit of sky.

Then full power and slide the nose down along the line of the lake for that first loop. A gentle backward pressure on the stick is enough to bring the nose soaring sharply upwards, while the g-suit grips my legs and four times the force of gravity pushes me firmly into the seat. I grunt as I tense against the force, meanwhile the horizon reels away, pointing us upwards into the blue. As we come over the top, the force diminishes and for a second all is peaceful as the Welsh countryside floats vaguely above me. Looking up I check that we are still lined up with the lake, and then the nose drops back towards the earth and the horizon tumbles past once more. Momentarily pointing straight down as the forces increase I pull back to level flight 15,000ft above Bala. Then I carry on into the rest of the sequence. Afterwards, when my instructor has seen enough, he lets me settle myself and the aircraft and call up the radar controller for recovery to Valley.

'Victor two seven, for identification turn left thirty degrees,' a glum sounding voice. I imagine him sitting in a dim room in front of his radar screen, a half-finished cup of luke-warm coffee by his elbow. If he's lucky he might escape the darkened room later on and spend some time in the glass-windowed control tower: but today with the rain lashing down, that too will be dreary. No sunshine

Mustang 2: one of my solo close-formation sorties over Snowdonia on a gloriously clear day. Anglesey is visible in the background.

for him today. I try not to sound too smug as I acknowledge his instructions. Eventually though, we reach the cloud tops and even I must say farewell to the sunshine, as the clouds enfold us. Now the instrument panel becomes my focus. I concentrate on flying as accurately as I can while the controller feeds us towards the airfield, which lies hidden still beneath the murk. Ten miles out, I am instructed to lower the gear and carry out my pre-landing checks. Then I am handed over to the final controller, another poor mortal for who this is just another grey day in a darkened room. A pleasant female voice starts a running commentary as she talks me down the glidepath on the runway centreline.

'Slightly above glidepath, adjust rate of descent … five miles from touchdown, left of centreline, come right two degrees heading three-two-five … four and three quarter miles, on glidepath adjust rate of descent … left of centreline correcting … four and a half miles, on glidepath …'

At 500ft the murk disappears and I look up from the instruments to see the lights of the rain-soaked runway ahead of me: And so back to the dreary world of terra firma.

Our local flying area from Valley covered most of North Wales and on occasions we ranged much farther. The West Country, southern Scotland and the Midlands all became as familiar to me as the Trent Valley had been at Cranwell. No two days were ever alike, and as the course progressed, the scope for variation became greater. Here one day and then somewhere doing something completely different the next. The highlights for me were the close formation and the low-level navigation phases. One fine November afternoon found me up at 35,000ft inching towards the two other Hawks of Mustang Formation on my first solo-formation sortie.

Almost within touching distance, they glisten in the bright sunlight, bobbing slightly on invisible currents of air, trailing dazzling white banners of vapour. Seeing another aircraft in flight at close quarters is a mystical experience: there is no impression of speed, and it just seems to hover there like some kind of illusion. Close-formation flying is hard work, involving constant minute and gentle corrections and total concentration. All this effort is invisible to the casual observer: the Welsh farmer, if he happens to look up from his tractor, would just see three white lines chalking themselves across an otherwise faultless sky. Time to tail chase: one after the other my companions roll into plan form and then, with thin wisps of white streaming from the wingtips, shrink into the distance. A long plume of vapour follows each one. My turn: pressure on the stick and the horizon swivels and disappears over my right shoulder. The familiar g-force pushes against me as I follow the twisting contrail-lined avenue left for me, the horizon swaying drunkenly as I chase the other two downwards, back upwards and then down again. We continue in a long succession of lazy loops and barrel rolls. I am working hard trying to stay in the right position, cutting corners to catch up when I need to, and lagging behind the leader's manoeuvres if I'm getting too close; somewhere in all that frenzied manoeuvring I find time to think 'surely this is the recreation of the gods!'

Just a few of days later, when most people would be cursing in the early morning traffic jam, I am heading north at 20,000ft toward the Mull of Kintyre on the west coast of Scotland. This time it is a solo-navigation exercise. Letting down through a thin layer of altostratus I find myself a few thousand feet above the majestically calm blue-grey waters of Loch Linnhe. A solitary ship heads seawards, the long vee of its wake creasing the water. Ahead the granite pillars of Mull disappear into the clouds, while to the right the long finger of Lismore Island beckons me towards the start point of the day's low-level route. A quick check of the map: I streak past the lighthouse on Lismore's fingertip; height 500ft, speed 420kts. Tucking into the right-hand shore of the loch, heather and pine trees flick past in a blur of purples and greens.

A right-hand fork at the head of the loch leads to into Loch Leven. Heading east, I dart across it and up onto Rannoch Moor, a red-and-white flash over the heads (and sometimes below the feet) of hill-walkers as I continue eastwards over an alternating floor of open water and bracken-soaked moorland. Occasionally I pull out the folded map, to re-check the heading or the time to the next turning point, and then quickly tuck it back under my left thigh. Hugging the hillsides, I flash along the line of the valley following its sharp turn past Pitlochry, until I reach the lush pastures and comparative flat of Strathmore and Fife. Farms and villages replace the rugged landscape in the scenery as it rolls by. Now that I'm out of the highland valleys which have kept me pretty much on the right track, I need to concentrate more on navigation. With no large hills to stop you drifting off the planned route, the lowlands are full of opportunities to find yourself somewhere where you shouldn't be! To navigate at this speed you need to think big. Large hills or tall masts make ideal landmarks. I check the map: look ahead for the next landmark, then stuff the map back under my thigh. Too much map reading is a sure way to get completely lost. Yet here is the paradox of low flying: try to find something small and you cannot, but just happen to glance in the right direction and you can see minute detail: a bus stopping for passengers in a country lane, a child waving from a school playground as I streak past, a young mother pushing a pram along a path.

Soon I pass to the east of Kirkcaldy and pop up to 1,000ft to avoid the seagulls on the Firth of Forth, giving me the chance for a quick check that I am well clear of Edinburgh. The island of Inchkeith, like a green battleship in the midst of the cobalt-blue waters of the estuary, marks the safe passage across and on the far side I drop back down to low level, skimming over the tidy countryside to the south of Edinburgh. Way out to the left the Cheviots rise to meet the clouds, almost forming a barrier to the south, but I still need to keep a sharp lookout for any Tornados and Jaguars that might be coming out of the murk from the range at RAF Spadeadam. Looking out and navigating and flying at low level at seven miles-a-minute is pretty hard work and it takes all of my concentration to

A BAe Hawk from RAF Valley over North Wales. (Tim Ellison)

keep up. Heading west, I find myself among the rolling Tweedsmuir Hills of the Scottish borders near Hawick. Now my course is taking me across the valleys, rather than along and the 'roller-coaster ride' up over ridges and down the other side is a lot less comfortable. Although the line on the map has me cresting a series of ridges, I find that by weaving slightly I can avoid the highest hilltops and stay in the lower ground. But the world seems to be moving past a bit too quickly for comfort and my brain is reaching overload as I try to keep track of where I should be going. At last I reach the comparative flat of Dumfries and Galloway. Here navigation suddenly becomes much easier with big lakes, big hills, and big masts all around. I fumble for the map under my thigh to double check my position and am relieved to find that I am still pretty much on track, despite the weaving. A quick check of the fuel gauges tells me that there is just enough to stay low for the last run towards Burrow Head. Then full power, ease the stick back and trade all that speed for height. Back up to 20,000ft and home for lunch!

The instructors on our squadron at Valley were a great bunch, most of who had previously served together on the same Lightning squadron. The boss was a giant of a man known to us as 'Desperate Dan' on account of his uncanny likeness to the cartoon character. His attitude was that students should be seen and not heard until they had proved themselves worthy of being heard. True to form, he completely ignored our presence for the first couple of months on the squadron. However, we realized that we were doing OK when he intimated to AJ at the beginning of December that he wanted a Christmas tree on the squadron, but that he wasn't prepared to pay for it. That night the nine of us were crawling through the local nature reserve, armed with axes and saws.

Dan loved the tree and after that we could hardly put a foot wrong. A month later, however, we nearly blew it. After a week of rain and low cloud, with the forecast for it to stay that way for some time to come, we had an impromptu party in the mess bar and got completely wrecked as we worked our way through the barman's cocktail book. Of course the next morning, to our horror, the sun was shining brightly and nine very jaded students sat at met briefing.

'Right, hands up if you are unfit to fly this morning,' said Dan.

Nobody moved. We couldn't possibly admit that we'd rather be in bed for another eight hours!

'Last chance, if you're unfit to fly put up your hand.'

There was a slight uneasy fidgeting, but no hands.

'Right, you lot, I know that you were all in the bar last night and I know that none of you are fit to fly this morning. Your course flying has been cancelled today and I'm disappointed that none of you had the integrity or common sense to admit that you couldn't fly this morning. You're all banned from the bar for the next two weeks. Now we're all going on a five mile run and anyone who comes in after me is banned for the two weeks after that as well.'

At that point I think that most of us would have relished the prospect of never going to the bar ever again in our lives. But with our sports kit on and with fine sand blowing around our ankles we trotted along the beach thirty minutes later, the old competitive spirit returned, and only two of our number came in behind

A Hawk, just airborne from the westerly runway at Chivenor, climbs over Braunton Burrows. It was a huge psychological step to fly a camouflaged aeroplane.

the boss. We all learned a lesson about flying and drinking and he seemed to have forgiven us!

At the end of January it was time for my Final Handling Test. In the back seat was the Chief Flying Instructor (CFI) – the man who would decide over the next hour whether or not I would get my 'Wings.' It was one of those rare days on Anglesey when the sun was shining as I lined up on the south-easterly runway. We got airborne and as I accelerated after retracting the flaps, the throttle lever was pulled firmly shut.

'Simulated engine failure!' intoned the voice from the rear cockpit. Instinctively I pulled the nose up, trading speed for height and began a right-hand turn back towards the airfield. There, almost magically, I found myself perfectly positioned for a glide approach onto the crosswind runway. I told ATC my intentions and, holding off the other aircraft in the circuit, they cleared me to continue. The gods were smiling on me that day, as I pulled off what was probably the best practice forced landing that I'd ever flown. After a copybook roller landing I took off again.

'Very nice,' just two words from the voice behind me but I knew from that moment, for the first time ever in a test, that whatever I did thereafter, I had passed! We climbed into the upper air and overhead my old friend Lake Bala I was able to demonstrate that my stalling was adequate, that my steep turns were average and that my aerobatics were agricultural. Next, down to low level to find a target in the Yorkshire Dales: I missed it. Bang! Another simulated engine failure just west of Harrogate. Speed for height and we zoom above the solid clouds as I make a call on the distress frequency for a steer to the nearest suitable diversion airfield. According to the controller the nearest one is Linton-on-Ouse, quite a few miles away. I head towards it, but are we going to make it? Then through a gap in the clouds I recognize RAF Dishforth adjacent to the traffic-laden A1 trunk road. I swing round towards it and tell the distress and diversion controller that I'm going to Dishforth instead and he needs to let them know I'm coming. My second simulated forced landing of the day is not as polished as the first, but it is good enough and as we climb away, the CFI switches on his microphone: 'OK I've seen enough – take me back to Valley.'

The fast-jet course had been hard but enjoyable and often exciting work. At the end of it came the ultimate prize – a set of RAF pilot's wings. Once again we had pulled each other through the inevitable struggles and all nine of us were still there on 3 February 1984, our 'Wings Day'. It was certainly the proudest day of my life up to that point, the achievement of an ambition set nearly twenty years beforehand. There had been times, particularly at Cranwell when I wondered if I'd ever make it this far. Passing this series of courses, as I had, required a certain amount of pure flying skill, but more than anything else it needed the qualities of determination and tenacity.

Up until the end of the Valley course, the emphasis had been on learning to fly. But in military aviation, flying is not just an end in itself, but the means to attack a target. The next logical step was to learn how to use the aircraft that we had just learnt to fly, as a military tool. That next step was carried out at the Tactical Weapons Unit (TWU). Two such units existed, one at RAF Brawdy on the Pembroke peninsula near St David's, and the other at RAF Chivenor near Barnstaple in North Devon. My first stop was neither of those places, in fact, but the Aircraft & Armaments Experimental Establishment (AAEE) at Boscombe Down because of a backlog in the training system. Here I spent six months as an odd-job man for the Tornado Operational Evaluation Unit (TOEU), a small cadre of experienced Tornado crews whose job was to trial various new tactics and weapons and to decide how best to use various modifications to the aircraft. They were a friendly team and they made me feel welcome. I was given various projects to keep me occupied, including helping Vic, one of the navigators, with his Open University homework! During my time I was taken for two backseat rides in a Tornado as a reward for my hard work. But although I had been made welcome, I missed my friends and it was a very lonely six months. I was pleased when it was all over and I headed for Chivenor and the next rung of the ladder.

Chivenor shared the same exciting atmosphere as Valley, and two refinements improved it further. Firstly it was a tiny station – you could easily walk around it – so it had a very 'village-like' feel about it. Secondly it was run by the front-line RAF Strike Command rather than the more academic RAF Support Command.

This meant that the Hawks at Chivenor were not painted in the eye-catching red-and-white finish of training aircraft, but were a dull grey and green camouflage, like 'proper' warplanes. It was an important psychological step for us would-be fighter pilots. Where the flying-training syllabus at UAS, Cranwell and Valley had all been very similar in content, but carried out at ever increasing speeds, the syllabus at Chivenor was like nothing we had seen before. Here an ability to fly the aircraft was taken as read, and we were expected to use our skills to learn the rudiments of tactical formation, air combat and weapon delivery.

Just as at Valley, I was lucky to arrive on the 'good' squadron. The other squadron at Chivenor was not a happy place and the instructors used the rather unhelpful 'I can do it, why can't you' method of instruction. Just after we arrived we dropped in on a stressed-looking JC, now on the course ahead of me, in his room, preparing for a 'chop ride' the next day. We all rallied round and the usual remedy of a jog around the airfield followed by beer and sympathy apparently did the trick: JC passed the course and later went on to fly Phantoms, Jaguars and F-16s. The course members were made up from my Valley course and by now we had almost become a family. Again we were always there for each other when the going got tough.

After a brief ground school we started flying. Some general handling revision and an instrument rating and then we were into the course. The first skill that we needed was how to fly in tactical formation: this was completely different to the close formation that we had learnt at Valley. Leader and wingman flew on parallel courses a mile apart, each able, by craning their neck round to check the 'kill zone' right behind the other's aircraft. In theory, if flown properly it was impossible to sneak up behind such a formation, but of course the pilots also had to navigate and look everywhere else - as well as behind – so reality made it less vulnerable. There was also the complication of turning corners – if the leader simply turned, the wingman would suddenly find himself well in front, or well behind, the leader and the critical cross cover would be lost. The solution was the 'double assisted turn,' a bewildering method in which both aircraft turned towards each other and crossed over before turning back towards the new heading and rolling out once again in battle formation. The turns were flown at an aggressive 4-g and then with two aircraft pointing at each other at closing speeds close to 900kts, there was a massive scope for hitting each other! The first few trips at Chivenor were designed to ensure that we always knew who was avoiding whom. Our low-level navigation skills were honed, too, at first on our own, then as pairs of aircraft flying in the recently learnt tactical formation.

Low level flying was something of a challenge at Chivenor, not least because apart from the fancy new paint scheme, our new warplanes also carried a gunpod under the fuselage and weapons pylons under the wings, all of which caused more drag and thus a much higher fuel consumption than we'd been used to at Valley. A further complication was that the aircraft had an appalling gyro compass which was liable to spin round uselessly at the critical moment, usually when you needed to check the heading after you rolled out of a turn. In fact one or two aircraft had been modified with the more reliable compass we had used at Valley, but inexplicably

Norman and Me, about to set off for a 'composite' gun and bomb sortie over Pembrey Ranges.

these were always allocated to the staff pilots. Finally, the camouflage paint job was so good that in formation the element leader often simply disappeared against the background, making station keeping virtually impossible!

With more practice we learnt to work around these new challenges, but inevitably as soon as we had almost mastered one new skill it was time to move onto the next one. Indeed that was the pattern at Chivenor and the mental workload on every sortie was extremely high. As well as flying an aircraft at seven miles-a-minute, perhaps only at 250ft above the ground, you had to juggle the tasks of looking all around for the 'enemy,' navigating accurately and keeping formation. All this takes a massive amount of processing power in the brain. On many occasions, if someone had asked my name while I was flying I wouldn't have known the answer because I was literally working to my mental capacity.

My own favourite discipline at Chivenor was air combat and it was the only thing all through my training in which I excelled. Starting at about 15,000ft in the now familiar tactical formation, we would turn away from each other, then reverse the turn to end up pointing head-to-head, a position with no advantage to either one. The aim now was to manoeuvre behind the opposition's tail and shoot him (with the camera) while he tried to do the same to you.

Mid-October and I'm on my first solo one-versus-one air-combat sortie. Head on the other Hawk flashes past, but in the instant of crossing I see him start to manoeuvre. I pull up high and left into an oblique loop, my neck twisted over my shoulder to try and keep sight of him.

Under the g-force, my head in its heavy flying helmet weighs over five stones (70lb) and all that weight is taken by my twisted neck, causing an involuntary scream from the pain, but I know that I've got to keep looking if I'm to have any chance of winning. The nose comes down and I see him coming up at me in a left-hand turn. With the nose almost vertically down and his flightpath now predictable, I roll quickly to grab a handful of advantage, and as we cross the second time, I see that I've already got some angles on him. I keep rolling and pulling with the wings just 'burbling' in the lightest hint of buffet on the edge of the stall – their way of telling me that I'm getting the best lift out of them. A glance to make sure that we're well above the 10,000ft base height: it is 'the ground' today, so if I descend below it I've crashed and lost the fight. More grunting and screaming as the g-forces build up and we flash past each other a third time. No change in angles, but I've still got the advantage. Upwards again, all the time rolling to keep myself pointing ahead of him.

We continue round, each trying to gain a little on the other, trying slightly different gambits. A little more use of the vertical, or unloading to 0-g for a second to accelerate up a few knots of airspeed. But always back to the relentless 6-g and always back to the slight burble of buffet. Pull too much and the wing will buffet and stall, too little and you won't be turning as well as the other man. Playing the buffet needs a delicate touch. There is a time for coarse manoeuvring, but you have to know when – air combat is not for the hamfisted. Mentally, too, air combat is a careful game of patience, stealing a couple of degrees of advantage here or perhaps trading some angles for a bit more separation there. If you try to grab too much you inevitably end up sailing out right where you don't want to be – in front of him!

Then some luck – I've managed to manoeuvre myself into the piece of sky directly between the sun and him.

'Lost Tally,' he calls – he can't see me any more, and I see him roll wings level and dive towards base height.

'Continue,' I call, trying hard not to let a trace of excitement into my voice. I relax the g-forces so that the aircraft can accelerate and get back some of the energy used up in the hard manoeuvring. Staying high, I stalk him, while he, turning this way and that, tries to get sight of me once more. Eventually I am high directly above him and shove the nose vertically down, the throttle right back so that we don't go zooming past. He sees me as I swoop down and breaks to the left. But it's too late I stay with him long enough to track him, camera running, through the break.

'Knock it off,' time to set up again. At Chivenor, air combat was called 'The Sport of Kings' and how right that description was.

The weapons range at Pembrey was our focus for the middle of the course. It was the first time we had fired anything from an aircraft and was another important psychological step for us. On the Hawk, the gun was mounted in a pod under the fuselage and the practice bombs, just 3kg 'flash-and-smoke' spotting charges, were loaded under the wings. We started learning weaponry by firing the gun at hessian panels held between posts on the beach. My first trip to the range was with Spike on a sortie which marked almost exactly the halfway point of the course. We headed across the Bristol Channel at a leisurely 1,500ft below a grey overcast, aiming for the dark cliffs at Worms Head on the Gower Peninsula. From there we crossed Burry Inlet and beyond it I could make out the disused airfield at Pembrey. A large forest extended from the airfield and as we neared it the rough area of the range was visible as a spur of golden sand at the tip of the inlet. I still couldn't see the targets until Spike took us around the airfield onto a short base leg. And there they were, two tiny-looking white squares, with white dotted lead-in markers showing the correct line of attack. We tipped in towards them in what seemed to be an almost vertical dive as Spike delivered his Qualified Weapons Instructor (QWI) patter on how to strafe. In the last moments I felt an incredible sensation of ground rush just before we pulled up at a stomach-churning 6-g. Nose up until we get to 1,500ft, then a 4-g turn crosswind, roll out, pause, then another 4-g downwind and Spike runs through the checks. Two more 4-g turns in quick succession and suddenly we're diving earthwards again. Just as I feel the rush again there is a loud rattling 'ratatat' from somewhere under my feet, and then the g-force comes on again as we rocket back up towards safety. A satisfyingly acrid waft of burnt cordite fills the cockpit. I'm in an aircraft that has fired a gun! It's an incredible and almost surreal feeling. Four more turns at 4-g and it will be my turn.

I found the sighting very difficult to judge and as a result was not very successful at strafing, which was particularly difficult in the Hawk: the cannon had a relatively low muzzle velocity so in order to hit the 15sqft hessian target

Lined up on the runway for my SAP 2 sortie, Rammo in the back seat.

you had to open fire at about 350yd. If you were still firing at 300yd, you were deemed unsafe and sent home! At the speeds we were flying the bracket for firing was only a second or so long. Being something of a coward, I always opened fire well out of range. The added problem with my method of opening up way out of range was that even if the cannon shells hit the target, they wouldn't register with the 'acoustiscore' system. This was a microphone at the base of each panel which counted the number of shells it 'heard' going past. Because of the cannon's muzzle velocity, if you opened up out of range, the shells were going too slowly by the time they reached the target to register on the acoustiscore! However, despite my relative lack of success, at least I wasn't unlucky like Jules, who was on the course behind me at Chivenor. He nearly managed to shoot himself down on the range, when a shell ricocheted from the strafe target and hit his aircraft as he pulled up from the pass. The bullet bounced round the cockpit, missing his head by inches on three occasions, before firing the detonating cord designed to shatter the canopy in the event of ejection. Left in an open-top Hawk, with small pieces of the shattered canopy embedded in his face, he very calmly and courageously brought the aircraft back to Chivenor. There were many beers drunk in the bar that evening. After that, Jules was sent to the Air Defence Phantom where he would never need to strafe again!

After a couple of sorties' worth of strafe, we were introduced to bombing. We started with dive-bombing, which followed a very similar range pattern to strafing. The targets for our bombs were circles of old oil drums. This, I found a

little bit easier. Whenever the weather was good enough we went to the range. After dive-bombing came level bombing, a particularly demanding exercise in precision flying as the smallest error in height, speed or pitch would cause massive errors in the fall of the bomb. The Hawk was not fitted with a radar altimeter, so instead each aircraft had a calibrated height to fly on the altimeter. Although it was a rather 'Heath-Robinson' arrangement it seemed to work pretty well. The range sorties also included a couple of 'composite' sorties with strafe and dive-bombing in the same detail. Having been streamed to fly the Tornado, I flew one of these with my navigator Norman. The final weaponry event was air-to-air gunnery, which was carried out against a 20ft banner, towed behind another Hawk. The cannon shells loaded into each aircraft's cannon were painted with a different dye: when (if) a shell hit the banner it left a trace of colour around the hole, so that the number of hits scored by an idividual aircraft could be counted. Red was always a popular colour as it showed up well (especially for a surreptitious check as you left the range) but green was another good one as it was suspected that when the flag landed on the grass after it was released over the airfield, it picked up a bit of grass stain, which always helped! It was always an exciting moment when the flag-tow recovered back to Chivenor and dropped the flag. It would be retrieved by ATC who would deliver it to the waiting throng. The flag would be laid out on the grass in front of the squadron offices and the QWIs would start to count the holes.

German Tornados on the Tri-National Tornado Training Establishment, RAF Cottesmore. (John Butler)

The grand finale of the course was the Simulated Attack Profile (SAP) phase. This was flown in pairs, at low level with two pop-up dive attacks on targets in the low-flying areas. Typically the targets included bridges, buildings and electric substations. Halfway through the phase a 'bounce' aircraft was brought into the scenario: the bounce would try and shoot down the strike aircraft, so the strikers had to make sure that their formation and lookout was immaculate. Once they saw the bounce the pair had to manoeuvre to counter the threat, before fighting their way back towards their target. The SAP phase brought everything together: formation, low-level navigation, air combat and weaponry. It was undoubtedly the most demanding phase of the course but it brought with it an incredible sense of achievement and if you had the spare mental capacity to notice (most of us did not!) it was great fun, too! The penultimate SAP was the last trip that counted and it included a timed First-Run Attack (FRA) on the range was well as the field target and, of course, a bounce. The final sortie was a bit of a 'freebie' – a staff-lead four ship in which the students flew in the Number Two and Four slots, again with a bounce and another FRA. It was mind-boggling in complexity and served to remind us that despite the hard work and almost vertical learning curve of the previous four months, we had only just reached the lowest rung of the ladder!

About two thirds of the way through the course, we were told where we would be going at the end of it. Normally this decision was not taken until after all the flying had been completed, but our course included an experiment to try and crew up trainee navigators with pilots for the last few sorties, so that those destined for the two-seat world would get used to this way of operating. We had been joined at the beginning of the course by five navigators fresh from their training school at RAF Finningley. We were wary of them at first, not least because to be seen socializing with navigators might be to invite a two-seat posting prematurely. For fast-jet pilots, the very zenith of achievement was a posting to a single-seat aircraft like the Harrier or Jaguar, and such postings were hotly contended. I was not overly bothered by this machismo and found the navigators, particularly a pleasant Scot by the name of Alan, to be good company. Both Alan and Cookie were bound for the Tornado, a posting which would have delighted me. I had moved on from my earlier dream of flying Phantoms when I realized that it was low-level flying that I enjoyed most. Over a beer one evening Alan and I decided that if there were any choice, he and I would ask to be crewed together.

When the day of our role-disposal came, we pilots were lined up in the bar and a small innocuous drink and a pint of beer were placed in front of us. We were told to down the small drink in one, and seeing that this was no particular challenge, we did so. Almost instantly a burning sensation seared its way down and we had to drink the pint of beer straight away to soothe our throats and get rid of the awful taste. The small drink was chilli vodka brewed by the navigators and the pint of beer had at the bottom a note with our aircraft type and the name of navigator. I had a double take when I peered into the bottom of my glass: the first thing I saw was the name of Norman, a Buccaneer navigator. I had nothing against Norman, but I really didn't relish the thought of the ancient Buccaneer. Then, as I looked closer, the beer-foam slipped down a little more and I saw that I was posted to the Tornado. Alan and AJ had been crewed together, as had Cookie and Trevor and they would end up a course or two ahead of me on the Tornado conversion. However, I would catch up with AJ, Alan and Cookie again later when we were all posted to the same squadron at Brüggen, where, eventually, I would be crewed up with Cookie. I finished the rest of the course with Norman, before we parted our ways and I headed off to the Tornado.

The Tornado was designed and built jointly by the Italians, Germans and the British and some great intellect decided that since the aircraft was produced tri-nationally, it followed that the aircrews should also be trained tri-nationally. The result was a rather curious course in which the inflexibility of the Germans and the relaxed nature of the Italians were hosted by the British. It achieved very little, since each nationality (except perhaps the Italians) then had to undergo their own course to learn what was needed before moving on to a front-line squadron. However, for us Brits it was a very welcome break from the pressures of RAF flying training, even if it was only a temporary respite. The staff on the next course, UK-only Tornado Weapons Conversion Unit (TWCU), were reputed to believe that it was their duty to supply the ration of 'hard time' we had missed from our European partners, as well as giving us a full ration of their own.

The front cockpit of a Tornado: It is dominated by the circular 'moving map' display in the centre and the Head-Up Display (HUD) immediately above. To the left are the flight instruments; the engine instruments are to the right. The screen above the flight instruments is the E-scope and the one above the engine instruments is the radar warning display. The throttles and wing-sweep lever are on the left console with other systems on the right.

The Tornado was as much an increase in complexity over the Hawk as the Robin had been over the glider. A similar bout of self doubt seized me as it had done eight years previously, so it was probably a very good thing to learn the groundschool in the relaxed Italo-Germanic atmosphere. The simulator sessions, so often a beasting session in the RAF, were particularly superb. Sitting in the simulator was just like flying the real thing in thick cloud. The cockpit was a faithful replica of the real thing; all the switches and controls worked properly, and massive hydraulic jacks tilted it around to make it feel as if you were really flying. The only thing lacking was a view of the outside world, as the canopy was a dull opaque grey, much the same shade as the inside of a dark rain cloud. We were given ten 90-minute sessions in the simulator to learn the comprehensive checklists and get used to the procedures before we were allowed in a real aircraft. After the ten simulator sorties I felt just about ready for the real thing.

Eventually the great day came. My flying instructor and I were dropped off at the engineers' line hut where we inspected the aircraft's engineering logbook and

Crewing-in at TTTE: a German student clearing a German Tornado at TTTE – British groundcrew of course! (John Butler)

exchanged some pleasantries with the groundcrew, then proceeded to walk the 100yd across the concrete apron where our aircraft stood amongst the neat line of Tornados. Unfortunately, while we were in the line hut the heavens had opened and we made the walk (running was out of the question with all the bulky gear we were wearing) in a downpour of tropical proportions. By the time we had reached the steps of the aircraft, I was completely soaked. We opened the canopy, jumped in quickly, then closed it again before any more water could flood in, and continued the intricate process of strapping in. This is usually done with the canopy open and one of the groundcrew to help, so it was quite a job to do it alone with the lid closed. By the time I had done up the last strap, I was in quite a sweat. I then busied myself with the tortuous task of firing up the machine, a good thirty minutes' worth of work for a new boy like me. At last I had got us ready to taxi and was able to look up from the instrument panels for the first time. I thought I was back in the simulator: all the controls and equipment were working as advertised, but I couldn't see a thing outside – we were completely misted up! All the moisture that had evaporated off my sweaty flying suit had condensed on the inside of the canopy.

Eventually I managed to clear a small area of the front of the canopy and we were able to taxi gingerly towards the runway, with me peering out of the tiny transparency. On the ground the Tornado was nothing like the Hawk's bone-jarring ride, it loped along with a spongy springiness as the undercarriage oleos smoothed out the bumps. More checks before we reached the runway, then we were cleared for take-off.

I couldn't fail to be impressed by the surge of power as I pushed the engines into reheat, only to be pushed back into the seat myself by the acceleration as the Tornado thundered down the runway. I pulled back the stick and the aircraft lifted off cleanly and rose eagerly into the air: And I might as well have been in the simulator once again. We had climbed straight into thick cloud, where we remained for the next fifty minutes. The altimeter told me that I had climbed to 25,000ft, and the moving map display showed me that I was touring the skies over Lincolnshire, but all I could see of the outside world was the swirling grey mist. Eventually after a radar talkdown we popped out of the cloud again at around 200ft, the airfield lights shining bright in the damp air, and I plonked the aircraft onto the glistening runway.

The whole thing had been just like simulator sortie number eleven!

I was crewed up for the course with a US Air Force major on a NATO exchange posting. I think he found being flown around England by an *ab-initio* British student pilot in a European-built aircraft to be a surreal experience, poor chap! We were allowed to fly together only after each had done some time with staff instructors and reassured them that we weren't going to kill ourselves. After what seemed an incredibly short time under supervision, we were let loose on our own. Mike and I had a great time flying around together, but I still cringe when I think of the two of us flashing around in an aircraft so complex that neither of us fully understood how it worked! However, we achieved the exacting standard required of us and said our farewells as I headed for the dreaded Tornado Weapons Conversion Unit (TWCU), and he for his desk at NATO.

At this stage it would be useful to take a tour of a Tornado. The first thing that strikes you about the aircraft is the enormous tail fin, which dominates the side view of the aircraft, giving rise to the aircrew's imaginative nickname for it, 'The Fin'. Although the Tornado is quite big, nearly 55ft long in fact, the fin gives it an overall squat and angular appearance. The second feature of note is the wing, or more specifically the 'swing wing.' The swing wing is the 1960s' answer to the problem of the swept wing: to go really fast you need a sharply-swept wing, but the problem comes when you slow down to land as a swept wing doesn't work particularly well at low speed and the aircraft then flies like a pig. Nowadays, the problem has been overcome by clever aerodynamicists who didn't find aeronautical engineering as 'dry' as I had, but the Tornado solution was to have a wing that was virtually straight for take-off and landing, and could be swung back to give a more swept wing at higher cruising speeds. Swivelling pylons on the wings meant that anything mounted under the wings always faced forwards, no matter the angle of sweep. Usually there was a fuel tank and an electronic warfare pod slung under each wing, and air-to-air missiles could also be carried.

This left the underside of the fuselage for carrying bombs; more usually, though, we carried a dispenser for the same 'smoke-and-flash' practice bombs we'd used at Chivenor, or yet another fuel tank. Thus virtually the whole underside of the aircraft − wings and fuselage − had things dangling off it. This made the Tornado look particularly pugnacious but also created a huge amount of aerodynamic drag. It was always a mystery to me why the designers hadn't made the thing with an internal bomb bay, which would have cut the drag and made the aircraft go further and faster.

At the back of the aircraft, under the huge fin, were the jetpipes for the two engines. If the pilot wanted lots of extra power and wasn't overly worried about how much fuel he used, he could select reheat on the engines, at which the jetpipe nozzles would open up fully and raw fuel would be pumped at a fantastic rate into the hot exhaust gas from the engine, where it would ignite. The result was a spectacular sheet of blue flame out of each jetpipe, a spectacular rate of acceleration as the engine power doubled accompanied by a spectacular increase in the noise; more critically, there was also a spectacular increase in the fuel consumption. We used reheat for every take-off, but only sparingly in flight, because of the gargantuan fuel penalty. On those occasions when there was fuel to burn, the acceleration was truly phenomenal.

At the front of the aircraft, under the sharply-pointed radome were two radars. One was the ground-mapping radar used by the navigator to help him find targets. The other was a Terrain Following Radar (TFR), used by the autopilot to fly the aircraft at low level in cloud or at night. This was really the whole crux of the Tornado: the RAF was committed to flying and fighting at low level, but the weather in northern European meant that for more than half of the year this wasn't possible. With Tornado, darkness or low clouds were no longer a limitation, and the RAF now had the capability to attack twenty-four hours a day all-year round.

When you get close up to a Tornado, you become aware of its size and bulk. The cockpit is 8 or 9ft off the ground, and you need a ladder to get into it. In fact there is another way, involving clambering up onto the tailplane and then walking along the spine of the aircraft, a route marked at regular intervals with small notices saying 'No Step'. Although probably meant as an instruction not to tread on the various parts, we interpreted them as indicating where to go if there were No Steps with which to climb into the cockpit!

Once in the cockpit, you are aware of sitting quite high. The cockpit is comparatively roomy, especially compared to the close-fitting Hawk. The ejection seat is reasonably comfortable, with an electric motor to adjust the seating position up and down. Strapping in is rather like getting into a bowl of spaghetti. First a chunky metal attachment fitted with one's oxygen hose, g-suit hose and intercom wire clunks into position on the left of the seat, connecting you to the aircraft systems, then comes a series of straps over legs and torso which connect to a big fastener over the stomach to attach you to the integrated seat and parachute harness; finally leg and arm restraints clip onto each limb to ensure that they don't flail wildly about if you are unlucky enough to have to use the seat. The seat is fired by pulling a yellow and black-striped D-handle just between your legs.

The pilot's cockpit is dominated by the glass screen of the Head-Up Display (HUD), just in front of the windscreen, so you have to look through it to see out of the front; just beneath it is the 12in diameter moving-map display. On either side of the display, are all the other important instruments, all easy to see. The consoles running along the sides of the cockpit contain numerous switches for less important systems, or ones that don't need constant monitoring. The whole array is well-laid out and most things are easily at hand.

Your left hand falls naturally to the throttles on the left console, at mid-thigh level, while your right falls to the stick, which is between your legs. The reason the HUD dominates the cockpit is because it is the prime instrument for flying the aircraft. All the information you need, speed, height, attitude, weapon aiming and lots more, is projected onto the glass screen, so that when you look through it the information appears as green symbols on the far horizon; using the HUD is instinctively easy. The moving map is a projection of a normal low-flying chart, which moves with the aircraft so that when you look at it, it shows you exactly where you are on the map. This assumes of course that the navigator has kept the aircraft's computer properly updated, because if he hasn't the moving-map world can be somewhat at variance to reality!

The navigator sits immediately behind the pilot, so his forward view would be obscured by the pilot's ejection seat, if his own displays weren't already in the way. Controlling the aircraft navigation systems and most of the weapon selection and aiming are all carried out by the navigator.

The Tornado cockpit would eventually become like a second home to me, but when I arrived at TWCU at RAF Honington for the final phase of my training it was still a place of mystery. As advertised, the staff were quick to remind us we were back in the RAF and that we should therefore expect the usual harsh treatment. In many ways it was a bit like going back to Cranwell and I cannot say that I enjoyed my time there. I still found the aircraft intimidating, with a Jet Provost-like mind of its own in comparison to the agile and obedient Hawk.

The bulk of the course was an introduction to the many and diverse methods of dropping bombs from a Tornado. We practised the various profiles on the weapons ranges in the Wash, where an assortment of orange-painted hulks lay forlornly on the mud flats. Apart from the familiar methods of laydown (in other words flying straight over the target) and dive-bombing which we had already done on the Hawk, we were taught an interesting and highly entertaining method called 'loft'. Loft involved charging towards the target at nearly 500kt just 150ft above the Wash, while the navigator marked the target on the radar. At around four miles short of the target, you lit the reheat and pulled upwards. Having done its calculations, the computer then released the bomb at the appropriate point so that it would fly the remaining three miles or so to the target; meanwhile, as soon as the bomb came off, you overbanked to a semi-inverted attitude, pulling the aircraft smartly back down to low level and then scuttled off in the direction you'd come from, without having to overfly the target. This would be a particularly fine idea if the target was shooting back! Needless to say this method could be rather (literally) hit and miss, and the recovery manoeuvre also gave great scope for killing yourself if you got it wrong.

My problem was that my brain found space for all this new information by dumping the stuff it had learnt on earlier courses! I could fly a decent loft attack but then I couldn't fly a circuit. After nearly hitting my leader during a pairs take-off, I had to fly an extra close formation sortie, after which came some extra circuit trips. Despite their harsh rhetoric, the instructors rallied around to help me. Or most of them did. At one briefing for a night-flying sortie, a particularly obnoxious navigator dramatically announced that he wouldn't fly with me because I might kill him; he then flounced out of the ops room like a petulant teenage girl. In the embarrassing silence that followed it was clear that the rest of the staff would have been quite happy if I had killed him! Then the avuncular unflappable Keith stepped forward and invited me to take him flying instead. For this his reward, after a 1½ hour night TFR during which we almost went supersonic accidentally over the Vale of York, was a Direct Hit (DH) from our loft pass. I think that Keith was so pleased at getting a DH that he forgot that I'd almost taken us through the sound barrier. As we had climbed over the North York Moors, the autopilot had selected full power, but unfortunately did not deselected it as we descended towards the lower ground on the other side. Going downhill with full power on the Tornado accelerated well, but I was concentrating so hard on other things that the first I noticed was the deep hum, like an organ pipe, as the supersonic shockwave formed on the canopy! Luckily, yanking back the throttles was all that was needed to stop us shattering all the windows in Pickering.

For the rest of the course I was crewed up with Huggy, our course commander, who took me aside and said, 'don't worry, Mike, we'll get you through!' He was true to his word, as were Tom, Den and Al who had the misfortune of sitting in the backseat while I struggled around extra circuit sorties like a basic flying training student, and Macalps and Ricky who took me under their wing and saw me through the operational phases of the course. I could not have asked for more, but my overwhelming emotion was sheer relief rather than gratitude, when I successfully finished the course.

two

THE FIRST CRUSADE

At the end of the course in October 1985, I was delighted to be given the posting of my choice to the Crusader Squadron, at RAF Brüggen in Germany. The unit was the third squadron at Brüggen to re-equip with the Tornado. Here I was reunited with AJ, Alan and Cookie from my Chivenor course as well as JB, Jeremy and Rambo who were all of a similar vintage. I was also pleased to discover that my flight commander would be Vic, whom I knew from Boscombe Down days. The Boss, a tall ex-Jaguar pilot called Joe, had previously been at the Personnel Management Centre (PMC), so he had been able to handpick most of the squadron members. I suspect, though, that this did not really work out as he had hoped: in practice it simply corralled lots of large egos into a confined area. The senior Flight Lieutenants were unhappy because they all thought that they should have been promoted long ago and the Squadron Leaders were busy scoring political points off each other. Unfortunately Vic came off rather badly here, as he suffered from two career-limiting character faults: firstly he was outspokenly honest and always said what he really thought, and secondly he was invariably right.

Paradoxically the part of the squadron over which the Boss had no choice, worked very well together: we 'First Tourists' were already quite a close-knit team and our little group just attached itself to the rest of the squadron. With no pretensions about careers and still in the throes of childishly naive joy at surviving the flying-training system, we took everything at face value and threw ourselves into our new environment. I think that over the next two years the Boss got to love us, but I also know that I personally caused him many pangs of exasperation.

At that time the Cold War was in still full swing: the Russians were expected to swarm across the Inner German Border at any moment. Brüggen, bastion of the RAF's front line, sat on the Dutch border to the west of Mönchen-Gladbach, poised

A Tornado in one of the Hardened Aircraft Shelters (HAS) on a frosty morning at the Crusader's site. (Mike Lumb)

ready to strike at Warsaw Pact forces in Eastern Germany and Western Poland. If RAF Valley had engendered a sense of excitement, Brüggen exuded a powerful sense of purpose: a fortress of barbed wire, concrete bunkers and drab green buildings lurking menacingly along the edge of a pine forest. In the Quick Reaction Alert (QRA) shelters at the end of the runway at Brüggen, fully-armed aircraft were at fifteen minutes' readiness to launch. The station had, over the previous two decades, established a reputation for excellence throughout NATO in the annual Tactical Evaluation (Taceval), which tested the entire station's ability to fight a war. There was massive pressure to keep the 'excellent' scores and not to screw up. Sirens would regularly summon us at 02:00hrs in the morning for no-notice exercises and the threat from the Russians was so real that when the siren went, you got to work by the quickest possible means. Once there, the first question was always 'Is it real, or exercise?' Even exercises were taken deadly seriously at Brüggen. As a result, over the next few years I was to spend many hours wearing my 'tin' helmet and gas mask when most sensible people were still tucked up in bed. I also spent numerous weekends manning an aircraft in the QRA shelters. But it was all exciting stuff.

The runway at Brüggen lay east-to-west with the squadron dispersals at each corner. Each squadron comprised nine Hardened Aircraft Shelters (HAS), a supposedly bomb-proof structure that could accommodate a single Tornado. There was a Personnel Briefing Facility (PBF), which was locally known as 'the Hard' and contained all the planning facilities and the operational and engineering controllers who ran the flying programme. Two other long, low huts, which were probably intended as temporary structures when they were built in the 1950s, were known as 'the Soft' – one for the engineers and one aircrew. Our one contained the crewroom in which off-duty crews could lounge with a cup of coffee and talk about flying. The centre of our social life was the Officers' Mess, another dull green single-storey, and very temporary-looking, building on the north side of the airfield. Here the epicentre was the bar, where the unfeasibly large Driek and matronly Hannah-Lohre served foaming beer at unbelievably cheap prices. The bar was always buzzing and when I first arrived it was *de rigeur* for everyone on the station to call in there on the way home. It was a wonderful opportunity for everyone to meet up and discuss the day's business.

When I arrived at Brüggen there were two sets of Crusaders: us, the new boys, working up to becoming combat ready with the Tornado and the old hands of the Jaguar squadron, which was still operating from the other side of the station. They were waiting to be disbanded once we were ready to take their place in the front line. But any thoughts that the 'old' and 'new' squadron should get on together for a seamless transition of the squadron's 'number plate' were soon scotched: our Jaguar-flying colleagues made it very plain to us that they regarded us as second-class citizens, to be ignored at all costs.

My front-line flying did not get off to the best of starts. On my first familiarization sortie, Hylton, the pilot flight commander, deemed my circuit flying to be in need of further practice and invited me to do it again. Second time round, with The Troff, our warm-hearted Geordie flying instructor, I managed adequately enough and a few days later I set off for my first familiarization trip with a navigator in the back seat. This didn't go too well, either. I was used to flying at 250ft over terrain in the UK that gave some sense of perspective, but low flying in much of Germany was limited to 500ft and even with the Radar Altimeter (Rad Alt) I found it difficult to estimate such a relatively large height over the vast flat plain of northern Germany. As a result, whenever I went near one of the small ridges on the route I triggered the Rad Alt warning, which I had dutifully set to go off just below 500ft. This was considered a major black mark by the navigators' union and I was made to fly the sortie again, this time with Hylton in the back seat. I was beginning to feel as if I was back at Cranwell again, peering over the slippery slope that would lead to a career change. It was a sunny October day when Hylton and I got airborne and threaded our way north-eastwards to our main operating area on the plain to the north of Osnabruck ridge. We sped eastwards towards the Dummer See and I was relieved to have got this far without the Rad Alt warning sounding once. As ever in Germany, a thin grey haze blurred the horizon making it a little harder to match the outside world with the map. I tried to resist the temptation just to look at the moving map and concentrated as much as I dared on the outside world. I was looking out as much as I could, trying to find landmarks in this unfamiliar landscape and trying to spot other aircraft, too. Then out of the corner of my eye I just caught a speck before the aircraft jolted with a loud 'thump!' Instinctively I climbed away from the ground and checked the engine instruments. We'd just hit one of the enormous buzzards that circle lazily over the German countryside – rather inconveniently at about 500ft. The nearby *Luftwaffe* base at Hopsten was the obvious diversion so we headed there and landed uneventfully. When we inspected the damage we found that the bird had hit the forward fuselage just behind the nose cone, where the impact had ripped off a huge metal panel. Luckily both bird and panel had then missed the engines. No wonder it had been such a loud thump! My third attempt at the trip was successful, after a 'top tip' from Steve to set the Rad Alt warner at 100ft, rather than 500ft. 'That way you won't frighten the navigators if you clip the odd ridge and if you do hear it go off you know to pull hard,' was his friendly advice. Sadly this technique probably cost Steve his own life some two years later when he flew into the ground on a clear summer day.

Looking back, it's hardly surprising that I was finding it hard work when I was flying only seven times a month! Furthermore some of these sorties had been cut short because of aircraft snags, including the nose-gear sticking down after take-off on one flight. At the end of the November, I was programmed to fly as one of a pair of aircraft for a land away to RAF Coningsby to do some flying in the UK. This was quite a regular method of flying when the Low-Flying System (LFS) in Germany was closed because of one of the numerous German Bank Holidays. The first indications that things were going to go awry were when I lined up on the runway: as I applied the brakes the aircraft stopped, but its position on the moving map display carried on motoring westwards! The Inertial Navigation System (INS) had failed, leaving us in a reversionary mode in which, amongst other inconveniences, the display in the HUD would wallow around, rather than staying fixed in the right place. No problem: we were number two of a pair, so all I had to do was hang onto my leader's wing until we got to Coningsby. But about halfway there and still

At low level in Germany

in cloud, both my navigator Bob and I could smell fumes in the cockpit and we both started to feel unwell. Our leader told us that RAF Coltishall was the nearest suitable airfield and advised us to divert there. It was a weird, almost out of body, experience flying on instruments that were wobbling around at the same time as I was suffering from symptoms similar to a mild hangover! We got an excellent talk down and landed on one of the runways at Coltishall – though which one I had no idea, as I was so disorientated by the time we landed! On shut down we were picked up and whisked off to the medical centre by the station ambulance with blue lights flashing. At this stage I was feeling rather heroic, but the bubble was soon burst by the engineering officer who had just inherited our aircraft. When we had landed, Les had been reasonably sympathetic and promised to put the aircraft into his hangar; but now he needed us to help him. Firstly he needed the canopy to be closed manually and secondly he needed all the safety pins for the weapons pylons. Unfortunately Bob and I were completely unable to help him with either query. Neither of us could recall how one closed a Tornado canopy – we had been shown once, six months previously at RAF Cottesmore but had not had occasion to do it since then! Nor, despite a telephone call home, could we locate the safety pins; these were hidden in an obscure camera bay. Despite searching all over the aircraft, we could not find it. Les was by now getting somewhat grumpy, because the annual inspection of his hangar was due that afternoon and our aircraft, with its open canopy and lack of safety pins, was going to cause him to fail it. Eventually, but not before he had intimated that he thought we were a pair of 'muppets', he managed to find some spare pins and a responsible adult who knew how to close the canopy.

That evening we bought him lots of beer, which went some way to assuaging his feelings and which, as it happened, cemented the beginning of a long friendship.

My next sortie with Bob was not much more successful. It was my first flight after the Christmas break and I'd not flown for fourteen days. Once again we were Number Two for a pairs take off. I took the middle of my half of the runway, in a loose echelon, my head in line with the leader's mainwheels. The leader holds his gloved fist up, twirling his index finger to instruct me to run up the engines and light the burners. The burners light and the Tornado dips forward, as the thundering power strains against the brakes. A check of the engine instruments and a 'thumbs up' on the coaming: The leader taps his visor and after an exaggerated head nod he releases the brakes. I do the same, and we surge forward. My head is continuously moving: check ahead to make sure we're keeping straight, then across to the leader check his wheels are still in line, then back ahead, while all the time my left hand juggles the throttles gently to keep me in the right position. The leader rotates and I ease back the stick to match his pitch angle. I see the oleos on his wheels stretch and then the wheels lift off the ground. Another head nod and his wheels retract, with mine following a fraction of a second later. I'm locked onto the leader's head now, awaiting the next nod, which will tell me to retract the flaps. I see the nod, reach outboard of the throttles and move the flap lever up, trying not to wobble in position as the aircraft trim changes. So far so good, I'm sticking in there, still sitting slightly wide and forward of the close-formation position: I'll move inwards (and therefore a touch backwards) as we come out of burner at 250kt. A white plume of unburnt fuel streaming from the vent under the jet pipes tells me that the leader is coming out of burner and I gently pull back my throttles. BANG!! The aircraft shudders and a sheet of bright yellow flame shoots out of my right intake, briefly obscuring my view of the leader. An expletive slips unconsciously from my mouth and I can feel my heart rate accelerating. The right-hand engine has surged. I ease up and away from the leader and he disappears into the murk. Once we're safely clear of the other aircraft and the ground I check the instruments again. The engine looks OK now, and my heart rate begins to drop back to normal. But Bob and I aren't taking any chances and we ask the radar controller to feed us in for a precautionary single-engine approach. Twenty-five minutes later we are back on the ground and I've missed out on another sortie!

We received more new aircraft over the winter months and by January I was getting more flying time. I was even beginning to consolidate the skills I was learning, rather than barely managing to keep up, which had been the case up until then. Most of our day-to-day flying was in West Germany, over which we were allowed to fly at 500ft. In addition there were eight LFAs where we were allowed to fly down to 250ft. The skies were full of numerous other NATO aircraft, some of them other ground-attack aircraft who would avoid us, and some of them fighters who would attack, trying to get a camera-shot kill. On the rare clear days the sky seemed black with aircraft; in the more usual German haze you couldn't see as many, which was much more frightening since you knew they were still out there somewhere! We enjoyed a friendly rivalry with the air defenders flying Phantom fighters out of Wildenrath, just down the road from us. The game was to try and sneak up behind a Phantom, since the Tornado could turn much better than a Phantom and he couldn't get rid of you once you were there with a finger on the camera button. On the ground the defensive belts of Surface-to-Air Missiles (SAM), and the countless numbers of ground troops provided us with lots of practice targets to attack with our cameras. A number of weapons ranges in Germany, Belgium and Holland also provided us with targets to attack with our practice bombs. With so much choice right on our doorstep it wasn't difficult to put together a suitably taxing yet enjoyable training sortie.

Our bread-and-butter range was at Nordhorn, on the Dutch border to the northeast of Arnhem. The target was a bus in the middle of a large circle, which sounds easy enough, but trying to find it on a murky German day from the attack height of 150ft at 480kts could be a challenge. The UK ranges I'd used previously were all on the coast, so if nothing else, the shoreline gave a pretty good idea of where you were. Nordhorn was just another nebulous part of the nebulous German plain. Where the Initial Points (IP) for UK ranges were huge bridges or lighthouses, the IP at Nordhorn was an anonymous and easily-missed minor road junction. From here you headed virtually due south, dropping down from 1,500ft to 150ft. About a mile short of the target was a line of cottages, which we thought must have been inhabited by deaf Russian spies: no-one else would have put up with being overflown at ultra-low level by NATO jets every few minutes. Luckily the cottages provided a bit of a line-up feature as behind them the target was conveniently masked until the last moment by trees. The further complication was that because the Tornado stores management computer had a habit of randomly dropping stores every now and then, we were not allowed to make any switches live until just before weapon release, so in those last few frantic seconds you had to correct any line up error and adjust height and speed while simultaneously making the Master Armament Safety Switch (MASS), the Late Arm (L/A) switch and the stick top Weapon Release Button (WRB) live – and then drop the bomb. Eventually you got to know the layout of the range pattern pretty well, but as a new boy I found the place to be completely bewildering.

If Nordhorn range was almost impossible to find, the Belgian range at Helchteren was a much better prospect. Here the main challenge was staying out of the control zone of Maastricht airport, but assuming that one did so, a massive well-marked lead-in took you to a huge yellow board which was almost impossible to miss. There was also a Dutch range at Vliehors, amongst the sand flats on the tip of Vlieland Island, which, though not as easy to find as Helchteren, did benefit from some very generous Range Safety Officers (RSO). 'OK you missed the target, but I'll give you a direct hit on the offset.'

The exercises were coming thick and fast as we approached the squadron's initial Taceval at which NATO would decide whether we were good enough to be declared combat ready. Unfortunately the weather was not on our side. The winter of 1985/86 was a bitterly cold one: there was a heavy snowfall over northern Europe and even the lakes in the local area were frozen with thick ice. The station ring road and the carparks had become skating rinks. While others scurried around and worried about the problems caused by the weather, the Boss came to the sensible conclusion that things had reached the 'too difficult' stage. He called us into the crewroom.

'We can't fly at the moment, so I'm closing down the squadron,' he announced. 'There is good snow on the slopes at Winterburg, so I'm ordering all of you to get across there and fill your boots with skiing. Everyone back here in three days' time – and no broken legs.' After some horse-trading about who was going to drive, we headed en masse for the slopes and a welcome break from the drudgery of preparing for exercises.

When we got back, we were quickly into the thick of it again. On the exercises most of the flying was restricted to the experienced hands, as they knew what they were doing and wouldn't mess it up. As a result, I spent most of my time hiding in the recesses of the 'Hard', trying to avoid any 'silly jobs' and getting some sleep. Then in mid-February came the Taceval. I managed to keep a low profile throughout the proceedings, so on last day I was surprised to find that I had been allocated an aircraft for the final mass launch. I noted, though, that I was crewed with Dick, a very experienced navigator, who was undoubtedly there to make sure that I didn't get into any trouble. We came to cockpit readiness in the darkness of the early hours and strapped into our ejection seats with the 'telebrief' buzzing loudly in our headsets. After the roll call by the strike controller had confirmed that everyone was on state, we were left to contemplate the passing of time inside our chilly little concrete world. Our ground crew lounged nearby, dozing fitfully on the hard floor. The hours passed slowly, the coldness and discomfort interrupted occasionally by a comms check or a broadcast of the airfield weather details. The latter was very useful because, sat in our secure HAS with the armoured doors locked, we had absolutely no idea what it was like outside. Then suddenly the telebrief burst into life... 'This is Red Door, Exercise *Green Arrow*. Execute reference time...' I gave the ground crew a shout on the intercom and they jerked into life, with one racing towards the doors, standing ready to open them. The controller read down the list of strike missions with a release authenticator code after each one. In other shelters, crews were checking their authenticator codes, confirming with Red Door and had started working their way through the calculation which would give them their take-off time window. When he got to our number, instead of an authenticator the controller simply said 'hold,' before continuing down the list releasing other missions. When we heard the reference time, Dick and I had already started on the sums for our take-off time and we realized that things were beginning to get tight. If we didn't get released soon we'd miss our take-off slot. Around us the other HAS doors were opening and aircraft were nosing out to join the herd heading like a pack of lemmings towards the runway. Once released, crews worked out their take-off time and taxied out using silent procedures, getting to the runway using the 'first come first served' method. It was usually a scrum at the end of the runway as everyone jostled for position. But today we would miss out on the excitement – we'd already missed our take-off time.

Then our mission number is called out with the instruction 'launch to vertical dispersal.' This means that we are not going to be used today, but that we must get airborne and hold in a safe area to keep our weapon system out of reach of incoming Soviet strikes, so that it can be used later. I'm disappointed not to be doing a 'proper'

Doug and myself on our way to Akrotiri.

launch, but in the next moments I've got both engines running and the shelter doors have rolled open to reveal a dirty grey winter's day, with snow still lying thick on the ground. I'm moving forward, the adrenaline pumping now we're off, as Dick tries to reign me in, reminding me that it is just an exercise, not a real war! We race out to the runway, lining up almost simultaneously with a Tornado from the other side and then we thunder airborne. As I climb through layers of wispy cloud, Dick is fighting a valiant rearguard action, trying to get me to slow down and at the same time to get clearance from Air Traffic Control (ATC): despite the silent exercise procedures he has noticed that our holding pattern is actually in the middle of the Dusseldorf Control Zone and we'll be none too popular if we just go blundering into it. Of course I'm blissfully ignorant of this small detail (we had never practised this procedure before) and I'm going there anyway – luckily Dick smoothes the way before I upset anyone. Eventually after an hour's worth of drilling holes in the sky we are recalled and that is the sum of my contribution to the squadron's successful Taceval. That night the bar is a busy place.

The reward for passing our Taceval was to take our place manning the Quick Reaction Alert (QRA). Each squadron at Brüggen kept a nuclear-armed aircraft constantly at fifteen minute's readiness to launch against targets on the other side of the Iron Curtain. The duty itself was a twenty-four hour stint in the QRA area, a cluster of HAS fortified heavily with barbed wire and guarded by armed policemen. After checking into QRA in the morning, the first duty was to take over responsibility for the weapon system from the off-going crew. Although we had practised the drills many times, there was still a moment of awe when you stepped into the HAS and saw the real bomb nestling malevolently under the aircraft. That was the moment when you realized the enormity of what you were doing. Once the formalities were completed and I had become the temporary owner of an explosive quantity of uranium, there was nothing else to do for twenty-four hours, except watch videos and wait for World War Three to start. After the novelty of doing it once, QRA became a chore, and it became quite usual for the flight commanders to find some reason why one of the junior boys should do their duty for them. As one of the junior boys, I spent lots of time there!

Shortly after the Taceval, and perhaps as a reward for not cocking things up too badly, I was amazed to find myself programmed for the squadron's first Overseas Training Flight (OTF), a long weekend in Cyprus. The OTF concept was justified because crews needed to be able to deploy to unfamiliar places and to cope with the unusual demands of ATC. Although at first this might seem a weak reason, it was actually a very good one, as the RAF was to demonstrate when operations started in the Middle East five years later. Either way I was not complaining: I recognized a good deal when I saw one and I couldn't believe my luck at the prospect of a weekend in Cyprus, where it had to be warmer than freezing cold Germany! The team was a good one: Snowy was the lead pilot with Alan in his back seat. I was crewed with Doug, a very experienced and laid-back navigator who didn't seem at all fazed that last time we flew together the nosewheel had refused to retract! And having been posted to Cyprus in the mid-1970s, Doug was the perfect tour guide. A few days later we are heading back to Brüggen after a fine weekend. Snowy and Alan lead us through a beautiful clear sapphire-blue sky, while below us the Cyclades drift lazily past, silver beaches glittering along turquoise-green shores. Doug and I hang off their wing in a comfortably loose formation and I savour the moment. My warplane might be stuffed with oranges and jars of coccinelli, but it is still a warplane and in a moment of revelation at 20,000ft over the Aegean I finally realize that I've actually achieved that ambition born twenty years previously; and now I even have an opportunity to savour the moment, too. I also realize that despite my inauspicious start to the tour, the Boss has decided that I am worth sticking with, and that I now fully belong to his squadron.

Back at Brüggen the squadron was concentrating on the work up for the (non-nuclear) attack role. Most of our sorties were flown as pairs, with a bounce to keep us on our toes, but with lots of poor weather and the usual German haze sometimes it was a challenge to get the job done. I was taught a very good lesson early on.

It is a grey day as we get airborne from Brüggen and thread our way past Venlo and Laarbruch towards Wesel and Borken. Here the muddy brown Rhine, flowing languidly between the factories and smokestacks, marks the start of the LFA. Baldy drops down to 250ft, my signal to move from the loosely swept formation into battle formation 4km abreast of him. The visibility is poor in the haze. The grey shape of Coesfeld appears out of the gloom. I hit the stopwatch. The town clarifies into focus and colour as it gets nearer, just as the forests and fields merge back into the greyness behind us. Baldy and I go either side of the town and I notice the stopwatch just passing twenty-five seconds. That puts the visibility just above our legal minimum of 5½km. I close a little on Baldy – it wouldn't do to lose him in the mist. This is a typical German day. All the smoke and fumes from the industrial area of the Ruhr stagnates below a dirty tidemark at 10,000ft, leaving a hazy grey fishbowl beneath. On some days you can even smell the pollution through the air-conditioning system. All too soon we reach the end of the LFA and pop back up to 500ft to squeeze past the control zone around Munster airport. Ahead is Osnabruck sitting on the end of the Teutoburg Ridge.

Beyond that the North German plain stretches, completely flat, on through Poland and Russia as far as the Urals. Perhaps today the ridge will mark the boundary with clearer air, as it sometimes does. We aim for Smokey Joe, a tall chimney belching out more filth just to the east of Osnabruck to keep us clear of the town. Easing up to stay 500ft above the ground, we are very close to a broken murky layer of cloud, which is merging into clumps of haze. Baldy turns towards me and I check back towards him aiming to cross just behind him. Once past, I haul back firmly towards a northerly heading and we roll out in reasonable formation, dropping down from the ridge.

If anything the visibility is even worse here. A strobe on the radar warning display tells me of an F-16 coming the other way. I see him as he emerges from the gloop and passes a couple of hundred feet above me, waggling his wings to show that he's seen me. Unconsciously, I close up the formation and Baldy instructs the bounce to stay away from us. Muddy brown fields and bare trees loom out of the

At low level in Germany on a typically murky day – more often than not the visibility in north-western Germany hovered around the minimum of 5½km which we needed to fly legally at low level.

murk ahead and flick past back into the murk behind us. So many German days are like this – an amorphous grey haze which might be suitable for low flying, or might not. With weather on the limits today we have to decide what we can get out of the sortie. Somewhere up ahead is the target whose demise we have been planning in minute detail for the last few hours. After so much work and effort, there is a real pressure to push on regardless. Who wants to have nothing to show for a day's work? The weather might just improve, or we could just plug in the TFR and plough on through the haze. The only problem is that we don't know who else might be stumbling around ahead of us – helicopters or light aircraft, other Tornados or perhaps just other fast jets pushing their luck to reach a target. And if we do press on, but find the visibility gets worse, we will have to pull up into the civilian airspace around Bremen and Hanover, exploding like a pair of greyhounds set loose among a flock of sheep.

'Turn-about port, go,' Baldy has decided that it is unworkable here. We flash past Osnabruck once again, this time heading south. The visibility is marginally better here in the Gutersloh 'bowl', an area of flat land bounded on three sides by hills and on the other by the sprawling industrial cities of the Ruhr. It is soon obvious that we will not be able to cross the high ground to get out of the bowl and the bowl itself is such a small area that we cannot get much done there. All this is only dimly apparent to me at the time, my brain is busy enough just trying to keep in formation and look out. A few more turns as Baldy manoeuvres the formation around and I gamely fight to keep in position.

'Close, go.' I move into close formation on Baldy's wingtip. He chops us across to Clutch Radar, the military radar unit who control the approaches to all RAF Germany airfields. We climb through the haze to 9,000ft, back towards Brüggen. Now I realize that all the manoeuvring, seemingly at random to me, has put us in exactly the right place for an easy pick up for Clutch Radar. It has also got us in position to take advantage of a little-known pathway across the airways near Dusseldorf. This was not one of the most exciting or productive sorties that I ever flew, but it provided me with a lesson I never forgot. There was always pressure to get the job done, but sometimes even the legal limits were still not good enough on the day. Baldy had known when to give up, and what's more he had kept us safely and firmly under control and he had brought us home tidily. Military flying is a uniquely unforgiving business and knowing when to call it a day and go home before it's too late is the mark of a true professional. The obituary lists are full of men who pushed the limits to try and get the job done.

A week later it was time to have my Instrument Rating (IR) renewed. Snowy straps into the backseat and we roar airborne for a very busy two hours. There is a solid overcast, so most of the instrument flying will be 'for real' inside real clouds. The first event is a single-engined heavyweight Precision Approach Radar (PAR), a talkdown from a ground controller and the most usual way to get into Brüggen on a murky day. I bring the left throttle back to idle and increase the power slightly on the right engine. Unlike many twin-engine aircraft the Tornado flies pretty well on one engine; on some types the second engine is merely there to accompany you to the crash site after the first one fails. We are vectored downwind at a stately 300kt

Gear and flap down, I'm approaching the start of the glidepath during a PAR 'talkdown' approach.

— faster than with two engines — to keep our energy high enough to manoeuvre. It is an old fighter pilot adage that 'speed is life' and that's certainly true if you're only on one engine! The Tornado is pretty easy to fly on instruments: everything you need is in the HUD and if you keep the aircraft symbol lined up with the horizon line, the aircraft stays level. If you want to fly a 2½° gildepath, you simply put the aircraft symbol halfway to the 5° dive-angle bar. On base leg, I trickle the speed back so that when the approach controller lines us up with the runway centreline and hands us over to the talk-down controller we're back at 210kt. When the talk-down controller says 'begin descent now' I drop the gear and the speed bleeds back towards our threshold speed. We fly an accurate but otherwise unremarkable approach to decision height and I go around. The thing drilled into us here is to select 'combat power' on the good engine, and there is an impressively reassuring push in the back as the burner lights and pushes us up and away from the ground. Once we are cleaned up, Snowy lets me have the other engine back and we climb up and join an airway route, which takes us up towards Hopsten. Here I let down for a Tacan approach. The PAR was easy: someone else gave me a running commentary on how to fly the ideal glidepath. This time I have to work it all out myself using ranges and bearings from the Tacan beacon at Hopsten. Again, once we're on the centreline it is pretty straightforward and we fly down to the minimum descent height.

Instead of a full overshoot, though, we fly out into the LFA to the north of Hopsten at low level. Below the cloud base the area is workable for the next phase.

First it's steep turns, flown entirely on instruments at 420kt and 500ft with 60° of bank. One way all the way round, then reverse and back the other way. Then we fly a loft-recovery manoeuvre, drilling into me the need to fly it solely on the head-down instruments. Back to another steep turn: halfway round Snowy shouts 'low-level abort – go!' I roll the wings level and pull back to 4-g, at the same time pushing the throttles into burner. At 30° nose up the Tornado punches up through the cloud layer and rockets heavenwards. Up in the blue skies at 15,000ft, Snowy takes control and invites me to close my eyes while he flies some very agricultural aerobatics from the back seat. It's not that he is an agricultural pilot: he is just trying to get me a bit disorientated. This is my opportunity to show him that I can recover from any 'unusual positions' I might find myself in if I get distracted or disorientated on instruments. 'Open your eyes and recover' instructs Snowy. The nose is pointing steeply down and the airspeed is building rapidly. I sort this out using the head-down instruments, as the HUD is far too sensitive, being intended for use in more dignified flying. I slam the throttles back to idle and pop the airbrakes out at the same time as I roll towards the horizon and pull firmly up towards it. Snowy takes it back. Next time we're pointing skywards with the speed bleeding off drastically. Full dry power, roll towards the horizon then pull down to get the nose below it and once the speed is safe roll back the right way up. Soon Snowy is satisfied and we start an approach into Brüggen, this time using the head down instruments. This is harder work than using the HUD – it is 'proper' instrument flying like I learnt in the Jet Provost and Hawk. It takes a bit of time to get used to it again – and to get out of all the bad habits engendered by HUD flying! And just to make it 'more interesting,' or so he claims, Snowy invites me to fly another Tacan for this approach. In fact it is not a bad way to fly a Tacan approach, since the display is right next to the Artificial Horizon, which I am now using as my prime instrument. I follow a twelve mile arc until we reach a point due east of the airfield, then turn west to line up with the runway which is out there somewhere beyond the clouds. We go around from that approach for two more PARs. The first is with the wings swept all the way back to 67°. At low-ish speeds the aircraft flies like a delta wing and I fly it using Alpha (angle of attack). We fly downwind at 300kt, slowing to 215kt for the approach – about 55kt faster than usual. The technique on the final descent is a bit different: I control the rate of descent only by putting on more power or reducing it, and I use the stick to make sure that the nose is always pointing up at exactly 16° Alpha – no more, no less. Swept-wing approaches always seemed a little esoteric and pointless to me then – little did I know that I'd have to do one for real almost exactly eight years later! The final approach is in mechanical mode – where the usual computer-controlled flying control system is bypassed and control is by a direct link with the tailerons. In this configuration the Tornado flies like a complete pig, or, more accurately, a nodding dog, with the nose continuously bouncing up and down. We land with Snowy satisfied and me 'legal' for another year.

Spring brought Exercise *Mallet Blow*, a large week-long exercise run twice a year by the RAF in the UK. We bombers had to run the gauntlet of fighters manning Combat Air Patrols (CAP) along the east coast in order to attack targets on the unfamiliar range at Otterburn, high up on the moors to the northwest of Newcastle. Here the targets were defended by batteries of Rapier anti-aircraft missiles, and once we had escaped their notice, we had to get past the electronic warfare range of Spadeadam, with its array of Soviet-style missile radars, before braving more fighters guarding the valley between the Lake District and the Pennines. Given that *Mallet Blow* had an uncanny knack of coinciding with atrocious weather one can understand that the exercise sorties could be hard work! I was very fortunate, though, that my first *Mallet Blow* sortie, and my first fourship in a Tornado, was flown on a beautiful day.

We are in wide 'covert' formation – close enough to warn each other about fighters closing in but far enough apart that the fighters will only be able to find one of us. Heading northbound fifty miles off the Lincolnshire coast, the front pair are smoking dots just above the horizon. Our element leader is two miles abeam us on the right, slightly offset from the front pair. Below us a small drifter rolls gently in the sea-green swell as we sweep past 250ft above its mast. High above, a thin veil of cirrostratus softens the sun's glare. It also gives a conveniently light backdrop against which incoming fighters should show up well.

Craning my neck round, I check behind Number Three's tail, then scan slowly round to the left. Then I see them. Two dark shapes rocketing towards us from eight o'clock high. The distinctive arrowhead silhouettes of two Lightnings: silver supersonic interceptors of the sixties, now drab camouflaged but just as lethal. Instinctively my left hand rams the throttles forward, thumb jammed on the transmit button.

Silence nothing comes out. I try again. Nothing: my microphone has failed. Frantically, I bash the canopy with my knuckles to get Terry's attention, gesticulating with forefinger towards the closing fighters.

'Buster,' shouts Terry and the formation scatters. I have already checked towards the Lightnings as the other three disappear into the distance behind a shimmering haze of burners. The fighters cannot have seen me – they streak over the top in pursuit of the others. And they're shifting – 600kt plus by my reckoning. We watch the distance close rapidly.

Another curt instruction from Terry and Number Three pulls up waggling his wings. The Lightning knows that he's been spotted and that a bomb would have been dropped in his face, which would give him something to think about. In answer the Lightning zooms upwards and wheels off to the east. His mate hauls off the front pair and dashes after him. They are worried now about the missing fourth Tornado that they have not seen yet (me!). Being shot down by a missile-armed bomber sneaking up behind them would be the ultimate disgrace for a fighter pilot. Their threat swiftly diminishes into the distance.

'Tail clear' calls Terry and the formation slowly merges back together. Today's target is a small Bailey bridge in the middle of the artillery range at Otterburn. It is not a target of choice for us – for real we would expect to go against something larger – but good practice. It is not ideal, either, that the target co-ordinates are a little vague. Tornado's precision depends on having a pretty good idea of exactly where to find the target. Today Terry will get me into the right area, but it will be

Exercise Blue Moon: *with Rambo and Wez on my wing at low level over Denmark.*

up to me to find the bridge. It certainly does not help that now I cannot talk to him; even in ideal conditions the crew has to work closely together, and we are still quite new to this game.

'Phantom spike two o'clock – move left,' calls one of the front pair. The formation slews to the left in response. Without a radar warning receiver in our aircraft, Terry and I remain blissfully ignorant as to whether we have been also locked on.

'Buster,' throttles rammed forward again. In the distance a Phantom cruises casually down to the right of us like a grey shark. We wait for him to hook behind us, but he does not bother. Either he has not seen us, or, more likely, he has already taken the shots unseen from head on.

North of Newcastle the formation scatters once more – this time to generate some spacing between us over the target. If someone is dropping a stick of bombs ahead of you at low level, you need to be at least twenty or thirty seconds behind or you run the risk of being damaged by debris from the explosions. Terry and I cross behind Number Three in a wide turn out to sea to get our spacing and run through our checks. Terry does the talking while I respond in silent charades. Then it's time to turn in.

Terry squirts the radar at the Amble lighthouse to fix the navigation kit, Alnwick flashes past and suddenly we are crossing the rolling moorland of the range.

'Four clear hot,' calls the RSO. Switches live. Terry's target bars are sitting just below the crest of a small hill. I don't see a target. Then I'm aware of a mass of old tanks and muddy craters. It's around here somewhere. Nothing is clear – just a subliminal blur of monochrome as I search frantically for the bridge. Twenty seconds to go. Nothing, then I spot a vague shape out further right. There it is! Grey lattice work, tiny against the surrounding 'moonscape'. I yank the Tornado viciously across, to put the bomb fall line in the HUD over the bridge. My thumb is on bomb release button as the sight passes through the target with a few seconds to spare! After that hard manoeuvre, the weapon aiming computer would be working hard to release the bombs accurately, but at least with a stick of eight 1,000lb bombs we would have made a mess of the place! I crest the ridge beyond the target and dive into the next valley, suddenly remembering the Rapier missile batteries which are defending the target area.

Hugging the fir trees, we scuttle off down the valley towards safety and the rest of the formation.

In the middle of May we're off to Sardinia for our annual Armament Practice Camp (APC). Our temporary home for two weeks would be the large airfield at Decimomannu (Deci), which sprawled amongst the dusty olive groves on the central plain of Sardinia, to the northwest of Cagliari. Just inside the main gate, which was guarded by sullen Italian conscripts, a large sign proclaimed that Deci was 'Where the Free World Trains to Fight.' It was run quadrinationally by the British, Americans, Germans and Italians, and it frequently also hosted the French, Canadians, Dutch and Belgians, among others. Going to Deci was rather like going on a Mediterranean activity holiday: a busy time flying in the daytime and a relaxing social scene in the evenings. Some of us flew the squadron's aircraft down, while others and the ground crew went by transport aircraft. Once there, we were quartered in a rather squalid accommodation block, which boasted its very own bar, known to all as the 'Pig & Tapeworm.' The Pig & Tape was, in reality, just a large room, empty but for two huge fridges which were stocked with cans of beer. It was decorated with murals painted by all the RAF and RN units that had been to Deci and was the scene of many a debriefing; it was also a great place just for letting off steam. Around the corner was the much more up-market Quadrinational Officers' Club, run by the Italians. For some reason it was a tradition when visiting the club for us to drink cappuccino and Sambuca, two things we never drank anywhere else. The result, after the first evening's inevitable over indulgence, was a very poor night's rest as you lay on the bed with eyes wide open thanks to all the caffeine, while the room span madly thanks to all that Sambuca. There were usually quite a few bleary red-rimmed eyes at met brief on the first morning!

Apart from drinking Sambuca, the reason for going to Deci was to use the excellent range on the west coast of Sardinia. Capo Frasca was one of the few ranges in Europe where virtually every possible weapons delivery profile could be practised. The bombing targets and strafe panels were set out on the top of a headland surrounded by 300ft cliffs. This had caused problems more than once in the distant past when the occasional Starfighter pilot, used to the sea-level ranges in northern Europe, had let down over the sea to 200ft on a hazy day and drilled a neat hole just below the top of the cliffs. For us, though, the range at Frasca was a wonderful opportunity to practice all kinds of esoteric methods of dropping bombs and firing guns.

Me, Dermot and the 1,000lb concrete bomb that we were about to drop at Frasca Range, Sardinia.

We flew in fourships at Deci, launching in waves to use the thirty-minute range slots allocated to the squadron during the course of each day. With a very full range programme catering for the needs of four nations at a time there was no time for any flying other than the transit to and from the range and twenty minutes of mayhem on the range itself. The airfield itself was continuously busy, too, as relays of fourships from all the detachments there departed towards, or recovered from, the range.

The sun is shining again and I'm Number Three as we fan out heading towards the coast. We're crossing a range of low mountains west of 'Point Golf' the small town of Guspini, grey rocks and green bushes roll past as we follow the slopes down, diving gently and letting the speed build up towards 450kt. With my left hand I slide the oxygen regulator on the side of the seat out of 100 percent oxygen and back to 'air mix.' I seem to be allergic to something in the trees or the grass at Deci: on the ground my nose is streaming, but ten minutes' worth of 100 percent oxygen is enough to clear my nose and sinuses and I can breath normally again. It adds to the satisfaction of flying! Ten miles west of Guspini the hills end abruptly in tumbling cliffs and at once we are over the sea, glittering blue in the sunlight. As we cross the coast we all swing northwards, putting us in a loose chain at 2,000ft heading towards the tip of the peninsular in the distance. This sortie is devoted to dive-bombing. First we'll drop four bombs in 'reversionary mode' from a shallow 5° dive, and then we'll drop the other four from a steeper 25° dive using the 'full kit.' The reversionary method means that we're using the aircraft like a big Hawk, and I'll be aiming the bomb using a fixed sight in the HUD just like I was taught at Chivenor: Except I'm going to cheat. The aircraft symbol in the HUD shows me exactly where the aircraft is pointing, so provided I put it in the right place just above the target and make sure that is a 5° dive, all I have to do is 'pickle' the bomb off as the sight passes the target and I'll get a good hit.

The first pass is 'dry' as we check the target area and that there is no shipping in the Gulf of Oristano beyond the range. 'No sheeps in the bay,' calls Ivor, the leader, and we follow round the pattern. It's quite hard work trying to fly accurately and keep an eye out for the other three in the range pattern. Reversionary dive-bombing is pretty much all 'pilot stuff' so Dermot, a tall Irishman who takes very little seriously, amuses himself in my back seat with a tirade of abusive banter about my flying. I don't mind, though, firstly because the reversionary bombing is one of the few things I'm quite good at, so I can tell him to wind his neck in, and secondly because I know that he'll defend me to the hilt in the debrief. Such is the nature of crew loyalty: whatever arguments may happen in the air, once on the ground the crew sticks together. The scores today are OK. Then we move up to 5,000ft for the steep dive. The RSO decides that he can't see us as we tip in at the top of the dive, so he can't clear us 'hot.' The solution is for us to dump a blip of fuel as we tip in producing a white flash just behind the aircraft as the fuel evaporates. My turn: just short of the target I roll almost inverted and pull the nose down steeply, simultaneously changing hands on the stick to reach for the fuel-jettison panel on the right console. A quick blip, then change hands again to roll out pointing at the target, closing the throttles, calling 'Paris three in hot,' and making the switches live.

The dreaded flat turn at Decimomannu as seen from my back seat – Ivor and Vic lead Baldy and Dirty John as Number Two through Alpha South. As usual, I'm hanging back a bit in the Number Three slot!

Busy times: Dermot has marked the target with the radar, but now I must move my left hand again to the hand controller and refine his mark exactly onto the pile of white oil barrels in the centre of a large circle that marks the target. Dermot then fires the radar ranger. While all this is going on we are hurtling towards the ground in what seems like a vertical death dive! I press the stick top to 'commit' the attack and as the bomb comes off I pull hard to point back up towards the sky and safety. The RSO scores the bomb (it's not bad) and as I climb back up towards the circuit height I hear Rambo, in the Number Four slot, tipping in. But Rambo is having problems. 'Two thousand at six,' calls the RSO as Rambo pulls off his attack: he's dropped nearly a kilometre short of the target. The same thing happens on the next two passes. Dermot and I are giggling like schoolgirls by this stage. We realize that Rambo's back-seater has forgotten to deselect reversionary mode, so every time he commits to what he thinks is an automatic computer-driven attack, he is simply 'pickling off' a bomb in reversionary mode.

The range slot is over and we hear a formation of German Phantoms calling to join. As he comes off his last pass Ivor starts a gentle right-hand curve over the Gulf of Oristano and from our last passes each of us cuts the corner of his trajectory, so that we end in a loose echelon by the time we coast in at the east of the bay. Once we're past the mountains on the western side of the island we pass a point called 'Alpha North' and head southwards, tightening up into close formation. For some reason, every recovery to Deci is flown in close formation and the two 90° turns at 'Alpha South' and 'Initials' are flown as flat turns – manoeuvres that we have never been taught in flying training and which the RAF never flies anywhere else in the world. To me it seems like madness – perhaps as much as anything else because I find flat turns unbelievably difficult and also rather frightening! In a 'normal' formation turn you simply stay in the same plane as the leader, so from your cockpit the side-on view of the leader looks exactly the same but the background alters; in a flat turn you stay in the same horizontal plane, so you have to look up through the top of your canopy at the leader's belly as he turns against the same background. There is nowhere to escape to if you think it's getting too difficult, because there is another aircraft under your own belly! You also have to put on power because you are flying a wider circle and you have to move forwards a bit because you'll inevitably drop back as you roll out. You're also pulling 2-g as you go around a steep turn and with none of the usual references to keep you the right distance out, it becomes a bit of guesswork as to whether you're in the right place. Add to this that as Number Three (Dermot and me) you have to account for any wobbling on the part of Number Two. Number Four is OK as he can hang slack at the back and as long as he nips into the right place when everyone rolls out; nobody knows where he was during the turn! As the aircraft roll out it seems as if Number Two's wing is going to hit us on the top of the canopy, which used to scare the hell out of me! Yes, Number Three was the worst place to be.

We come through Initials and I grit my teeth and close up to Number Two's belly, trying to look past him to make sure that I keep Ivor's aircraft lined up with the horizon. The leader starts a slow rollout and I can feel myself relaxing – ever so slightly – as we all end up in a much safer-feeling echelon. We cross the runway threshold: Ivor breaks away and I start counting. Ten seconds, Number Two breaks and I instinctively turn my head forward to make sure I keep in a straight line. Ten seconds and it's my turn: 2-g, throttles back to idle, airbrakes out and wings forward as I turn downwind.

An interesting physiological phenomenon during a detachment to Deci is that everyone complains after they use the toilet that their excrement is black. The old hands point out that it is a well-known saying in aircrew circles that 'when you pass south of the Alghero Tacan beacon your shit turns black.' However, I suspect that it has more to do with the local wine, known affectionately as 'Deci Red' which is available from the RAF mess hall in five-gallon plastic jerry cans. It is probably not for the connoisseur, but after the second pint it can taste quite passable. At the weekend we head off for expeditions to the local resorts, always accompanied by at least one freshly-filled plastic container of Deci Red. Late in the evening of the middle Saturday Alan, AJ, Cookie and I are meandering along a deserted country lane. We're heading back to the resort at Villasimius after a pleasant expedition to a local bar. It is beautifully warm and above us the stars sparkle brightly in a clear sky. A gently zephyr carries the aroma of cut grass from the fields along the way. Cicadas sing loudly along the roadside verges, harmonizing with Cookie's bawdy rugby songs, while the sea murmurs against the coastal rocks a mile or so away. And I remember thinking 'life doesn't get much better than this.'

Back in Germany, our attack work-up continued through the summer with lots of fourships. I was declared combat ready (attack) in July, just before I headed south to Bavaria for a fortnight of much deserved (or at least I thought so) leave. The autumn brought the return of night flying – and also our first NATO squadron exchange. The idea of the exchange was that two squadrons from different nationalities took it in turns to host each other for a week. During that time we were expected to fly and socialize together and thereby find out how best to work together in time of war. Our exchange was a one-way detachment to a USAF Phantom squadron at Spangdahlem, in the Eifel just north of the Mosel valley. The Boss chose all of us 'first tourists' for his 'away team' with just a few responsible adults to keep us in check and we were determined to enjoy ourselves. The USAF squadron commander appeared to have come up with a similar gameplan and our hosts were a handful of the most junior members of his squadron. Although the social scene was suitably busy and boisterous, we saw little of the US commander who was a reformed alcoholic; this put our Boss off his stride a bit, as he appeared to be an aspiring one! One evening we all trooped round to the commanding officer's house for a barbeque which finished promptly at about 8.00pm. That was about the time that we were used to getting started. Doug, my tour guide from the Cyprus trip, insisted that we take a crate of beer with us as recompense for such a ridiculously early finish!

One minor victory for the first tourist pilots at Spangdahlem was a revision of the Boss' decree that junior pilots should not be allowed to have 'Green' instrument ratings. We all had 'White' ratings which in practice meant that we were not allowed to descend below 400ft on an instrument approach; the Green rating, which denoted an experienced pilot, allowed the holder down to 200ft. When we came back from our first trip on the exchange, we found that the high ground of the Eifel had clouded over and Spangdahlem was socked in with a cloudbase around 200ft. Knowing the hassle it would cause if we all diverted, we all pressed on and got safely down. None of felt that we had taken any risks: we had all demonstrated during our recent instrument ratings that we could fly (several) approaches to Green limits. Of course the Boss could not condone such wilful breach of the rules, but there was a quietly whispered 'well done' and when we got back to Brüggen we discovered that we had all been miraculously scheduled for a Green rating test.

Night flying on the continent was a rather tedious chore. It involved a couple of set routes, the 'Night Charlie' which flew anti-clockwise round northern Germany and routed through the range at Nordhorn and the 'Night Bene' (or 'Benny') which flew clockwise through Belgium and the Netherlands, routing through Vliehors range. They were all designed for use by non-TFR aircraft droning round at around 2,000ft and offered very little training value. They were also flown under radar control, which seemed rather bizarre for supposedly tactical training, but which did offer some amusement on one dark night. Tasked with a Night Benny, myself and Loins were allocated the callsign 'Mission 1111' and we spent the evening trying to see how many different ways we could say the digits as we checked in with the different radar units. One-one-one-one, one-treble-one, eleven-eleven, one-double-one-one … well, it kept us amused for 1½ hours.

The UK offered a much better quality of night flying and we frequently spent our evenings flying 'high-low-highs' to make use of the LFAs and ranges in the country. The only drawback was that the long over-sea transit at each end of the sortie meant that we had to wear an immersion suit, known colloquially as a 'goon suit', in case we had a snag and had to eject over the sea. The goon suit was a heavy rubberized one-piece garment designed to keep you dry if you had the misfortune to parachute into the sea. To put it on, you had to climb in through a diagonal opening which stretched from right shoulder to left hip and then push your neck up through a tight rubber seal at the neck. There were similar seals at the wrists. The suit was then closed up with a heavy zip. The whole dressing process was made more difficult by first having to don a cumbersome 'bunny suit' which was there to keep you warm in the freezing waters of the North Sea. The 'Hard' was rarely as cold as the North Sea, so when we were night flying the flight-safety equipment area was usually occupied by a bunch of hot, sweaty and increasingly irritated aircrew, all attempting Houdini-like contortions as they tried to 'dress to survive.'

Once strapped in to an ejection seat the goon suit/bunny suit combination didn't feel too bad. Also the start of the sortie was easy enough – a climbing-turn towards Laarbruch and then a handover to Dutch Military Radar for the transit across the Netherlands at around 20,000ft. Some pilots used to hand-fly, but I used this opportunity to engage the autopilot so that I could relax and enjoy the view outside. Sometimes there wasn't much to see apart from the amorphous inside of a cloud, which pulsated luminously with the aircraft's own strobe light; sometimes, though, on a clear night, there was a lot to see. One night, I became aware of a pale fluorescent glow above us. We were approaching Mike Charlie Six, a waymark in space known only to navigators and radar controllers, which is the crossing point from Dutch to British airspace. At first the phenomenon seemed no more than the fleeting sensation of some sixth sense feeling, but gradually it grew stronger until I realized that we were looking up at a shimmering jade green curtain, dancing across the heavens: the Northern Lights. We watched in silence, since the majesty and mysticism of the spectacle above us was beyond words. But then it was time to get back to work: heads in as we concentrated on getting close to the dark world beneath us, nature's wonders temporarily forgotten. On another evening we had just crossed the Dutch coast on a clear and crisp winter night. I was admiring the panorama of East Anglia, which spread out before us. Moonlight tinted the water, defining the coast and the Norfolk Broads, while the pinpoints of light which dappled the land, marked the towns and villages. Suddenly a bright cluster of lights exploded into view ahead of us and seemed to hurtle towards us at breath-taking speed, then vanished as quickly as they had materialized. 'What the hell was that, Wez,' I asked my navigator. Wez,

Myself and Doug, letting down to low level.

burdened with the responsibility of navigation hadn't been looking out. 'Dunno,' he answered helpfully. Then on 'Guard,' the distress frequency, I heard 'Mayday, Mayday, Mayday, this is Saxon Two – I've just collided with my leader and I think they have ejected.' It had not been a cluster of lights heading towards me that I'd seen, but the fiery wreckage of an aircraft tumbling vertically earthwards: I had witnessed a mid-air collision over 100 miles away.

Usually, though, the high-level transit was somewhat less exciting or scenic. We were always alone during the transit, regardless of whether or not the low-level part of the sortie was to be flown as a singleton (one aircraft) or as a formation. As a formation we would carry out the transit in a two or three minute trail. Often, if we were flying a Simulated Strike Profile (SSP), we might be in a stream of aircraft flying the same route. The advantage of this arrangement was that it simplified the planning for everyone if there was just one plan and we didn't have to deconflict from each other. The disadvantage was that if the route strayed too close to a town or village, there would be a sheaf of low-flying complaints the next day. People didn't seem to object to being overflown by one Tornado, but perhaps understandably they got fed up after a stream of four or five (or ten, on one Wing exercise launch). The only exception was the Home Counties – the 'Gin and Tonic Belt' as we called it where even a single sortie, which had been planned with extra care to avoid the hotspots, would generate more complaints than Northumbria would produce in a year. It seemed that while the stockbrokers were happy to enjoy the fruits of democracy, they were not willing to pay the price in the form of some occasional noise from those who defended it.

Sometimes we managed to get more useful time at low level by landing in the UK during the daytime and launching for a low-high sortie back to Germany in the evening. It was for just such a profile that Dirty John and I led a pair into RAF Leeming in North Yorkshire. The Central Flying School (CFS) had recently moved out and the place was virtually deserted. After dinner in the 'Marie Celeste'-like Mess, we headed back to the aircraft. We would be Number Two for the night trip, which would be flown in parallel-track formation. The concept of parallel track was that two individual routes would be planned, parallel to each other and two miles apart. As the aircraft flew their own routes they would be in battle formation with each other. Since we could not fly cross-over turns, the aircraft could keep roughly abreast of each other by planning minor changes in groundspeed and limiting the turns to relatively ones. This technique was known, even to navigators who had only known decimal coinage, as 'Thrupenny-bitting.'

It is dark as we strap in under the floodlights. Canopies closed, ejection seats live and engines running, and then it is time to taxi out towards the runway. Night flying is a mystical experience. Everything seems calmer and quieter: communications, so terse and sharp in daytime, assume an almost reverential tone at night. The airfield itself is transformed into a magical place. As we leave the brightly lit apron behind us, it is like venturing into space. The rest of the airfield is invisible in the darkness, save for the dim blue taxiway lights that seem to hover over a void. As we follow the path traced out by them, a small pool of light precedes us, where the beam of our own taxi light falls onto the ground. The rest of the airfield seems to be cloaked in black velvet, but at least we know that we are taxiing on concrete. In the cockpit I have turned the lights down as low as I can, so that I can still read the instruments in their dull glow, but I still have some night vision to help me see into the dark world outside. When we get there, the runway is more brightly lit, clearly defined by the string of pearls laid along each side. Our leader departs just a head of us in a shimmering flame of afterburner and we take the runway. Dirty John counts down to our take off time, burners light, brakes off and we also thunder down the runway. Airborne, climb to 3,000ft and we head towards our low-level entry point north of Catterick. Below us houses, hamlets, villages glide past, spots of light that, without being fixed in a visible landscape, might equally be thousands of feet or thousands of miles away.

Dirty John quietly says farewell to Leeming radar and we check in on the formation frequency. Ahead of us our leader confirms that he is on his 'time line.' We run through the TFR checks and as we approach the start point we can see the lights of our playmate approaching his own one. The autopilot takes us down towards 1,500ft, the highest clearance we can select. I check that it is working OK. On the E-scope, just under the coaming on the left of the instrument panel, the terrain returns are showing clearly as a thickly-curved luminescent green line. A test pulse every few seconds indicates that the scope is functioning correctly. In the HUD, a letter 'T' in the top right-hand corner shows that the Flight Director (FD) is following the TFR commands and I can also see that the autopilot, in turn, is obeying the commands of the FD. In the backseat, Dirty John confirms that we're on track and on time and he peers into his radar, giving me a commentary of what it is showing him. Out on our left, a set of flashing lights confirms that we're nicely in formation. I take the height down a notch and re-check everything. These are still relatively early days with the TFR, so we always take it gently. Eventually we are down at 750ft, which for the moment is as low as we're allowed at night. And for the moment it seems plenty low enough! There's not much cloud tonight as we work our way northwards up past Newcastle towards coastal Northumbria. The built up areas between the Tees and the Tyne stand out brightly off to our right, while to the left the Pennines and Cheviots loom unseen beyond the flashing lights of our leader. Below us the ground is faintly visible under the soft radiance of the moon and stars, the lights of occasional house or vehicle giving it a little more texture. The ground undulates in a series of gentle ridges, which show up on Dirty John's radar as 'cut off' where the radar can't see beyond the ridge. As we approach each one he calls down the miles. I reply when I can see the returns on my scope and confirm that the autopilot is reacting to the terrain until John calls, 'painting beyond.' That means that we've almost crested the ridge and the radar can see the ground beyond it.

When we were planning this sortie, the challenge for the navigators was how we would get from line abreast heading north past Newcastle, into line abreast heading west across the Scottish borders. There's not enough space to 'thrupenny bit' through 90°, but the boys have come up with a clever solution: they have incorporated a target, an anonymous bridge over a small river to the northwest of Coldstream, for a simulated attack. From being in line abreast, we have to arrange ourselves to overfly the target forty seconds after the leader. At the pre-planned split point, our routes diverge: the leader accelerates and heads towards the target while we generate some spacing by heading off towards the coast. Then we, too, accelerate to 480kt and turn for the target. A low-level night attack is all the work of the navigator – I'm just there to switch on the autopilot. It is up to him to find the target on the radar. As he moves his radar marker, the autopilot responds obediently. Looking through the HUD, I can see the green target bar marking where Dirty John thinks the bridge is located. The aircraft flies itself towards the mark, offsetting slightly into wind to allow for its effect.

Off target we head to the rejoin point, and surely enough we see a set of flashing lights converging towards us from the south. The hills are a bit less gentle in this part of the borders and there is more of a sense of urgency in our commentaries as we fly among them. I find myself almost retracing the route I once flew on one of my solo navigation exercises from Valley – except this time its almost pitch black and I am relying on an automatic system to keep me clear of the ground. I'm no Luddite, but it is still a slightly scary thought. In my Hawk, the tall mast at Barrow Head had marked the end of the low-level route, but now, standing invisible somewhere ahead of me it is the fix point that Dirty John is going to use to make sure that our 'kit' is fully updated when we get to the range. A small green cross appears in the HUD field of view. It moves slightly then stops. Above it, as we get closer, I can see a vertical line of red lights above it and the cross itself sits on the dim outline of a small hillock. It is a pretty good mark.

Another 'split' puts us in a sixty-second trail heading over the sea towards Jurby Head, the northernmost tip of the Isle of Man. The range at Jurby lies along the

Airborne from Deci: AJ and Dermot heading for a punch-up on the ACMI range.
(Andy Jeremy)

west coast of the island. It is not a popular range with navigators because, although there is a distinctive 'wine glass' pattern of buoys and target rafts on the radar, it is also very easy to mistake one of the many fishing vessels in the area for the target raft. It is not a popular range with pilots because at night there is no artificial light, so you can see nothing outside: it is completely black. The loft recovery becomes a particularly scary manoeuvre when the things that you might hit are invisible! There is also the small matter of the long bum-numbing, bladder-stretching transit home. After a dry pass, we have enough fuel for one hot one. On the range I can descend to 400ft. I've switched off the TFR and once we're on the correct Line of Attack for the target I use the Rad Alt to descend rather gingerly towards the sea. It is invisible in the blackness somewhere beneath us. I centre the aircraft symbol in the HUD over Dirty John's target mark. We're now pointing at the target at 480kts, exactly 400ft above the unseen wavetops. In the HUD the timing circle starts to unwind, counting down to the pull up point. As the timing circle approaches the pull up marker, I push the throttles through the gate into reheat and move my hand to the hand controller just aft of the throttles, index finger poised on the phase change button. There is a firm push in my back as the burners light and at the same time I trigger the phase change. An elastic triangle with a dot at its apex appears in the HUD; by tracking the dot with the aircraft symbol I'll be pitching upwards at exactly the right rate for the weapon-aiming computer to drop the bomb accurately. The bomb comes off with a barely detectable jolt, but this time instead of overbanking and pulling back towards the sea we keep going upwards. The nose is pointing well and truly skywards as the Tornado climbs. The incandescent flame of the burners lights the night sky behind

Low level over the Black Forest: JB and Jeremy southwest of Stuttgart on a rare clear day. (John Butler)

us; the undersides of the wings and the fuel tanks are bathed in its luminescence. The altimeter winds rapidly up to 20,000ft in just a couple of minutes. I bring the throttles out of burner and the aircraft seems to sag with the dramatic reduction in thrust before it settles into the cruise. I plug in the autopilot and try and get comfortable for the long slog back to Brüggen.

The huge excitement in the New Year was that we were off to Deci once more. It was not for the range at Frasca this time, but for the Air Combat Manoeuvring Instrumentation (ACMI) range off the west coast of the island. The ACMI range was primarily intended for use by the air defenders, but we mud-movers were also allowed on it every now and then. At its heart was a telemetry system which picked up the data relayed from a pod carried by each aircraft. In the ground station, all that data produced a real time three-dimensional picture on a huge display screen, showing the positions of all the aircraft on the range and how they were manoeuvring. You could view the range from a God's eye view or you could see it from the perspective of the cockpit of any of the aircraft. It seemed like an incredibly complex arcade game, but it was actually an invaluable tool for working out what exactly happened in a fight involving lots of aircraft and therefore piecing together a meaningful debrief. Previously, there was enough of a grey area as the various participants tried to put together what they could recall of a combat that the fight was often won or lost during the debriefing. Now, ACMI's 'eye in the sky' ensured that the truth was clear to everyone!

We were accompanied by three Harriers from Gutersloh. After starting off by fighting each other, we worked up to two-versus-two combat with the Harriers. During one of these sorties Alan very kindly tried to inspire me by playing the soundtrack to the film Top Gun on the cassette tape usually used for loading the route into the main computer. My recollection of these combats was of two very manoeuvrable but not very fast Harriers going round in tight circles while the faster but much less agile Tornados slashed past in huge arcs, rather like ice-skating hippos. It was, however, tremendous fun!

At that stage of Tornado operations it still took some thirty minutes to align the aircraft's inertial platform before each sortie, which was the source of much amusement to the Harrier boys, who only took about a minute to fire up their jets. On the last morning, I had won the privilege of sitting in the back seat of the two-seat Harrier during the grand finale of the detachment, a four Tornado versus two Harrier combat. When the Tornado crews walked to their aircraft, I was strapped into the back of the Harrier, but then Cliffy, my chauffeur for the trip disappeared. The clock ticked down to the check-in and there was no sign of Cliffy. As I peered into the distance I could see two people standing in front of the line of Tornados. It was the two Harrier pilots, Cliffy and Wack, having an exaggeratedly relaxed chat and cup of coffee, apparently without a care in the world or any realization that they were due to check in for a combat sortie in the next few seconds. After the first Tornado taxied out, they looked at their watches, nonchalantly wandered across to the Harriers and jumped in. Here the nonchalance immediately wore off and I was aware of a frenzied activity in the front seat. Cliffy checked in and we taxied out in perfect order immediately behind the fourth Tornado. Round one to the Harrier pilots!

On the range itself the sky seemed to be full of Tornados whizzing past, burners blazing, while the nimble Harriers ducked and dodged out of their way, claiming the odd shot if a Tornado was foolish enough to try and 'mix it' too closely. One Tornado did look as if it was about to get lucky, though, and as he closed for a missile shot Cliffy said, 'Right, this'll show him,' followed a few seconds later by 'Oops,' as the Harrier flicked sideways then started tumbling. It certainly worked: the Tornado was last seen high tailing it into the distance, trying to get as far away as possible from the nutcase in the Harrier. 'Perhaps we won't do that one again,' suggested Cliffy. I could only concur. By now everyone is running short of fuel and the two formations head back towards Deci. On the recovery into, Wack closed into echelon and I was struck by how tiny a Harrier was. I felt that I could almost put out my hand and touch the Number Two as he sat locked onto our right wingtip.

The weather had been great for most of the week, but towards the end it clouded over. One morning we came in to find a solid layer of low cloud and reports that the ACMI range was also unusable because of cloud. Rather than sitting around, some of us were tasked to fly one of the low-level routes around Sardinia. Loins and I were allocated a triangular route which ran northeast from Deci to the east coast and then westwards to the west coast, before returning to

Deci. It was pretty obvious as soon as we got airborne that the low cloud over the low-lying central plain would become thick hill fog amongst the mountains further north. We plugged in the trusty TFR and then followed an exhilarating 30 minute ride in which I felt equal measures of pure terror, as we hurtled towards huge rocks, and utter marvel, at the ingenuity of the aircraft designers, when we missed them. There was quite a wind through the mountains and the aircraft, normally so solid and smooth, rocked and bounced its way through the air currents. We were in and out of cloud as the route took us down steep-sided gorges. Walls of grey rocks rushed past, alarmingly close and as we pushed over one ridge, we would come out of cloud to find ourselves pointing directly at another one. After ten minutes we were spat out of a remote canyon to find ourselves at 500ft over a dirty green sea, flecked with spume. Like a punch-drunk boxer warily circling his opponent, the aircraft flew us in a wide left-hand turn, continuously buffeted by the wind, before pointing us back towards the mountains. Loins kept up his running commentary on the radar picture and just before we re-crossed the coast, we were pulled upwards into the 'clag' once more. In the corner of my eye I could see cloud and granite flashing past underneath us, but still the TFR kept us on the route, keeping us exactly 500ft above the unseen ridges. The whole experience gave me great confidence that the system worked well and could be trusted.

Unfortunately the few months after our return from Deci marked the nadir of my flying career. Perhaps I had become complacent now that I thought that I knew what I was doing, but whatever the underlying reason I managed to have a string of incidents caused entirely by my own carelessness. Any one of them might reasonably have led to an early posting to somewhere unpleasant, had it not been for the fact that the Boss believed strongly in looking after his own. The first, and most serious, incident was when I nearly wrote off a Tornado by running it off the runway. I'd come back from a singleton trip to southern Germany and I was feeling very pleased with myself for having negotiated our way through the inflexible USAF air-traffic control procedures to get down to low level in marginal weather. Despite all the difficulties Old Mikeham and I had got the job done when lesser men would have given up and gone home. I celebrated our feat by doing some circuits at Brüggen with the remaining fuel. On the final landing, I decided to practise the art of aerodynamic braking. On landing a Tornado one had to lose about 150kt to get to a reasonable taxi speed. The Tornado brakes were good for parking but not much else, so the usual way to stop after landing was to rock the throttles outboard, thereby selecting reverse thrust on the engines, which in turn slowed the aircraft very efficiently. If instead you used the aerodynamic braking technique, then after mainwheel touchdown you raised the nosewheel off the ground to an exaggerated nose-high attitude so that the drag of the aircraft's planform slowed it; at the same time you flicked the 'taxi nozzle' lever which opened the jetpipes fully to reduce the engine thrust. Unfortunately, I touched down so gently that the spoilers that were supposed to deploy along the wing to keep the aircraft on the ground did not do so, and instead the aircraft skipped airborne again when I pulled the nose up. Our second touchdown was halfway down the runway and we were still motoring. I decided to abandon aerodynamic braking and go for the reverse thrust. This might have worked had I remembered

The Beagle and me: The long-suffering Beagle was given the job of keeping me on the straight and narrow for the first part of my Crusader tour.

to deselect the taxi nozzle, which overrode reverse thrust. But I didn't and we were still travelling down the ever-shortening runway while I tried to work out why we weren't stopping. There were still a couple of options open to me: I could drop the hook and catch the overrun cable, or call for ATC to raise the overrun barrier, a cable and canvas net at the end of the runway for just such an eventuality. However, I chose none of these sensible options and instead stood on the brakes and tried to turn off the runway at around 40kt. I might just have got away with it had the white stripes of the 'piano keys' on the runway threshold not been wet; but sadly they were and, with a sickening juddering, the aircraft span round to the right like a car on black ice. 'Bloody hell, Mike,' exclaimed Old Mikeham helpfully. At which point one of the mainwheels dug into the grass sideways and, with an expensive-sounding crunch, the machine came to a sudden halt.

Tornado on the break: AJ and Loins break into the circuit. (Andy Jeremy)

Shortly afterwards I was invited to stand to attention in the Boss' office while he described in excruciating detail what he thought of me. He also told me that I was to visit the engineers in aircraft servicing flight and make myself known to them; I was then to visit them regularly, with crates of beer, for as long as it took to repair the aircraft. Luckily the engineers were quick workers and my visits over the next couple of months only cost me a few crates of beer. I was also interviewed by the station commander. I realized that, thanks to Joe, I had got off very lightly when this latter interview took place not in the station commander's office, but in neighbouring urinals in the mess toilet at 'Happy Hour'. 'You'd better not try to drive one of my Tornados across the grass again, young man,' declared the station commander sternly. 'No, sir,' was my meek response. The following Monday the long-suffering Troff climbed into the backseat of a Tornado and declared me safe to fly again and that was the last that I ever heard of the matter.

The next incident was with Bob, who seemed to have an uncanny knack of making things go wrong for me. It was the 5th Anniversary of the first Vulcan raid on the Falkland Islands. Bob had been part of that crew and they were holding a reunion at RAF Waddington over a weekend. The Boss said he could get to Waddington by Tornado if he could find a pilot. A weekend in 'Blightly' sounded like a good deal to me so I immediately agreed to fly him. We set of with the intention of doing some low-flying before we reached Waddington so that we had flown a useful training sortie rather than just a transit flight. We let down into East Anglia and as we headed north and westwards the dark grey cloudbase lowered towards us. Eventually it became clear that we could not fly the route that we had planned and as we passed east of Peterborough we had to choose between two options: we could pull up into the cloud and get a radar handover to Waddington, or we could continue straight to Waddington at low level. There were problems with both options. We were below the Cranwell instrument pattern and on the radio we could hear a rather under confident student pilot somewhere above us, so pulling up towards him did not seem very sensible. However, the problem with staying at low level was that there was a newly established 'one way street' at low level in the gap between Cranwell and Coningsby and of course it went the wrong way. Actually on my map it went the right way, but it had recently been reversed. Bob called up Cranwell and announced our intention to fly at low level northwards through the gap and the Cranwell controller indicated that she had no objection to us doing so.

At Waddington, Bob went for his reunion lunch and afterwards I was invited to join the crew at the pub in the local village. The Vulcan crew looked after me incredibly well, filling me with lots of beer and taking in good heart my 'I'm a fast-jet pilot and you are only a bunch of V-Force losers' banter. Actually as the afternoon progressed into evening and I discovered what they had achieved during their mission to Port Stanley: I wound my neck in! The next day I was greeted by a very serious looking Bob. 'Oh dear,' I thought, 'I must have overstepped the mark yesterday.' But that was not the problem. The problem was that some officious ATC controller had reported us to the RAF police for violating the one-way rule through the Cranwell and Coningsby gap. A couple of months later I was interviewed at Brüggen by a particularly pompous RAF policeman about my 'flagrant breach of Low Flying Regulations.' I could have told him that my map had the arrow pointing in the other direction, but that would have landed Bob in it and I thought that I owed it to him for all the times that navigators had stuck their necks out for me. So I kept quiet and 'Mr Plod' read me a very formal police caution before warning me that I was in deep trouble. Rather dejectedly, I left to join the rest of the squadron who had deployed that morning to Deci.

When I got there the Boss didn't seem very bothered. 'I shouldn't worry about it,' he said enigmatically and then he walked off to speak to someone more interesting. And once again I heard nothing more about the matter. But then bad things always come in threes, so I should have been ready for something else...

We were at Deci for another two weeks of dropping things at Frasca. One morning I was due to lead the morning fourship when Reg, the squadron QWI provided a fast-ball. 'We've just got clearance to use the laser rangefinder with strafe, so I want you lot to do some laser strafe on your sortie' he exclaimed excitedly. For this detachment I had been crewed with the Beagle, a very experienced navigator who was there to keep me on the straight and narrow. The Beagle did not seem too phased at the prospect of leading the squadron's first ever laser-strafe sortie, so we briefed our team and set off. The first setback for the day occurred when there were only three aircraft serviceable. The fourship became a threeship, a pattern that we'd all eventually get very used to.

'Frasca, Paris, three aircraft join for level, glide and strafe,' my left hand leaves the transmit switch and wipes the drips of sweat from my eyes. Although it is still early in the day, the sun beats down from a bright azure-blue sky as we leave the mountains at 'Point Golf' and head west toward the coastline.

'Rrogerr, Paris forra bom-bing left-a range-a left-a pattern, strafe left-a range right-a pattern,' responds the Italian RSO.

'Paris bombing left-left, strafe left-right,' responds the Beagle. Now we are approaching the coast-out point and the Beagle and I run through our game plan. We mustn't score too highly on the squadron Pigs Board, a record of everyone's mistakes and misdemeanours which hangs behind the ops desk, so we rehearse the order of events and who is going to do what during each pass. Most importantly, we remind ourselves who is going to check which switches. And, of course, we go through all the laser switches very thoroughly, because we DON'T want to make a mistake with that.

The bombing part of the sortie goes well; some reasonable scores there and now onto the strafing. I come right after my last bombing pass into the strafe pattern. Downwind at 2,500ft; the Beagle and I run quickly through the checks, there's Number Two off target now, just need to keep an eye out for the other one. As Number Three comes off his attack, I roll in for the safety height pass.

'Paris one – In, safety height pass,' I tell the controller.

'Roger, yorra clear.' We drop down to 350ft to check that the strafe panel looks OK and that the bay beyond the headland is clear of shipping.

'No sheeps in the bay,' I call back in time-honoured fashion, as the strafe panels flash past beneath us. A steep climbing turn to the right, and we're downwind again, ready to start shooting.

In the Tornado, the cadence for a strafe pass should be: turn finals, halfway round start the descent, roll out pointing at the target, check dive angle, 'Paris one - In hot, Lima,' weapons safety switches live, 'laser's firing,' from the Beagle, check speed, throttle back, gun trigger live, 'Clear 'ot,' track the target, 3,600yds, shoot – brrrrp – recover, pull 4-g, to 15° nose up, straight ahead to 1,500ft, 'Paris One, no 'its,' turn downwind. It all takes about as long to actually do it as it does to read it, so you're pretty busy.

And that's how it usually went. Except that today, instead of 'No 'its' or even (dream on) 'Ten 'its' as the RSO scored my first pass, there was silence.

'Paris two – in hot, Lima.'

Silence.

'Paris two off dry.'

'Paris three – in hot, Lima.'

Silence.

'Paris three off dry.'

My turn again 'Paris one – in hot, Lima.'

This time it's met by an urgent cry of horror from the RSO: 'Paris lead, you 'ave keel-ed two 'orsses,' at which the Beagle, helpfully, bursts into hysterical laughter. He

A Crusader's Tornado jet on the line at Deci (Mike Lumb)

is reduced to a gibbering wreck for the rest of the sortie, and offers no more help other than the occasional loud guffaw from the back seat. The other two can't keep their mirth to themselves, either, and all their subsequent radio calls are punctuated by puerile sniggering. I am mortified. Luckily we soon run out of ammunition and range time.

Now word travels fast, so I am rather worried to see the Boss waiting for the formation as we taxy in. But no! He's come for a glass of bubbly to celebrate the first use of the laser with the local 'wheels'. Phew, I think, I've got away with it! But, as I turn to walk back to the line hut I pass my trusty steed from that fateful sortie, I glance up. There – already – just beneath the cockpit are two horse symbols painted in 'day-glo', courtesy of the fast-thinking ground crew!

The ciné room was packed out for the debriefing as various QWIs clicked through my film frame-by-frame to see if they could find any horses, but alas none could be seen! The reason for the untimely death of two wild horses, which had foolishly decided to graze near to the strafe target panels, was a fault in the software for the laser rangefinder. Apparently, the range staff ate well on fresh horse steaks for the next few weeks. Luckily the Boss found this one quite amusing, so once again I got away with it.

In comparison to that ill-fated sortie, the rest of the detachment went quite successfully, though sadly the Beagle and I broke our aircraft on the 'Competition Sortie' at the end of the detachment, so we were could not participate.

Over the summer I did most of my flying with Cookie. It seemed that after our adventures at Deci the Beagle thought I was OK to be set loose with a more junior navigator. Or perhaps he simply decided that I was beyond helping. At any rate Cookie and I started our work up to become pairs leaders, flying sorties across Germany and the UK over the summer months and landing away at faraway places like Lechfeld, Bremgarten and RAF Lossiemouth in Scotland. Although we knew each other very well socially, at first we did not really 'gel' together very well as a crew. I thought that Cookie was a bit of a back-seat driver and I found myself double checking his navigation. What that really meant was that neither of us fully trusted the other. By our second month, though, we had worked through our differences: we had leant to trust each other fully and as a result we worked together as a good team. And I had finally realized how fortunate I was to have been crewed with a truly excellent navigator.

In mid-September we led a number of sorties on Exercise *Cold Fire*, a large NATO exercise which involved most of the land and air forces in Germany. The last one was an early start: we left the HAS in darkness with the merest tinge of dawn on the eastern horizon. It was the day after Cookie and I had passed our pairs lead check, and it was our first 'real' lead. My call to ATC requesting to 'Taxi for the dawn patrol' was met with a chuckle over the radio from Ramco, my housemate, who was leading another pair from the Blackhand Squadron just behind us. For the first ten minutes or so we stayed at 2,000ft: the LFAs were not yet open, so we enjoyed a leisurely transit in semi-darkness towards the Osnubruck ridge. 'The LFAs are open – let's get down,' announced Cookie and we eased into low level in the still of the early morning. Bathed in the half light of dawn, the towns and villages of the north German plain were beginning to wake up. Tendrils of smoke drifted vertically from the occasional chimney, avenues of trees cast long shadows over dew-covered fields and the streams and ponds breathed mist into the calm air. I looked out to my left. I hadn't had to say anything: Smudger was already there, as he always was, perfectly placed just before you needed him to be there. An experienced formation leader, Smudger was always the perfect Number Two. Today's target was an army engineer regiment laying a bridge across the River Weser. Approaching from the still darkened western sky at 250ft we would remain invisible to them until the last moment. On the other hand, they would be easy to spot against the dawn. And there, exactly under Cookie's mark, I could see a cluster of people busily working among half-erected steel bridges on the banks of the silvery water. Moments later we flashed overhead, the morning tranquillity shattered by the thunder of our engines. In one movement, a hundred startled faces swivelled upwards to look at us, pink discs picked out by the sun: they had not expected us to start so early, nor to pounce on them without warning! We regroup and swing back to the west. The ranges are still closed, no one else is flying, and breakfast awaits us at Brüggen!

We spent the next month in North America for what was to be a spectacular climax to my first tour. The first stop was Goose Bay in Canada for a two-week work up for our participation in Exercise *Red Flag*, an ultra-realistic training exercise held in the Nevada desert near Las Vegas. Actually, the time in Goose was more of a

'You 'ave keel-ed two 'orsses!' Two horse symbols in 'day-glo' paint on the side of my cockpit commemorate the last of the three misdemeanours which marked the nadir of my flying career.

work down, as we would be learning the art of ultra-low-level flying, down from our accustomed 250ft to an eye-watering 100ft over the ground.

Goose Bay, at the southern tip of Lake Melville in the midst of the wilderness of Labrador, was a relic from the days when transport aircraft couldn't cross the Atlantic all the way from the USA in one hop. Later it became important when nuclear bombers couldn't make it all the way from the USA across the North Pole to Russia and back. Then, in the late 1980s it enjoyed a reprise when its isolation made it the perfect training area for the RAF and *Luftwaffe*. The citizens of Western Europe were increasingly intolerant of noise from low-flying jets and the vast tracts of uninhabited countryside around Goose Bay were ideal for practising ultra-low-flying if the weather was good enough or Automatic Terrain Following (ATF) if it

was not. In Europe we were not routinely allowed to use the TFR in cloud in case there were other aircraft around who didn't realize that low clouds and fog might be full of Tornados. At Goose Bay we had exclusive use of the training areas, so we knew that nobody else would be around.

One minor inconvenience was that despite the emptiness of the surrounding countryside, the Canadians had some very restrictive noise rules: we had to avoid fishing camps and designated wildlife sites by ten miles. Thus single fishermen, who might not even be there on the day, were afforded more protection from jet noise than whole populations of villages in Wales or Lower Saxony! The Canadians were also running an experiment on the effects of jet noise on the local caribou. There were two herds which were tracked daily by satellite. We were to try and overfly one herd and had to avoid the other one. It was a great theory, but more than once I heard the anguished cry of a navigator 'Oh no. We've just wazzed the wrong caribou.'

Goose Bay: the Tornado line. The lack of snow narrows the time this was taken down to only a few days in the year! Although I enjoyed my first few detachments to the base, there was not much to do there and I grew to hate the place. (Dougie Roxburgh)

There were two massive training areas, one to the north and one to the south of Goose Bay. Both areas were huge tracts of rolling wooded hills intersected by lakes and meandering river valleys. In the northern area the trees became progressively smaller and smaller as you progressed northwards, until eventually there were none, just bare rock and – even in the summer – ice. The Canadians advised us not to try and judge our height by looking at the trees, because 100ft over the tall trees of the southern area would equate to about 10ft in the northernmost reaches! By far the best flying to be had in the northern area was Harp Lake, a fifteen-mile finger of water about half a mile wide and surrounded by 2,000ft sheer cliffs. It was exhilarating to drop into the gorge and skim across the water with the vertical rock faces towering above on both sides, so we tried to do it as often as the plan would allow.

Operational low flying, as flying down at 100ft was officially termed, was thrilling and exciting, but very hard work with disastrous consequences if you got it wrong.

The fact that no one did actually kill themselves doing it in Goose Bay is testament to the excellent training and high standards of our flying skills. There were the occasional close shaves and some aircraft – usually *Luftwaffe* Phantoms – sometimes recovered to Goose with bits of conifers hanging off them.

The first time I tried flying that low I found it incredibly difficult: firstly a sense of self-preservation (and mine is very strong) made me very reluctant to go much below 200ft and secondly the concentration was such that I couldn't look anywhere but straight ahead and needed the navigator to do everything else. The feeling of the ground just 100ft away rushing past at 420kt is quite a frightening experience at first. After a few practices, though, I got my comfort level down to 100ft and could happily fly the aircraft and look around me at the same time, as the green carpet of trees rolled past just beneath my feet. If we ever went to war during daylight, we would have had to fly confidently at heights below 150ft to survive the defences, so the ability to fly low was a vital skill.

To start with the flying at Goose Bay was simply a handling exercise, as both pilots and navigators became competent and confident at very low level. We practised formation turns and manoeuvres, sometimes with entertaining results. During one early sortie with The Troff leading, I was expecting to 'shackle' in which both aircraft turn towards each other, then reverse and roll out in the same direction they were originally going having effectively swapped sides in the formation. In fact the Troff called a 'rotate' in which both aircraft turn towards each other and then continue to complete a 180° turn, so that they can go back the way they had just come. I was working so hard that my brain simply could not process the new instruction, so I flew the shackle anyway – and soon we were hurtling away from each other in opposite directions. It took us ten minutes to work out what had happened and get us back together again! This detachment gave us first tourists a glimpse of a very different side of the Troff. Until then, we through-and-through 'steely' fighter pilots (for that is how we saw ourselves) regarded the Troff a little disdainfully as a 'mere flying instructor,' albeit a very experienced one. At Goose our jaws dropped at his charismatic leadership and tactical innovation – and we realized that we had completely underestimated the man!

The only problem at Goose was the lack of anything to use as a realistic target. In Germany we had any number of bridges, SAM sites or deployed army units, but in Labrador there was absolutely nothing. In a typical 1¼ hours sortie from Goose Bay you would see no sign of human habitation, no evidence of human presence. Nothing; in fact it was quite likely that no human had ever set foot on some of the land that we flew over. So we had to be inventive: eskers (long winding ridges of stratified sand and gravel) became runways, small islands became bunkers. It worked reasonably well at night on the radar, where one blob might look much like any other, but in daylight it was a lot less convincing.

By the second week we were flying in fourships, with a bounce trying to stop us reaching the target. One bright morning we headed into the northern area, using The Troff's new tactic of flying all four aircraft in a wide line abreast. Fighters were used to us operating in a card formation, or in a trail formation, so punching through the line in one wide rush was bound to take them by surprise.

Young Crusader 'Top Guns' in front of an F-14 Tomcat – myself, Alan, Cookie, JJ, Simon and JB visiting the US Navy Top Gun School at NAS Miramar, San Diego in the week before Exercise Red Flag *started.*

Fighters were also loath to commit themselves to attacking another aircraft until they could be sure that no one was behind. As we sped in our line, hugging the ground as closely as we could we could see the bounce lurking above, trying to see us against the ground. The dark grey and green camouflage of the Tornado was especially effective against the Labrador landscape and we were pretty much invisible even to each other. As he was on the same radio frequency he knew that we could see him, but he could not see us! Eventually he started dropping down on where he thought we should be. The first time it happened we all slowed down and the bounce very conveniently flew right in front of one us, presenting himself as a wonderful target! The second time he had learnt the lesson. 'He's on us!' shouted Cookie. I pushed the throttles forwards, but kept them short of burner: the bright flame would have been a tell-tale against the dark background. I knew that if I kept low enough, he wouldn't be able to see me sky lined and nor would he be able to find me using the infra-red missile seeker head. I was looking forwards, using every fold in the ground as cover: at 100ft even the smallest valley offers some terrain

Exercise Red Flag: *the airfield target at Tolicha Peak, looking back along the line of attack that Cookie and I used. A full-size replica of a Warsaw Pact airfield, it had been bulldozed out of the desert and was easily visible from above. Unfortunately it had no vertical extent, so it was almost invisible from ultra low level!*

masking. We crested a low ridge and ahead I could see a large river valley, known to us as 'Star Wars Valley'. The valley was quite wide, between steep wooded sides, with the river meandering along the bottom, alternately tumbling white over rapids and then flowing in deep-green curves around glacial hillocks. I dropped into it, with the bounce close behind and slightly offset to our right, but still unable to see me. I kept us tight into the left-hand side with the fir trees flicking past our wingtip at 500kt, so that I would always have a dark background beyond us. All the while Cookie twisted round in his seat to look back and give me a commentary on what was happening behind us. After a few minutes there was a brief silence. Then, 'Mike, just look to the right a moment,' said Cookie – and there, a few hundred feet abeam of us, was the bounce! He must have seen us at the same time because in the next moment the aircraft pitched abruptly nose up and disappeared heavenwards like a rocket!

Once we had finished the Operational Low Flying (OLF) syllabus we did a little bit of night flying, which was something of an anti-climax after the day flying. With no artificial light anywhere, it was also a very dark experience! That left us with a few days to kill and no more flying to do. It was looking like a grim prospect until Alan and JJ found an ingenious alternative. They had discovered that a USAF C-141 Starlifter transport aircraft would be routing through Goose on its way to Las Vegas and they persuaded the Boss to let us hitch a lift. So six of us; myself, Alan, Cookie, JJ, JB and Simon left the dubious delights of rural Labrador behind us and headed for the bright lights of Las Vegas. We enjoyed a fantastic few days of freedom during which we travelled to Los Angeles and San Diego. The undoubted highlight was a carrier qualification party for some US Navy pilots from Naval Air Station Miramar; we decided to leave when the police were called for the second time!

Back at Nellis Air Force Base (AFB), on the northern outskirts of Las Vegas, we were reunited with the rest of the squadron for Exercise *Red Flag*. Hosted by the US Air Force, this massive exercise was held in an area about the size of Wales in the middle of the Nevada desert. Here they had assembled an army of Soviet missile systems defending a number of full-size mock-ups of airfields, railway yards and other realistic targets. The defences were bolstered by a squadron of fighters which operated to Soviet tactics and to cap it all, the whole range was covered by the same telemetry-data system used in the air-combat range at Deci. Taking part in Exercise *Red Flag* was reckoned to be the closest you could get to going to war without actually doing it. It wasn't without risk, either, and over the years more than one fighter pilot had ended his career by spreading himself across the Nevada desert.

Usually the sun was shining in the Nevada sky and a 'package' of fifty or sixty aircraft would form up at the eastern end of the ranges ready to push westwards towards the target areas. This was the American way of fighting an air war. Having learnt through trial and error in Vietnam, US forces had become the world experts in getting large groups of aircraft operating together. It wasn't just a matter of sending in the bombers. To succeed in attacking a target successfully, a small core of strike aircraft would need the support of fighter sweep, 'Wild Weasel' defence-suppression aircraft, airborne jammers, and Airborne Early Warning (AEW) aircraft also at times a close-fighter escort. Getting all that lot together was an incredibly complex business, and needed a lot of practice. We knew that if we ever went to war, the *Red Flag* experience in planning large packages would be invaluable.

The planning might have been complicated, but the flying was out of this world – every schoolboy's dream. We flew only one sortie a day, usually as a six- or seven-ship formation for 1¼ hours of adrenaline fuelled pandemonium. The range work was thrilling, exhilarating and exciting, but the recovery was often just as frantic as fifty-plus aircraft, all short of fuel, jostled for priority on the way back to Nellis AFB. The rule was to latch on to the nearest aircraft and follow them in, but you needed to be on your toes: there were two parallel runways at the base and you often didn't know which runway, or which circuit direction, to use until the last moment!

I managed to disgrace myself on the first sortie with a 'Switch Pigs' – a mistake with the weaponry switches that meant our bomb didn't come off the aircraft, but having learnt a hard lesson, Cookie and I got to be pretty good. By the time we set off to bomb Tolicha Peak airfield in the middle of the week, we were truly in the groove.

Images from my HUD film taken during my Exercise Red Flag *sorties. The aircraft is flying at just over 100ft at a groundspeed of some 480kt-plus.*

Ahead of us our formation leader starts a lazy orbit as we reach the holding area. We're in a dusty brown desert valley 100 miles north of Las Vegas. I'm sitting some 200yds behind Mol, my element leader, the middle pair of a sixship tasked against the airfield. Sitting behind me Cookie has just checked out all his kit – now it's my turn. I bunt downwards to check out the air-to-ground weapons systems, then ease back up and double press the button on the front of the throttle. A small green diamond appears in the HUD, and I fly that onto Mol's jetpipes. I'm rewarded by a loud growl as my missile sees him. It's all working as advertised. A trill from the radar warning receiver tells us that one of the back pair is trying out their missile on me. As our loose formation orbits 1,000ft above the valley floor, we catch the occasional glimpse of other aircraft flashing past us as they await their push time. High above the sun shines brightly in a perfect azure-blue sky. A glorious day for sun-worshippers, but not for us – it will be virtually impossible to see the 'Red' fighters today against the brightness and they will be able to see us and our shadows, dark against the desert. Our camouflage, perfected for European terrain makes us conspicuous from above over the low ground, especially against the bright yellow of the dried lakebeds. It is only amongst the grey, bush-dappled mountains that we can blend chameleon-like into the background. Unfortunately we have to cross the flats to get to the targets, which, of course, are also set out in the flat ground. Let's hope our escorts get to Red fighters first!

Push time approaches. The formation rolls out on a westerly heading, thin smoke trails emerge from the aircraft ahead, wings sweeping back as they accelerate. I push the throttles forward and set the wingsweep lever half-way back. We drop down towards the desert floor, fanning outwards towards our position two miles abeam Mol. Today's tactic is to keep the formation as short as we can, with only ten seconds or so between succeeding pairs. We're all bunched up in comparison to our normal formations, but there is comfort in being in the midst of a herd. Even so, it's sometimes difficult to see the front pair tail-on against the ground. It's only when they cross the ridgelines that I see them clearly.

'Steering is in for the first waypoint,' says Cookie. The first few minutes are always quiet, an opportunity to get back in the groove at low level. I settle down to a comfy 200ft and set the speed to centre the timing index in the HUD. In a while I'll gradually ease myself down to 150ft, but with the desert whipping past at 450kt, even descending that last 50ft takes a bit of effort. The whole area, about the size of Wales, is a succession of mountain ridges running north-south across a plateau of muddy sand and salt flats, some 6,000ft above sea level. This sortie, like all the others, will become a series of rushes across the salt flats. After a couple of minutes of flat desert, we approach Mount Irish, a squat sprawl of hills rising to about 3,000ft above the desert in places.

'Come left and you can follow the valley,' instructs Cookie. I bring the nose round a bit and see the valley he wants. The ground has been rising gently to meet me. A beep from the low-height warning prods me back up to a sensible height. Sandy-coloured salt flat gives way to grey rock in the periphery of my vision as we scoot into the valley. No more than a small fold in the rocks it is more like a grey Tornado-sized corridor through the high ground, an ideal place to hide from prowling fighters. A clamour of American voices on the radio tells us of a dogfight developing over the farms – an area just a few miles northwest of us. I want to move further south, but that way is the forbidden area, known as 'Dreamland'.

Dreamland is a strict no-go area. We're not to overfly it, even in an emergency, and we've been warned of dire consequences if we get too near the place. A hapless US Marine Corps crew has already been sent home for getting too close. In fact we are briefed that if we have an emergency on the range we are to eject from the aircraft rather than overfly Dreamland. Rumours abound of what may lurk in Dreamland. My favourite was from an US colonel, 'I don't know for sure, son, but I guess if Elvis is still alive that's where he lives.'

We're out of the hills again, skirting the air battle raging over the farms out to our right. Brown desert stretches ahead, almost perfectly level until the next mountain range explodes vertically from the flats. To our left the granite mass of Bald Mountain appears as an impressive sentinel guarding the northern boundary of Dreamland.

I'm vaguely aware of a black speck scuttling across the desert two miles north of us – Mol on his track. I quickly scan the sky above him for any sign of Red fighters that might have escaped from the melee over the Farms. High up in the far distance the sun glints off jinking fighters in a couple of silver flashes. They're all too busy and too far away to trouble us for a while. But my number one priority is to keep looking out ahead and makes sure we don't collect the desert floor as we rush across it! By now I can happily sit at 100ft over the flats.

'Just going heads-in for a fix,' announces Cookie. Up ahead is a massive bombing target which belongs to the Fighter Weapons School, which use the ranges when *Red Flag* isn't in town. The target is a huge dartboard of concentric circles on the dry lakebed, with a radar reflector in the bullseye. It's designed for use from 20,000ft, rather than 100ft, but a quick squirt with the radar is enough for Cookie to update our navigation kit.

Then it's into the next mountains – a ridge only 8,000ft high, but steeper than the first hills we encountered. We pick a route through making the best use of the maze of little canyons to stay off the ridges as much as possible. This is the final frontier. We both know that the belt of ground defences starts on the other side of this range. Without saying anything, an air of excited apprehension seizes us both. As we come up towards the last ridge I roll the aircraft aggressively and haul the stick back, so that we cross the ridge semi-inverted, just 100ft above it, already dropping into the valley beyond. Rocks skim past just above our heads.

'Yee-ha,' I shout at Cookie. Apart from being mightily exciting, the manoeuvre has ensured that we were only exposed over the ridge for a few seconds. We could still surprise the defences yet. Diving down we prepare to set off across the next salt flat.

Suddenly the radar warning receiver lights up – there's a strong green strobe and a shrill warning tone in my headset.

'Sam eight – come left,' shouts Cookie, but I'm already heaving the aircraft hard left at 4-g and trying to stay low. I know that Cookie is shoving out a dose of radar-confusing chaff from the dispenser on our right wing. If we are lucky, a combination of that and my hard manoeuvre might break the radar lock before the operator gets a missile away. The spike on the RWR lingers for a second and then disappears. Safe for the moment: Another 4-g turn and we're heading back in the right direction, racing low across the level salt pan. It's devoid of any cover – we really don't want to get caught here.

Then another spike and shrill warning, this time left of the nose. An anti-aircraft gun has locked onto us. Another violent jink and scintillating cloud of chaff: the jammer on our left wing should help lose this one, too.

'Fly lower,' shouts Cookie, the first time that anyone has said that! I realize that I've succumbed to the natural tendency to climb slightly as I've been manoeuvring. I shove the nose down to get us back as low as I dare to go, with the throttles wide open. We stay at 100ft, streaking just above the ground. It's save yourself time. I've no idea what has happened to Mol. He's probably jinking away to avoid his own missile sites. For us the sanctuary of next mountain range beckons. Just as we get there another system locks us up, but like a cat pouncing at a tail disappearing into a mousehole, he's too late. We dart into a convenient canyon. With a lump of granite between him and us he can touch us no more. By now the adrenaline is really pumping.

Out over the next salt pan, I look to my right and find that I'm still in perfect formation with Mol – this despite our weaving around.

'OK, there's Mol in our three o'clock,' I tell Cookie, proud of my achievement.

'That's not Mol, that's Mol – over there,' shouts Cookie. Although I can't see him pointing, the awful realization dawns that I'm in completely the wrong bit of sky! Looking across I can see a small black dot scuttling over the desert in my one o'clock position. There's nothing else for it. I slam the throttles into reheat and feel the reassuring push as we surge forward.

At 600kt, the scenery really motors past. A couple of Triple-A sites try to snatch at us, but at that speed we're out of range before they can touch us. Cookie punches out a squirt of chaff just to makes sure. We come steaming back into formation just as an F-5 of the Aggressor Squadron drops in behind Mol.

'Mol, flares,' shouts Cookie. Mol pulls up, wings waggling and a stream of flares pumping off his wing. For real he would also have dropped a bomb which would have exploded pretty much in the Aggressor pilot's face. That would put him off his aim if nothing else. Conceding defeat this time, the F-5 pulls up and then disappears skywards in search of easier prey.

Nearly there, just a slight ridge to crest before we're on our target run: This is where things are very different to what we're used to. In Europe, we would thumb our way along a detailed map for the last couple of minutes to find the target. With so many easily identified features in any 10-mile stretch of European terrain, map reading is pretty straightforward even at 500kt. From the backseat, too, there are usually plenty of things which will show up nicely on the radar. But not in the Nevada desert. Most of it is totally featureless. Even if something does show up, the maps are so old that you can never be too sure of its exact co-ordinates. Luckily the targets are BIG, but even so, there is the added complication that most of the *Red Flag* targets had been made by bulldozing shapes in the sand, so there is no vertical extent to them. They are easily visible from 20,000ft, but not from a sweaty Tornado cockpit rocketing along just 100ft above the ground.

Cookie does his best on the radar as we thunder towards the target area. Tolicha Peak is a full-size replica of a Soviet airfield in East Germany. Just the sort of thing we'd have been sent against if war ever broke out in the Central Region. My target is the hulk of an aircraft on the far runway threshold. The time-to-go circle in the HUD unwinds swiftly, counting down the last sixty seconds before we reach the target. Cookie and I make sure all the weapon switches are made so that we can get a bomb off. The Tornado has a plethora of safety switches, all of which have to be made before we can drop a bomb. They have been designed to make sure that you don't drop a bomb by accident in peacetime, but the result is that come war – or realistic exercise – it becomes incredibly complicated to get your job done! In the excitement it is all too easy to miss one switch, just as we did on the last sortie. After the public humiliation that followed we will not be making that mistake again!

Over the last ridge, and there is the airfield ahead of me. Cookie has done a great job – we're perfectly lined up. In the distance I can see the black blob which is my target. I have to take over now to pick up the exact position. Before I have time to do anything, we're locked up again. I stick the Tornado on its wingtip pulling hard, and then reverse just as aggressively towards the target. I line up on my aiming point, wings level, and speed stable.

Bombs gone! We race straight ahead off target to clear the defences, then two hard 90° turns and we're heading for home. Out to my right I see another Tornado hugging the ground. Is it Mol? I don't know and I don't really care. We've planned to rendezvous in orderly fashion off the target, but with everyone jinking around to escape ground threats, the practice has become to find any other Tornado and head east as fast as possible. I'm certainly not hanging around here any longer than I have to. I latch onto the aircraft I can see and station myself in formation two miles off his left wing.

A hard turn towards me, probably avoiding a missile site; I come left, too, and reverse back as he does to keep the formation together as we run the gauntlet of the defences once more. The route home takes us north of our inbound track in a similar series of dashes between mountain spines. By now the fighters have used up their fuel and gone home leaving us with just the ground threats to negotiate.

In no time we have reached safety and the eastern edge of the exercise area, and here the real adventure begins! Sixty aircraft from scattered formations, all short of fuel jockey for position as they all converge on Nellis AFB. I pull up just as my anonymous buddy does and barrel towards him, trying to find out who he is. It seems he has the same idea and both aircraft zoom upwards, corkscrewing round each other like a pair of playful dolphins. Now I'm close enough to read the letters stencilled on his tail fin and at last I know that my companion of the last few minutes is Steve, one of the front pair.

'I'll follow you, Steve,' earns me a double click on the microphone in acknowledgement as he rolls out and points towards Nellis.

'I think he's still got a bomb on,' observes Cookie. I close up the formation and drop slightly so we can get a clear view underneath. Joy! There, hanging accusingly from Steve's aircraft is the bomb he should have left on Tolicha Peak airfield. How awful to take pleasure in someone else's misfortune, but the sight fills me with glee! Steve was one of our most outspoken critics after our 'Switch Pigs' on the last sortie. Poetic justice has been done and Cookie and I snigger all the way home. He can buy the beer tonight on the Las Vegas strip.

The middle weekend of the detachment gave us a bit of a clue about the weather prospects for the second week. We drove through the desert for six hours to see the Grand Canyon, but when we got there all we could see was the inside of a cloud! Low clouds and driving rain meant that we only managed two sorties in that second week. On the final day the rains continued, but the Boss managed to persuade the Americans that TFR-equipped aircraft should be allowed to use the range. Cookie and I launched as Number Four of a fourship. After taking off at thirty-second intervals we cut the corner slightly and caught up with our element leader, Nid, as he climbed towards the holding area at Student Gap.

Out on the range we could see layers of grey stratus clinging to the mountain slopes; below us thin banks of mist obscured the valley floor as we followed Nid in a gentle orbit. In short, it was an ideal day for TFR operations. While Cookie busied himself checking out his kit, I switched on the TFR to check that the system was OK. As I made the switch, the central warning panel leapt into life: the 'lyre bird' alarm sounded loudly in my ears and the red 'TFR' caption illuminated the cockpit.

Me and Cookie looking pleased with ourselves after the last Exercise Red Flag *sortie.*

The TFR was broken. The first rule of an 'electric' aircraft is that if something doesn't work, recycle it. The switch went off and I counted three bananas before switching it on again. Lyre birds sounded and red lights flashed once more. It was definitely broken. Cookie and I had a quick conference and we decided to press on anyway. We reckoned that the Americans were too easily intimidated by the weather and we'd be able to sneak along below the cloudbase. The only problem was how to get into low level with no TFR to see us down safely.

I pushed the throttles forwards and eased us into close formation on Nid's right wingtip. Two heads turned towards us to see what we were up to and we signed that we wanted to go down on their wing. A few minutes later we were descending through the layers of cloud. What neither of us realized at that point was that that Nid's TFR did not work either! We were mightily unimpressed to find out this small detail much later in the bar. In those moments of ignorance, though, we felt very pleased with ourselves as we approached our start point in good order under a dark, but not-too-low, overcast.

Crossing the first salt pan is easy enough. It is just like a typical day in Germany, except the ground is a sandy colour instead of green fields. Up ahead, though it looks more ominous: the weather is waiting for us up on the hills near Mount Irish. Once again Cookie directs me towards a valley which leads up to a saddle, the only chance of us getting through the ridge line. I pull the nose round into the valley and we soon find ourselves flying up a long tube with granite floor and sides and a thick grey cloud forming the ceiling. As we get higher, the valley narrows and the cloudbase lowers; the tube closes in around us, tightening its grip and adding to the impression of speed as we race upwards. The aircraft symbol in the HUD sits on the opening of the tube, so I know that we can just squeeze ourselves between mountain and cloud. In training this is called 'letterboxing' and is strictly *verboten* (forbidden). On the frontline it has just become a necessary technique. We're not through yet, though: I mustn't balloon over the ridge or we'll end up in the cloud. Just before we reach the ridge I roll semi-inverted and pull down the far side. The cloud shrinks back above us and we're back in the clear, skimming over the next salt flat. On the far side it is a grey panorama of rocks, rain and cloud and even the salt flats, so brightly yellow in the sunshine of previous days, have become a dull anonymous khaki.

The next mountain ridge plunges darkly into the overcast, while, elsewhere, lighter grey shafts of rain obscure the horizon. There's no need to letterbox through the next ridge. The route takes us around it, skirting the hills and keeping to the low ground to the north. By now Cookie and I are feeling pretty confident: from here it's low ground all the way to the target. We just need to negotiate the ground threats in the next valley, which shouldn't be much of a challenge at 100ft! Surely enough, as we round the top end of the ridge a Firecan gun radar locks onto us. A gentle weave from me and a bundle of chaff from Cookie soon persuade it to look elsewhere and we sweep past, passing swiftly beyond its reach. This third salt flat is different from the others, though. The cloudbase seems much lower here and it soon becomes clear, as the cloud ceiling gently lowers towards the floor, that we are 'letterboxing' on a grand scale. Cookie tries to persuade me to fly lower, but I know I'm already as low as I dare to go. Eventually, the inevitable happens and I find myself in cloud at 450kt just 100ft above the very hard ground. This is where the automatic habit bred in training kicks in: instinctively my left hand pushes the throttles into burner while my right hand hauls back on the stick to 30° nose up. Almost instantaneously we're up at 15,000ft, safely away from the ground. The RWR lights up as we suddenly become the focus of all the missile systems in the area, but we are beyond caring now. The game is over and we are just interested in getting back to Nellis.

A month later I was sitting in the crew room at Brüggen, waiting to be called into the office of the Executive Officer (Exec). The rumour was that some of us would get our next postings. I was confident of mine. I had already decided that I needed a change from life on a Tornado squadron. That summer I had volunteered to go to the CFS to become a flying instructor and since volunteers from the fast-jet world were rare and the Troff had kindly given me a good write-up, I knew that I'd be spending the next summer teaching students how to fly while I enjoyed life in the Vale of York. So with great confidence I strode into the Exec's office so that he could confirm my starting date.

'Mike the Knife, you are going to the Goldstar Squadron straight after Christmas,' he announced. My smug self-satisfied smile vanished abruptly.

'But, sir, I'm going to CFS,' I blurted out. The Exec raised his hand. 'If I were you I'd think myself a very fortunate young man,' he said. 'The next person in here will be considerably less happy than you are.' And he was right on both counts: I was lucky to enjoy a fantastic tour with the Goldstars, over the next two years, and poor old Rambo left the office just after me with a posting as a simulator instructor.

three

STARS OF GOLD

News of my imminent posting was followed swiftly by an invitation to the Goldstars'
'Lunch of the Year.' It was a tradition on most squadrons that all the officers sat down
together periodically to eat and, inevitably, to drink to excess – before retiring to
the mess bar for 'Happy Hour' and yet more outrageous behaviour. Lunch of the
Month usually came around about once every couple of months; Lunch of the Year
combined the pleasures of December's Lunch of the Month with some Christmas
cheer. It was always a fine occasion! The only problem was that, with the Christmas
stand-down fast approaching, both squadrons' Lunches of the Year were on the
same day. When I mentioned the invitation to Joe, he pointed out that I was still
a member of his squadron and that under no circumstances would I be permitted
to attend another squadron's event. He was, of course quite right and I should also
have shown more gratitude to the man who had kept me on his squadron when
others might have got rid of me, but I did feel a bit hard done by. I telephoned
Pete, the Goldstars' Boss, on the morning to present my apologies and he told me
not to worry about it. A couple of hours later, we had just sat down for the first
course when the door of the crewroom was flung open and a thunderflash came
sailing into the room. After a loud explosion, three burly figures wearing gas masks
and balaclavas burst through the doorway, dragged me out and bundled me into a
van waiting outside. We then set off at high speed for the opposite corner of the
airfield: with typical panache the Goldstars had decided that I was coming to their
Lunch of the Year after all!

I had enjoyed the company of some very good friends amongst the Crusaders,
but my tour there had left me feeling a little unfulfilled. In retrospect I realize that
I had needed those two years to consolidate my basic skills, but at the time I had
so desperately wanted to move on. I wanted to run before I could walk! What I
did not appreciate then was that the experience I had gained while under Joe's

command was the foundation upon which I could build in later tours. But my frustration was also a symptom of the slightly dysfunctional management of the squadron. I liked all the flight commanders as individuals: they were all first class aviators and they were all great social company. It was just that somehow they never quite cracked the concept of working together! The Goldstars, on the other hand, were a very different prospect: under the charismatic leadership of Pete, the whole squadron 'gelled' together well, morale was skyhigh and the flying was great. I was quickly made to feel very welcome and I realized that I had joined a crack unit. I was also struck with renewed enthusiasm for Tornado flying, just as I had been reinvigorated when I got to Valley for my advanced training.

One of my first few sorties with my new squadron was with Loins, a fellow ex-Crusader. Loins' introduction to the Goldstars had been rather more dramatic than mine: he'd had to eject from his aircraft during his arrival check! On this January evening, in 1988, we were tasked with a (hopefully less exciting) high-low-high sortie to use the UK night low-flying system and the East Coast ranges. We took

Exercise Red Flag *again! A Goldstar Tornado on the line at Nellis AFB, Las Vegas.*

off in the late afternoon and an hour or so later we dropped into low level in mid-Wales, just as the sun was setting. From there we meandered eastwards at low level, following a route which would eventually take us to the Wash and the range at Wainfleet. We headed through the Welsh Marches in the fading light of dusk. By now the street lamps and house lights were beginning to blossom around us but there was still enough ambient light to make out the ground features. We crossed the River Severn near Tewksbury threading our way between the silhouette of the Malvern ridge to our left and Bredon Hill, tinged with the last glow of daylight, on our right. I even had time to think how pretty England looked in the twilight. Then there was a loud thump and the familiar smell of barbequed chicken. We had just hit a bird and it had gone into the engine. No big drama, but we would have to divert somewhere to get the engine checked over.

'Well,' said Loins matter-of-factly, 'we're pretty much equidistant between Brize Norton, Lyneham and Shawbury – where do you fancy going.' We quickly discussed the various pros and cons of each option and the decision was swung by the fact that one of my coursemates from the previous year's jungle survival course was based at Lyneham. He had promised me a beer whenever I was next there and now we had the perfect opportunity. It was only after we had landed from an uneventful PAR that I realized the major fault in our decision-making process. It was dark by now and when we taxied off the runway onto a wide pan we could see under the floodlights that everyone was wearing gas masks! Lyneham was in the midst of a serious exercise. We were technically exempt from this, but all the station facilities, including the mess bar, were closed for the duration. Things were not looking good. Luckily my ex-survival course colleague lived off-base and a telephone call later, Loins and I were sampling some very pleasant ale in a local village pub. Since we had nothing else to wear, we were still dressed in our smelly flying suits, much to the interest of the locals! By the next evening our engine had been checked over and declared undamaged, so Loins and I booked ourselves a range slot and prepared to finish off the previous night's work. But luck was not with us on this night, either: almost as soon as the wheels were up we were told that all Brüggen-based aircraft had been recalled and that we were to divert immediately to the *Luftwaffe* base at Nörvenich. An hour later we touched down at Nörvenich. Here we discovered the rest of the Wing, most of who had been there for several hours thanks to thick fog at Brüggen. And now, thanks to German hospitality, they were very merry indeed! We made our way home by coach, on a slow fog-bound journey, which was delayed even more by numerous pee-stops.

Most people would have thought themselves fortunate to fly in one Exercise *Red Flag* at Nellis AFB in their career: I was about to do it twice in six months! The Goldstars were due to participate in Exercise *Green Flag* in April, so very soon after my arrival on the squadron, crewed this time with the Gerbil, I was busy with another workup and qualification for Operational Low Flying (OLF). This time, rather than the empty wastes of Labrador, we detached to RAF Leuchars to use the Tactical Training Areas (TTA) on the Scottish borders and in northern Scotland. Although these areas were much smaller than those at Goose Bay, they offered much more scope for decent tactical flying. For a start they were full of realistic targets, including, in northern Scotland, some inflatable tank targets provided by Henry our indefatigable army major. The resident Phantom squadrons at Leuchars gleefully provided us with fighter opposition and the Electronic Warfare Range (EWR) at Spadeadam gave us practice against ground threats.

The border country was familiar territory, albeit not from quite so close to the weeds. Down at 100ft, the Gerbil and I discovered the nuances of low ridges and small gullies that were not apparent even at 250ft. The northern-most parts of Scotland were a completely new experience for me. To the west of the Great Glen, the deep valleys intersecting the mountains of the Western Highlands provided exhilarating and spectacular flying. And just as the trees in Labrador become shorter as you go north, so, too the mountains of Scotland diminish northwards, before blending into the flat 'moon country' of Cromarty and Sutherland. Here the moorland is virtually devoid of features or contours. The only cover to be found was in the few shallow valleys of burns running off the moor or the occasional sparse woods and, just like the more northern parts of Labrador, it was easy to get suckered into flying lower than you should – especially if you were being chased by fighters! There were other hazards, too, like the massive power lines from the Dounreay nuclear power station ran through the middle of the area. In many ways it was an ideal training ground: you really had to be down amongst the weeds to get any benefit from terrain screening, but you also had to be on the ball to keep yourself safe.

The flying in Nevada was just as exciting second time round. This time the weather was better, and I flew nearly twice as many sorties as I'd managed on my previous visit to Nellis AFB. In the second week we flew one mission armed with a couple of live 1,000lb bombs. The Gerbil and I were Number Seven – right at the back of the formation – so we should have had a good view of the proceedings. If the most important thing with a live bomb (in peacetime at least) is to make sure that you don't drop it where you shouldn't, the second is that you drop it at the right time. During routine raining we always had a sizeable time gap between aircraft attacking the same target so that the second aircraft was not damaged by all the debris thrown into the air by bombs dropped by the first aircraft. Timing discipline was drilled into us. After all that practice it would be interesting to see how it worked in real life! I was expecting to see huge explosions and clouds of debris just ahead of us. Our target was part of the 'industrial site,' a massive array of containers and piles of scrap metal laid out to represent a factory and railway marshalling yards. We were to attack one part of the array at the same time that Dick, our element leader, bombed another part about half a mile abeam of us.

In the end we never saw the fireworks and explosions that we anticipated. We were kept so busy by the ground threats on the way in that we didn't see the bombs dropped on our target before us: they were obscured by the same folds of rock that we were hiding behind to avoid the enemy radars! Just after we left our IP, Dick was locked up by a radar and was forced to manoeuvre hard towards us, so I checked towards him and swapped sides. We were just arranging to swap targets too, when we were both locked up again, but more hard manoeuvring put us back on the correct sides of the formation! We crossed the low ridge twenty seconds short of the target in an orderly half-mile line abreast streaking over the desert at 540kts. The only evidence of the attacks made by the five aircraft ahead of us was a thin whisp of charcoal-black smoke drifting a few hundred feet over the target area. Lining up with the Gerbil's mark on a pleasingly large pile of scrap metal, I made sure that the switches were live. I had to pull up slightly to make sure that we did not drop the bombs from too low, otherwise they would not fuse properly. The 'time to go' circle in the HUD unwound rapidly while the desert floor continued to flash past underneath us at breath-taking speed. Two huge thumps shuddered through the aircraft telling us in no uncertain terms that the bombs had come off the pylons as advertised. Out of the corner of my eye I could see that I was still in good formation with Dick, but there was no time to try and look back to admire our handiwork. I was concentrating on getting away from the target as quickly as possible, staying low and keeping some cross-cover for Dick.

Flying over Chicago: my Tornado over the city on a lovely spring morning.

I enjoyed some amazing flying during the detachment and there was some fantastic off-duty moments, too, ranging from a drive across the desert to Los Angeles for a *Pink Floyd* concert, to a squadron black tie night out, which ended with us putting the leftover 'kitty' on the roulette table and winning back the cost of our evening's entertainment! At the end of the detacthment we spent three days flying the aircraft across the US, back to their summer home in Goose Bay. The first day of the transit was a tedious 2¾ hours clinging to my leader's wingtip in close formation through unrelentingly thick cloud. On the second day, though, the skies cleared for the leg from Omaha, Nebraska to Utica, New York State. This time it was my turn to lead two hours' worth of relaxed, loose formation. With no clouds to spoil the view, I could admire the spectacular scenery, which more than made up for the hard work of the previous day. For me, the most memorable sight was the city of Chicago sprawling beneath us in the sunshine of a bright April morning.

In the crewing reshuffle that followed *Green Flag*, I was crewed with Loins and much of my flying for the rest of my tour with the Goldstars was with him. We were a great team, each one aware of the strengths and weaknesses of the other, instinctively compensating where necessary and accentuating strengths of our crewmate; the team was, I believe, better than the sum of its parts and I thoroughly enjoyed flying with Loins.

It is difficult to describe a daily routine a Brüggen, since no two days were the same. Every day the cocktail of exercise tasking, the annual training syllabus and aircraft serviceability would be mixed slightly differently and of course the weather, which was probably the single greatest influence, would be different too. The daily flying programme was published the evening before on the noticeboard in the Officers' Mess, but what actually happened on the day often bore little resemblance to the original plan. The person who had to juggle all the various competing, and often contradictory, factors was the 'Auth' (duty authorizing officer). The Auth, who was responsible for the day-to-day running of the flying programme, worked from the ops desk in the squadron 'Hard'. In a slightly darkened room, the ops desk sat under a huge Perspex board on which the aircraft, the crews and their task were written in chinagraph pen. Radios, telephones and squawk boxes kept the Auth in touch with the outside world. Take-off and landing times were recorded on the board in neat chinagraph, by an operations assistant who helped with the admin of running the flying operation, for example by making low-level bookings or filing flight plans. The engineering co-ordinator 'lived' in an office next-door, interconnected by a hatch.

Met (weather) briefing was the morning communion for us. The call to prayer was not the toll of a church bell, but the Auth's countdown of 'five, four, three, two, one – Hack.' For every brief started on the exact second with a time check. Then the disembodied voice Met forecaster would emanate from a small green spherical speaker next to the telephone. He would intone the synoptic situation and the weather cross section, while the Auth reverently laid out the appropriate slides on the overhead projector. Everyone in the room watched and listened in hushed concentration. At the end of the brief the Auth would utter his pronouncement on what the flying programme would really look like and then the planning room would explode into activity.

If the weather was good enough in northern Germany we would plan to fly there; if it was not we would look further afield, perhaps to southern Germany or perhaps back to the UK. Next we would see if we had any range details booked – typically it would be Nordhorn and we would aim to fit that into the sortie profile. So now we had a take-off time, a general area to fly in (let's say northern Germany) and a range slot (Nordhorn) and we had to fill the time between take-off and the beginning of the range slot with the best training value we could. We would also choose two targets from the large map of Germany on the wall of the planning room in the Hard. The map showed the position of various 'NATO-approved training targets' which were generally military installations. With a country full of army units and SAM sites there was no shortage of choice. For example, we might pick an army barracks in LFA 3 to the east of Paderborn and a HAWK missile site in LFA 1 to the east of Ahlhorn. And as Loins was deeply interested in Electronic Warfare (EW), much of our tactical flying would inevitably route past the EW site at Borgolzhausen on the Teutoburg Ridge a few miles northwest of Bielefeld. The next 1½ hours would be filled with frantic activity: the attacks would be planned, formation splits would de designed to ensure that every aircraft attacked from a different direction and that each one had the correct time separation from the others. Then a route joining all the targets and ranges would be drawn up taking a meandering course to give the bounce crew a chance to get ahead so that they could set up for another ambush. If there was no bounce, a telephone call to Wildenrath would tell us where the Phantoms were intending to ply their trade.

One pilot would work out details of the radar offsets to be used to help find the target while another collected all the information needed for the briefing, and filled out the overhead projector slides ready for formation leaders to use. Meanwhile, the navigators huddled around the computerized map table measuring the tracks and distances. It was policy on the Goldstars to make every plan 'IMC-capable' so that it could be flown in bad weather or at night; of course we could not have flown the route in those conditions because of peacetime rules in Germany, but at least we were always in the habit of planning for the worst case. Usually the route was planned with parallel tracks, which was quite a time-consuming task. Just like the met brief, formation briefings started precisely on time, with the lead pilot counting down the seconds to the 'time hack.' He would then brief the 'domestics,' details of the departure and recovery, the formations and tactics to be used en-route, before the lead navigator ran through the route, timings and fixes for the sortie.

In a final out-briefing the Auth checked that that every detail had been properly covered, and then signed the authorization sheets. Then we 'walked.' If the aircraft were in a nearby HAS we might do so literally, but for the further HAS sites the squadron driver would drop us off in the aircrew minibus. In the HAS, the two-man 'see off team' would meet us and while the navigator got into the back sat and started up 'the kit', the pilot checked and signed the aircraft Form 700, which detailed the servicing that had been carried out on the aircraft and any faults that it might be carrying. After that he would carry out his 'walk around' check to see that all was in order and remove the safety pins from all the pylons. The Tornado was something of a pig to start up: electronic equipment often needed to be recycled and one sometimes had to wrestle the engines to get them started by unloading generators and other sundry equipment. Such techniques were not in the owner's manual, but the alternative was a disconsolate walk back to the crewroom. It was a joke (though not a very funny one) in the Tornado force that we briefed as a fourship, walked as a threeship, taxied as a pair and took off as a singleton and there were indeed days like that. Most of the time, though, we managed to coax our beasts into life and after checking in on the squadron frequency we nosed carefully out of the HAS and onto the taxiway where we met up with the rest of the formation.

Today we are just a pair. Our wingman follows us out from the Goldstar site for the short taxy to the easterly runway and within a few minutes we're airborne. We clean up and sweep the wings back to 45°. Our wingman slides back into a looser arrow formation. We stay at 1,000ft and 360kt in deference to the locals who get upset by the noise we would make if we were lower and faster. Not that we would want to be lower or faster today: it is a typical summer's day in Germany and anything more than a few miles away blurs into an amorphous purple-grey haze. Just south of Monchengladbach we pick up the autobahn and follow it southwards. Its grey ribbon leads us between the major built-up areas and then into open countryside. Here we drop to 500ft, still following the departure route, which is closely defined in the Flying Order Book (FOB). The final landmark is a huge open-cast mine, which provides lignite to the power stations that lie between Dusseldorf and Koln. It is a massive hole in the ground, a mile or so across and as we fly across it the Rad Alt tells us that we are over a 1,000ft above the quarry floor.

A Goldstar Tornado in its element: me flying through the Lake District at low level with Wriglet in the back seat.

The haze lifts a little. Without needing to be told, Number Two widens out into battle formation and we cross the Rhine a little south of Köln (Cologne), in a 4km line abreast. Away from the industrial urban sprawl of the Ruhr we are in bandit country. It is open airspace and it is full of military aircraft. Some want to find us to attack us, others are on their way to their own targets and are trying to avoid us, but all of them seem to be hurrying towards or away from the LFA. Low Flying Area 3 sweeps in a broad arc across the Sauerland from Meschede past Winterberg and almost as far as Hameln. It is the only LFA in Germany which is not as flat as a billiard table, so it is always busy. Today is no different. As we descend into the area, we pass a pair of F-16s who are just leaving it and once as we are down at 250ft I see a Harrier scooting across in front of us. Instinctively, I start looking a few kilometres either side of him for his Number Two. I don't see him – maybe he is on his own.

We tend to choose our targets in the low-flying areas because it is much more realistic to attack them from that height. Today's target lies forty miles into the LFA, but that is only five minutes' flying time at our attack speed of 480kt and almost as soon as we enter the area our Number Two disappears into the distance. He is flying the split that will generate his forty-seconds spacing behind us over the target. Meanwhile we accelerate up to 480kt and head straight towards the Initial

Point (IP), a small mast on a hilltop with a distinctively edged wood. I recognize it and pull my target map from under my thigh. The 1:50,000 scale map is folded into a semi-rigid rectangle of paper displaying the track between IP and target. I check the heading written in large black numerals next to the square that surrounds the IP. Meanwhile, Loins has also found the IP with the radar and is marking it in the HUD with a small green cross, which sits exactly at the base of the mast. I take a good look around us. This is the most dangerous time for us: my concentration is about to be drawn into the narrow track from the IP towards the target and I will be focussed on locating the target. Meanwhile, Loins is heads-in looking for the target himself using the radar. Our wingman is too far away to give us cross cover now, so no one really is looking out properly.

After checking that it is all clear around us, I blip the camera so that we can prove that we found the IP. As we sweep past it, I hit the stopwatch. I check the map in my left hand, and see the black line drawn from the IP, its ten-second markers like the rungs of a ladder. Then I look ahead to find the distinctive features that will ensure that the aircraft is following that black line. The target area shows in the HUD with a gapped bar indicating where the aircraft thinks the target is. At the moment the actual position is hidden behind a ridge, but the marker shows me where to expect it to be. Meanwhile, I make sure that I'm flying exactly the correct ground track. In normal transit flying it doesn't really matter where you are, as long as you're in roughly the right bit of sky; if I'm dropping a bomb I need to be precisely in the right place. A few metres left or right and bombs will miss the target.

We crest the ridge and the target is right there on the nose two miles away. That's fifteen seconds to line up. As usual Loins' mark is right in the centre of the barracks. I decide to target a particular building so I take over the target marking. I stuff the map back under my thigh and my left hand grasps the hand controller just aft of the throttles. It's the shape of a large door handle. My forefinger naturally falls on a push button on the underside, which I press to take control of the target marker; then my thumb flicks a circular switch, known as the 'Chinaman's Hat', on the top to slew the mark to the right place. Loins locks on the radar to give us an accurate range and I blip the HUD camera again to film the last ten seconds of the attack. Off target and we're both heads out; we are both very aware that our concentration on the target has compromised our look out for the last couple of minutes. It is all clear and we extend rapidly away from the target area. From the split point just after we entered the LFA, we flew a straight line to the target and our wingman flew a dogleg; now we swap over and each fly the mirror image of that pattern: a straight line for him, a dogleg for us. On the map it looks like a drawing of a pair of spectacles. Just after we turn back towards the re-join point, we pick up our wingman slowly closing on us.

Back in good order, we leave the LFA and ease back up to 500ft. Once again we need to keep a sharp lookout. The route takes us across the large bowl between the Sauerland, the Ruhrgebeit and the Teutoburger ridge. It is the playground for helicopters: Gazelles and Lynx from the Army Air Corps base at Soest and also Pumas and Chinooks from RAF Gutersloh. It is also full of fast jets transiting the area. The helicopters should all be beneath us – they tend to inhabit the layer between the ground and 250ft, but you never know and in any case they're incredibly difficult to see. I am aware, too, of the dangers of gliders on a day like this. I can remember watching Rambo flying past a small hillock not far from here and seeing a flock of gliders suddenly appear all around him, as the sunlight caught them, like a massive sparkling shoal of silver fish. I crane my neck, checking all around us and Loins calls up the electronic warfare range.

In comparison to the facilities at Spadeadam, Borgolzhausen is very basic. A gun radar detects us, we allow it to lock up, and then we start jinking and throwing out chaff to practise breaking the lock. I look across at Number Two doing the same thing. He rolls and jinks – it is like watching an antelope trying to rid itself of a swarm of black flies. Soon we're past it, we have crossed the Teutoburg ridge and we reach the North German plain. North of the Teutoburger the weather is sometimes better, as the ridge can act as a barrage holding back some of the industrial pollution from the Ruhr. Today it is workable, but the visibility is still only a little above the legally minimum 5km.

This swathe of land which extends all the way from the Dutch coast to the Urals is, in aircrew parlance, 'as flat as a witch's tit.' In comparison to the rolling countryside further south it seems almost featureless. With no hills or valleys, it seems easier to navigate around here by looking inside the cockpit at the moving map display, but that is an appalling habit to get into. In fact, when you get used to it there are lots of

Personal pilot: After leaving my broken Tornado in his hangar at RAF Coltishall during my early days at Bruggen, I caught up with Les again when he took over as the Senior Engineer Officer (SEngO) with the Goldstars. I became his 'personal pilot', flying him to various destinations! (Les Hendry)

distinctive features to help with orientation if you navigate heads–out. We fly towards one of them, the Dummer See. It is an almost oval-shaped lake, some two miles across but reputedly only about 3ft deep! It is a busy centre for windsurfing and sailing – and as one of the easier features to find on the North German plain it is also a magnet for fast jets. We need to fly over it to update the height channel in our weapon-aiming computer. Once again I accelerate to 480kt and I see Number Two closing in so that he, too, can over fly the lake and update his computer. We screech across a flotilla of windsurfers, but they are so used to jet noise that no one even looks up.

Then there is a short leg eastwards before we split again for the second target. This time we're looking for a HAWK site, one in the long chain of missile batteries which runs the length of West Germany, some fifty miles back from the Inner German Border. The drills are the same for the attack run, although this time we are twice as high and the ground is flat. The only difficulty as far as navigation is concerned is the haze, which merges the nondescript terrain into a bland nothingness. It is difficult to make out any detail to match to the line on the map. Eventually, I see the HAWK site appear under the target bars in the HUD. It is a 'B' shaped installation; a well camouflaged clearing covering a couple of acres. A large olive-green dome covers the radar halfway along the straight edge of the 'B' and smaller domes mark the launchers located on the curved eastern edges. I decide to go for the radar head. The sighting picture is a bit more difficult this time: because we are higher we have to make more allowance for crosswind while the weapons fall, so I find myself offsetting uncomfortably upwind of the drab-green dome.

Once again we re-join into formation and then turn westwards, dropping down to 250ft as we enter LFA 1. We set off towards the Peheim mast to see if we can take the Phantoms by surprise. On this flat plain, the tall TV-transmitter mast at Peheim is a natural landmark and it is the obvious anchor point for air defenders. There is usually an almost continuous CAP of fighters there; as one formation goes home another arrives to take its place. We mud movers never really know what to expect: maybe a couple of RAF Phantoms, or some from the *Luftwaffe* bases at Wittmund or Hopsten, or USAF F-15 Eagles from Soesterberg or maybe a mixture of all these. In our authorization sheets we were cleared for 'evasion' or defensive manoeuvring. Heavily-laden bombers don't want to take on more agile fighters in a turning fight, they want to run away from them so that they can get through to their target and that's what we usually practise. But now that we have theoretically expended our weapons, we decide to take a more aggressive approach.

The axis for the CAP at the Peheim is southwesterly, but we are approaching it from the northeast, at 90°. We push the speed up to 450kt so that we have a bit more energy if we need to turn hard. The RWR is quiet, so it looks like the Phantoms have gone home – or perhaps we have managed to sneak up on them undetected. The mast appears out of the gloom and I look hard to see any other aircraft. Then I see them! Two Eagles, cruising at about 1,500ft are directly ahead of us. They start a left turn that will take them onto the 'hot' into-threat leg of the CAP, not realizing that the threat is coming up fast behind them. I double press the air-to-air button on the front of the throttles to get a missile sight in the HUD and pull up to get a radar lock on the nearest Eagle. That's when they realize that we're there. The Eagle cranks into a hard left turn and I try to follow. But just then some sixth sense tells me to slacken the pull and as I do so the light-grey belly of a Phantom suddenly appears from under our nose. I push hard, ruddering right as I do so and the Phantom flashes past our heads. I can see every oil stain and rivet as it goes by. That was a close one! With the nose now pointing downwards and the wings nearly level I get a grandstand view of what is happening. We have stumbled into the middle of a huge 'fur ball' of manoeuvring aircraft. Phantoms and Eagles are 'turning and burning' trying to get the better of four more Tornados, some Dutch F-5s and even a couple of Belgian Mirages, which for their part are all trying to get the better of the air defenders! I count about twelve aircraft around me, all manoeuvring hard. Having had one close shave, discretion seems the better part of valour and I point towards the first clear bit of sky that I see and bug out as fast as I can. Our wingman follows close behind. Loins and I decide to run away bravely and see if we can get onto the range at Nordhorn a little earlier than planned.

Nordhorn, so difficult to find in my first tour, seems pretty straightforward now. I have been there so many times that I can find all the landmarks: the tiny clearings in woods and the minor road junctions. We charge through for a FRA, and then pull up into the academic pattern for three more passes. Bombs gone and it is time to recover to Brüggen. There is a bit of low-flying to be done as we transit LFA 2, but not for long as our recovery route into Brüggen starts in the middle of the LFA. Unfortunately that point coincides with another CAP anchor point, so sometimes we have to suffer the irritation of being intercepted by the Wildenrath boys as we are slowing down and pulling up to go home. Usually a waggle of the wings is enough to let them know that we're not playing, though. We cross the Rhine near Wesel and fly towards Venlo. Here we cross the Maas, then turn to follow it south towards Roermond, where we re-cross the river at a convenient railway bridge which points us directly towards Brüggen. Number Two closes into a tight arrow. Any aircrew outdoors on the station will be watching recovering formations with critical eyes. We fly over the runway threshold at 500ft and 360kt and I pull up and right into the break. Throttles closed; airbrakes out, wings forward and manoeuvre flaps down. A steep decelerating curve brings us downwind, abeam the threshold at 1,000ft. Below 280kt I extend the flaps to 'mid' and below 235kt the gear comes down. The speed bleeds back, I turn finals concentrating now not on speed but on Alpha (angle of attack), or in the HUD. I push up the power to hold 10 units and roll out to put the aircraft symbol in the HUD onto the numbers.

We taxi back to our HAS after 1¾ hours of busy flying, looking forward to a well-earned cup of coffee. But the work is not over yet: the debriefing is to come. With paperwork completed and coffee mugs full we will sit in the briefing room and reconstruct the sortie. We will go through it in fine detail, dissect every aspect of it, picking out the lessons, discovering what we could do better next time. Then, once the films have been developed, we will go through each simulated attack and each pass on the range, sometimes frame-by-frame. Once again we want to find out what we got right and, more importantly, what we got wrong so that we will not make the same errors tomorrow. And tomorrow we will do something very similar – yet which will also be something very different.

Goldstar Squadron Photograph. I'm second from left sitting on the wing (without my customary moustache). On the left of the front row, Baggers leans nonchalantly against the fuel tank next to Pete our charismatic Boss.

Late one morning in May, the crash alarm sounded and the station tannoy announced that a Tornado aircraft had crashed off base. In the three years since re-equipping with the Tornado the Wing had already lost two aircraft and in both those accidents the crews had ejected safely. We expected the same, but this time, sadly, it was different. Steve, my mentor from Crusader days, had lost his life flying into the ground after bouncing a formation at low level. The whole thing seemed distinctly unreal to me: Steve had been one of those larger than life characters, an ever-cheerful extravert and an incredibly talented pilot, who had seemed to be indestructible. And I had reason to be deeply grateful to him. He had taken it upon himself to turn me into a decent ground-attack pilot, using a mixture of charming persuasion, harsh bullying and brilliant personal example. He had hammered me mercilessly when I screwed up, praised me generously when I got things right and was always a friendly and welcoming face in the crew room or the bar. Perhaps more than anyone he had helped me grow from bare adequacy to credible competence. No, it didn't seem true that he had gone. On the day of Steve's funeral, Ramco and I strolled through the pine trees down the gentle slope from the Officers' Mess towards the church. The sun smiled down on us as we walked stiffly in our best uniforms that had been made-to-measure for our former slimmer selves. We bantered with each other light-heartedly until we got to the church door. Here the temperature mysteriously dropped by several degrees and we were suddenly both struck by the awful reality and seriousness of what was happening. In an instant two jaunty fighter pilots had been transformed into two small boys, lost in a grown-up world. Steve's was the first and the hardest of a number of similar funerals I attended over the next few years.

We were back in Goose Bay just over a month later. Despite June nominally being a summer month, it was still cold and in places there was even snow on the ground. For most of the first week at Goose the weather forced our hand and the flying was mostly in cloud using the TFR. For many crews this was the first time they had been able to use the TFR in daylight in cloud – Loins and I had already experienced it during our dash across Sardinia a couple of years beforehand. We routinely flew in pairs, with the two aircraft on parallel tracks.

And so we might spend 1½ hours flying around the wilds of Labrador, with the view from the cockpit alternating between the thick mists inside the cloud that sat on the high ground and the plush green carpet of fir trees which covered the sweeping valleys. Dipping out of the cloud to cross one of the many valleys, it was reassuring to look across and see our wingman in perfect formation a mile abeam us, anti-collision light flashing bright red against the deep green of the trees. The forest stretched on either side as far as we could see, punctuated by rivers and lakes, but ahead of us, where it rose towards the next ridgeline, it merged into the grey overcast. Hurtling straight towards a hidden, cloud-covered hill certainly concentrates the mind! In those moments, Loins' and my whole focus would be on our radar displays, watching closely to make sure that the aircraft climbed above the unseen ridge. My right hand would be on the control column, fingers poised over the autopilot cut-out button, ready to pull back the stick as hard as I could. Occasionally the cloud would be a little thinner and through the mist we would see rocks and trees skimming past just below us, before a denser bank of fog drew its cloak around us. As we ventured further northwards the vista of trees was gradually replaced by a desolate wilderness of bare rock and ice-covered lakes. Paradoxically the ride over this bleakly forbidding landscape was smoother than over the softer wooded country: the relentless erosion over millennia had ground the surface into gentle curves and it was not unusual to find ourselves just under the cloudbase, skimming over miles of flattened basalt.

At the end of the week the weather improved in time for the Goose Bay Air Day. Our contribution to the event was a close formation flypast by four aircraft in a box formation. Unfortunately during the practice, after a very punchy break into the circuit, I snapped the gear down at exactly 325kt instead of exactly 235kt as I'd been briefed. It was a case of numerical dyslexia when I saw the right digits in the HUD. I visited the groundcrew that evening with a crate of beer to apologize for causing them extra work, but luckily they found it rather amusing and were grateful for something to do over the weekend!

After the success of his inflatable tanks earlier in the year, Henry decided that he should take a Laser Target Marker (LTM) to the small range that had been established in the southern area. I thought that he was a brave man because, apart from leaving himself vulnerable to our ineptitude, he was also heading for 'bear country!' The range comprised a stack of oil drums in a small clearing in the forest – hard to find but better than nothing. Loins and I visited Henry at the start of the week with an inert 1,000lb bomb loaded underneath our Tornado. This practice weapon was the same size and shape as a real bomb, except that it was made of concrete instead of high explosive. We delivered it onto his laser mark from a mini-loft attack, pulling up just short of the target into a low wingover. Once the bomb had come off, I reversed the turn to parallel our original track so that we could watch the results. We saw our bomb impact amongst the oil drums, just as we had expected, but then came something that we had not expected: I suppose we should have realized that 1,000lb of concrete traveling at nearly 500kt was not going to be stopped by a mere pile of oil drums. It kept on going! We watched in amazement as the bomb careered through the trees for another mile or so, taking down anything in its path like a line of dominoes.

The Canadian theme continued on our return from Goose Bay with a squadron exchange with a Canadian CF-18 Hornet-equipped squadron from Baden Solingen. Among the aircraft they brought with them was a two-seater and there were some back-seat rides for the lucky few. One of the lucky few was to be a huge toy panda bear, which sat in our crew room. It had been a squadron mascot from years beforehand and it had its own logbook, recording a long flying career in Canberras, Phantoms and Jaguars. The Canadians decided that the Panda's logbook should also contain the Hornet. I learned one evening late in the week that I was also to be one of the lucky few. What I had not realized until I was being strapped into the back of the aircraft was that the panda and I would be sharing our first Hornet flight! We taxied out with me crammed into the tiny rear cockpit, clutching a huge panda which seemed to take up more space than I did. I had to peer over its shoulder to see out of the front. We took off and climbed to high level, heading down to southern Germany. Once there we would go looking for a fight with any mud movers in the LFA east of Dinkelsbuhl. The Hornet was an awesomely capable air-defence fighter, so if anyone was using that LFA, it would not be their lucky day.

While Grass, my pilot, stuck to his leader's wingtip for the transit, I busied myself getting the panda out of my way by squeezing it between the side of my ejection seat and the canopy. We both finished our tasks at about the same time: I stretched out in my new-found space and Grass widened into tactical formation, accelerating to 420kt. At low level the weather was clear beneath a sheet of high alto-cumulus. We headed towards the 'Battleship' – a long wooded hill with a tall mast on top. From a distance the hill looked just like the silhouette of an old battleship and being in the middle of the LFA, it made an ideal anchor point for fighters on CAP.

Almost as soon as we established ourselves on station, the radar painted a pair of aircraft fifteen miles away, heading towards us. They made an inviting target and our Canadian heroes went straight on the offensive, widening out into pincer movement that would bring them in from either side right behind the unfortunate pair. Just before the final hook, Grass rolled the wings level to check that there weren't any trailers. 'Jeez,' was all I heard before the burners lit and we pitched up at 6-g towards the vertical. It hadn't been a pair of unsuspecting mud movers that we had found: we had just tangled with the front of a 'gorilla' of twenty-plus aircraft from the NATO tactical leadership programme! Now eighteen of NATO's finest

A full war-load of eight 1,000lb bombs underneath a Tornado. All those bombs cause a huge amount of drag, but there was a satisfying thump when they came off! (Dougie Roxburgh)

fighter pilots were lining up behind us trying to get some gunsight film of two dumb Hornets which had blundered into their path! We soon ran out of fuel and with tails between our legs, we climbed back to medium-level for the long transit back to Brüggen.

A week or so later Loins and I set off for an afternoon high-low-high sortie to use the range at Cowden, just off the coast between Hull and Bridlington. We'd done the same thing the previous evening and dropped some good bombs, so we felt that we were in the groove. After letting down to low level over the sea north of Cromer, we headed towards Spurn Head. Loins got his side of the house in order, updating the weapon aiming computer's height channel and taking a radar fix to ensure that computer knew that it was in the right bit of sky. I checked my switches and squeezed off a few seconds of film in the HUD camera to check it was working. Then I busied myself looking for other aircraft joining or leaving the range at Donna Nook, a little way off to our left. It was a lovely summer evening, pleasantly warm with hardly any cloud and the sunlight glinting gently on the swell of the blue water. We were about to call the range for clearance to join when the lyre bird warning resounded in my ears, the red attention-getters flashed urgently on the coaming and the red 'APU FIRE' caption lit up on the warning panel. With heart pounding I pulled up to 2,000ft. There had been a number of unexplained Tornado accidents recently where control of the aircraft had been lost because of a fire in the rear fuselage; usually the only symptom just before a catastrophic loss of control was this warning caption. The Auxiliary Power Unit (APU) – is a small jet engine at the back of the aircraft, which was used to power the generators on the ground and supply air to start the main engines. Since it could only be used on the ground, one would never expect to see the fire warning in the air. Instinctively I pointed the nose towards Coningsby, the nearest airfield, but still some forty miles distant. At the same time, I hear Loins put out a 'Mayday' call. Having had to jump out of a Tornado once before, he was pretty twitched and his voice was several octaves higher than normal; I, too, could feel the ice-cold grip of fear slowly take hold of me. I tightened my straps and tried to run through in my mind exactly what I'd do if I felt myself losing control of the aircraft. How much time would I have if the aircraft suddenly pitched nose down? The North Sea, so refreshingly inviting just a few moments beforehand, now seemed cold, grey and forbidding. We didn't say much as we headed straight towards Coningsby, but we knew that we had to get the aircraft onto the ground as soon as we could. I think that Loins had one hand on his ejection handle for most of the approach – I know that I would have done in his position. The ten minutes it took us to get to Coningsby were probably the longest and most frightening ten minutes of my life.

The next day, after the engineers had inspected our aircraft, they informed us that the warning had been a spurious one caused by oil leaking from the APU onto its fire detector. They cleaned up the oil and assured us that all was well – so we took off again to fly home. Ten minutes later, exactly the same warnings sounded! This time at least we were ready for it and a rather calmer Loins and I diverted to RAF Marham, where the engineers were used to working on the same type of aircraft. It took them three days to fix it.

The back seat ride in the Hornet was the closest I had ever come to the NATO Tactical Leadership Programme (TLP). This month-long course held at the *Luftwaffe* base of Jever was designed to train the senior formation leaders of combat squadrons in the art of working effectively in large 'packages' of tactical aircraft. Aimed at the top level of pilots and navigators, TLP was something to aspire to. You had to be pretty good to get a place on the course and I assumed that the bar was set well above my level. So I was greatly surprised and flattered to discover that Loins and I had been allocated a course in the autumn. After a busy summer, we joined three other RAF Germany Tornado crews, two *Luftwaffe* Tornado crews, four RAF Jaguar pilots, four Dutch F-16 pilots, two Canadian Hornet pilots, two RAF Germany and two *Luftwaffe* Phantom crews. Loins and I had our very own Tornado for the whole month, which was great, except that only one afterburner worked. You are supposed to have two for take-off, but somehow we got by!

After a week of academics spent examining weapons and tactics in great detail, the flying phase started. The initial sorties were relatively simple, but the complexity quickly built up. We started in sixships and soon built up to the full twenty-ship 'gorilla' like the one that I'd encountered in the Hornet. Every sortie was subsequently reconstructed debriefed in meticulous detail. Cameras set up on all the targets measured our time-over-target accurately so that it compared to the plan. Everyone's weapon aiming film was inspected in minute detail to determine whether or not the correct weapon delivery parameters had been met – both for air-to-ground attacks and air-to-air claims. The sorties took some two hours to plan and about the same time to debrief, so it was a very full day's work. We were all under the microscope and, despite the occasional cock-up, Loins and I did pretty well.

The weather broke in the last week of the course and on what turned out to be our last trip; Loins and I were towards the back of the gorilla. By now the engineers had fixed our burner, so we got airborne more easily than usual in the early afternoon and headed out on the 'timing trombone' – a long U-shaped route running east-west designed to let everyone get airborne in an unrushed sequence and then get together, cutting the corner if necessary, to form a tight package. Once we were all in position, the huge formation swung southwards, cruising under a slate-grey overcast.

The fenland and peat bogs of Jever give way to the flat fields on the north German Plain, still glistening after the morning's rain. We speed past Osnabruck, crossing the low ridge and dropped into the bowl to the east of the Ruhrgebiet. There is a wonderful feeling of empowerment, for it truly feels that nothing can stop this great juggernaut of nearly twenty aircraft. On our right-hand side the sprawling conurbation littered with black slag heaps and dirty grey factories contrasts with the bucolic farmland stretching away to our left. A little further to our right industrial chimneys belched out plumes of filth into the atmosphere, but at least it means that there would be no fighters from that direction! We reach the foothills of the Sauerland and start a gentle easterly hook back up through the hills of the LFA around Winterberg. At the front of the gorilla, the two *Luftwaffe* Phantoms provide our fighter sweep, followed by the Dutch F-16s, who combine their excellent air-to-air capability with a particularly aggressive attitude.

The weather has only just cleared from this higher ground of the Sauerland and layers of dirty grey 'scud' loiter above the peaks. Fog still lurks in the valleys, its silvery tendrils clinging onto the autumn-tinted hillsides, making it difficult to see, sometimes, where the cloud stops and the ground starts. We expect that the fighters will be waiting for us here, so we weave our way through the hills, making the most of the terrain cover. I can just see the Tornado ahead of me, a small dark shape occasionally silhouetted against the lighter grey as it crossed a ridge. To our right our own wingman also disappears behind the hills that separate us, reappearing every now and then to clear a ridge, like a leaping steeplechaser.

In the back seat, Loins is busy with the radar. He has a gift for getting the best out of the radar and although it is designed for mapping the ground, he has perfected a technique for using it to find aircraft a head of us. He scans ahead while I concentrate on the low flying. Today the RAF Phantoms and the Canadian Hornets are the baddies.

'I've got them, twenty miles ahead, just left of the nose,' calls Loins. Two strobes on the RWR confirm he is right. Then the tactical radio channel bursts into life – the fighters have found the front of the gorilla. The air defenders pitch into the melee, but we decide to run away bravely: our job is to get to the target. 'Move right,' from someone in our formation. I ease the stick right and pick a route through the lower ground about 30° off the nose. This way we should avoid the enemy fighters while they are tied up with our own escort. Also, we push the speed up to 450kt. From just being 'busy,' Loins and I become 'very busy' now. I've got to keep us low without hitting the hills amongst this ambiguous fog and cloud and I mustn't collect our wingman either, who is unseen somewhere out on our right; Loins has got to work out how we are going to get back onto the correct timeline for our target run. And we both have to look out for fighters! 'Tally – nine o'clock' calls Loins. I glance to the left and in the distance I can just make out the menacing grey shape of a Phantom passing down our left side. But he does not react and nothing shows on the RWR, so he hasn't seen us. He disappears again into the murk.

Suddenly, we burst out of the rolling hills to the west of Hameln onto the billiard table flat of the north German Plain. The contrast is stark and rather unsettling, because it coincides with the edge of the low-flying area. From being hidden amongst the folds of the ground, almost wearing the terrain, we are suddenly 500ft above it, although it feels much higher. We cannot help feeling almost naked from the lack of cover. By now the radios have gone suspiciously quiet and, strangely, the fighters seem to have completely disappeared. We speed towards the target airfield at Diepholz and deliver our attack, careful to avoid the HAWK missile sites to the north and east as we come off the target.

When we arrived back at Jever we discovered why the fighters had suddenly disappeared: one of the RAF Phantoms had crashed and the exercise had been stopped. Somehow we mud movers had all missed that call. The aircraft had suffered a surge on one engine and it seemed likely that the crew had mistakenly shutdown the other one. Unfortunately without any engines, even the Phantom's brutish aerodynamics could not save it from the effects of gravity. Luckily the crew had ejected safely, which became a good enough reason for us to retire to the bar and celebrate their good fortune in surviving. The beer drinking was time, too, to reflect on our own fallibility and the thought that in the world of fast-jet flying we were all living just a razor's edge away from calamity.

There was more opportunity to work with other nationalities and their different aircraft types before Christmas. The squadron headed for Deci and another visit to the ACMI range in December. Here, instead of limiting ourselves to 'in house' flying, we mixed it with Italian Air Force F-104S Starfighters, USAF Eagles and French Air Force Mirages. The Italians were amusing but rather frustrating. Every fight on the range started from a head-on pass. From head-on the needle-like Starfighter was almost invisible, but we could see them coming from miles away thanks to the long plume of black smoke from the engine. The Starfighter was very fast in a straight line, but it couldn't turn, so they would come at us supersonic, and then blow through into the far distance on the same straight line. Not much of a dogfight! Ten minutes later they might be ready to come back from the opposite direction. Occasionally we could claim a head-on kill, but mostly these engagements were rather a waste of time!

Maybe the USAF crews said the same about us. The Eagle had fantastic radar, powerful engines and a wing the size of a tennis court, making it ideally suited to medium-level manoeuvring. In contrast, the Tornado had been optimized as a low-level bomber, so we found ourselves fighting well outside our comfort zone, but right in the middle of theirs! Dogfighting with an Eagle was incredibly good fun for the few seconds it would take him to kill you, but with a bit of practice we learnt a few tricks. The first, which the Americans themselves were keen on, was to have a 'scenario' where, for example, two Tornados would have to run from one end of the range to the other using low-level 'bomber' tactics, rather than trying to mix it, and the Eagles would have to try and stop us. It was an aerial version of the game 'British Bulldogs'. Quite often, by thinking laterally and being unpredictable we were successful in evading them. We usually insisted that on the last run the Eagles were the bombers and we were the fighters! This way of handicapping the Eagles resulted in some pleasing shots.

The French seemed to have distilled the best bits of both of the other two: even smaller than the Starfighter and just as manoeuvrable as the Eagle, the Mirage was deadly. Peachy and I learnt the hard way on our first fight with them.

'Fight's on, fight's on,' from the ACMI controller, 'Napes – on your nose now thirty miles, pair in battle formation, look high.'

I hit the stopwatch. Our closure rate is sixteen miles-a-minute, so we should merge in less than two minutes. I look ahead and upwards, moving my head around the HUD and the canopy arch. Every few seconds I look across to my wingman, in battle formation to our left, and check the sky above him; nothing.

'Twenty miles – on your nose – still high.' Seventy-five seconds to go.

In the back, Peachy stops trying to find them on the radar and joins me looking out.

'Fifteen miles, they're widening slightly. Napes, to you, one right of the nose and one at eleven o'clock, both high,' the controller tells me.

A minute away, I'm searching frantically.

'Merge,' calls the controller, followed shortly by 'Napes you're dead.' I do an aileron roll to acknowledge the kill. 'You're both dead, roll out south and we'll set up again.' None of us had seen anything!

We set up again and the same thing happens. These Mirages must be invisible!

On the third merge I see it, a flash of grey hurtling vertically down on my wingman.

My 'Break left,' almost coincides with the inevitable 'You're both dead,' and now the Mirages are out of fuel. At least we've seen them now and I feel that my eyes are calibrated to look in the right place for something the right size. It is very different from looking for an Eagle! We fly the next few sorties as four Tornados versus two Mirages and soon realize that we'll get the best training value by adopting a similar scenario-based approach that we used with the Americans. All the while it's a learning curve and we get better and better at dealing with the Mirage.

On the last day, Matt and I are down to lead the four-versus-two and we decide that it is time to have some fun. We pop across to talk with the Mirage pilots.

'Right, guys,' explains Matt, 'this time you two are the bombers and you have to get across the range without being shot. This time we will be the four fighters trying to stop you!' We also restrict everyone to rear-hemisphere shots – no more head-on-shot-and-blow-through, the Mirages will have to turn and burn if they want to get behind someone to get a kill. A Gallic shrug and a sardonic smile and *les garçons* wander out for a pre-flight *Gitaine*. Thirty minutes later, two small specks in a wide line abreast are racing towards us across the thin sheet of altocumulus, which lies like a chiffon veil across the base of the range. With the morning sun behind me, I should be difficult to spot as I pull down into a steeply descending right-hand turn towards them. If the plan works I will curve down behind them for an easy tail shot. My wingman follows me down in loose trail and a couple of miles behind us the rear pair is covering our tails, ready to engage if things don't go our way. But of course it was never going to be that easy in reality – inevitably the Mirages see us and turn hard towards us! I screech over the lead Mirage in a minimum separation pass pointing at his Number Two, while my own wingman deals with the leader. The second Mirage and I pass each other in a hard climbing

The participants in the NATO Tactical Leadership Programme Course 4/88 in front of our aircraft (Phantom, Jaguar, Tornado, F-16 and F-18) – Loins and I are on the far right.

turn, vapour streaming off our wings. Not surprisingly my new opponent turns better than me, so I unload and run, leaving the rear pair to tangle with him. Once I'm safely out of the fight, I pitch back towards the swirling melee. In the last few seconds the airspace has exploded into a massive 'furball' of manoeuvring aircraft, like some kind of out of control solar system with different orbits all intersecting at different angles somewhere in the middle! The other three Tornados, relatively big with their dark paint sharply contrasting against the light-grey cloud, are easy to spot and between them the Mirages are small grey flashes, intermittently merging with the background as they turn. I stay high for now, looking for my chance to drop in from above. I know that the Mirages can turn better than I can, so I aim to come in, take a shot at one and then blow through before the other Mirage can catch me. In the end it comes down to numbers – the French pilots working on their own can't keep track of all of us, but we have eight pairs of eyes keeping track of them! Beneath me a Mirage turns hard towards another Tornado, flashing his jetpipe towards me. I swoop down, put the missile head onto his tail and pull the trigger.

'Good kill, Napes,' from our range controller. The Mirage aileron rolls out of the fight while I also bug out, trying to keep clear of his mate. It is not long before the fuel gauges tell us all it is time to go home. Afterwards the French pilots seem to have enjoyed themselves as much as we did. And, however unrealistically, at long last we've shot down two Mirages!

Over the next few months Loins and I started our work up to become fourship leaders. The New Year also coincided with the start of the exercise season, not that it ever really finished. We had become the night specialists, covering the night shift on exercises. It was not a bad deal: we usually missed most of the daytime's hardship of endless air-raid warnings and gas mask wearing. Usually after a relatively low pressure night sortie (more often than not back to the UK to use the night LFAs) we spent the small hours planning the next day's sorties for the day team to fly. In the early hours of the second Wednesday of the year, the steam hooter called us all in for a station-generated 'Minival.' Two nights later,

Me and Les (top) lead a fine formation of Goldstars over the Aegean Sea.

on the last night of the exercise Loins and I got airborne into the dusk of a cold hazy winter evening.

It is Thursday the twelfth of January 1989: ominously tomorrow will be Friday the Thirteenth. The climb-out takes us north over Laarbruch, before a handover from Clutch Radar to Dutch Military Radar. We're used to it, as we've done it a thousand times. In the usual routine, once we level off at our cruising altitude I check the fuel. I change hands on the stick so that I can reach towards the fuel gauge on the right-hand side of the instrument panel, with my right index finger. The gauge reads the total fuel automatically, but I have to press buttons underneath it to make the needles show the contents of the various tanks. The left underwing tank needle points firmly to the full mark: for some reason the transfer valve has not opened, so the tank is not feeding. Without that fuel we can't get to the target and back, so with a curse of frustration Loins and I turn around and head back home. I plonk the jet back on the runway after a PAR just forty minutes after we took off. Back in the 'Hard', dressed in 'war suits' and tin helmets Loins and I busy ourselves getting things ready for the next day. There's not much planning to be done, because the last day will be spent waiting at cockpit readiness for the Mass Launch to follow the pre-planned 'equivalent' routes. With no mission planning to do the night is a long one, made longer by our early return, but eventually Baggers, our ferociously gifted Warlord, appears. We hand over to him and head off to our respective homes for some overdue sleeping. It is past three o'clock in the afternoon before I rise from my bed and wander down to the kitchen for a much-needed cup of coffee.

'Ah, Mike – sorry I didn't disturb you, but I guessed you needed the sleep,' says my housemate Perky who is already boiling the kettle.

'No worries,' I reply, rather wondering why he should feel the need to apologize for something he hadn't done. I wonder, too, why he is not back in the mess bar like everyone else probably was by now. I reach for my mug.

'Why don't you have a cup of coffee and I'll drive you into the mess in a couple of moments,' suggests Perky gently, before continuing 'I'm afraid there's been an accident today.'

'Really, what sort,' I ask off-handedly, spooning the coffee granules into my mug.

'The Crusaders lost a jet this morning.'

Naturally I assume that two more of my colleagues have jumped out of a Tornado, and earned themselves a Martin Baker tie from the ejection seat manufacturer. I pour the water into the mug while my mind slowly tries to come up with some appropriate banter about what a bunch of losers my ex-squadron are, but Perky interrupts the thought process.

'The crew didn't get out – they were both killed,' he says quietly.

'Oh shit,' is the best I can manage. Then the thunderbolt strikes.

'I'm afraid it's worse than that. I'm sorry, mate, it was Alan and Smudge.' The coffee, suddenly unwanted, swirls slowly in the mug on the counter. Perky, ever thoughtful, ever kind had come home early and waited for a couple of hours for me to wake up so that he can tell me himself. He knew that Alan was such a close friend and that Smudge, too, was a good buddy from Crusader days.

'Right – you need to go to the bar,' instructs Perky decisively and, like a mother hen, he hustles me into his car. On the drive through the local village we see AJ and Julia walking dazedly towards Alan's house and I know that I need to be with them and not in the bar. I get out of the car and join them, finding that Cookie and Chrissy are already there. There follows a surreal and deeply depressing evening in the company of two of my best friends and their wives – and the new widow of another one. The over-riding feelings are of utter disbelief and bewilderment.

At around 11.00am that morning, while I was still fast asleep, Alan and Smudge had been heading westwards towards Nordhorn as part of the mass launch. They were feeling pleased that they had attacked their exercise target exactly on time. By now the early morning mist, which had delayed the launch, had thinned, but a milky haze still lingered, and southwards against the glare of a low sun the visibility was down to the limits. As they cruised along, exactly 500ft above the fenland of Northern Germany they started getting ready for the attack on the range. Twenty miles southwest of them, four *Luftwaffe* Alphajets were racing northwards for a simulated attack on the airbase at Jever. They, too, were at exactly 500ft above the ground.

Alan was busy setting up his cockpit for the range detail. Smudge squinted against the glare as he looked around for other aircraft, but he probably never saw the grey speck hurtling out of the haze towards him at a closing speed of 600kts. By a chance in a million, the eastern-most Alphajet was on an exact collision course, which also coincided precisely with a blind spot behind the Tornado's canopy arch. Certainly the German pilot never saw them. He thought he had hit a bird. He was lucky; he survived. Alan and Smudge were not: the wing of the Alphajet sliced through their cockpit killing them both instantly and reducing their Tornado into a mass of flaming wreckage.

Smudge's funeral a week or so later was difficult, but, strangely, Alan's was not. At Alan's funeral I felt no emotion at all. Nothing – I was completely numb. At first I felt guilty because I knew that I should have had been grief stricken at the loss of such a close friend, but then I realized that my brain had decided that the whole situation was far too painful to manage and that, as a result, it had simply deleted the whole episode from my consciousness. It seemed a heartless state of mind, but it provided an effective way of coping in what would otherwise have been impossibly difficult times.

Over the next few months Loins and I were kept busy and by springtime we had qualified as fourship leaders.

The squadron exchange with an Italian Air Force squadron based at Cameri, near Milan and equipped with the F-104 Starfighter, offered prospect of a pleasant break from the daily routine at Brüggen. We knew that an Italian air-defence squadron was unlikely to take life terribly seriously, so we deployed there in something of a holiday spirit. My own trip down was in the back seat of a Tornado with Batty, the squadron QFI, driving. This was by way of a rear-seat familiarization ride. It was interesting to have a go in the navigators' office, but I did not find it a very comfortable experience. To start with the view from the back seat was more restricted than I was used to: the pilot's seat blocked most of the view forward and the engine intakes blanked out most of the downward view, too. As a result I found the rear cockpit to be a bit claustrophobic and without the forward view it made me feel a bit queasy, too. All in all it made me very relieved that I was not a navigator!

Our first sortie from Cameri confirmed our assumptions about our hosts' attitude to life. Loins and I were in a pair led by Jerry for a familiarization sortie around northern Italy. We were to be led by a pair of Starfighters, who took off just ahead of us. One of the Stafighters had a problem and returned to Cameri and it took a further ten minutes or so for the other fighter pilot to find us while we flew lazy orbits over the River Po. What a good job we were not Russian bombers! When he did find us he decided that since the Tornado had better navigation kit than he did, we should lead him, so Jerry set off for the mountains to the north of Turin. I followed in a loose arrow formation just off Jerry's right wing and in my mirrors I could see the Starfighter trailing me in turn, slightly offset to the right. We climbed steadily following the slope of the mountains towards their summits, our speed gently bleeding back as we gained altitude. Even with the wings forward and manoeuvre flap set, I could feel the aircraft wallowing slightly as it slowed in the rarefied air. The saying 'speed is life' was never truer than with the Starfighter, which was probably happiest around Mach 1 and did not cope terribly well with slow speeds. In the mirror, I could see our Starfighter escort wobbling precariously as he tried to stick with us. I wondered if Jerry was doing this on purpose. Eventually, the Starfighter pilot decided that he had had enough of struggling with his machine close to the stall and he also returned to Cameri, leaving us to our own devices!

It was a beautiful morning in the high Alps. A temperature inversion at around 10,000ft had trapped the dust and dirt beneath it, forming an opaque sandy-coloured floor, above which the snowcaps glistened white against a crystal sky. After crossing the Aosta valley at 15,000ft we were once again in amongst the peaks and jagged ridges – and the breath-taking beauty of the mountains. Jerry led us eastwards to follow the Italian border, passing Mont Blanc and then the Matterhorn which, poised sphynx-like, off our left wings made a spectacular backdrop to Jerry's dark-painted Tornado. I followed Jerry low over a snow-covered col as we traversed the southern slopes of Monte Rosa, just below the peaks. We kept close to the left-hand side, where the dazzling ivory of the main summit towered above us. It was strange to see the radar altimeter reading 250ft while the head-down altimeter told us that we were at 15,000ft! We sped over the snow, pursued closely by our own shadows which skimmed across the whiteness just beneath our tails. As we passed below a large mountain hut, presumably used by climbers, I hoped that they were not too displeased at the sudden appearance of two jets which had shattered their peace!

After Monte Rosa the route took us downwards into a deep valley. Snow gave way to the green of fir trees and the aircraft became more responsive as we descended into thicker air. After a few minutes the long valley widened onto *Lago* (Lake) Maggiore and so, in only a short time the vista had changed from Alpine peaks and precipices to the flat calm of the lake. We roared over the water at low level in the same loose formation, swooping past the magnificent *palazzo* (palace) on Isola Bella, banking gently to follow the low hills leading us towards Como. Here the scenery was different again. Deep, green-watered *Lago* di Como lies in a

A Goldstar Tornado over the Alps, with wings swept back to 67°.

steep-sided valley, but a valley that was very much alive. We swept into the valley, ducking under a small floatplane which had just taken off from the lakeside, and we easily overhauled the white-bowed hydrofoil ferries speeding up the lake. Small towns and large mansions flashed past on either side as we followed the course of the lake winding its way northwards. At the tip of the lake we turned to follow a wider, less intimate, valley eastwards, before looping back south and westwards over the much smaller *Lago* d'Iscea and then into the flatter terrain near Bergamo. By now the fuel gauges were telling us it was time to go home. We were getting close to the civilian-controlled airspace around Milan, so Jerry called ATC advising them of our presence and our intention to recover to Cameri. The unexpected response was an invitation to fly over the new airport at Malpensa 'as low and fast as we liked.' Obviously it would be rude not to accept such an invitation! I was concentrating hard on Jerry to stay in formation but I could feel that I had pushed the throttles up to the reheat gate to keep up with him as he led us down to the deck. The new terminal and a handful of parked airliners flashed past in a blur before we pulled up into a big lazy wingover which placed us perfectly at initials for the runway at Cameri.

The rest of the week's flying was very similar: the Boss had realized that there was little tactical value to be had from the flying at Cameri, so instead we concentrated on flying some of the ground crew on short trips around northern Italy as a way of thanking them for their hard work over the year. It was a gesture that was greatly appreciated by the lads. To thank our hosts for their hospitality, we put on a 'typical British' dinner for the Starfighter pilots and their wives. Shifty and Gav the Nav did a fantastic job roasting a huge joint beef to feed us all. On our little table one of the Italian wives was very complimentary about the main course and politely asked what she might expect for dessert. Loins then decided that this was a great opportunity to practise his Italian. When he told her it was strawberries and cream the poor girl nearly choked on her wine; apparently the Italian words for 'strawberry' and 'penis' are very similar and Loins had chosen the wrong one.

Back at Brüggen, we had a change of command: Pete left us and was replaced by (a different) Jerry. Pete had been a truly fantastic Boss: a charismatic leader who was the best pilot on the squadron and who led from the front. We all loved him and would have followed him anywhere. Taking over from Pete was always going to be a difficult job, but it was something that Jerry was able to do very successfully. Perhaps the secret of his success was that he didn't try to do things Pete's way: his own style was very much more laid back and 'hands off.' But it was no less effective – something that was demonstrated decisively eighteen months later with the award of a Distinguished Service Order (DSO) for leading the squadron through the Gulf War.

I spent a few days at the end of the summer at RAF Valley trying to fire an air-to-air missile. Life-expired Sidewinder missiles were quite a rarity, so it was a real privilege to get a slot at the Missile Practice Camp (MPC). It was said that firing a Sidewinder missile was even more spectacular and exciting than firing the gun, so I was looking forward to the experience! The firings took place in Cardigan Bay and were run very tightly by the range at Aberporth. The staff there

Low level in Italy: myself with AJ2 in the back over Lake Garda.

controlled a remotely-piloted Jindivik [an Australian-built target drone], which towed a target flare on a long cable. The idea was that the heat-seeking missile would lock onto the flare rather than the drone; however this theory didn't always work in practice and over the years a number of Jindiviks had found a final resting place at the bottom of Cardigan Bay! The routine was to launch in pairs from Valley: the lead aircraft was the firer and the second acted as the 'photo chase' to film the missile as it came off the rails, using the HUD camera. Sometimes there would also be a second missile-armed aircraft, acting as a spare if the primary firer had a problem. The sun shone and it was gloriously warm while Teddy and I hung around the crew room waiting impatiently for our turn to shoot. After two long days our names appeared on the flying programme as primary firer. The chase pilot was to be Macalps, who had helped me through my TWCU course a few years beforehand. Now a flight commander on a Laarbruch squadron, he had fired his own missile a few days previously. I was very keen to show Macalps how much I had improved since we had last met, and I was determined to make him proud of me. But the road to Hell, as they say, is paved with such good intentions.

On the day we had a very thorough briefing from the MPC staff. We went through the sequence of events and I was reminded that I must fire from above the target at a high angle off and preferably from a distance which was comfortably in the heart of the engagement envelope. None of this was surprising, for we had practised this very profile in the weeks beforehand. But even though the whole profile was pretty familiar, by the time I was racing across Cardigan Bay towards the flare, I was pumped up with adrenaline. Time then seemed to accelerate into a kaleidoscope and everything started happening so quickly that I soon found myself behind the aircraft and no longer master of my own destiny. In a few microseconds, the carefully rehearsed sequence completely went to pieces. I barrelled into the launch, finding myself lower than the target, at a shallow angle off and closing rapidly towards minimum range. A sensible person would have broken off at this stage and set up again in a more leisurely fashion, but by now my common sense was trailing several miles behind the aircraft.

'Store away,' I called as I pulled the trigger and broke away in a hard right-hand turn. Then time started to slow down again and I remember feeling distinctly underwhelmed at the firing. There had been no great flash-bang – just a disappointingly thin trail of smoke in the distance. After that hectic few seconds of excitement, the whole thing was suddenly a massive anticlimax.

'Mike, did you actually fire on that pass,' enquired Macalps.

'Affirmative,' I responded, wondering how he could not have noticed. There was a short pause.

'Would you just check if there is anything on your pylon,' Macalps persisted.

The missile pylon was not visible from the cockpit with the wings swept back, so I moved the wing-sweep lever forwards to 25°. The wings motored forwards and I looked across to the right wing. There, still firmly on the pylon, the seeker head of the missile sat accusingly. Oops! We carried out the misfire procedures and landed dejectedly back at Valley. There had been a number of technical faults with the missile launcher rails over the summer and I'd like to believe that my misfire

Goldstar crews on Missile Practice Camp. Back row l-r: Mike, me, Dick, AJ2; front row: Tony, Teddy, Willy, John – and the missile I didn't fire!

was caused by just such a snag. I suspect, though, that the more likely reason was some sort of 'Switch Pigs' on my part! The thin trail of smoke that I had seen was the trail left by the target flare. The whole episode was incredibly embarrassing – particularly as I had screwed up completely in front of Macalps!

Luckily I got another go in January. By now summer was a distant memory and September's gentle sunshine had been replaced by a howling crosswind. As we descended towards Valley the angry-looking sea was white with foam whipped up by the gale. Heavy surf pounded the beaches at Rhosneigr and towering waves hurled themselves against the blackened rocks of South Stack. It seemed like a good day for a radar talkdown rather than trying to struggle with a visual circuit in such conditions. On the final approach we were buffeted by the gusts and there was so much drift that I had to look out of the side of the canopy to find the runway! The day-glo orange windsock stood stiffly at a rightangle to the ground and also at 90° to the runway. It took a good boot full of rudder to straighten the aircraft onto the runway. Luckily the weather had calmed down a bit two days later and I set off for the range once more …

'Alpha check'

Bertie and me on our way to fire a missile at Aberporth Range: I got it right this time!

'Bravo'

I call, 'Valley radar – alpha and bravo airborne for the range.'

It's a pale winter day. The sky is clear, but the winter sun is too weak to brighten it much. Three thousand feet below, the Irish Sea is a deep blue-green. From Valley we are cruising across to Bardsey Island on the tip of the Lleyn Peninsular, the entry point to the Aberporth range which fills most of Cardigan Bay. Behind me sits Bertie, a new flight commander on the squadron who combines the distinction of being one of the scruffiest people in the world with being one of the nicest. Today Bertie and I are going to fire a Sidewinder missile. This time, Bertie and I are going to get it right.

Abeam of us, just to our left are Dick and Matt, taking the photograph of us for posterity. They are the photo-chase. When we are on the range, they will follow us in and use the HUD camera to film our missile all the way from leaving the rail to (hopefully) hitting the target. The controllers at Valley direct us across to the range frequency and we check in.

'Roger, alpha and bravo; hold Bardsey. Confirm alpha firer, bravo chase.'

'Affirm, hold Bardsey,' says Bertie cheerfully. We reach Bardsey and start a gentle orbit. Down below the monks from the priory are clustered around a boat, taking it down a slipway to the sea. As we swing round we can see the whole length of the Lleyn with Snowdonia rising in the distance. Then Anglesey lies wide open before us, and finally we're back to Bardsey. The boat is a little nearer the water now. Around a couple more times. The boat is in the water.

'Alpha steer one eight zero degrees.'

Bertie acknowledges, and we start running through the checks to make the missile ready to fire. Dick slots in behind us. I push the throttles forward to 450kt. A couple more adjustments to our track as the controller juggles us into the right position. He is trying to arrange it so that the Jindivik crosses perpendicularly to us exactly two miles ahead of our nose. Then it will start a left hand turn.

'Alpha, target eleven o'clock, four miles, call visual.'

On the horizon, just left of the nose, I spot a bright orange speck.

'Alpha visual,' I call with a touch of excitement, and then make a double press on the front of the left throttle. The HUD changes to an air-to-air sight, a small diamond showing me where the missile is looking. In my headset a slight background growl as the missile sees the sunlight reflected off the sea. The Jindivik crosses in front of us as advertised.

'Alpha flares,' I call.

A bright light appears behind the Jindivik. It's the flare pack. I'm supposed to hit that, not the Jindivik (like Dick and Wally did!).

'Punch, clear to fire,' orders the controller.

The Jindivik, now out in my two o'clock, starts a gentle left turn. I extend forward for a couple of seconds, and then pull hard right to put the diamond on the flare. The growl suddenly gets much louder, almost drowning out every other sound. I tap the switch on the front of the throttle once more to lock the missile seeker onto the flare. At the same time I'm rolling left to keep tracking the flare. All at once the growl is replaced by a ferocious barking. I feel as if I'm holding back an angry rottweiler. The diamond is now locked on to the flare and I slacken the turn and pull up slightly to give me more space. Now for the most difficult piece of co-ordination I have ever attempted. I have to leave gaps in my transmissions so that the range controller can stop me if he needs to.

Left thumb on transmit button, 'Firing,' release the button, right hand curling round the trigger, pause, left thumb again, 'Firing,' release button, blip the HUD camera with the right forefinger, pause, thumb again, 'Now,' release button, right finger pulls the trigger, then right hand pulls the stick back to break away.

Simultaneous shouts of 'Wow'… 'Jesus Christ' from both of us. The missile has accelerated from standstill on the left wing, just 10ft away from us, to Mach 3 in its own length and is rocketing away from us at breathtaking speed, trailing a thick plume of white smoke. I have never ever seen anything move so fast. Although the missile was only 10ft long and quite slender, the shock of acceleration makes it feel like a huge locomotive rushing past us. Because of our breakout manoeuvre we don't see the missile strike, but Dick films it all the way till it hits the flare.

It is a very relieved (and exhilarated) me who climbs out of the aircraft after the flight – and I wonder how I could have mistakenly believed that I had fired on the previous attempt! As Macalps had told me after my last try, 'you will KNOW when you have fired a missile.' And as usual he was absolutely right.

Between missile camps we had had our usual visit to Goose Bay. The novelty for me this time was that I was being worked up as a bounce pilot. I now had the opportunity to play at being a fighter pilot! Being the bounce was a great job: you didn't have to worry much about the planning and in fact you didn't even need to be there for that bit, really. All you needed was a map of the route which the formation would be flying and the times that they would make each turning point. Then you and your navigator would find a quiet corner and work out a plan. You would aim to hit the formation about four or five times, coming in each time, if at all possible, from a different aspect. The idea was not to score 'kills' but to exercise their lookout skills and make sure that they could react correctly to the threat. Quite often I would aim to pass through the formation and then disengage once they reacted, rather than mixing it in an unrealistic (but doubtless childishly enjoyable) dogfight; occasionally I would need to turn the formation through 180° just to give me time to run ahead to set up the next ambush.

Sometimes we would set up a racetrack CAP at low level across the planned route in the hope of seeing the formation skylined over a ridge as they headed towards us, or, if the weather was good enough, we might CAP at 10,000ft above the route and drop down from above. A third technique was to come in from the beam, preferably using some small valley to hide in until the last moment. This method could be spectacularly successful or spectacularly disastrous if you got the timing wrong and appeared in front of the formation perfectly placed for them to shoot you! The keys to success as a bounce pilot were a good lookout – and a good navigator!

The navigator detailed to show me the ropes was one of the best: Peachy, advocate and champion of 'The Big Picture' and a man of immense ability, kept me on the straight and narrow over the two weeks at Goose. We started off working

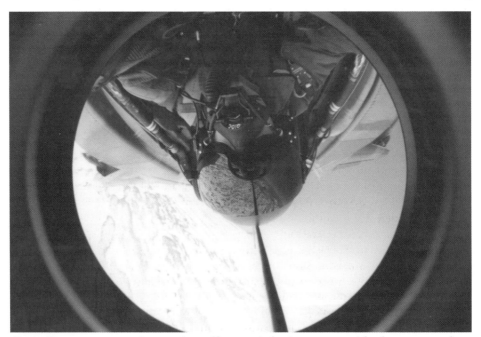

Goose Bay scenery: an impressive self-portrait by Lummy, upside down somewhere over Labrador. It might be white underneath, but it could still be summer there! (Mike Lumb)

against a pair, then through two pairs at once and eventually against a fourship. In the southern areas the succession of low ridges running across the wilderness provided numerous opportunities to CAP ahead of the formation for, at only 100ft above the trees, they were incredibly difficult to see unless you could skyline them. The Tornado camouflage was particularly effective against the Labrador treescape, so a high-level CAP only worked if the route went across one of the many lakes in the area. Of course the pair knew that, too, so they would try and keep to the shores, preferring to weave around the lakes so that they could blend in with the terrain. The resulting game of cat and mouse might involve feinting towards the pair even though you couldn't see them, to provoke them into manoeuvring off track so that they would then have to cross water to get back onto their route! Further north, the bare rocks worked in my favour, especially as the lakes were frozen and the landscape was dusted with the first snows of the autumn. From high above, an aircraft at low level stood out as a dark speck gliding swiftly over the lighter rock. The heat from the engines, too, contrasted sharply with the bitter coldness making it easy for the missile seeker head to lock on from miles out. In these conditions I would tip into a long dive as soon as I saw one of the pair and lock the missile head onto him. Then I could concentrate on looking for the other one without fear of losing the first. Once I'd found the wingman I could commit to the attack: into burner, wings back accelerating to 550kt, dropping onto my prey like a thunderbolt. Occasionally the first thing that the pair would know of my presence was my voice on the radio calling 'Fox Two on the left-hand man,' my finger on the camera button as I recorded the shot. More often than not, though, I'd be seen and the wingman would turn hard towards me, menacing with his missiles. A hard check towards him, flash past him in a minimum separation pass then blast into the distance using my massive speed advantage to disengage, while the pair got themselves back together again and I set up for the next bounce. It was the sport of kings!

The sport continued through the winter months back home. One favourite area for low-flying and evasion training was the Belgian Ardennes, a fairly large area in which we could low fly down to 250ft. Although there were LFAs in Germany for the most part they were over flat terrain and were restricted by avoidance areas and airfield control zones. Added to that we used them so frequently that we knew pretty well where the bounce could try to engage. The Ardennes, by contrast was free of avoidance areas and its rolling countryside, intersected by some deep-sided river valleys made it ideal evasion country.

On one pleasant February day with not a cloud in the sky and the merest haze fringing the horizon, Shifty planned to lead a pair into the Ardennes. Gav the Nav and I followed the planning process and plotted as we went how best to keep them on their toes. We would hit them, we decided, with a bang almost as soon as they entered the Ardennes. With the briefing over, Gav and I set off a few minutes ahead of the pair, taking a leisurely cruise down past the Aachen chimney and then turning westwards into Belgium. Gav the Nav is one of those delightful people who are naturally talented but don't know it: you would never know from his modest and unassuming nature that he is an exceptionally good navigator. Once in the Ardennes, Gav directs me southwards, paralleling one of the deep valleys off on our right-hand side. Five minutes later Shifty checks his formation in on the squadron tactical frequency and we check in with him, too. The game is on! Gav and I swing back northwards, accelerating to 480kt and dropping into the valley. The low winter sun is behind us and our heads are sitting just above the valley parapet as we speed past rolling forest on the plateau that surrounds us. We will have a good view of the pair, but they probably will not be able to see us coming. If Gav has timed this right we will get them exactly as they cross the same valley just south of Verviers. Gav gets it right.

'Tally,' we both call to each other at the same time. Shifty's team are two fast-moving dots emerging from the thin haze just above the horizon in our two o'clock, heading west. After a few moments the dots coalesce into Tornado shapes and we can see that we're on a perfect intercept. I slide down a little in the valley and push the throttles forward, just short of the reheat gate. A few seconds later, the southern-most Tornado flashes over our canopy and I pull up into a hard left-hand turn. Our extra speed means that I roll out exactly in the six o'clock of the northern-most Tornado. I'm just about to call the shot when the 'lyre-bird' sounds and the 'APU FIRE' caption shines brightly on the warning panel.

'Knock it off,' I call to a surprised pair, who hadn't even realized until then that they were engaged. I pull up and away from the ground and Gav gives me a course towards Liege, just twenty miles to the north. What are the chances of two spurious APU fire warnings in as many years? Pretty slim I think and probably much less than the chance of a real rear fuselage fire. By the law of probabilities, then, this has to be a real warning. By now Gav has got a frequency for Liege and has put out a Mayday call; Shifty has closed to give our aircraft a quick checkover.

'There is no sign of fire or smoke,' he tells us reassuringly. I'm not taking any chances, though, especially as kapton (insulation) burns smokelessly. Liege vectors us towards the runway by the shortest route, but I can see that it will take us right over the city. It is not worth the risk.

'Negative,' I call, 'We have indications of a rear fuselage fire and we might lose control of the aircraft. We're going to position for a visual circuit to the north of the airfield.' Gav and I tighten our straps and we curve round to land on the military runway, hotly pursued by a fleet of fire engines: Drama over. And perhaps time to buy a Lottery Ticket, too: it was another spurious warning caused by another oil leak!

It was around this time that Taff got married in Stranraer. Some members of the squadron got there by car, but a handful of us travelled by Tornado. It was late Friday afternoon that we launched from Brüggen – after the aircraft had done their proper work for the day. In the back of my aircraft sat Wriglet, a pilot who was serving a 'sentence' as a simulator instructor. For him even sitting in the back seat of a real Tornado was an exciting break from the simulator. The plans started to go awry when we could hear an emergency locator beacon almost continuously on the emergency frequency. After a high-level transit across Holland we checked in with Eastern Radar, who identified Dick's aircraft as the source of the distress signals. We later discovered that the ceremonial swords he had loaded beside the ejection seat in the rear of the aircraft had snagged on the cable for the distress beacon and set it going! However, by now Dick was heading home to get the problem fixed. Things were going to be tight and it looked like Taff was going to get married sans sword! Meanwhile, the rest of us descended to go low level near Harrogate, in a loose trail about a mile apart, for a run across the Pennines towards the Lake District. We headed up Windermere and then along the valley past Thirlmere and Basenthwaite, the snow-clad hills brooding high above us in the dull evening light. Streaking across the Solway Firth, pausing only to fly as low as we dared over Taff's in-laws' farm, we reached West Freugh. As we touched down the tower controller asked if there was a Flight Lieutenant Napier on board the aircraft. When I answered in the affirmative he responded with a telephone number that I was to ring immediately. 'Oh no,' I thought, 'what have I done now,' I wondered if I could have overflown a prohibited area as we flew through the Lakes. And then I thought that if I had done so, how could they know it was me? Curious and rather worried, I found a telephone in the hangar and, with some trepidation, I rang the number.

'Hello there, it's JD at Innworth,' said the voice at the far end. 'How do you fancy being posted to Chivenor as a TWU instructor. I've got a slot at the beginning of June if you're interested,' Chivenor – the dream posting! I very gratefully accepted his offer and went to tell the others of my good fortune. The next piece of good news was seeing Dick's aircraft touch down, complete with its cargo of swords, shortly afterwards.

I finished my second tour in almost exactly the same way that I had started it (and ended my first) – with a *Red Flag* exercise in Nevada. Once again we carried out our work-up from Leuchars. This time there were no Phantom squadrons: they had been disbanded pending re-equipment with the Tornado F3, although a small cadre of crews still flew a handful of Phantoms from the 'waterfront.' In practical terms this meant that we get to use one of the empty HAS sites for our operations and our fighter opposition was supplied from the new Tornado F3 squadrons which had just formed at RAF Leeming.

On the previous *Red Flags* I had seen, we had flown the exercise sorties as a large seven or eight-ship formation. This time the Boss took the more sensible view that we would fly the task as two independent fourships, an altogether much more practical approach. The weather was kind to us, too, so we all enjoyed a very full flying programme. All too soon it was the last sortie of our detachment.

Eight Tornados circle over the familiar dry lakebed; eight crews waiting impatiently for the seconds to run down to the start of our last sortie of the exercise. About a mile away and a few thousand feet beneath us the four jets of 'Limey' section, led by the Boss, are dark shapes above the light sand. Their task is to loft live 1,000lb bombs onto the airfield target just east of Stonewall Mountain to suppress the defences so that Hydra section can run in to attack targets on the airfield complex. Carts and I are Hydra Three. This time we are just carrying a practice bomb. A few hundred yards ahead of us, our leader Drewbags and his wingman, the Station Commander, fly a lazy orbit, trailing the other formation. I look up into my mirror which reveals Gasher sitting loosely off my starboard wing. At last 'push time' approaches and the front four drop toward the desert floor then fan out into a wide card formation as they head for their start points. Then Drewbags, too, swings onto a westerly heading and dives towards the surface, a silent signal for us to slide outwards into our tactical formation. In my HUD the green pointer of radar altimeter unwinds slowly as I descend; subconsciously I push the throttles forward to peg 420kt and on the opposite side of the HUD the timing index centres itself, announcing that we were exactly on our time-line. Once we have levelled off at a comfortable 100ft I steal a glance out to my right, where I can see Gasher in perfect formation a mile or so away.

Our routing today takes us further north than previous trips, which has the dual advantage of keeping us away from the usual haunts of the fighters and of offering some more gently undulating terrain rather than the usual extremes of salt flat-followed-by-mountain of the more southerly areas. Low, rolling scrub-clad hills fills the miles between us and Quinn Canyon, a sprawling range of high mountains which dominate the north of the exercise area. By now Limey section is far enough ahead to be invisible to us as they hug the desert and even the rest of our own are difficult to spot as we all weave our way between the knolls and hillocks.

We are listening to the broadcasts by the AWACS controller, transmitting the positions of enemy fighters as he sees them on the radar.

'Four to sixship east of Helen heading for Cedar,' was the call as we entered the exercise area. I registered the information and decided that it was probably not an immediate threat to us on our route. But something is certainly happening up ahead: we hear the front four reacting left in response to some sort of threat. Drewbags moves us right, away from whatever is taking an interest in our colleagues, and towards the northern boundary of the exercise area. I concentrate on keeping us low while Carts keeps a good lookout. We crest a low ridge and I can catch a glimpse of the others ahead.

'One, two – got 'em all,' I say to Carts.

'Next heading, please,' I ask

'Next track is two six seven – pretty much straight on,' replies Carts. There is almost continuous conversation between us as we share what we are doing, what we can see and what we think we need to do next. We're chatting away calmly and anyone listening to our conversation might think that we were in the crewroom having a casual chat over a cup of tea, rather than streaking across the desert in a Tornado at nearly 500kts! A few minutes later we reach the foothills of Quinn Canyon.

'This is Quinn where they're supposed to be,' says Carts.

'No – more towards the farms, I think,' I reply, but I am almost immediately interrupted by the AWACS controller: 'low contact over Quinn.'

'Aha – a low one,' from Carts and then suddenly the radar warning receiver lights up: A bright-green line on the scope shows that something is behind us and a high-pitched trilling noise in our headsets tells us that we have been locked up. My instinct is to turn to put the strobe onto our beam, but quite correctly Carts decides we are much better off running: 'No – go ahead – don't turn – run out,' he shouts excitedly. I push us into reheat and we surge ahead towards the cover of higher hills and deeper valleys, with an as yet unseen fighter in hot pursuit. The radar warning trills intermittently as he tries to keep the lock on to his fleeing target. I see a gap

Exercise Red Flag *again! At Nellis AFB in the cockpit of a Goldstar Tornado.*

in the ridgeline ahead and point us towards it. It leads into a valley running almost perpendicularly beyond it, so we should be safe in there.

'I'll take us down here and round the corner – we should be alright in the weedosphere,' I tell Carts, 'Might be an F16,' I add, optimistically wondering it it's actually an over-zealous 'friendly' escort.

'Well it's giving indications of an F15,' Carts dashes that hope with a slight strain in his voice as he twists round in his seat trying to see our attacker. We're thundering along at 550kt now and as we approach the gap I roll crisply onto our right wing, pulling 4-g to get round the corner, keeping the Tornado as low and as close to the edge of the ridge as I dare. We shoot through the gap and find ourselves running along the bottom of a narrow valley, with a wall of limestone between us and the fighter. We have broken his lock and he will have lost us visually, too, if indeed he actually saw us!

'He's not locked now – I see nothing behind,' reports Carts.

'OK – fuel's four-eight, we should get ourselves sorted back into formation after this,' I respond, as for the next thirty seconds or so we weave and roll our way through the maze of canyons, ridges and peaks at a break-neck pace.

'We're getting close to the northern boundary now,' says Carts.

I reply, 'Yeah … happy with that,' then say, 'actually we've probably overtaken the rest by now. They should materialize over this next ridge.' Ahead of us is the last ridgeline before the inevitable wide expanse of salt flat. Although our tactics on the way in to the target are pretty much 'every man for himself,' we still need to get the formation together so that we can give each other cross-cover. I ease the nose up so that we will just clear the top of the ridge and then roll the aircraft rapidly left. We crest the ridge almost inverted; pulling hard to keep close to the rocks and make sure we are not skylined. Suddenly we're out from among the hills and we're scooting over the open desert again at 100ft.

'I'll do the height fix over this bit,' from Carts, 'OK – there's one of them out left.'

I see him at the same time and answer, 'Yeah got him – that's Drewbags ... and the Stashe is about level with us, so Gasher must be slightly swept ... OK – got Gasher now.'

I jink outwards slightly so that all four of us are once again in a wide card formation, but then I see Drewbags curving out to the right. 'Where's he going,' I ask.

'I think he's just easing out to the right,' suggests Carts, 'we've still got a bit of space.' I'm not convinced because I think that we're heading out of the exercise area, but our conversation is curtailed by the return of the fighter which had been chasing us. The radar warner blossoms again and a high-pitched trill sounds in our headsets.

'Napes rackets four o'clock – knee-capping right,' I let the others know that we're locked up and we're manoeuvring.

'You can't kneecap right,' exclaims Carts – he's also realized that we're on the northern edge of the range. So push the throttles forward once more and we carry on running. 'We're jamming and we're chaffing,' he says, but the lock is still there.

'OK – he's got to be high out there in the six o'clock,' I tell Carts as I weave a little, making the most of what meagre terrain cover there is, 'I'll manoeuvre back this way, back with the Stashe and then reverse back.'

The fighter behind us is probably out of range to shoot at us at low level, but we've got more company: 'Hydra – high over the nose,' calls Drewbags suddenly from ahead.

'Yeah indicating just left of the nose,' confirms Carts, '... OK visual with him.'

I shout almost simultaneously, 'Visual with him high.' The airwaves are getting busy.

'Limey – track twelve,' the front four are running along track now.

From Drewbags, 'Eagle over Hydra – bustering out.' They're all running away in the secure knowledge that the fighters are only going to tangle with the back of the formation!

'He's turning after us,' says Carts with a sense of urgency in his voice.

'Yeah – there's a pair,' I've seen another menacingly grey flying tennis court coming our way. They're staying high, trying to get visual with us before they commit. '... OK I've got the guy over us now'

'I've just got the one in our six – you need about five-fifty knots.'

'Yeah coming up,' I reply with the throttles pushed firmly into burner, 'I'll take us a bit round this hill and see if that helps' Now we're amongst the hills again and we're in with a chance.

'Still six o'clock – we're chaffing,' reports Carts, but the radar warner is still trilling away. The radio is alive, too, with calls from the other Tornados as they react to threats ahead of us. Another ridge approaches.

'OK – over the ridge I'm going to roll to the left … round … should see him – can you have a look out the back.' The ridge flashes past, a blur of green bushes and grey rock. The radar warner goes quiet.

'I'm looking,' calls Carts, 'OK I can't see anything following us – he's certainly not close. I can't see anything out there and it's clear on the scope.' We're in another low valley now, feeling safe enough to turn back onto our track. I turn us onto a southerly heading that will take us down into the heart of the range complex; Carts tells me that after all that high-speed dash we're running about twenty seconds early.

'I'll pick up the rest of the boys at the end of the valley,' I tell him.

'One on the left, just crossing the ridge,' says Carts as he spots the first one.

'And one low on the ridge,' I add.

'Yup,' is the short response from Carts,

The fighters seem to have left us, so we must be we entering the lair of the ground-based defences. Now we have to run the gauntlet of guns and SAMs. Almost immediately, there is a spectacular eruption of yellow smoke up ahead – the tell-tale sign of a SAM launch.

'Dick's jinking left,' on the radio – presumably it was fired at him. It was a 'Smokey Sam Simulator', a large pyrotechnic that looks exactly like a missile launch and it appears pretty realistic to me! A few seconds later another one blossoms out to our left, adding to the heady atmosphere of excitement and fear.

Over the next couple of minutes we thread our way down through the hills along the edge of the mountains so that we can retain some sort of terrain cover, while we weave past SAM sites and gun positions. Streaking low across the ground, making the most of every dip and ridge to screen ourselves, it seems that we're on almost on top of the defences before they are aware of us. Most of the attention comes from behind as we charge past, but even so the trill of the radar warner sounds almost constantly. As one site is defeated, another takes its place. Periodically Carts punches out a cloud of chaff. Our problem is that we're still early after all the running from the fighters. We have got to generate sufficient delay between us and the aircraft ahead or we will get tangled up in their attack. We don't want to slow down too much, either, because that would make us sitting ducks: Carts suggests that we extend southwards slightly before we turn west towards the IP for our attack, but we can't stray too far south or we'll run into more missile sites.

'OK do I want to start coming right, now,' I ask

'Yeah – come right now,' says Carts. I start a long, gentle turn to the west, which will help me to lose a couple more precious seconds and also make it easier for me to keep the height down. There's always the tendency to balloon upwards in hard turns and right now I need to keep our belly as close to the dirt as I can. The radar warner sounds and I tighten the turn a little to follow the contours into a small depression. Gasher darts across our path ahead, extending further south, making his own arrangements to get onto his time line. We cross half a mile behind him.

'I'll get behind this ridge of high ground,' from me, as the radar warning sounds again.

'We're early thirteen, so a quick left and right jink,' instructs Carts.

We manoeuvre and are rewarded almost immediately by another lock up, this time from missile-guidance radar of a SAM 6. Carts lobs out more chaff, I keep the Rad Alt needle pegged at 100ft and turn slightly to keep the strobe within the coverage of our jamming pod. We break the lock and roll out, hurtling westwards towards our IP. With the mountains behind us, we are dashing over a nebulous flat bowl of desert, a panorama of sand, gravel, rocks, yellows, pinks and dirty browns all pelting past at eight miles-a-minute. In the distance the large peak of Stonewall Mountain gives an idea of the general area of today's target in an otherwise indistinct landscape. A little nearer to us, the shapes of small hillocks some miles ahead are the only features good enough to use as navigational features. One of them is our IP.

'We're a little late now,' exclaims Carts.

'Yeah, it's coming,' as I push on the power and watch the timing index drift into the centre, 'Three-six on the gas... looking better now.'

'That's where it should be ... just over here somewhere,' I continue, looking ahead for the IP. The radar warner sounds again. 'Sam three ... no problem dropping down a bit,' I tell Carts. I realize that I've climbed slightly to 150ft as I've been concentrating on trying to find the IP. I ease us back down. Then I see it. 'That's the IP coming up here.' I check the speed and start the stopwatch, confirming with Carts that I can see the others ahead of us disappearing into the distance.

'That looks about right,' agrees Carts, but with little opportunity to update the navigation system he is worried that it might have drifted. 'I don't know how good the kit is ... I rather suspect that we're a bit right of track here.'

'Limey, bombs long on target, long on target,' calls Dick over the radio.

'That gives us some idea of where they ought to be,' I say to Carts. 'OK, I've got this ... got the general area of the target.'

'OK,' he acknowledges, as he concentrates on getting something workable out of his radar picture. As we race across it, the ground is rising gently towards an escarpment. The airfield lies in the low ground beyond the ridge, at the foot of vertical sandstone cliffs. Deep ravines cutting back from the edge of the escarpment give us some navigational features, but the success of the attack will depend on me seeing the target in time.

In the HUD a small cross denotes an offset. I can slew that mark onto a small feature on the attack track to update the kit, but there's not much point: I'm about to see the target area in all its glory and I might as well wait and simply mark the target.

'Cancelling my part of the offset,' I tell Carts.

'Limey two slow speed egress,' I hear on the radio. So someone has used up his fuel and is beginning to hurt 'Limey one copied.'

I look left towards Gasher, who is where I expect him, a mile abeam of us.

'We're well sorted from Gasher, anyway,' I inform Carts.

'When you can see the target give me a shout and I'll give you the laser,' responds Carts

We crest the cliffs, the radar altimeter swings rapidly up to 300ft and in an instant the whole target array is laid out in front of me. A huge airfield has been bulldozed into the desert in the shape of an 'E', tilted so that the main runway runs northeast-southwest. Our particular target is the hulk of an aircraft halfway down the eastern-most limb and I pick it up easily.

'Dinky – dink – dink,' I mumble to myself as I trigger the phase changes with my left hand on the hand controller just behind the throttles. I slew the target bar in the HUD over the target and make sure I've got a good mark on it. I decide to stay in our shallow dive, rather than get down onto the deck because it makes everything much easier. Another glance left to make sure Gasher is still clear, then check that our speed and dive angle all look good.

Carts calls out, 'Laser.'

'Thanks a lot, that's good,' I see a good laser lock in the HUD and the time-to-release circle unwinding rapidly.

'Filming,' my right forefinger triggers the HUD film. 'Committing,' the thumb holds down the weapon release button on top of the stick; 'bomb gone,' I haul off due north and get back down to 100ft.

'OK keep going straight… OK turn now,' Carts directs me round so that we hook up with Gasher off the target.

We look around for the rest of the formation.

'Got one out to the left,' I call to Carts.

'Flares … look at those flares,' shouts Carts – as up ahead a Tornado treats us to a magnificent fireworks display. A trail of incandescent yellow blobs traces the path of the aircraft, which is almost invisible against the hills beyond. This is rather better organized that my first Exercise *Red Flag* and we're heading eastwards as eight Tornados in an orderly bunch. It's taken just sixteen action-packed minutes to get this far and now another six or seven minutes more will see us safely out of the exercise area.

'That's three-two on the gas … can we use the heaters at all,' I ask.

'Yup, yeah don't worry about that,' Carts reassures me, 'I'll let you know when we're getting tight.'

After fighting our way to the target, it all seems a bit quiet now. A few radars had looked at us in the target area, but now the ground threats seem to have given up. But the fighters haven't! Our short interlude of calm is shattered by excited calls on the radio.

'Limey four – Fox two, Eagle going north,' then followed by, 'Hydra, two Eagles coming your way, one high, one low.'

'Tally-ho one right at one o'clock to Drewbags,' is the reply.

'Two Eagles left nine o'clock to Limey Four.' Sounds like there are three of them, but I can't see anything yet.

'Looks like they're chasing you down Limey,' I hear from Drewbags.

'Roger,' I hear Dick respond, and we hear the calls from the four aircraft of Limey section as the melee develops. While two of the Eagles tangle with the Limeys, their mate heads down towards us. The RWR lights up.

'Counter port – Gasher,' calls Gasher, turning hard away from us. Burners in, we turn, too, punching out a trail of chaff. I try to keep the height down, but it's not easy while I'm pulling 4-g and trying to keep tabs on everyone else!

'He's off you Dave,' calls someone and I see Gasher turning back eastwards. 'Gasher track twelve,' he confirms. That is one Eagle defeated but it's not over.

'Eight o'clock to Limey four,' from up ahead, followed by, 'High to Drewbags, coming down track right-hand turn now… he's committing,' and once again we are locked up.

'High Eagle, right two,' calls Carts and another hard left turn puts him on the beam. The Eagle stays high and blows through, disappearing westwards.

'Where's Gasher now,' I ask, having lost him in that last manoeuvre.

'In our right one,' replies Carts.

'OK got him now.' We had both turned left, but I turned further, so now he's right of the nose. We both reverse the turn back towards the east and back into formation. Just in time, it seems, for the last Eagle has had enough of the front four.

'Eagle pulling off downtrack from Hydra,' calls Drewbags, '… coming your way three and four.'

'Over you, Napes,' calls Gasher. I see it. The Eagle comes screeching towards me, a huge light-grey predator passing only a few hundred feet above my head. With a closing speed of over a 1,000kts, it's an impressive sight!

'Past us now,' calls Carts twisting round in his seat to give me a commentary. I manage a quick glance over my shoulder just long enough for a subliminal impression of a planform Eagle seemingly standing on its wing behind us. 'He's in a left turn after us,' continues Carts, '… you can buster out this way … he's off us now.'

I look left and see why he's hauled off. Gasher has seized the opportunity and his Tornado is banking vertically as he pulls across to get a shot on the Eagle.

'Gasher's going for him,' I chuckle. We're safe again but we've used up a lot of fuel: Carts tells me to fly at 480kt. It's much faster than our normal cruising speed, but after charging around for the last 20 minutes it seems like a very sedate pace. A few more minutes and we reach the eastern boundary of the exercise area.

'Hydra pulling up,' calls Drewbags, 'right-hand turn call aboard.' Ahead I see a line of flares and close on that. Gasher is trailing me and as we close in he calls, 'Hydra's aboard.'

'Hydra Stud seven – go.'

'Hydra'

'Two'

'Three'

'Four'

'Nellis, Hydra three one, four Tornados.' It's Taff's voice.

'Hydra squawk, five-four-three-one and ident, runway two one, altimeter three-zero-zero-two.'

'Copied and we're ten miles north of Texas lake with four,' replies Taff.

'Hydra three one, radar contact; climb and maintain sixteen thousand, cleared to Arco.'

Suddenly, flares begin to spurt from the pods on the front pair. I realize that it's the last sortie of the detachment and the flares will be thrown away if they're not used. I ease back and enjoy a second impromptu firework display. What a great way to finish a tour!

four

HEAVEN
IN DEVON

Chivenor – that jewel in North Devon. Lying inside a sweeping curve of the River Taw just beyond Barnstaple, Chivenor was the place where everyone in the RAF yearned to be posted. For pilots the flying was exceptional: demanding, exhilarating and sometimes downright dangerous, it was, above all, fantastic fun. For non-fliers the tiny base enjoyed the intimacy of a village community: it was small enough to walk from one end of the camp to the other in five minutes and everyone knew everyone else, bringing a sense of belonging that was not to be found elsewhere. And for fliers and non-fliers alike the airfield was situated in the most beautiful part of the country, teaming with pubs, restaurants, beaches, cliffs and spectacular coastal scenery. I arrived there early on a summer's evening and received my arrival bollocking within minutes of parking my car. A very grumpy Officer Commanding Operations Wing (OC Ops) considered that I'd driven my sports car too fast around the Officers' Mess car park (actually I doubt that I exceeded 5mph!). Thence into the mess bar, where over a few beers I was reunited with many familiar faces from the last few years: Snapper, Gibbon, Woody, Robbo, Spot were amongst the sea of flying-suited bodies crowded into the bar that Friday.

Before teaching the course I had to pass it again, though, so I spent the next two months in student mode re-learning the skills I'd lost in five years of lazy Tornado flying. No navigator, no HUD, no moving map – it was back to the basics of map, stopwatch and looking out. The Hawk was just as wonderful as I remembered it, a close-fitting 'garment' that one slipped into and wore into the air. After the Tornado it was intimate and frisky, making the Tornado seem staid and matronly. The biggest culture shock for me in the first few sorties was close formation: I was used to a rock stable machine with instant engine response, but the Hawk bounced around up and down, left and right and the engine seemed so sluggish that it was easy to get completely out of sequence: full power when you needed idle and vice-versa.

Strapping into a Hawk at Chivenor.

But after an hour with Bruce, our patient Australian flying instructor, I got the hang of it. A light touch on the stick and a bit of anticipation on the throttle seemed to do the trick. I soon grew to love the Hawk's agility and I got a real sense of satisfaction from flying it well in close formation.

Little had changed at Chivenor in my five years' absence, except that the aircraft were now painted in a sleeker-looking air-defence grey instead of the green-and-grey 'mud-moving' camouflage they had worn previously. They all had a decent compass too, so the days of making a best guess at the direction while the gyro compass span in slow circles were over. The course syllabus was virtually unchanged and it was a wonderful opportunity to do it all again with enough skill and experience to be able to enjoy it properly. The pace was relentless, though, often with two or three high-workload sorties a day and not without incident.

One bright June day I started the low-level phase. After a g-loaded, neck-straining, grunting fifty minutes of the air combat sortie in the morning, there's just time for a quick bite before a low-level navigation sortie. The afternoon's route has already been planned, so with hands full of maps, sandwich, briefing slides and coffee, I head into the briefing room. Today my Number Two is Joel, the French exchange instructor. Between mouthfuls of sandwich and coffee I run through the brief.

Soon we're airborne. We've attacked the first target near Hereford successfully and now we're passing Ludlow on the Welsh Marches. Still fresh from the Tornado and used to luxuries like a navigator, a moving map and a HUD, I am finding doing everything myself rather hard work. The weather is still OK, but the sunshine in Devon has given way to a thin layer of cloud at about 4,000ft and a touch of haze in the distance. Ahead the distinctive Clee Hills (for some reason known as 'Sally's Tits' to generations of air force pilots) is our next turning point. I know where I am and can't possibly get lost now: a good time to set up the bombsight for the next target. Another good look around. Joel's tail is clear and we're not going to fly into the ground. Head in the cockpit, looking at the sighting controls low in front of the stick. THUD! A sharp jolt rocks the aircraft. Birdstrike! Instinctively, I pull up and slam the throttle closed. I check the engine instruments, and they look OK for now, but I can't be certain that the engine hasn't been damaged. In a Tornado it doesn't matter much because there are two engines, but in the Hawk, with just the one engine, a birdstrike is a rather more serious proposition.

'Blue two, I've hit a bird,' I call, 'two fifty knots.' Joel must be wondering what on earth I'm doing up here. For my part I'm trying to trade speed for height and get as high as I can while staying under the clouds.

'OK, I give you visual inspection,' replies a thick French accent. I see him closing up to take a look at my aircraft. The speed is trickling back to the best gliding speed as I stay level just beneath the cloud deck.

Joel eases into close formation and gives my aircraft a good look over on both sides and underneath.

'No damage visible,' his accent reassures me.

'Shawbury is your nearest, about twenty miles north,' from Cleaves the trainee navigator sitting in Joel's back seat.

'Ta,' I acknowledge, gingerly increasing the power just enough to maintain level flight. I figure that I don't need any more power than that. If the engine is damaged there is always the chance that it might surge as I open the throttle, however gently. But I'm in luck, the engine responds obediently. My next task is unravelling the map. It has been folded tightly to make it more convenient to use in a small cockpit. I need to open it out so that I can find my way more exactly to Shawbury. That's easier said than done. It's a two-handed job, and I need one hand to fly the aircraft. Map unfolded, it's time to chop us across to the Shawbury controller. Cleaves must be reading my mind. Just as I'm thinking I need to find the Shawbury frequency, he calls up with it. Navigators have their uses!

'Pan, pan, pan, Shawbury this is Chivenor blue section. Two Hawks recovering to you, leader with a birdstrike.'

'Roger, blue, your pan call acknowledged. Head zero-two-zero, airfield eighteen miles, runway one nine, call visual.'

I turn gently right to pick up the controller's heading, with Joel following in a very loose formation. Suddenly I realize exactly where I am even without the map. From school days in Shropshire I recognize the Long Mynd. Hell! We shouldn't be there – we've flown straight through a glider sight. Over my shoulder I can see a glider high above us, so I know they're flying today. They won't be pleased to have a pair of Hawks going straight over their airfield. It's too late to do anything about it now. I'll telephone and apologize when I'm down. Ahead of us I can see Shrewsbury clearly, but I'm far too busy to try and make out the little school where I had filled interest books with aircraft pictures all those years ago. I'm searching the green fields beyond for the runway at Shawbury. It's amazing how difficult airfields can be to see sometimes. I see it! At first it is just a dull-grey mark running across a large field. As I get closer the airfield buildings and taxiways start to stand out.

I call, 'Blue section visual.' Joel hangs back out of my way. He will land once I'm safely down. Now a dilemma: When we practice forced landings we normally do it from 4,500ft overhead the runway, with the speed back at gliding speed. The other option, for poor weather days, is to arrive over the runway threshold at 1,000ft at 300kt, bleeding the speed off in a flat circuit. Today I'm not placed in either of these 'ideal' situations and I'm even approaching the airfield from the wrong direction, so I'll have to improvise. First, though, a low-speed handling check I need to make sure that the gear and flaps are not stuck and that they also haven't been damaged by the bird. I bring the speed back gently and check the controls. So far, so good: Gear and flap both come down as advertised. I move the control column round once again to confirm that the aircraft responds correctly. It all works.

I coast in towards the airfield and fly downwind at 1,500ft. From there I've pretty much intercepted the familiar forced-landing pattern, so I close the throttle and glide downwards in a gentle circuit. When I judge that I'm definitely going to make it I select full flap and push the nose down into a steep dive towards the runway threshold. A check back on the control column puts me back on the ground safely. I look around at the airfield: it's the same one that I had visited from school for that first flight in a Chipmunk fifteen years previously. Did I really imagine then that I'd be returning years later at the controls of a fast jet? All that remains is that grovelling call to the Long Mynd gliding club. The man there is happy to forgive, though, when I explain my predicament: another day's work for a fighter pilot. I record those dramatic moments carefully in my logbook: 'Low level, pairs lead – divert Shawbury.'

I flew my last sortie of the course almost exactly two months after arriving, leading a pair for a simulated attack profile with a timed FRA at Pembrey and a bounce to make us fight our way around the route. It was quite a workout and I was certainly a much better aviator for having done the course again. Now I just had to learn how to instruct. The instructors for this part of the course were experienced hands who had seen it all before. After teaching me to fly the Hawk from the rear seat (not too difficult) we spent the next two weeks navigating at low level or combatting at medium level. For much of the time they played at being students making the grossest errors imaginable. 'Surely no-one could be that inept,' I thought. Then I flew with Gilbert.

Gilbert was my first student, a cheerful soul with the rolling gait of a trawler man and the chatty confidence of a car salesman. We were programmed to fly the first sortie of his low-level navigation phase. The first sortie was flown dual (with me in the back seat) as a singleton. This was probably his first low-level navigation sortie since his final navigation test at Valley some months before, so it was really a shakedown and a safety check before continuing on to the rest of the phase. For that Gilbert would be flying solo with his instructor in another aircraft. We planned, we briefed and then

Instructing – that's me in the back seat this time!

we strapped into our little Hawk, with me in the still-slightly unfamiliar back seat. After take-off the route took us over the Saunton Sands, past Baggy Point and then a right turn northwards over the Bristol Channel. It was a pleasant summer's morning as we skimmed across the sea. Gilbert was clearly trying hard to impress: wave tops flashed past close beneath the wings and the horizon seemed uncomfortably high around us.

'Gilbert,' I enquired trying to sound as calm as I could, 'how high do you reckon we are now.'

'Oh sorry,' responded Gilbert firmly grasping the wrong end of the stick, 'I'll get down lower.'

'No, no,' I said quickly, 'I think you're a bit low, actually. How about easing it up a bit, I think you're at about fifty feet at the moment.'

Having survived the Bristol Channel we crossed the Gower peninsular and then into South Wales towards our first turning point at the Ammanford mast. This is where it got really interesting. Gilbert suddenly veered off in a completely different direction to the one on the map. It was as if he had turned his map through 90°! Intrigued, I thought that I'd watch and see what happened next. I unfolded my map so that I could keep track of our progress and make sure that we didn't go anywhere that we shouldn't. Soon the rear cockpit was full of map as I thumbed my way along Gilbert's random meanderings. The two signs that a student doesn't really know where he is are firstly that he starts to slow down and secondly that he eases the

A dual sortie at medium level – this time I get to sit in the front.

height up as he frantically looks for something he might recognize. It wasn't long before the speed was trickling back towards 360kt and we were up at 6 or 700ft! Still, at least he wasn't back down at 50ft!

Then just as I was convinced it was all going pear-shaped and I would have to intervene, a miracle happened. There, just a few miles out to our right, was the IP for our attack run. We were coming at it from a completely different direction, but it was easily recognizable. Gilbert suddenly saw it, hoiked the aircraft round towards it and off we went, back along the black line on the map that we had planned. Of course once we got back to Chivenor he was convinced that he'd flown the entire route correctly!

I flew two more low-level sorties that day, with two other students and the next day I set off to teach my fourth student how to do pop-up dive attacks. Andy was a very different kettle of fish to Gilbert: having come top of his course at Valley he had spent a couple of years instructing and, as I discovered watching from his back seat, he was an absolute natural pilot. The weather had broken since the previous evening and although we had planned two different attacks in areas where the met man had said the weather would be best, the cloudbase was too low for us to fly either of them. We had also planed a third 'laydown' or level-bombing attack against a warehouse on the Somerset levels and when we got there we discovered that the weather was a little better. The cloudbase even looked high enough to get in a dive attack. A short conference, a few calculations and some chinagraph scribblings on the map later and we'd come up with a bastardized plan. I took control and flew along the new line on the map towards our 'best guess' pull up point. I pulled the stick back firmly at 4-g and we zoomed upwards towards the overcast. Looking out of the side of the cockpit I found the warehouse and rolled to the left in a tight wing-over that would leave us diving straight at the target from about 2,000 ft. That was when we went into the cloud. With anyone else I would have rolled back upright, climbed away and headed home, but instead I counted three bananas and we popped out of the cloud again and found ourselves nicely placed for the attack. I rolled level, put the pipper onto the target and uncaged the bombsight so that it dropped to the correct depression. We dived steeply towards the target until the sight tracked through it and then recovered to level flight. Hey presto a workable, if rather agricultural demonstration of a pop-up attack.

'Shall I just demo that again a bit more tidily just to make sure you've got it,' I offered.

'No thanks – I've got it,' replied Andy, who then proceeded to fly an immaculate dive attack, without going into cloud this time, as if he'd done it every day. I decided that the best instructional technique in his case was for me to watch and learn!

Through the rest of the summer and autumn I filled my boots with flying, usually flying two or three trips a day – compared with two or three a week I had been used to at Brüggen! Apart from weaponry on the range, which was the jealously-guarded domain of QWIs, I taught the whole syllabus, so my flying day might encompass anything from teaching battle formation or flying cine-tow for the junior course to low-level attack sorties or air combat for the senior course. Each day was different from the previous one and no afternoon was the same as the preceding morning, bringing an incredible variety to the job. I also learnt the landscape of the West Country and Wales so that I knew it intimately. Hills and mountains, woods and forests, rivers and streams, masts and aerials, unique bridges and distinctive villages became the familiar friends that showed me exactly where I was.

Towards the end of the year, when I'd found my feet, I started to get my share of the 'staff only' sorties. One of the first adventures was two weeks spent at Coningsby flying Saudi Arabian pilots and navigators around the UK as part of an orientation course before they converted to the Tornado F3. Each one was given four sorties in the back of a Hawk, to get used to the procedures for low flying in the UK and to get a feel for the geography of the country. We ranged at low level all over the country, covering Wales, central and northern England and southern Scotland. The Arabs were all happy to sit in the back and watch the scenery roll by, and even the pilots did not seem too bothered about flying the aircraft themselves. But the verdant majesty of the British landscape certainly got their attention. On one sortie as we sped across Wales at low level all I could hear over the intercom was a quiet voice intoning, 'Many, many sheep … many, many sheep.'

For me the highlight of the time at Coningsby was being able to borrow a Hawk over the middle weekend to visit my girlfriend in Yorkshire. The loan had been agreed early in the week when the sun was shining, but on the Friday the whole country was blanketed by thick fog. Flying was cancelled for the day and the others all headed off home, leaving me behind with my Hawk – and an instruction not to do anything stupid. By using a fairly liberal interpretation of the met forecast I decided that the weather at my destination, RAF Finningley, would be just within limits, so after lunch I strapped in, fired up the engine and taxied out into the gloom. Despite the mist I could see far enough to navigate myself slowly along the taxiway and out onto the runway. Nothing else was moving at Coningsby and, rolling onto the runway threshold, I was invisible to those in the control tower.

'Charlie two-one clear take-off, at your own discretion,' called the tower controller, making sure that I understood that it was me that was solely responsible for whatever happened next. I released the brakes and pushed the throttle all the way forward. It was easy enough to follow the large white centreline markings as I accelerated down the runway, but even so it was a relief to get off the ground and retract the gear. At about 200ft I was suddenly in the clear. Beneath me a dazzling white shroud smothered the landscape as far as the eye could see, while above me the sun shone brightly in a clear, azurine sky. It was a sky that was empty, because everyone else had already gone home! In the distance the occasional chimney or mast poked above the fog and the power stations along the River Trent advertised their presence with a line of tall white plumes. Although I was flying at only a few thousand feet, the limitless cloudscape made it feel as if I was much higher and I could easily have believed that I was at 20, 30 or even 40,000ft. The trip to Finningley was only a 15-minute hop (instead of a 2 hour drive along fog-bound roads), but it was long enough for me to wonder if I'd been sensible launching airborne on such a foggy day. I was completely alone in a pretty basic aircraft with no fancy instrument flying aids – and I still had to get back onto the ground! I called Finningley radar for a PAR and was given an excellent talk down. Of course when I reached my 200ft decision height I had only just gone into the cloud, but I could make out the runway lead-in lights glowing through the murk, giving me just enough detail to find the runway.

Flying solo in a Hawk at medium level: The gun pod is clearly visible under the aircraft.

Later that month, I had a wonderful couple of days doing two-versus-two Dissimilar Air Combat (DACT) with Fleet Air Arm Sea Harriers from RNAS Yeovilton. The Hawk and Sea Harrier were ideally suited opponents: with its great thrust-to-weight ratio the Harrier went up and down very well, while with its great wing the Hawk went round and round very well. The Hawk could out turn the Sea Harrier, but the Sea Harrier could out climb the Hawk, so the art for the Hawk pilot was getting the opposition to try and turn with you. The Harrier that had appeared so small from the cockpit of a Tornado now seemed quite large in comparison to the Hawk, so seeing them before the merge was quite easy. We usually chose to come in high, so that we could store some energy in our height and because we could usually see the Sea Harriers quite easily against the ground or low cloud; the Sea Harriers came in low to use their radars looking up to help see our minute Hawks. And then the fight would start. Usually it degenerated very quickly into two individual fights in close proximity but, like a good barn dance, we could swap partners if we saw an advantage. It took a lot of concentration fighting your own opponent while trying to keep tabs on your mate's progress and it was physically hard work, too, holding the aircraft in the lightest buffet; rarely coming below 4-g, but it was exhilaratingly good fun, too!

Another enjoyable task for staff pilots was to fly the daily weather ship, which took off early each morning in time to report back to the morning met brief. It was an unwritten rule that the weather ship took off at exactly 07:50hrs and it was a matter of pride that one released brakes at the end of the runway at the exact second. People wandering into work for the 08.00hrs met brief would unconsciously glance at their wrists as the weathership powered up and charged down the runway. Once airborne the task was to check all the LFAs, the medium-level airspace and the range patterns in time for a report to be sent via ATC. I usually climbed into the overhead to check the local medium-level weather, before descending to low level over the sea under the watch of the radar controller at Chivenor. I'd then dart into North Devon for a quick check of the low-flying area and then head northwards across the Bristol Channel to Worms Head and through the range at Pembrey. Here a report of the conditions and cloudbase helped the QWIs decide which weapons events could be launched for the morning wave, or whether the aircraft and students should be rescheduled for something else. If it was an air-to-air firing day, I'd take a quick look at the conditions over the sea to the west off Lundy Island. Then it was a matter of finding out how far one could get into Wales at low level. It was a serious and responsible duty (for the success of the first waves of flying depended largely on the report), but once the work was done – or if it was obviously going to be a beautiful flying day – it could also be an opportunity for some licensed hooliganism. One routine port of call was a hippy commune in a secluded valley to the southeast of the Lampeter mast. The brightly coloured tepees were too much of a temptation for us and the hippies must have become fed up with being woken each morning by a very low-flying Hawk roaring overhead. If the weather was good enough to get to the Hereford area, I always took delight in beating up RAF Hereford. It was home to the RAF Administrative Branch and I thought that the 'scribblies' should be reminded what the real RAF was all about! Starting with a bit of altitude I could get almost 500kt out of a Hawk, which was enough to make my presence felt as I rocketed over the parade square at 250ft.

Dinghy drill, on a much nicer day than we had at Chivenor! When you are bobbing around in a dinghy, a bright yellow Westland Wessex helicopter is the most wonderful sight in the world.

The 'weathership' was also a wonderful opportunity to say 'thank-you' to all the non-fliers who worked so hard to support the operation at Chivenor. Anyone who wanted to have the 'Hawk experience' could put their name on the list to fill the (otherwise empty) back seat of the weathership and we rarely flew alone. My first passenger was a young girl from the telephone exchange called Mel, who whooped and screamed with excitement all the way as if she was on a fairground ride!

I was horrified to see my name on the list for dinghy drill on a particularly dirty wet and windy December morning. In Germany, because most of our flying was supposed to be overland, we had some sort of dispensation to do dinghy drill in the swimming pool. Of course now I was under UK rules which meant that I now had to do it every couple of years in the real sea. Even so I had expected to do it on a pleasantly warm, calm summer's day, not in freezing, rough water in the teeth of a howling gale! A group of us trooped unenthusiastically onto the drab-green RAF bus which delivered us to the lifeboat station on the other side of the estuary, in Bideford. My overwhelming emotion as we boarded the lifeboat was, 'I can't believe they're making us do this.' The feeling of detached disbelief continued for the next thirty minutes as the boat worked its way from the relative calm of the estuary to the heaving swell of the open sea. The boat was rocking alarmingly, to the great delight of the lifeboat crew who seemed to enjoy our discomfort. Eventually we were given the signal and reluctantly we made our way on deck. Here the only relief was the sight of a Westland Wessex Air-Sea Rescue (ASR) helicopter approaching, its bright paint a radiant yellow against the slate-grey sky and the menacingly dark grey of the sea. By now the continuous roll and pitch of the boat was beginning to make me decidedly nauseous, so I wasn't really too upset when a firm boot in the backside propelled me overboard. Actually, after the initial shock of a mouthful of ice-cold brine, it was not too bad in the water. The cumbersome combination of 'bunnysuit' and 'goonsuit' worked as advertised and kept most of me warm and dry. I clambered into my dinghy, expecting to spend a miserable hour or so waiting to be rescued. In the event, I was only in it for a minute or so before an orange-suited winchman appeared in front of me, on the end of a cable attached to the helicopter. He tucked a strop under my arms and suddenly I was in mid-air, being hauled into the helicopter. Here I joined a handful of my damp-looking colleagues. The helicopter was unbelievably stable after thirty minutes or so of pitching and rolling lifeboat, also a welcome draft of jet efflux warmed us through the open doorway. Life was definitely beginning to look better! Then, just ten minutes after being booted off the lifeboat, the helicopter had deposited us into the car park of a pub near Bideford where the landlord was clearly expecting us. The marathon beer-drinking session which followed more than made up for the earlier inconveniences of the morning! Despite the ominous start this had been quite the quickest and most painless dinghy drill I had ever done.

One very welcome arrival over the winter was Cookie, my good friend and partner in crime from Crusader days. He had come from Bahrain where he had deployed with the rest of Brüggen's 'A Team' in response to the crisis in Kuwait. A couple of months later it felt utterly bizarre for both of us to be watching our former colleagues on television while they took part in the Gulf War. I thought of that final *Red Flag* sortie with the Goldstars: here I was, less than a year later, watching news reports as my old squadron returned from action on the first day of the war. I saw crews who, during my time, were too junior even to participate in a *Red Flag* exercise, going to war for real! It was an odd mixture of emotions that I felt. On the one hand I wished that I could have been in the Gulf doing the job for real and playing my part on the squadron which had meant so much to me. There would have been professional satisfaction, too, in doing the job for which I had trained for so long. There was also the question of whether I really would have had the courage to do the job well while being shot at; you can never know until you've tried it, no matter how good or unflappable you may think you are. There was part of me, too, that felt that being bloodied in battle was the mark of a real military aviator. On the other hand I was very grateful for being in the safe comfort of North Devon, not being shot at!

This latter point was driven home to me when Cookie and I flew together to Marham in the early spring, for Max's funeral. Max had been a navigator from Crusader days, whom we christened 'Max the Chat' for his propensity for using twenty-seven words when just one would have done. Ten years older than us, he had spent most of his flying career sitting backwards in the bowels of a V-bomber before converting to the Tornado. Sadly he had been killed in action during the Gulf War. Max was a gentle soul untouched by the arrogant self-confidence that afflicted the rest of us and I thought it was an unutterable tragedy that such a noble man should have met his end over some worthless piece of Iraq. The reception after his funeral was the usual polarised event, with his grieving family at one end of the room and at the other, a bunch of his aircrew mates, all desperately trying to conceal their excited delight at seeing each other again. It wouldn't do to seem too happy at a funeral! At any rate Max would have enjoyed the party.

With spring approaching the 'exercise season' started and four of us, each with a student navigator for company, deployed to Wattisham for Exercise *Elder Joust*. This exercise was a workout for the UK's air defences, which included Wattisham's two resident Phantom squadrons. With the HAS sites on the airfield in use by the Phantoms, we were relegated to a dispersal on the far side of the airfield, just off the taxiway. On the first morning The Llamaman and I watched jealously as the other two were launched to a CAP on the coast while we were left to sit around, supposedly at fifteen minutes' readiness to launch. It was a pleasantly warm April day, with the sky freckled with small cumulus over a slight haze. Although we were disappointed not to be flying, it didn't seem too much of a hardship to be waiting, 'Battle of Britain' style, for the call to scramble. As we lounged on the grass next to the aircraft we noticed a distinct lack of information from the Air Defence Operations Centre (ADOC) and to us ex-mud movers, the whole set up seemed to be rather haphazard and chaotic. Somehow Harv, who was our detachment commander, managed to purloin a copy of the in-coming raid plan, so he knew, even if the ADOC apparently did not, that we would be attacked by the Dutch air force at some stage during the morning. With no direction from the command chain, Harv decided to be proactive and suggested that we come to cockpit readiness independently. Soon we were sitting strapped in, canopies open, listening to the radio with a finger poised over the start switch. What a good job we had done so…

'Scramble – two Hawks,' calls the voice of someone taken completely by surprise. Canopies slam shut, ejection seat pins are stowed and engines are turning. Two minutes later I am following The Llamaman onto the easterly runway. Full power – Llamaman's head nods – brakes off, we roar down the runway. Airborne – gear up – flaps up – Llamaman banks away and we 'Playtex' into battle formation. Just in time, for the first F-16 rockets through the space between us: he would have hit us both if we hadn't separated!

'That was bloody close,' exclaims Baldheed from the backseat. The Llamaman sees another F-16 and turns hard after it, I keep climbing in a gentle turn to get some energy as I check that Llamaman's tail is clear. Then I see the next F-16 appearing out of the haze close by. I reverse the turn in a tight barrel roll and shove the sight onto him hoping for a head-on shot before the range closes. He sees me and pulls

Myself and Baldheed over East Anglia during Exercise Elder Joust.

off his attack, turning hard towards me. He flashes past our canopy in a minimum separation pass, vapour pouring off his wing like a cataract as he turns: he's got the speed, but I've got the angles. We screech across the airfield locked in full-blown air combat just a few hundred feet above the ground. As I look up through the canopy I can see the pale upturned faces of our groundcrew watching from the dispersal that we left only a few minutes beforehand. I hope that no one important is watching because they will probably notice that we are breaking all of the rules by combating this low! Meanwhile, Llamaman is dealing with the fourth F-16 and I leave my one to point eastwards, desperately trying to get some more speed so that I can intercept the next Dutchman before he reaches the airfield. I bend the throttle forward with all my strength, trying to will a little bit more acceleration, swearing under my breath at the lack of reheat. I've not gone far before another F-16 emerges from the greyness, crossing the nose a couple of miles away. This time I've got more displacement. I pull up slightly and then arc downwards for a shot from his two o'clock. With the benefit of good air-to-air radar he knows I'm there, and I'm enough of a threat to make him haul off his target run and turn towards me to spoil my shot. We cross and, once again, I've got the advantage of the angles. He reverses and suddenly we're over the airfield still at low level, rolling closely around each other in tight barrel rolls. But the massive performance advantage of the F-16 soon begins to tell and he disengages, disappearing back into the 'gloop' before I can shoot.

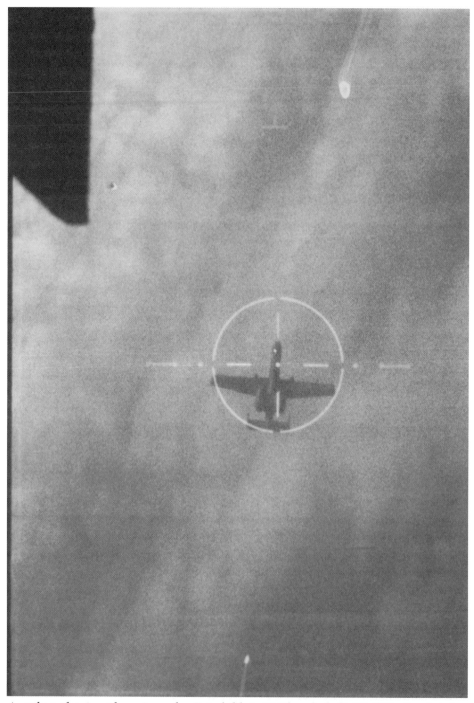

A rather pleasing plan view of a Fairchild A-10 Thunderbolt III ('Warthog') taken through my gun sight. I had to work hard to get it, though. (Crown Copyright/MoD)

We swing eastwards for the third time, but all the Dutchmen have disappeared. As the last F-16 thunders away we re-group and set up a CAP some five miles east of the airfield. From frenzied activity the sortie quickly reverts to tedium and after ten minutes of boring holes in the sky, The Llamnaman decides that we have had enough and recovers us to Wattisham. Back at our dispersal the ground crew are chuffed at the private airshow they enjoyed while the rest of the station was taking cover in the concrete bunkers!

Over the next couple of days we launch a few more times at the behest of the fighter controllers, sometimes for a base CAP, defending the airfield, sometimes to hold a CAP on the East Anglian coast. None of the sorties provides the same excitement as that first one, but there are some interesting moments. One morning we are sent to identify a low-level contact over Norfolk and find a curious looking Italian Air Force Piaggio Avanti reconnaissance aircraft with backward-facing (pusher) propellers; that afternoon we tangle with two USAF F-16s at 20,000ft off Cromer. On the last day all four Hawks head out to Blakeney Point to make up a mixed-fighter force CAP with four Wattisham-based Phantoms. I'm on The Llamaman's wing again, in the back pair of the four. It's another lovely day and we pick up the Phantoms from several miles out. We slot in behind them and Harv calls aboard. After another orbit of the race-track pattern there's a startled cry on the radio 'Counter port – bandits six o'clock.' The Phantoms start a hard turn and we tag along behind them, quite comfortably hanging onto their tails in our agile Hawks, looking all around and wondering where these bandits are. Then the truth dawns that the Phantom crews have only just seen us and they think that we're the enemy!

'Knock it off,' calls Harv in a patient and soothing tone. The Phantoms slacken their turn and rejoin the CAP orbit. Meanwhile, I spot a lone Hunter passing a few thousand feet directly beneath us.

'Red four, tally three o'clock, one Hunter heading east at low level, engaging,' I call. I overbank to the left and let the nose drop, rolling out in a steep dive behind the Hunter. I put the boresight onto the Hunter's jetpipe and wait for the range to come down. To my right, trailing me by a 1,000yds is The Llamaman who has come down with me to clear my tail. Two miles, and a good overtake. 'Fox two, re-joining the CAP.' The Llamaman and I swing back towards the others, converting our speed back into height so that we slide in tidily behind the two Hawks. Suddenly there is another excited clamouring from the Phantoms. Apparently they have just seen a Hunter at low level.

'God help us all,' I murmur to Baldheed, wondering if this is really the best that the air defenders can manage. We drone around the CAP for another tedious twenty minutes. It was a relief to get back to Chivenor later that day.

June brings summer sunshine. Surfers surge into the sea at Croyde, bikini-clad beauties fill the beaches and blue skies herald more superlative flying. And for added interest a USAF A-10 Thunderbolt II (Warthog) squadron from Alconbury joins us for a week-long 'squadron exchange.' For us instructors it was a great opportunity to escape from student flying for a time and do some more 'real' flying. The A-10 drivers were a fantastic team. The USAF can sometimes be rather weird – sometimes very straight-laced and sometimes not particularly good. This lot were different. They were a very lively bunch and they were very good, too.

My first sortie with them was a two-versus-three evasion sortie. Two Hawks would bounce a trio of A-10s on a low-level route, working together as a pair and doing our devious best to get in amongst the Americans. The lumbering A-10 was a massive aircraft and we could see them easily from miles away as they cruised at a leisurely pace through Wales and Herefordshire. Speeding along in our tiny (and we hoped invisible) Hawks, we tried every trick in the book, but we could never get close. Their lookout was fantastic and they picked us up on every intercept before we could get a shot. We also learnt quickly that despite its ungainly appearance, the A-10 was a remarkably agile machine. It was armed with a phenomenally-powerful cannon in the nose and you really did not want that pointing at you!

I learnt the same lessons at medium level during a couple of two-versus-two air-combat sorties. We were well-suited adversaries, two aircraft that could turn well and while the A-10 had the advantage of greater power, the sleeker Hawk could fly much faster. We would smash into the merge as fast as we could, trying to keep as much energy as we could. Some of the American pilots were exceptionally talented and it was impressive to see such a big aircraft being chucked around with confidence. I remember closing on one A-10, convinced I'd got him right where I wanted him, only to watch in disbelief as this massive aircraft performed an impossible looking 'wifferdingle', rolled out behind me and called a kill! However, honour was restored on the next split when I managed to get some pleasing gun-camera film with the gun-sight pipper firmly locked onto his cockpit.

We decided to finish the week with an all-Hawk four-versus-two sortie: a fourship of Hawks would set out to attack a railway maintenance yard near Hereford, while the other pair would be the fighters trying to stop them getting through. There would be a free back seat in each Hawk for six A-10 pilots to join in the fun. Nick got my back seat.

On the runway, lined up as a fourship and I am Number Four, wingman in the back pair. I start my stopwatch as the front pair roll. Twenty seconds later, with an exaggerated nod of his head, Magoo releases the brakes. I stick with him as we roll. Gear up, flap up and I slide into a tight echelon. As we cross the Braunton Burrows at 200ft flying at 300kt, Magoo smacks his Hawk onto its wingtip, and we Playtex into battle formation 2,000yd apart. Ahead I can see the lead pair turning north. As we pass Baggy Point, Magoo starts a hard turn behind me. I wait until he's in my seven o'clock then haul round in a 4-g turn. We roll out behind the front pair in an offset card formation. The Hawk is tiny and well camouflaged in a light-grey colour which merges well with the slightest hint of haze. Sometimes it is incredibly difficult keeping your own wingman just 2,000yd away in constant view. Trying to keep sight of the front pair, which are virtually end-on to us, is nearly impossible, even on a bright day like today. We skim across the Bristol Channel, making for the Gower Peninsula. My head is constantly moving. Check the lead pair, and adjust formation if I need to. Check Magoo and the sky behind him. I crane my neck round to have a really good look back there. Then high above all of us to check there are no fighters above us. Out to the front again: Check my height and heading; a look at the stopwatch, then a quick glance at the map. Then back to check the front pair again. Unlike the Tornado there is no clever navigation

At low level on a staff continuation sortie – myself and Hooch.

kit, or a navigator to help. I have to do it all myself, with just a map and stopwatch and a pair of eyes. The front pair pulls up to coast in, adjusting their track to take them past Llanelli up towards Llandeilo. A last good check behind Magoo and we follow. As we approach Llandeilo we turn right to follow the valley northeast up past Llandovery. My head is rotating as I check the sky. They have to be somewhere around here. Then it happens.

'Red one and two counter starboard,' is called from the front pair. They start a hard turn towards a Hawk dropping in on them from high right. I make sure we're not going to hit them, and crane round to check Magoo's tail. It's still clear.

'Three and four pressing towards the target,' and suddenly the sky is 'wall-to-wall' full of Hawks. The front pair flashes past my right-hand side, hotly pursued by another Hawk. As I look left, I see the other fighter dropping in on Magoo.

'Red three and four counter port.' I pull 4-g as the horizon rockets past. The bounce aircraft sees me turning towards him and comes off Magoo, turning hard and high towards me.

'Off you Magoo; keep turning.' The bounce blows through high above me. He's no threat now.

'Magoo roll out track six.' We roll out in battle formation heading back the way we came, just in time to meet the front pair coming the other way. Once again they flash past, but their bounce has also headed off.

'Magoo turnabout starboard, track twelve.' I grunt heavily against another 4-g turn as we haul back round. Halfway round I see Magoo tail-on in the turn, but then I lose him under my nose. I overbank slightly to pull into the valley. I catch a glimpse of Magoo cresting a ridge in the distance. He's now in the next valley across. He's making best use of the terrain, but it means our cross cover may suffer a bit. I roll out, check the map and stopwatch and work out where I am. The front pair is nowhere to be seen. They are now well ahead of us. The only thing now is to make sure that they stay that way, because we can't see them anymore and we don't want to clap hands over the target. Builth Wells whizzes past. I pull up to crest the ridge and check left to find Magoo. I can't see him. No worry, he's probably there somewhere. I check heading and stopwatch again. Check the fuel. There's still a bit of spare for fighting our way home: Still no Magoo.

I call, 'Magoo, lost visual'.

His unpromising reply is, 'Likewise.'

'What's your position,' I ask him. Soon it transpires that he is somewhere ahead of me. Now we are split up and sitting ducks for the fighters. I set a new heading straight for the IP where the target run starts. By cutting corners and going as fast as the Hawk will let me, we might just get back together. I am working like a one-armed paper hanger now. Apart from the physical exertion of pulling this little aircraft round corners at 4-g, the cockpit is roasting hot under the bright sun. Added to that, the bumps of low-level turbulence are continuously buffeting us. I now have to navigate off the pre-planned line as we cut the corner to the IP, as well as trying to build a mental plot of where the front pair and Magoo are in relation to me, each other and the target. At the same time I have to make sure we don't fly into the ground and keep my eyes out to make sure we don't get caught by the fighters with our knickers down.

'Switches,' this call means that the front pair is leaving the IP. They are a minute or so ahead of me now. Magoo is somewhere between us. How could we have got split up like that? I realize that the aircraft I saw as we turned back was probably the front pair's bounce leaving the fight. Presumably we had got out of position in that first manoeuvre and Magoo had made a similar mistake with another aircraft. Easy to do with six identical aircraft, and when you have to base your decision on a glimpse of a small aircraft a mile away. We need to get our story straight before the debriefing!

'Magoo, extend off target, I'll meet you at the next waypoint,' I instruct. At least that will get us back together as a pair. The IP appears on the nose amongst the hillocks west of Hereford. I run through the weapons checks, making sure my switches are in the right place and the bombsight is set up correctly. We streak past the IP smack on track. My eyes dart from stopwatch to map to ground, as we follow a short black line across an Ordnance Survey map which ends at the target. Suddenly I see the target ahead, and stow the map back under my thigh. My right thumb uncages the sight. I concentrate on flying the pipper right through the building, keeping the aircraft straight and level as we thunder over the top. As we come off the target I realize that my plan to get us back together isn't going to work. There's a large rain shower over our rendezvous.

'Magoo I'll catch you on track.' I signal a quick change of plan, and then swing the nose round to point to where I think I might find Magoo. Eyes out searching for the others, I hurtle across the Wye valley, heading off to where it turns southwest to Brecon. A light-grey flash hugging the contours on the north of the valley catches my eye.

'Magoo waggle.' The Hawk obediently waggles its wings.

'Jink right, I'm rejoining from the east.' A quick jink and we're back in business. We round the valley towards Brecon in perfect formation and another flash reveals the position of the front pair in the distance ahead of us.

'One and two buster; dropping into your six high,' from Magoo. I look up to see what he has just seen. There high between us a small arrowhead shape is swooping down on the front pair. He is really shifting – a good 100kt faster than us.

Magoo calls, 'Napes, counter port.' I haul us into a 4-g break to the left in time to see a Hawk come rocketing past. The crafty devil was hoping to sneak in at low level while we were looking up! We keep the tight turn coming round, straining our necks to get a view of the fight down the valley. We catch up with the front pair at last and head on down track as a fourship once more. One last ambush has the formation dispersing again. This time we manage to stay in our pairs, constantly turning to keep out the threat. The two fighters take it in turns to harry us until they run out of fuel and pull up to head home. We have just enough to make it back across the Bristol Cannel to Chivenor. Running through initials to the airfield we are in perfect four-ship battle formation. Numbers One and Two are in a tight arrowhead with Magoo and me in a similar formation a mile abeam. We know that everyone at the squadron will be watching this bit, so it has to be perfect. Lead snaps into the break. I count three. Number Two and Magoo both break together, Magoo playing the turn so that his spacing behind Number Two is the same as Number Two is behind the leader. Count to three once more and it's my turn, throttle slammed shut and airbrake out to kill the speed. Just concentrate now on making sure my spacing from Magoo is perfect. We touch down in a tidy stream.

I wonder what Nick has made of all that. He is wide-eyed. In the A-10 he is used to all the fancy navigation kit of a modern warplane. He's also used to the world moving past at a more sedate 300kt, a huge aircraft to formate on, and one which is rock stable in turbulence. He admits that he found that fast-moving free play a bewildering experience. I don't like to tell him I did, too!

Each summer Chivenor hosted an air display and this year the line-up included some aircraft from the Czech Air Force, who arrived a few days beforehand. Unfortunately, their MiG-29 got soaked in the Devon rain and it spent its time at Chivenor in the hangar with all the inspection panels opened and electric bar-heaters underneath it in an attempt to dry it out! The other 'fighter' type was an L-39 Albatros, a training aircraft similar in size to the Hawk. I had understood it to be the equivalent of the Hawk, in terms of performance too and we had been briefed in Germany to expect missile-armed Albatros trainers to be flying as point defence fighters, much as the Hawks were used in the UK. However I was to find out that it was very different. The Czechs offered a back-seat ride for one lucky pilot and it was decided that the station commander would draw a name out of a hat in the bar of the Officers' Mess. A busy bar fell silent as the station commander pulled a piece of paper from the hat and unfolded it. He read out the name and everyone looked around to see the lucky prizewinner. However, it was soon apparent that he was not in the bar and the assembled throng became raucous once more with loud jeers and calls of 'Re-draw!'

The second name was also absent, so the station commander drew a third name. It was mine. The next afternoon I strapped into a very ancient-looking aircraft, complete with metric instruments and a pilot who spoke no English! I realized that it was going to be an interesting trip when my pilot tried to get taxi clearance from the approach radar controller rather than the local tower controller! Luckily the Llamawoman was the air-traffic supervisor and being a very sharp operator, she quickly realized what was going on. She smoothed the way for us with the tower controller and we set off around the airfield. Unfortunately we immediately hit the next snag. Being a coastal station, Chivenor's weather is affected by the sea breeze effect in the summer: first thing we'd use the easterly runway but as the day goes on, the wind reverses into a westerly. My driver from the land-locked Czech Republic had obviously never seen this phenomenon before and he set off for the runway which had been in use that morning but which by now was the wrong one. Chaos rained on the radar approach frequency as we tried to stop him! Eventually he realized what was happening and after a tight U-turn on the taxiway, we took off in the right direction. After we coasted in near Hartland Point, I was allowed to do a little bit of flying. Thanks to the metric instruments I had no idea of the speed or height we were flying. All I knew was that the controls forces were incredibly high and the aircraft felt worse than a Jet Provost on a particularly bad day. It was considerably less manoeuvrable than the Hawk and the pilot was adamant that I should not try a loop. Luckily the Albatros was not blessed with a very large fuel tank, so after a pleasingly short trip across north-west Devon it was time to go home. Back at Chivenor air traffic were by now fully prepared for radio calls on random frequencies and for general pandemonium in the circuit, so our recovery was relatively unexciting. I was relieved to get out in one piece!

After the excitement of the A-10 exchange and the air display, it was back to the routine of student flying. This was good news because our senior course was in the midst of the SAP phase, the part of the syllabus which offered the most demanding and rewarding flying for staff and students alike. Unfortunately though, within a few weeks the summer which had started so promisingly in June had deteriorated into cloud and thick haze and flying ground to a halt. One morning, after a couple of days of enforced sitting around the crewroom, I decided that I needed to do something. I recruited Magoo and Chapelli to the cause and persuaded the Boss to let us take three aircraft to Scotland to get Chapelli's SAP 6 completed. That afternoon we flew up to the Scottish borders at medium-level and then let down to low level near Dumfries for Chappelli's solo low-level evasion exercise, before recovering to Machrihanish. That evening we sampled the dubious delights of Campbeltown before retiring for the night. The accommodation at Machrihanish was pretty basic – my tiny room was in a Nissen hut where, despite it being mid-summer, the heating was full on! As my bed was pushed right up against the radiator, I didn't get much sleep and it was with bleary eyes that I met up with the others for an early breakfast. Soon Magoo and Chappelli were hard at work planning, but as the bounce at least I had a pleasantly easy hour or so. I invested my time drinking tea and slowly becoming more human as memories of an uncomfortable night evaporated in the sunlight of a beautiful sunny day. With planning completed I took off five minutes ahead of the others and climbed out to the north.

Just past Loch Lomond, I leave the restrictions of the Glasgow control zone behind and say farewell to the radar controller. It is a stunningly beautiful day in the highlands: there is no cloud to be seen and the visibility is unlimited. The horizon to my left is dominated by the Isle of Skye and out to my right I can just make out the Moray Firth in the far distance. From two miles up, the hills and mountains have flattened out and the view from the cockpit is like a huge coloured relief map. Just like a page from an atlas, the colours of the ground betray its contours: the lower-lying moors are a fresh green, while the higher ground changes from brown to grey and the lochs, deep blue and mirror-flat, lie amongst them like inlaid jewels. I take up station over Rannoch Moor in a gentle orbit at 10,000ft and compare the black line on my map with the green swathe beneath me. Once I've identified the path that the other two will take across the terrain below, I check the stopwatch against my wristwatch and adjust the orbit so that I'll be pointing up track when the pair should be approaching the moor. That way I can look forwards for them and play my turn to roll out almost directly above them; if I miss them I'll still have enough advantage of speed to catch them when I dive towards them. That done, I can relax slightly and take in the breathtaking views all around me: it is truly a privilege to see the world from this vantage point.

Magoo's voice interrupts the reverie, 'Blue check.'

'Two,' responds Chappelli.

'Three,' I call, 'weather is good in the operating area, game's on.'

'Roger – on time,' replies Magoo and I answer with a double click of my transmit button. I recheck the stopwatch as I swing southwards, should see them in two minutes; which is a long time when you're watching the seconds hand creep forwards. My eyes flick from stopwatch to ground to stopwatch with the regularity of a metronome. The time ticks down. I don't see them. Have I missed them? I turn northwards and now I stand the Hawk on its left wing and rudder the nose upwards as I scan the ground beneath me; nothing. I roll the other way and tread on the other rudder pedal. This time my peripheral vision picks up movement: just ahead of me, two light grey shapes are speeding noiselessly over Rannoch Moor heading towards the eastern side of Loch Ericht. Keeping them both in sight I push the nose forwards and select full power. And now I have to remember who is who. Ideally I will close on Magoo so that Chappelli has to spot me. Apart from being good training for the student's lookout, it is an unwritten rule that you don't embarrass fellow staff mates by surprising them on bounced sorties! I decide that Magoo must be on the left, so I point at him. At 550kt the Hawk starts fish-tailing: most of the aircraft have been bent by continuous g-pulling in the range pattern

over the years and like many of them, this one is not too happy at high speeds. I put the gunsight onto the left-hand aircraft. I'm diving steeply with a massive overtake, so Chappelli is going to have to look up quite high to see me, but he's on the ball today.

'Blue – counter port,' his distinctive Northampton accent comes excitedly over the radio and I see his Hawk turn hard towards me. I come off Magoo's tail, check towards Chappelli and then reverse into a high wingover as we pass.

'High above me, keep turning,' calls Chapelli. I keep the aircraft banked over but I don't pull: they see a planform and think I'm turning, but I'm not.

Botty and Harv at low level over the west of Scotland. Although most of our flying was over south-west England and Wales, we occasionally ranged farther afield to find good weather. In Botty and Harv the squadron benefitted from two highly-skilled aviators and excellent instructors.

'He's stretched – roll out track six,' from Magoo and as the pair starts to run away back up track, I take the opportunity to disengage. I roll the wings level and bunt at zero-g, heading out towards the west. It is a glorious day at low level, too. In the bright sunshine and almost infinite visibility the landscape seems to stand out with unusual clarity. At a comfortable 360kt the scenery rolls past majestically, a stately procession of moorland, farmland and forest, each defined by its own unique texture and shade of green. Reaching the Great Glen near Fort Augustus I turn right to follow the valley northeast. Now I am paralleling the pair's route, displaced a few miles to the west. They have had time to catch up, so I'm pretty sure that they are flying about five miles abreast of me. I bide my time, tucking into the right-hand side of the long, deep valley, taking cover just below the ridgeline. I check my fuel, glance at the stopwatch and then allow myself the luxury of a few more minutes savouring the fantastic view. A few hundred feet beneath me to my left, Loch Ness lies calm and still in the morning sun. Every now and then I pass a small boat that appears stationary on the water as I speed past and on the far bank there is the occasional glimpse of a car or lorry winding its way along the shore road: To my right, on the shoulder of the ridge, tightly-packed flocks of sheep race away from me across open moorland. Meanwhile, Magoo and Chappelli are doubtless working hard as they make their way towards their target, a railway bridge south of Inverness. Time to stop the sightseeing and go and interrupt them! I push the throttle forwards and accelerate towards 450kt.

This time I come in low, making use of all the cover provided by the low ridges that intersect the space between us. A minute ago I was a tourist, now I am a hunter, stalking the two Hawks just as a stalker might hunt deer in the countryside below. The only problem is that I don't know exactly where they are! Then there is a flash of grey a couple of miles away, a tell-tale movement to the right of the nose and I realize that (perhaps more by luck than judgement) I've hit them on a prefect 90° intercept. I pull clear of the ridge to give them a chance to see me and almost immediately Chappelli calls the counter. Sharp lad! This time I blow through and leave them to it – they need a chance to get to the target, so I disappear upwards into the sun, hoping that they don't see where I've gone to. I decide that from now on I'll follow them at medium-level and drop in on them from above. It's easier for me that way, because I can watch them all the time, a luxury that the British weather does not often afford. I can also enjoy the vista of the highlands laid out before me! I pick them up visually and watch them through their attack.

A couple more bounces and Magoo and Chappelli are running short of fuel.

'Sighters only,' calls Magoo, meaning that I can continue to bounce them, but they will just call the threat without reacting. It's good training for lookout, but not as much fun as full-blown evasion. I manage one more interception before they reach the end of the route. By now they are getting close to the bottom of their fuel tanks and as they prepare to recover to Machrihanish, I notice that I have still got stacks of fuel left. Forty miles northwest of me the Cuillins tower over Skye. I realize that this is the chance of a lifetime: I will probably never again have the same combination of my own aircraft and no other commitments, together with such beautiful scenery and such magnificent weather. The temptation proves too much and after informing Magoo that I'll see him back at Machrihanish for the debriefing: I head towards Skye.

The jagged shards of the Cuillins stand in a semi-circle curving slightly away from me, glistening jet-black in the bright sunlight. From a distance they form an intimidating barrier, but as I get closer they fade slightly in the sunlight into a less oppressive grey. They no longer seem threatening, but nor are they welcoming either. Instead they stand impressively tall and impassive; silent sentinels, custodians of some unimaginable treasure. I consider the best altitude to approach them: too high and they will become mere folds in the ground, too low and I might as well

Myself and Cookie in the nearest Hawk on our way to visit the Canadians at Baden Solingen.

see them on foot. I decide that a couple of thousand feet will be best and as I approach I pull close to the cliffs to follow the curve around the back of the range. Determined to have time to enjoy the view I've let the speed ease back to a relaxed 300kt and for a few minutes I am in full sight-seeing mode. Even at this height I am still dwarfed by the sheer rock faces that tower above me, but I am right there amongst them and I can feel the intimacy with mountains that only a golden eagle knows. It is at once a spectacular view and a truly spiritual experience.

At Chivenor we were much in demand as the RAF's only agile fighter and in the autumn four Hawks headed to Baden-Solingen for a week of two-versus-two air combat with the Hornets of the Canadian Armed Forces. One of the first people I saw at Solingen was Baggers, my old squadron-mate from Goldstar days. He was on an exchange posting with the Canadians and had been forced to affect a very bizarre and unconvincing pseudo-Canadian accent so that the locals could understand him! In the Hornet we found an opponent who could out-turn us as well as out-performing us in general and although the air combat was outrageously good fun, we definitely came second! One of the highlights of the detachment was a raucous happy hour on the middle Friday. This was notable for two events. The first was after a meal eaten by the whole Mess, sat along bench tables in squadron order, when a massive brandy glass holding the contents of several bottles of cognac was passed around the room from squadron table to squadron table, so that everyone could take a sip in turn. This moving ceremony was performed every Friday in memory of the Canadian fighter pilots who had lost their lives in Germany. The second event was a lively 'play scrap' shortly afterwards in which Cookie's flying suit was ripped to shreds.

On the Monday, Cookie was provided with a temporary replacement by our hosts, a Canadian flying suit complete, of course with Canadian pilot's wings. Now all correctly dressed, we arrived at the Hornet squadron in time for met brief. I was delighted to see from the programme that I was due to fly two two-versus-two air-combat sorties that day. Cookie wasn't so lucky, and it looked like a day on the ground for him. It was then that I spotted a familiar face on the far side of the planning room. I'd met the Major during the squadron exchange with the Goldstars a couple of years before. He was the epitome of a 'real' fighter pilot, with thousands of hours of flying behind him on the F-101 Voodoo, F-104 Starfighter and other such 'real men's' aircraft. He had the steely glint in his eyes, the square jaw and the purposeful grace of a tiger on the prowl. I went over to say hello, and was flattered by the flicker of half recognition in response.

'Just plannin' a pairs low-level affil trip. We've got a two-seater, do you want to come along for a ride,' snarled the Major. I'd have loved to, but I wasn't going to give up my DACT sorties! Then I thought of Cookie.

'I'm already flying today, but I'm sure that my mate Cookie here (gesticulating at the man in the slightly too big Canadian flying suit) would love to go,' I ventured. And so it was decided that Cookie would accompany the major on his trip. I left them to it and went off to have some fun myself.

Two sorties later, I was enjoying a well-earned coffee in the crewroom when the major and Cookie returned from their trip. 'That must have been interesting,' thought I, noticing that the major's steely glint had been replaced by a wide-eyed stare. He looked as if he'd seen a ghost!

'So how did it go,' I enquired of Cookie that evening in the bar.

'Well…,' said Cookie. It transpired that he'd had a fantastic time to start with. The two Hornets had been flashing around the low-flying area practising intercepts on a Lockheed T-33. It had all been going extremely well and Cookie had enjoyed playing with the radar. Then the T-33 went home and the boys in the Hornets decided to practise some formation flying. After some manoeuvring, the Major had enquired whether Cookie would like a go at flying the aircraft. Naturally Cookie seized the chance and, though he said it himself, was doing quite well. Then the leader called them into close echelon. The Major didn't express any interest in taking over control of the aircraft, so Cookie found himself doing his first ever close formation rejoin. He wasn't too sure what to do here, but he'd seen it done enough times before, so he applied full power, and pointed his jet straight at the leader. Luckily a nervous twitch at the *moment critique* saved them on the first attempt, and after narrowly missing the unfortunate leader, Cookie set up for another attack.

'Not quite so punchy this time,' suggested the Major in a laid back voice. The second go was much like the first, except that just moments before a collision must surely become inevitable, Cookie said 'Major, you do realize that I'm a navigator, don't you.'

The 'I HAVE CONTROL,' from the front seemed to indicate that he had not, whatever he later claimed. Things were a bit frosty for a while after that. But who can blame the Major? He was a single-seat fighter pilot on a single-seat fighter squadron hosting a bunch of experienced instructor pilots. He could never have expected to find a navigator lurking in the planning room, especially not one wearing a Canadian pilot's wings! Of course he assumed that we were all, like him, experienced pilots. Similarly, Cookie, a dyed-in-the-wool two-seat man assumed that everyone knew he was a navigator, despite his disguise as a Canadian pilot! I think we learnt about 'assuming' from that!

We returned from Solingen just in time for the squadron competition. Every staff pilot on the squadron took part in this competition, which started when each of us reported to the umpire thirty minutes before our individually pre-allocated take-off time. We were then given two field targets, quite literally gates in fields, one in Devon and one in Wales, each to be overflown at a specific time and we were also given the exact times to make two FRAs at Pembrey range, a lay-down pass after the first field target and a strafe one after the second. Our students had been deployed to the field targets, armed stopwatches and to check whether the aircraft overflew the target gate and to record the time.

There was just enough time to scribble some lines rapidly on a map before heading out to the aircraft. As I strapped in I realized that in my haste I had forgotten to copy the 'calibrated altitude' that I would need to fly to drop an accurate laydown bomb, but I did not have time to worry about it. Once airborne my route took me westwards, towards Hartland Point. I had planned the route in a series of right-angled legs, so that I could cut corners to make up time, or extend slightly if I needed to lose it. It seemed like an easy concept but I should have known the reality that my brain would be operating at massively reduced efficiency once I had climbed into an aircraft and that the easiest calculations would then seem impossibly difficult. I have never worked so hard in all my life trying to fly, navigate and work out all the timing constraints at the same time on such a complex yet scantily-planned sortie! My brain had simply run out of computing power to process all the inputs. Eventually somewhere to the east of Bude, I stumbled over the IP for the first target within a few seconds of the correct time and set off down the run. Halfway along I was suddenly filled with doubt – had I measured the track correctly, or were those woods on the left the correct ones? I hauled across to the woods on the left, had second thoughts and reversed back to join my original run with just enough time to see the target and line up with it. Phew! I zig-zagged my way northwards desperately trying to work out the sums to decide whether to turn early or late at each turning point.

At Pembrey I stayed high until I had lined up with the lay-down target and then dived down to fly as low as I dared, guessing at the calibrated height on the altimeter. The bombsight neared the target circle and I could see that it looked far too small. I must have been too high! I remembered the QWI adage, 'if you're low, let it go; if you're high, go on by,' so I counted three bananas after the sight passed the target

Self portrait in a Hawk cockpit.

and pickled off the bomb. The second field target was a disaster: I missed the IP and never saw the target, so with dented confidence I headed back towards Pembrey for the strafe pass. Strafing in the Hawk had never been my strong suite, but I hoped that I might get a few hits without getting fouled and that I might pick up some more points for being on time. It was with an incredible feeling of relief that I landed back at Chivenor about ten minutes later!

At five o'clock I headed to the mess bar where the results were to be announced. Some of the students from the first target were already there, with excited tales to tell. They had no idea which aircraft was which. 'And one pilot realized that he was about three seconds early, so he jinked off the target run halfway down and reversed back so that he overflew us exactly on time. He must have been really on the ball,' was one breathless story. I didn't like to shatter their illusions! My lay-down bomb was a good one too, so all those years of reversionary bombing at Nordhorn and Deci had not been wasted after all! In the end I came a respectable eighth out of eighteen overall, and considering that I was competing against a number of ex-single seat pilots and many who had been flying the Hawk for much longer than me, it was a result that pleased me.

The end of my tour at Chivenor was heralded by an instruction to report to the station commander's office immediately. Apparently some minor infraction or other had occurred on my watch and I was left in no doubt that I was about to receive a rocket for it. 'You're really in the shit this time,' were the Blob's cheerful parting words as I gave my boots a quick buff and donned my hat. A grim-faced station commander invited me to explain why I thought I had been summoned to his office. Standing stiffly to attention I stuttered through an explanation that although it was not my fault I was prepared to take full responsibility for whatever had happened. I didn't like to admit that I actually had no idea about what exactly had supposedly happened! At this point the station commander could not contain his giggles any more and thrust an envelope into my hands.

'Here,' he said, 'read this.' I opened the envelope and discovered that the signatory had the honour to inform me that Her Majesty was pleased to appoint me to the rank of Squadron Leader with effect from the end of the year. 'Congratulations,' smiled the station commander, 'you're posted back to Brüggen as a flight commander with the Crusaders.' On my return to the squadron I discovered that I was the only one who had not been in on the joke. 'So you'll be putting a barrel on for us in the bar tonight,' suggested the Blob expectantly. I did.

The Boss gave me free choice on the format and team for my last sortie at Chivenor. Having particularly enjoyed air combat in the Hawk, it seemed natural to choose a two-versus-two air-combat sortie; it was natural, too, that Cookie should accompany me on my final Hawk sortie. The Llamaman agreed to be my wingman and in another act of kindness from the Boss I was able to invite my housemate Cull from the other squadron to lead the opposition. The final player was Botty, a talented pilot for whom I had the greatest of respect: together Cull and Botty made two worthy adversaries. On the day The Llamaman and I took off first and climbed up though unpromising layers of stratus. Under radar control, we headed southwest over the sea beyond Bude where the weather ship had reported a clear area. True to his word the sky there was clear above 10,000ft. We bade farewell to Chivenor radar and checked in with our Ground Control Intercept (GCI) controller at Portreath. Meanwhile Cull and Botty had headed due west past Hartland Point; by the time they had checked in on their discrete frequency with their own fighter controller, they were in position at the northern end of the area as we turned to face them from the southern end.

I had allocated myself height blocks from 16 to 20,000ft and 26 to 30,000ft; the enemy had the 'ones-to-fives' blocks. For the first fight The Llamaman and I ran in at 20,000ft, at the top of that height block and pretty much in the middle of the airspace. That way we would be high enough to have an advantage if they came in low, but not too low to be disadvantaged if they came in high. Flying northwards, our eyes were peeled as the controller called out the ranges and headings. Cull and Botty had guessed our game plan and had taken the high option. They dropped down as they came towards us. We hit the merge in a wide battle formation and the fight immediately became two one-versus-one combats. Cookie and I found ourselves locked in a tight descending spiral with an anonymous opponent, wing buffeting gently at the point of stall as I tried to squeeze the maximum performance out of it. While we desperately tried to get behind the other Hawk: he, meanwhile, was hell bent on doing the same to us! Eventually he started gaining the advantage and when we reached the base height I had run out of options. It was not long

Some outrageous posing before my final trip at Chivenor. L-r: Llamaman, Cookie, Me, Cull, Botty.

before the controller told us that we were dead! It was only at the debrief that we found that our opponent was Cull: he knew immediately that it was us because he counted two helmets as we flashed past in that first merge, so he had taken particular delight in winning that first fight. Afterwards he was magnanimous enough to suggest that he had won because of his advantage of being on his own and thus in a lighter jet; I suspect, though that it was more likely the result of him being the better pilot! At any rate the next two fights went more my way and by the time we knocked it off for the final time I had thoroughly enjoyed myself. All that remained was a long straight descent into the easterly runway at Chivenor for a run in and break from close echelon starboard.

I must admit that I had not really thought this one through properly: the number four position in an echelon is right at the end of a long line and just like a whiplash, all the bumps and bounces get bigger and bigger towards the end! I stuffed the nose down and took us back through the layers we had climbed through earlier and it was only thanks to some phenomenal hanging in by Botty, that a very tidy formation arrived back overhead Chivenor and broke into the circuit! A few minutes later we were enjoying a glass of fizz with the rest of the squadron while, in accordance with tradition, I wore the contents of a fire extinguisher.

five

DESTINATION DHAHRAN

It was less than two years between my leaving Brüggen and returning to it. At first I thought that little had changed in my absence, except that there seemed to be more car parks. Even the station commander was the same. As I did my round of the station getting signatures on my arrival card, lots of familiar faces greeted me.

'Hello, sir, haven't see you around for a while – have you been away,' it was like coming home. But it didn't take long to realize that Brüggen had changed fundamentally in the short time I'd been away. I'd left in 1990, just after the Berlin Wall had come tumbling down. Since then the Cold War had been won and so had a rather hotter war in the Gulf. The Russians had gone home at last and Germany had been reunified. In my short absence, NATO's defences against the now non-existent foe had been dismantled with almost indecent haste. Now only a handful of the NATO jets that used to thunder round the German skies were still based on the continent. Most of the US aircraft had been withdrawn, leaving once-busy airfields now empty. Even the RAF contingent had been halved in size in less than two years. Just down the road Wildenrath lay virtually derelict, the Phantom boys now long gone. Up at Laarbruch the four Tornado squadrons had been disbanded and replaced by two Harrier squadrons, who themselves were displaced when Gutersloh closed. Only Brüggen had remained unscathed.

Low-flying below 1,000ft had been banned over Germany and the Low Countries, putting fast jets right where the weather was worst and where light aircraft fly. It was dangerous to fly there and the training value was severely limited. Not surprisingly the skies, recently so busy, were now virtually empty; while on the ground the once numerous army battalions were virtually non-existent and the missile sites lay empty. Even the exercises that had punctuated my first tours at Brüggen were a thing of the past. Without that focus, annoying and inconvenient though it had undoubtedly been, Brüggen had lost its strong sense of purpose. The aircrews were wondering what they were doing out there.

The result of these changes was a complete transformation in the emphasis on flying out of Brüggen. Most of the flying was now done in the UK. Sometimes we would land at an RAF base to refuel before returning, which would give an hour of useful low flying on each leg of the trip. If we couldn't refuel we would get just twenty minutes of low flying with an hour of high-level transit to and from Germany at either end.

One immediate result of the Gulf War was that all Tornado crews were now qualified in air-to-air refuelling. Previously this was the preserve of a very select few, for special occasions only, but now that tanking was a universal skill and more tankers were available, it provided a 'third way' to go flying in UK. The emphasis on night flying had increased too, partly because of the need to be able to fly in close-ish formation in the dark in order to be able to air-to-air refuel (AAR) at night, and partly because the UK night low-flying system offered infinitely better training than the continental system. Finally, crews were now trained in dropping bombs from 10 or 15,000ft as well as the 'traditional' low-level techniques with which had been familiar to me on my earlier tours.

The Crusaders were still based in the south-east corner of the airfield on the site which I'd known so well five years previously. The squadron looked a lot smarter than I remembered it. A brand new concrete bunker housing the operations and planning rooms stood in the woods behind the familiar office blocks and crewrooms. I had very mixed feelings about coming back. On one hand, I had always felt great loyalty to the squadron because it was my first and because of the close friendships I'd enjoyed there. On the other hand, I recalled that my tour there had ended with a sense of professional disillusionment. I was also aware that the new squadron Boss, Frank, enjoyed a reputation as a hard man, and I wondered how I was going to get on with him.

In fact I needn't have worried about that. True, Frank was an uncompromising 'Scouser', but his heart was very much in the right place and he ran a tight ship. He was also a stickler for getting it right and doing things properly. This rubbed off on the squadron, which had a much more positive feel about it than it had on my first tour there. My respect for Frank grew as I got to know him better, but he did seem to relish his hard-man image. 'I'm not here to win a popularity contest,' he once told me, which I thought was a shame: if the boys had realized quite how very deeply he cared about all those under his command they would have followed him much more willingly. For that their part, the boys were an excellent team with a lively bunch of youngsters; it was great to be on a good squadron once again.

I was to be Officer Commanding 'A' Flight, with responsibility for the day-to-day running of the operational side of the squadron. I was delighted to see that one of the other flight commanders was Doug, who had been with me on my first tour with the Crusaders. In fact he had been my tour guide to Cyprus six years previously. Doug took everything in his stride with a cynical pinch of salt and I was always glad of his self-deprecating sense of humour.

My first few months were spent settling in and finding my feet as a flight commander. I had to get myself through a short work-up before I could qualify as combat ready once again. I also had to renew my qualifications as a formation leader.

The latter was relatively straightforward, but in order to get combat ready I had to familiarize myself with the medium-level weaponry and the air-to-air refuelling. To my mind, the two most difficult things to master as a pilot are landing and air-to-air refuelling, or 'tanking' as we called it. The reason that these disciplines are so hard is because they are the only times when you have to fly an aircraft to within an accuracy of a few feet and a few knots. You cannot land left or right of a runway; if you pull out of your descent to land too late you'll crash into the ground, too early and the aircraft will stall, then crash into the ground. To land an aircraft you must put it down exactly onto the runway. Very similar things are true of tanking. You must fly your probe exactly into the refuelling basket at exactly the right speed. I found it tremendously difficult to get the hang of and every time I got to a tanker I felt there was a very real chance that I would be unable to hit the basket.

However, by the summer, as I headed off for a delayed honeymoon, I was a combat-ready Tornado pilot once again. Sitting in the luxury of a modern airliner heading towards the Maldives, I read through the Sunday newspapers. One story which caught my eye described how RAF Tornados were to deploy to Saudi Arabia to monitor the situation in southern Iraq. Apparently Saddam Hussein was involved in a major campaign to put down an insurrection by the Marsh Arabs who inhabited the wetlands between the Tigris and Euphrates rivers. The article described how the United Nations, and more particularly the Coalition who had fought Iraq barely eighteen months previously were very concerned about this development and that military intervention might be possible. It kept me interested for a couple of minutes as I read, but since it concerned Tornado reconnaissance aircraft, I thought no more of it, other than a passing wonder as to whether anyone I knew might be going.

Two very enjoyable weeks later, I wandered back into the squadron, much relaxed and sporting a golden suntan. In his office, Coulsy OC 'B' Flight, was working his way through an impressive-looking operations order, marked 'Operation *Jural*'.

'What's this then, Coulsy, anything interesting,' I enquired, trying to get a better view of the paperwork on his desk.

'It might well be,' came the reply. 'It looks like we'll be going out to the Gulf in November for a couple of months, so if I were you I'd plan on celebrating Christmas in Saudi! This is the Operational Order for enforcing the No Fly Zone over southern Iraq. The Boss has asked me to honcho our detachment there, so I'm just reading through it.'

Coulsy went on to tell me what had happened while I had been away, chiefly that six RAF Tornados were now based in Dhahran, on the Saudi coast near Bahrain. The United Nations wanted to stop the Iraqis from using aircraft and helicopters over the southern marshes and had declared a No Fly Zone (NFZ) below the 32nd Parallel in southern Iraq. The Iraqis were not allowed to fly any aircraft in this area. Coalition fighters were patrolling the area to enforce the NFZ, and our aircraft were being used for reconnaissance. The Tornados were using the video cameras in laser-designating pods to provide imagery of Iraqi ground forces in the marsh areas beneath the zone. The original plan to send only reconnaissance crews had been changed and now all the Tornado squadrons were taking it in turns to man the aircraft for three months. The present incumbents were another Brüggen squadron; they would hand over soon to one of the Marham squadrons, who would, in turn, hand over to us for our stint which would last from November to January.

'Each squadron needs to provide a flight commander to cover the detachment. I'll go for the first half and you get the second half,' he concluded.

My first reaction was one of excitement at the prospect. It would certainly be 'different' flying over Iraq and would make a change from the routine of 'high-low-highs' to the UK. It would also give me a bit of a flavour of what I had missed during the Gulf War and, with things still quite volatile out there, it might even provide some action. But in many ways it would be a step backwards into the 1920s. In those days the fledgling RAF had managed to keep its identity as a separate service largely because it had found a role policing the Middle East. In fact both the Tornado squadrons that I'd served on owed their continued existence between the wars to the fact that they had been based in Palestine and the north-west frontier of India respectively.

In those days the RAF kept a watchful eye on remote areas which traditional ground forces could not easily reach, and if things turned nasty they provided a means to punish the miscreants swiftly and powerfully. A village or stronghold could be demolished (with due warning of course to minimize casualties on the ground) leaving the locals so busy rebuilding that they had no time to cause any further trouble. Thus a degree of stability was brought to otherwise lawless areas. It also established a *modus operandi* which lasted well into the 1960s. Those sleek Hunters from Khormaksar, the very inspiration behind the wings I now so proudly wore, had been used for exactly the same purpose on numerous occasions.

There were many uncanny parallels between the air control of the inter-war years and our very own Operation *Jural*. Once again the aircraft would provide a means of watching over an area inaccessible to our ground forces. And once again Iraq would provide a *raison d'etre* for squadrons whose numbers had already been savaged by cost-cutting politicians. In fact, the pendulum, as we used to say at Brüggen – had swung full circle!

But apart from a strong sense of corporate *déjà-vu* and perhaps a chance of some action, I wasn't entirely convinced that our work over Iraq was a good thing. To me the very nature of our operation was somewhat dubious. Agreed, it had been given some sort of legitimacy by the UN (depending on how you interpreted the UN resolution), but it was still tantamount to interfering with the internal affairs of another sovereign country, however unpleasant those affairs might be. Only the Americans, the Kuwaitis and ourselves seemed to support the UN position unequivocally; the French had been persuaded into half-hearted support and the Saudis had grudgingly allowed us to use their air bases. No one else appeared to support the action.

The Cold War had been simple enough. We knew exactly who the baddies were and we knew that if we let then sweep into Western Europe, that would be the end of Great Britain as we knew it. There was an obvious and direct threat to our own country, which made it easy to envisage exactly who and what you would be risking your neck for. In the Gulf, matters were much less straightforward. There was no discernible direct threat to our own country and nor did there seem to

A pilot's eye view of Garvie Island in the last few seconds of a laydown attack. ('JJ' Burrows)

be one against her interests. The morality of defending one's homeland against the invading hordes was clear, but for meddling in Iraq, which was after all an independent country, it would be much more difficult to justify. So, too, would be taking any personal risks over Iraq.

As the plan for the detachment firmed up, my responsibility was to make sure that all the crews who would be going to Saudi were properly prepared. Much of that task was sorting out trivia like, for example, making sure that everyone would be current at night flying for the whole detachment and ensuring that all the annual check rides that would otherwise fall during it were brought forward. Check rides are the bane of the fighter pilot: instrument ratings, flying skill checks by the squadron flying instructor, tactical checks by the squadron checking officers all have to be done for every pilot at least annually and sometimes more frequently.

A more important goal in my view was to make everyone go through a work-up in medium-level tactics before we went to the Gulf to make sure they were fully up-to-speed on what to do and how to do it. Although our role at this stage was only that of monitoring, we might just be called on to fight. I decided to get all of us through a short work-up including air-to-air refuelling, live weaponry and reconnaissance from medium level, and some fighter evasion. We would also practise the attack profiles which would be employed if we were dropping laser-guided bombs. Unfortunately we lacked the vital piece of kit for this – a laser designator – so it was a bit like practising firing a gun by shouting 'Bang!' but at least we could get used to the profile and iron out any snags we found. At that stage the RAF only had four Thermal Imaging and Laser Designating (Tiald pods): one was at Boscombe Down where it was being worked on by boffins, and the remaining three were being used by crews in Dhahran.

The work-up started well. We got our hands on lots of tankers, though never a Victor which was what we would be using in the Gulf, and we all dropped live 1,000lb bombs on Garvie Island on the north-west tip of Scotland. There are many ranges on which one can drop practice or inert bombs, but Garvie is one of the very few places in Europe where real live bombs can be dropped. Garvie is a large granite lump a few hundred yards off the coast near Cape Wrath, it is impervious to the destructive power of even a live bomb, and is remote enough not to cause the public any worries or irritation. Our trips there gave us a useful feel for what operations over Iraq might be like: an hour's transit to the tanker, then another hour to the target area. After two long hours sitting in the seat, without the concentration of low flying to take your mind off how uncomfortable an ejection seat can become, there would be a flurry of activity to find the target and get the bombs off, followed by the dreary transit home.

When we arrived over Garvie it was hidden under a thick layer of stratus, so we had to drop the first bomb from low level to make sure we really had found the target. It wasn't that I didn't trust my navigator, Mal, but not unreasonably there are strict safety rules about dropping live bombs in peacetime! It was not difficult to find Garvie, in fact the only difficulty was deciding which bit of it we should bomb – having been used to targets made of oil drums or small boats, a whole island seemed a ridiculously huge one. The navigation kit looked in good order as we sped over the rock and we let our first bomb go. Then, having helped lower the island by another fraction of a millimetre, we climbed back above the cloud to drop the second from medium level.

The second bomb was an 'airburst', fused so that it would explode about 10ft above the rock. I'd wanted to see what it would look like when it went bang, but the cloud was going to make that difficult. Mal found the island once again as we ran in. The danger with a proximity-fused bomb is that once dropped it will explode if it senses anything nearby, so if it fuses straight away it might sense your aircraft nearby and explode almost immediately. This is exactly what happened to a couple of Tornados during the Gulf War, resulting in the loss of an aircraft over Iraq. With the benefit of hindsight, we knew now that the only way to avoid having to make a parachute descent over the target was to pull up and away as soon as the weapon came off the aircraft. As we got closer to the target, the bomb came off with a loud thud and I pulled away sharply, overbanking into a steep dive to get below the clouds. We popped out of the murky overcast above the choppy green-grey sea with the dark shape of Garvie a couple of miles out to our left, but even our rapid dive hadn't been fast enough. A dirty oily-black pall of smoke already hung over the island. Disappointed not to have seen my own explosion, I realized that if I extended upwind slightly before turning back, I would be well placed to see Number Two's bomb. I heard them call 'bomb gone!' to the RSO and hit the stopwatch. A few seconds later there was a massive flash over the island, as if it had been hit with a thunderbolt. If that was what one bomb would do, I could only begin to imagine the destructive power of a stick of three or four of them.

On other days we toured various airfields at 10,000ft and discovered how difficult it is to make out fine detail with the naked eye from that height. Finally we went through the motions of Tiald attacks until we'd got the drills right. The RAF was still in the dark ages of laser-guided weaponry, pretty much where the USAF had been twenty years previously in Vietnam, where one aircraft was needed to designate the target and another to drop the bombs. The critical part here is getting two aircraft in the right piece of sky at the right time, so that the designator has already found and marked the target by the time the bomber drops his bomb. But that is not all: the designator has then to keep the target continuously illuminated by the laser throughout the following thirty seconds or so it takes the bomb to fly to the target. All in all it was an involved procedure which took a lot of pre-planning to make sure that the relative positions of designator, bomber and target stayed within fairly tight limits. Even then, the whole thing would only work if no cloud or smoke obscured the target! Laser bombing was still a 'black art' as far as we were concerned and most of us had never even seen a laser-guided bomb.

Unfortunately, despite our impending operational deployment we were still vulnerable to the normal pressures on squadron. In the end we ran out of aircraft and time before we could all complete the work-up. As Frank, acutely aware of the conflicting pressures on the squadron, pointed out, there was only a very slight chance of real action in the Gulf, against an absolute certainty that we were required to complete the routine training of new crews. The fighter-evasion practice had to be cancelled and the remaining extra tanking and weaponry training had to be curtailed. At least there was some consolation that the last major event before the deployment was the ACMI range at Deci. Even so, when the first crews, led by Frank and Coulsy deployed in early November, we had only done what I considered the absolute minimum to be effective if we were called upon to fight. However, I had seen enough of Mal to feel supremely confident in his ability and I knew that whatever was ahead, we would give our best.

A couple of weeks later, one of the navigators about to deploy on the second wave went for a routine medical check. Unfortunately a slight anomaly was found and he was immediately grounded. A replacement navigator was needed in a hurry. The only man available at such short notice was my own navigator Mal, so he left almost immediately to fly with Marcus and with no more combat-ready navigators left amongst the Crusaders, I had to look to another squadron for a replacement. The surprising result of our plea was Platty. I had expected a like-for-like replacement for Mal: he was an experienced navigator well-established on his second tour, a four-ship leader and a veteran of the Gulf War. In short, he had the very sort of experience that I would need to support me as one of the executives on the detachment. Platty, on the other hand was a relatively inexperienced first-tourist with no qualifications as a formation leader. Being from another squadron, he was also a complete unknown. From his point of view, it must have been like being dropped into the deep end: crewed with a senior pilot, he would deploy with an unfamiliar squadron and be expected to plan and lead complex sorties. But if the prospect worried him at all, it didn't show. His easy-going character meant that he fitted easily into his new

Luxury accommodation at Dhahran 1: Khobar Towers, our home for the duration.

surroundings, while his casual laid-back attitude to life was probably a perfect foil for my own more serious nature.

The dawn on 9 December 1992 was cold, grey and damp. A lone, well-used Andover transport aircraft sat in the drizzle on the pan at Brüggen, its faded red paint glistening in the wet. A few hundred yards away, in a small shack bearing a sign grandly proclaiming it to be the air terminal, sat four aircrew, two pilots and two navigators. Having just kissed our wives farewell, Platty, Taff, Chris and myself were about to head off for our six-week stint in Dhahran. Chris was the other pilot, on his second tour: Intelligent, utterly reliable and with a dry wit, he was excellent company.

Taff and I had been on the Goldstars together, so we knew each other pretty well and had flown together frequently. He'd even shown me his parents' house on one trip. 'There it is,' he'd shouted excitedly as we flashed over the row upon row of identical-looking terraces in the Rhondda valley, 'the one with the red door.' Taff was also responsible for my record for being airborne in the shortest time after reporting for work. It was the morning of the Christmas Draw at the Officers' Mess and I sauntered onto the squadron aware that the only flying planned for the day was a pair going to Pisa for the weekend. Matt was already in the crew room, dressed ready to go when I walked in.

'Napes, we've only got one crew and I don't want to go on my own. The engineers say we can have two aircraft – why don't you come, too.' I wasn't overly bothered at the prospect of the Christmas Draw, as I didn't have a partner to take, and the thought of a weekend in Pisa suddenly appealed. The next person through the door was Taff, who didn't need much persuading either. Less than an hour later we were climbing through 10,000ft en-route to Pisa. It was only once we got there that Taff realized he hadn't told his girlfriend Mary, who was still expecting to be taken to the draw! I assume that he was forgiven on his return, since they married a year later.

At last we were called to board the Andover, which we were to share with a Medical Evacuation (Medevac) team for the flight to Northolt, the first leg of our journey. As the aircraft staggered airborne we were rather surprised when the loadmaster announced that our flight time to RAF Gutersloh, which lay in completely the opposite direction to RAF Northolt, would be forty-five minutes! The reason for this diversion was, in fact, to pick up the Medevac team's patient. We saw him in the terminal at Gutersloh when we got off for a leg stretch. He was hobbling around on his own quite happily as we headed for the coffee machine. Some thirty minutes later we saw him again as we re-boarded the aircraft, this time lashed to a stretcher and looking nowhere near as happy as the zealous Medevac team fussed around him. Eventually we reached Northolt and after much negotiating managed to get some transport to RAF Brize Norton, the jumping off point for our flight to Dhahran. The RAF certainly didn't wish to make this journey easy for us. At Brize we discovered that, in the great traditions of Transport Command, our flight would leave at 2.00am the next morning. Enough time for a last beer and curry in the local town, even with the usual report-in time several hours before departure! We were to regret both later as we spent the early morning heading eastwards in the dubious 1960s-style luxury of a VC10: burning stomachs and thick heads made sleep virtually impossible. Once again we were treated to an intermediate stop on the way to our destination. This time it was at Riyadh to drop off the Commander-in-Chief, who unbeknown to us had been travelling in the first-class compartment of the aircraft. We were let out into the VIP lounge for a very welcome and rehydrating drink of sweet tea in the bright sunlight. Most strikingly, we could see the huge number of USAF airborne command and control aircraft, which brought home the size of the operation and the US commitment. Forty minutes later we were landing at Dhahran.

Dhahran was a sprawling expanse of concrete which would have made London Heathrow look small. Apart from two long runways and an international air terminal, numerous taxiways and concrete shelters provided accommodation for the resident Royal Saudi Air Force units, as well as the visiting American, British and French Coalition forces. Taff, who had been there during the Gulf War, pointed out various landmarks to me as we taxied round. At last the VC10 came to a halt on the military apron and we were allowed out. At the foot of the steps, hunched slightly against the cool breeze was the very welcome sight of the Boss and the rest of the crews. They all seemed to be in cheerful spirits.

'Welcome to Dhahran,' said Frank, 'it's not bad here. There's no flying tomorrow, so we're all off to Bahrain now. Coulsy will sort you out.'

'See you when we get back,' echoed the rest of the boys.

With baggage retrieved we bumped our way across the airfields and through the many checkpoints towards our accommodation. Meanwhile, Coulsy outlined the plan for us over the next few days. We'd get unpacked and settled into our accommodation first, and then have a couple of hours of groundschool in the afternoon to introduce us to the Tiald. The next day would be taken up with briefings and reading through the various orders and instructions that we would have to read before we could fly.

At last we came to the domestic site, known as 'Khobar Towers'. This fairly large development of sandy pink tower blocks was built, apparently, at the behest of King Khaled for the Bedouins. The king's noble intention was to provide a permanent home for every one of his citizens, but unfortunately the Bedouin had decided that they much preferred their tents to the new tower blocks, and they never moved in. So in a country where it was quite impossible to conceive that the king might have got it wrong, the Towers had been conveniently forgotten and remained empty until the Americans arrived for the Gulf War and commandeered them. We were delighted to discover that, in true American fashion, the blocks had been furnished to a high standard and the whole complex had been provided with Americanized facilities. Even the underground car parks had been converted into a shopping mall and a gym. Among the accommodation blocks, the British had two towers (one for officers and one for airmen) and the French had one. The rumour – alas never substantiated – was that the French block had a well-stocked wine cellar! After surviving interrogation by two very officious RAF policemen, who seemed convinced that we were part of an international smuggling ring responsible for bringing alcohol and pornography into the country, we settled into a four-bedroomed flat which would be home to the four of us for the next six weeks.

That evening we were introduced to the culinary delights of the local town, Khobar, by a few of the boys who had remained at Dhahran. They would be involved in planning the op wave two days later, so would have to spend most of the next day in the planning room. We all visited 'The Grill' with its army of wok-wielding chinamen in the glass-fronted kitchen, which along with 'The Galaxy' Indian restaurant, which we visited the following night, offered much more tempting fare than the tasteless fast food available from the American 'eateries' on the base. I imagine that both establishments made a tidy profit thanks to the RAF while we were there. Khobar town was a short drive from the accommodation area, but we had a number of hire cars available to us, so distance and transport were not a problem. It was pleasant to stroll round Khobar of an evening. Although the place was bustling and although there were only the occasional black-draped women to be seen, the atmosphere was one of cosmopolitan friendliness. We went to eat there most evenings.

As we sat in 'The Grill' the boys filled us in with the detachment gossip and banter. Morale seemed high and everyone was enjoying their time in the Gulf, despite the lack of beer. Escape was possible across the causeway to Bahrain every now and then. There was a very restrictive RAF policy on such 'Rest and Recreation' visits, but so far it had not been rigidly enforced. As a result, most people could expect to get across to Bahrain for a taste of freedom every ten days or so.

We did not discuss the operation in any detail in such a public place, but we were told the top story of the detachment so far. Marcus and Mal had been on their first mission over Iraq, acting as wingman to a crew from another squadron. They had reached Tallil airfield, which the lead aircraft was to search for signs of Iraqi activity. Although it was the first time Marcus had been in that part of the world it was a chance for Mal to revisit one of his targets from the Gulf War. Looking

Marcus and Mal in the cockpit - they had suffered a catastrophic fuel leak and diverted into Kuwait just a few days before this was taken. (Marcus Cook)

down on the airfield as the leader completed his reconnaissance run, they chatted about what it had been like dropping bombs and being shot at. The leader came off his run and turned northwards, Marcus looked to check his fuel. Somehow the numbers didn't tally – ten minutes beforehand their remaining fuel had matched the planned figure, but now they were well down on the plan. At this point the leader, who was now no longer concentrating solely on his reconnaissance, called that Marcus and Mal appeared to be venting fuel. This confirmed their worst fears – they had a massive fuel leak.

They were now over hostile territory with no means of getting back to Dhahran and with every chance that the leaking fuel might ignite against a hot spot near the engine. The only chance was to head for Kuwait and hope that they had enough fuel to get there without it catching fire. The race was on. Marcus turned for Kuwait and accelerated – might as well burn as much of the fuel as possible rather than just losing it over the side. The formation leader handled the radio calls to alert the AWACS and scramble the combat-rescue helicopters in case they were needed. Meanwhile as they thundered towards Kuwait, Mal ran through the checklists. They managed to isolate the two sides of the fuel system so that the fuel destined for the left engine wouldn't gush out through the massive leak that was now apparent in the right-hand side. On that side, the fuel gauge was dropping quickly and it seemed certain that the right-hand engine would soon stop from fuel starvation. After what seemed like an eternity, they crossed into Kuwait – at least if they jumped out now they would be in friendly territory. With the two Kuwaiti military airfields out of action thanks to coalition bombing during the war, they decided to head for the International Airport at Kuwait City. However, their problems were not yet over. Firstly, the fuel leak had put the aircraft outside its normal centre of gravity limits and secondly they couldn't raise ATC on any of the frequencies. There simply was not time to carry out a check of the aircraft's handling with its seriously-abnormal centre of gravity and nor was their time to follow the usual courtesies with ATC. Marcus just turned towards the runway and landed without any clearance from the tower. As they taxied clear of the runway it became obvious why they hadn't managed to raise anyone on the radios – everyone had been warned of their approach and had all rushed outside to watch the crash! When Marcus shut down the engines, there was no fuel at all in the right-hand side, thanks to a fracture in the main fuel feed to the right-hand engine, a pipe of some 2in diameter. It is little short of a miracle that the right-hand engine didn't flame out or that the leaking fuel never ignited.

Two days after hearing this story, we had read and signed for all the orders, including one that directed us to ensure our urine was light yellow, so that we wouldn't become dehydrated. We had Saudi base passes to enable us to traverse the numerous checkpoints and we were the proud possessors of name badges in Arabic for our flying suits. The latter were hand-embroidered locally, and since none of us were Arabic speakers, we weren't entirely sure what the squiggley writing really said. An unpopular squadron commander on a previous detachment had sent a disgruntled minion along to get him an Arabic name badge. What he didn't know as he proudly wore his name badge in front of the Saudi base commander was that the minion had asked for the Arabic name to read 'Captain Fat Bastard.'

We had also learnt how the Tiald pod worked and how we would be using it over Iraq. The Tiald was intended as a laser-designator pod, for marking targets with a laser beam for laser-guided bombs. It had been in the early stages of development when the Gulf war started, and a couple of prototype pods had been rushed down to Saudi for use by the Tornado force as target designators. Here they had been highly successful. Now, in Dhahran we had three of the next generation 'pre-production' pods, two named 'Becky' and 'Rachel' were used every day, and a third one in pieces used to provide spares for the first two. However, we weren't particularly interested in the laser designating part of the pod: the bit that we were now interested in was the powerful video camera which was used to find the target in the first place. The idea was to use the camera like an 'airborne security camera' as we patrolled the sky. This was the result of some fast lateral thinking during the early days of the detachment when the Americans had banned aircraft from flying below 10,000ft over Iraq, ruling out the use of the low-level Tornado reconnaissance system. After their experiences losing aircraft to small arms fire in Vietnam, the Americans are very wary of taking unnecessary risks. Despite the fact that looking at the Tiald video camera in the air was like looking through the world through a straw, crews still managed to bring back useful video footage of the various points of interest against which they were tasked.

It is a tribute to the navigators using Tiald that it worked well in its new role and once again illustrated how RAF aircrew have to use their ingenuity to get by with equipment that isn't designed for the job.

Another very sensible rule which the Americans insisted upon was that aircraft should not operate alone over Iraq. Firstly, two aircraft could give each other cross-cover, particularly in the blind area directly beneath. Secondly if, for some reason, a crew had to eject, there would be someone on station immediately to alert the rescue team and provide 'top cover' if needed. The look out was particularly relevant for us, since the navigator was very much head in the cockpit while using Tiald and the pilot was also concentrating on flying smoothly and accurately to help him out. There wasn't much spare capacity for looking out and on our own we'd be sitting ducks if there was any ground fire. The solution was to fly as a pair, with one aircraft concentrating on the Tiald work and the Number Two as the 'shooter', providing escort and keeping a good look out. To add to the interest, the shooter crews were to carry a hand-held video camera, to film anything of interest. The hand-shot colour film would supplement the black and white Tiald video by giving a wider-angle picture and an idea of colour contrasts. That was the idea anyway!

Our combat-ready work up would comprise four sorties: two in Kuwait and two in Iraq. The first would be an introduction to the local procedures and a look at flying in the unfamiliar surroundings of the Middle East. The second would be an opportunity to play with a real Tiald pod and get used to its idiosyncrasies. We would then go 'sausage side' over Iraq as a shooter, before a final sortie using the Tiald for real. After that we would become just another crew to be fitted into the flying programme at the whim of the programmer.

Luxury accommodation at Dhahran 2: the operations block on the airfield.

The flying programme was decided by the headquarters in Riyadh, by means of a daily tasking signal, known for some reason as the 'Frag.' The Frag detailed which missions had to be flown by which units against which tasks. Our prime interest was our own tasking and that of the Victor tanker based across the causeway in Bahrain, which supported us on most missions. However, every time we flew we were just a tiny part of the 'big picture' of a vast number of USAF and US Navy aircraft, operating just as we had done on Exercise *Red Flag* as a mutually supporting package. Whenever we were over Iraq, there would be fighter sweeps, early warning aircraft, electronic jammers and Wild Weasels out there supporting us. If any aircraft were left over from the 'op wave' over Iraq, they could be used for training sorties in Kuwait. These trips were used for in-theatre training for new arrivals, like us, or to provide some low-flying practice and a bit of a change of scenery for the others. Eventually it would be my job to allocate crews to the flying programme and decide who did what.

The pattern of operations was a series of op days followed by a 'Down Day' with no flying, to let the engineers catch up with any necessary servicing. The timings of the sorties over Iraq each day were varied, as was the length of time between Down Days, so that the Iraqis would not know when or where to expect us.

To help with the day-to-day running of the operation, I was delighted to see a number of familiar faces, who were all on a three-month stint in Dhahran. Manning the ops desk most days was Keith, one of the more supportive instructors on the TWCU when I'd been a student on my first conversion course. He had 'escaped' from the conversion unit to Dhahran for a three-month stint as an operations officer. He didn't seem too downhearted at the prospect – perhaps he was pleased at not having to fly with students like me for a while! The operations desk is the heart of a RAF squadron. It is the contact point for the rest of the world, and it's here that all the day-to-day decisions about running the squadron are made. Manning the desk is a bit like crisis management and if it's done poorly, everyone suffers. Conversely a well-run desk makes life on the squadron much easier. I was pleased that we had someone sensible and level-headed like Keith doing the job.

On the intelligence side of the house, we were very fortunate to have one of the real stars of the Crusaders, Harry, our very own army major. Every ground-attack squadron had an army major attached to it as the Ground Liaison Officer (GLO). Harry seemed rather to enjoy the squadron and he made himself indispensable. He, too, had been on the Crusaders during my first tour, but while all the aircrew came and went, Harry stayed there and was now easily by far the most long-serving member of the squadron. An absolute gentleman, Harry looked upon us with benevolent indulgence, as a favourite uncle might look upon a bunch of 10-year-old schoolboys. For our part, the schoolboys adored their favourite uncle! He let us get on with our fun and games, but was always there in the background making sure that any loose ends we had missed in our excitement were tidied up before anyone noticed. The squadron owed him a great debt both operationally and socially. Here in Dhahran, Harry's job was to update us on what was happening on the ground in Iraq.

We also had two mission planners – navigators from other squadrons sent to Dhahran for three months to help with the operational planning. We were lucky to have two excellent characters who were real assets to us throughout the detachment. The first was our very own Rick, who must have found it galling to be there drawing maps for three months while all his mates came out for six weeks and flew their socks off! But Rick didn't let it get him down and got on with the job with his usual impressive enthusiasm. The other planner was Gordon, another old mate from my first tour with the Crusaders. Since those days, he had been exclusively on reconnaissance squadrons and was something of an enthusiast about the 'recce' world, almost to the point of being very boring about it if he wasn't kept in check! However, he'd had an exciting time during the Gulf War and the occasional modestly told war story made fascinating listening. Apart from their general interest to me, Gordon's stories did much to give me faith in the Tornado and particularly its electronic-warfare equipment. He had seen it in action for real and could vouch for the fact it worked better even than we had hoped. It was very reassuring

We managed to miss breakfast on our third day in Dhahran. By then the novelty of our new surroundings had worn off and the two-hour time change from home caught up with us. We made our way into work at a very leisurely 9.00am. The squadron operations (ops) block was back on the airfield, a couple of miles along the ring road that snaked its way through numerous security checkpoints around the airfield perimeter. The whole of the airfield was divided up into wired off security areas and we needed our base pass to get from each area into the next. In contrast to the two RAF policemen we had already met, and despite the dreary nature of their job, the US personnel manning the checkpoints were ever cheerful. Our progress was punctuated by numerous instructions to have a nice day. The ops blocks (ours, the Americans' and the French) were all sited just outside the access gate leading to the inner area, where the aircraft were parked.

Just across the road, but inside the wire, was the reassuring presence of a Patriot anti-missile battery. Our ops block was a tatty cluster of inter-connected Portakabins, looking for all the world, like a shanty town next to the neighbouring American building. But it contained all the normal functions of an RAF squadron. A locker room-cum coffee bar led into a wide corridor off which were a couple of briefing rooms and the intelligence room. The corridor then performed a U-turn past a couple of storerooms before leading into the planning room, then the ops room. A detached Portakabin housed an office for the Detachment Commander (DETCO) and a map store. Two similar shanty towns housed the tactical communications wing and the Reconnaissance Interpretation Centre (RIC), where the photographic interpreters did business, while 100yds downwind were the shared toilets. Our engineers had their offices in a suitably run-down shack inside the central area next to the aircraft.

The first stop was to check in with the ops desk. Here Keith confirmed that we were on the programme for our first sortie to Kuwait that afternoon after the 'Op Wave' (the aircraft operating over Iraq) returned. He suggested that we use the intervening time to finish reading the last couple of documents, check out our flying clothing and pay our respects to the DETCO.

I'd known the DETCO previously and remembered him as a nice guy. Now on a three-month detachment there, he was notionally in command of the whole RAF force there, including all the support staff, the engineers and the fliers. Nominally, at least, Coulsy was the next in the chain of command on the flying side. However, the Boss, also a Wing Commander of course, was also in town. Since all of the aircrew and most of the engineers were from his squadron, they naturally looked to him as their leader, and a strong character like Frank was never going to give up his own command easily. This put the DETCO in a rather awkward position, which wasn't helped by the fact that Vaughan, his immediate superior at Riyadh, was Frank's predecessor as squadron commander! The temptation for either of them to meddle in the dealings of the squadron was too much and the poor old DETCO was on to a loser from the start. This probably explains some of the strange decisions he was to make over the next few weeks. However, that morning he was all pleasantries as we renewed our acquaintance. I told him how much I was looking forward to acting as his deputy once Coulsy had done his stint.

The flying clothing (helmets, g-suits, and lifejackets) had been sent ahead of us from Germany a few weeks beforehand. Eventually we tracked it down, along with the flying clothing workers, in another Portakabin close to the engineers' set up, near the aircraft. Having reclaimed our possessions, we lined up to be issued with the extra kit we'd need in theatre. One vital piece of new equipment was an American-type survival vest, a number of which had been borrowed or stolen from our neighbours. This was like a 'fishnet' waistcoat, which contained enough pockets to hide all the added paraphernalia necessary to operating over hostile territory. The first thing to find a pocket for was a US-type survival radio, which we would need if we were unfortunate enough to call on the services of the combat rescue team. This was another area in which, thanks to their Vietnam experience twenty years previously, the Americans were streets ahead of us. The RAF search and rescue forces seemed to be limited to flying bright yellow helicopters around the coasts of Britain: no one seemed to have seriously looked into the possibility of rescuing downed aircrew on the 'wrong' side of the frontline. Here in Saudi, it was very reassuring to know that we had the support of the USAF combat rescue teams if we ever had to jump out 'sausage side'.

Another new toy was a hand-held Global Positioning System (GPS) station, which along with the silk map would provide a way of navigating home just in case we were not found by the rescue boys. With no comfortable place in the survival vest, I managed to squeeze my GPS into one of the calf pockets of my g-suit. I wasn't confident that it would stay there under the force of an ejection, but at least if it fell out it wouldn't cause me to break my leg on it when I landed! In case we came across any of the locals on the ground in Iraq (or in fact anywhere out in the desert) we were issued with a 9mm pistol, a 'goolie chit' and eighteen gold sovereigns.

The pistol was there to make us feel better, though we were all aware that it was virtually useless because of its extreme inaccuracy and propensity to jam at the critical moment. However, we carefully found space for two magazines in the vest. The 'goolie chit' promised a large reward to anyone who delivered us unharmed to the nearest British representative. Presumably we were to present this to the Arab who we had just missed with the 9mm pistol, and if that failed, we could persuade him with the gold not to kill us. The 'goolie chit' was a throwback to the 1920s when the RAF spent most of its time patrolling the bad lands of Iraq and

A French Air Force Dassault Mirage 2000 – one of the eight based at Dhahran.

Afghanistan. Here the tribes took delight in separating downed aircrew from their 'family jewels' before killing them, hence the term 'goolie chit'. I wasn't altogether convinced that gold would work, either, but at least I was temporarily the richest I'd ever been. We stuffed the rest of the pockets in the jacket and g-suit with as many foil sachets of water as we could stow.

Lunch was a surreal experience. A few minutes' drive round the perimeter road, in a secluded spot, was the Oasis, a US forces recreation centre, based around a large swimming pool. Loud rock music blared as hordes of troops, male and female, sunbathed in varying states of undress. I can only imagine that they must have been wearing a powerful insect repellent, because the only time I tried sunbathing back at the Towers I was plagued by a swarm of flies. This lot seemed unperturbed by such troubles. At one end of the pool a large barbecue had been set up, all under fine netting to keep the flies out. Over the inevitable burger and frankfurter we mused that it really was an oasis of California in the middle of Saudi Arabia! We were impressed with how much effort the Americans had put into making sure that their troops were well catered for and had recreational facilities. I doubt that Dhahran would have been as bearable without them.

Two hours before take-off, the Boss briefed us on the afternoon's flight. He and Coulsy would lead, with me and Platty as Number Two and Chris and Taff as Number Three. We would carry out a 'Kuwaiti Trainer', an area familiarization consisting of a transit to and from Kuwait and some low flying while we were there. As it was our first sortie, Frank ran through the local procedures in some detail. Then it was time to dress for action; flying suit, with all badges removed and pockets emptied except for a card giving name rank and number, then the pistol in a holster worn James Bond-style under the armpit, survival vest, g-suit and lifejacket. The whole lot weighed a ton! At least the short minibus ride to the engineers' shack was an opportunity to find out which over-filled pockets in the survival vest dug uncomfortably into one's anatomy before strapping into an ejection seat for two hours. Having repacked our vests more comfortably and signed for the aircraft, we ambled out onto the line.

The aircraft were neatly lined up on the taxiway 100yd away from a similarly neat line of French Air Force Mirage 2000 fighters. Four of our six Tornados were finished in a sandy desert camouflage, making them look very sleek and business-like; the other two were still in the traditional dark grey and green. All were loaded ready for action. I walked round our aircraft with the starting crew, giving it a final check and counting the safety pins which would be removed from the weapons pylons and shown to me once we had started up. I would expect to see seven. Large fuel tanks hung under the wings, half as big again as those we flew with at Brüggen. Live Sidewinder air-to-air missiles were loaded on the launcher rails just above the tanks. On the right wing, the flare dispenser bristled with live flares, each capable of decoying a heat-seeking missile. Under the cockpit, the gun panels were open so that we could check the high-explosive rounds loaded.

Platty was already strapped into the back seat and was firing up the navigation kit. It was great to get back into a Tornado once again, especially as I hadn't flown for three weeks. I settled myself down in what were now, after seven years and 1,300 hours flying time, very familiar surroundings and got on with the checks. A perennial problem for me was the secure radio, which had been fitted as a modification since the Gulf War. The HAVEQUICK (HQ – a frequency-hopping system) radio was an ingenious bit of kit, as it transmitted and received messages, it hopped across some ten different frequencies spending only a second or so on each. Provided another radio was tuned to hop across the same frequencies in the same order for the same amount of time, both radios could communicate with each other. Anyone else's radio, for example the enemy's, couldn't listen in to the conversation. Unfortunately, the HQ had been added to the Tornado very much as an afterthought. It had been placed in a very awkward position in the front cockpit at the rear of the right-hand console, just behind and outboard of ones buttocks. As a result, to see it or use any of its controls required twisting round and viewing it from almost upside down. As if that was not enough, it needed to be programmed, a procedure which took about a hundred button presses, each one of which had to be done in the correct order. The official checklist was not terribly good and various people had produced easy-to-read 'gizzas' as alternatives. I had tried the official list, and was on to my second gizza, but I could only rarely get the thing to work. I had begun to get superstitious about it: if I couldn't get the HQ to work, I usually had a rotten trip. Today I was confident that I'd programmed it properly.

Everything seemed to be going along very smoothly, and Platty and I were ready to go when the check-in time came round.

'Dundee, check,' called the Boss.

'Two'

'Three'

'Dundee, box two go,' the Boss called us over the HQ.

Silence, followed a minute later by: 'Dundee two on box one, any joy on box two,' enquired the Boss.

'Negative,' from me - I hadn't heard anything on the HQ box at all. Oh dear!

We taxi out, one after the other, past the Mirages and onto the northerly runway, to line up in a slightly swept echelon. The Boss' forefinger twirls the 'wind up' signal which I repeat to Chris. I push the throttles up to full dry power, check the engine gauges and look back to Chris. The nose of his aircraft is dipped as it strains against the brakes; his 'thumb up' fist is pressed against the canopy. I repeat this signal to the Boss. He waves bye-bye, selects reheat and thunders down the runway. The roar of his engines follows him into a shimmering haze as we are left rocking in his wake. Fifteen seconds later, I take my toes of the brakes and we charge forward to follow him skywards.

It's a beautiful sunny day as we leave the city of Dammam behind and head north up the coast past the port at Al Jubail. On our left is the tawny-coloured haze of Saudi Arabia and on our right the deep azure-blue of the Persian Gulf. I catch up with the Boss as we pass 10,000ft, and sit in a loose formation on his right wing as we carry on up to 22,000ft. Although we're travelling at over 400kts, there is no impression of speed at this height and the Boss' aircraft appears to be just hanging there, wings gently flexing as we ride the atmosphere's light undulations. As usual, I can't help looking for the wire that must be holding him up. Even at this height we can hear the muffled roar of his engines.

'Look at those tanks wobbling,' says Platty. The fuel tanks on the Boss' aircraft are indeed jiggling slightly in the airflow. A glance in the mirror and I can just see the noses of our tanks describing tiny circles, confirming that our tanks, too, are moving around. So this is normal for these big tanks. It's best not even to think about the stresses they must be putting on the wings!

Number Three joins us on the Boss' left and the three of us level at 22,000ft for the transit up to Kuwait. We chop across to the Kuwaiti ATC frequency and check in. Coulsy asks for clearance to fly round Kuwait at low level, which is duly given.

'You are welcome in Kuwait,' adds the controller encouragingly. The Boss wheels onto a north-westerly heading and starts dropping down to low level. This is a signal for Chris and me to ease back into tactical formation. I keep the Boss framed in the canopy quarterlight, and slide out until I am about two miles from him, swept back at about 30°. Chris stays level with me, a similar distance back from the Boss. Now we're in a loose triangle formation with the Boss at the apex and Chris and me on the base line. It's quite a comfortable formation to fly. The Boss can concentrate on navigating, safe in the knowledge that we're keeping his tail clear. As we descend the visibility reduces in a slight haze. Even a slight wind in these parts can pick up a fair amount of sand and dust.

Down to 500ft and we cross Faylaka Island, scene of heavy fighting during the war. The Coalition had led the Iraqis to believe that the main assault would come here and amphibious forces had landed here in a diversionary attack to keep up the impression. As we cruise over it we can see how fierce the battle must have been. The island is pock-marked with craters, a lunar landscape. Here and there shattered fortifications lie empty. Even nearly two years on, it is a scene of total devastation.

Suddenly we're over water once more. The water looks cool and inviting from the sweaty heat of a Tornado cockpit. Faylaka Island disappears behind us. Somewhere out on the left is the city of Kuwait itself, only five miles away but invisible in the haze. A wrecked naval ship, half submerged in the shallow water, flicks past beneath us. Ahead of us looms the huge viaduct which connects Bubiyan Island to mainland Kuwait. As we get closer we can see that the single span at each end of the bridge has been dropped. The bridge lies intact, but there is no way of getting on or off it. It just stands as a forlorn monument to the surgical precision of laser-guided bombs. Over the bridge and then on to a westerly heading and suddenly we pop out into clear air. Instantly a sharp horizon appears where desert meets sky, while behind it looks as if a curtain of sand has been drawn across our tracks. Now we can see more clearly, we drop down to 250ft, only climbing up occasionally to get a better view of some other relic of the war: Wrecked tanks, sometimes singly, sometimes in clusters, flash by.

The Boss alters course abruptly, then drops a wing as if he's just found something he was looking for. Then I see it. A huge satellite-tracking station is lying in shattered pieces on the ground. The whole place has been systematically wrecked. The buildings are charred ruins and the satellite dishes lie toppled in the desert. It is a breathtaking sight. It seems inconceivable that a structure so large can have been so completely destroyed. A couple of seconds later we cross the road running north towards Basrah. In the last days of the Gulf War the Basrah road had been the scene of carnage as Coalition warplanes found the stream of vehicles trying to escape northwards back to Iraq. Now the road is clear to traffic again, but on either side there are large piles of blackened wrecks which have been bulldozed off the road into huge square areas. Once again the sheer scale of the devastation defies comprehension.

The western part of Kuwait is a vast sandy plain. Surprisingly it is a bustling corner of the desert. Although there are no obvious tracks, the whole area is being criss-crossed by large trucks and articulated vehicles. It looks more like shipping on the English Channel on a busy day. It is not clear where the traffic is going, or where it has come from. The lack of road doesn't seem to be an obstacle. We still pass the occasional burnt-out tank, but herds of camels are becoming a more common sight.

'Dundee, loose line astern – go.' I see the Boss is now pointing straight towards a sprawling army camp and I need 500kt to keep up with him. This is home for a US Army regiment. It must be a pretty miserable home, too, out in the middle of nowhere, with none of the trappings of civilization that we enjoy in Khobar. One by one we screech over the top as a way of saying hello and assuring them they haven't been forgotten. I push us briefly into reheat so that they can get the full benefit of the noise! Whether the experience of being buzzed by three noisy jets is a morale-raiser or an irritant I don't know, but we enjoy it. It's that feeling of overwhelming power as you flash past a row of upturned faces. Now we are curving back round in a long daisy chain to do it all over again, this time heading back eastbound.

At 420kt, Kuwait is a tiny place. Only a couple of minutes after visiting the army we've arrived at the next site on our battlefield tour – the Ali-Al Salem Air Base. It is a large airfield with two long parallel runways pointing towards the heart of Iraq. Dispersed around the airfield are large concrete shelters for aircraft. Back at Brüggen, we operate from the first generation of HAS. These were built as a result of the 1967

Arab-Israeli war, when the Israeli Air Force wiped out most of the Arab air forces on the ground, on the first day of hostilities. Up until then, most air forces operated their aircraft from a large concrete pan, upon which the aircraft were neatly lined up. Events of 1967 changed all that and the shelters sprung up over all the airfields in Central Europe, on both sides of the Iron Curtain. At Brüggen ours are tiny, with just enough space inside for a Tornado. With only one set of armoured steel doors, the aircraft have to be winched into the shelter backwards. Second generation of HAS, like those in the UK are much larger – large enough to house two Tornados. But like ours, there is only one way into or out. Here in Kuwait, where money and space was no object, the third generation of drive-through HAS had been built.

From a distance it looks a truly impressive military airfield, but as we get closer we realize that it is completely unusable. At every taxiway intersection is a large crater which effectively blocks off the two sections of taxiway from each other. Like the bridge over to Bubiyan Island the runways are disconnected from the taxiways and lie utterly useless. Every single HAS has a hole punched through the roof, the doors blown outwards by the explosion that has taken place inside. The place is completely trashed. It is an impressive feat of arms. Such accurate bombing could only have been achieved using laser-guided weapons, but even so it would have taken several large scale and well-co-ordinated attacks to neutralize the airfield so completely and effectively. We fly past in a stunned silence. Three minutes later we come across a similar spectacle of destruction at Ahmed Al-Jaber Air Base.

The Boss peels off towards Kuwait City. At this point our tour of the Kuwait battlefield is over. We split into three individual aircraft for our recovery back to Dhahran. Night will have fallen by the time we get home and it is much easier to recover as singletons in the dark. For the moment I continue on at low level to get some spacing from the Boss. Below us, a herd of camels lopes along accompanied by its 'herd' of lengthening shadows; the desert here is a mix of black and dirty brown, stained dark by the oil-well fires which ravaged the area at the end of the Gulf War. I ease up the height to 2,000ft and call up Kuwait International to ask if I can shoot an approach. Once again the controller seems delighted to hear from us and we are made to feel very welcome. He cannot be more helpful as he vectors us round for an Instrument Landing System (ILS) approach. As we turn towards the final approach with the wings forward and flap down, I select the gear down and let the speed bleed back towards 180kt and we begin our final descent towards the runway.

'Dundee two you are cleared to fly by as low and as fast as you like,' calls the controller. I can't believe my luck. You don't get an invitation for licensed hooliganism at an international airport every day! Staying on the glideslope, I push the throttles forward and raise the gear and flap. As the aircraft picks up speed I sweep the wings back. I decide not to take him literally and limit myself to 250ft. It is the minimum height I've been authorized to on this sortie, so to go any lower would be unprofessional. Also, as I haven't flown for three weeks, it would be tempting fate: many pilots have killed themselves trying to be too clever with impromptu air displays. Aviation is a uniquely unforgiving craft. One mile out we're at 250ft, doing 500kt with the wings swept right back like a dart. As dusk falls, we streak across the line of staid-looking airliners and hurtle out over the desert once more.

'Dundee two are we cleared unrestricted climb level two seven zero,' I ask.

'Dundee two, that was a very good flypast, you are clear to climb unrestricted level two seven zero,' comes the reply. I push the throttles into reheat, pull the stick back and the Tornado rockets upwards, altimeter needle spinning madly round. Minutes later we're cruising homebound at 27,000ft. Looking down I can see that the ground is in darkness already, although we're still in daylight at our height and being treated to a stunningly beautiful sunset on the western horizon. Vermilion and ochre, burnished with copper slowly fade into mauve, then more swiftly into darkness as we start our descent.

That evening the four of us, Platty, Taff, Chris and I, went into Khobar to find something to eat. Morale was high after our first sortie in theatre and we chattered about the sights we'd seen in Kuwait as we drove around. Taff was our navigator for the evening. He had been there before during the Gulf War and he claimed to know where the good restaurants were located. I should have known better than to trust his sense of direction, having seen him in action in Goose Bay during a detachment with the Goldstars a few years before. Six of us had mounted an expedition from Goose Bay to Rabbit Island, a small, uninhabited finger of land ten miles out in the lake. We sailed out in two motorboats and set up camp for the night on the small beach on the south of the island. As the rest of us busied ourselves getting the campfire lit, Taff announced his intention to circumnavigate the island by boat. Having jumped into one boat, he immediately rammed the other, nearly sinking it, and then set off towards the east. Ten minutes later we were alerted by the noise of an outboard motor approaching from the west. Taff appeared round the headland and sped past our beach a few hundred yards off shore. We waved idly at him as we lounged round the campfire and were a little surprised when he carried on past and disappeared out of sight again eastwards. Ten minutes later he reappeared, breathless with excitement.

'You'll never guess what. There's another team camping on the beach on other side of the island,' he enthused.

'Taff, were there five of them, with one wearing a red T-shirt,' asked one of the others nonchalantly.

'Yes, how did you know that,' Taff was curious.

'It was us – you've been round the island twice, you prat.'

Taff's sense of direction hadn't improved any in the intervening couple of years and we were getting hungry by the time he found something he recognized. It was a Mexican fort, looking slightly preposterous in the middle of an Arabian street.

The next day was a Sunday, but weekends were meaningless to us. Sunday was a normal working day in Saudi Arabia, and in any case our work and leisure was controlled by the operational calendar, broken only by Down Days. Thus divorced from the normal cadence of passing time, it was very easy to lose track completely of which day of the week it was. For us it was the day of our second trip to Kuwait. This was to be our first trip with the Tiald pod, so we would have to wait until the morning op wave returned and the aircraft were refuelled before we could go. That effectively gave us the morning off. This was something of a luxury, since at Brüggen we would be expected to be in the squadron getting on with the myriad of administrative tasks and 'secondary duties' which fill a RAF officer's life. Here we

Rachel, one of the two Tiald pods we had at Dhahran; the other was Becky.

were free to do as we wished when we weren't involved in planning or flying. This morning we headed to the American PX store to stock up on breakfast goodies, so that we wouldn't have to rely on the tasteless 'gack' served in the American mess halls. We also invested in a small plastic Christmas tree to provide at least some festive decoration in our flat. Our shopping done, we retired to the flat to have a real cup of tea and to vegetate in front of the television.

The afternoon's planned route was the same as the previous day. With no further planning, we re-read the information about Tiald, then briefed for the sortie. The trip was one of mixed fortunes. The great news was that I got the Havequick to work, so I felt quite buoyed up as we taxied out. On our way up to the operating area Platty tried out the pod and seemed to have success as he looked at a couple of small islands off the southern Kuwaiti coast. The idea was to head up towards Bubiyan and then via the defunct satellite tracking station to the two airfields at 10,000ft, so that the navigators could continue to practise with their new toy. But the weather was nothing like the previous day's blue skies. Huge clouds billowed past and we couldn't get beyond Kuwait city.

I managed to find a hole in the clouds above Ahmed Al-Jaber and we managed to circle in the murk above it at about 8,000ft. I didn't want to go any lower because below that height there would be enough sand and dust in the air to damage the pod's optics. Although conditions were far from ideal, it was just enough to give Platty a taste of the Tiald. He seemed to pick it up pretty quickly. In the end, though, I think that Platty and Taff both suffered because they didn't get the time and conditions they needed on this first trip with the pod. The next time either of them would get their hands on a pod would be for real over Iraq. Nevertheless, we were quite pleased to have salvaged something from the day. Once Platty had got what he could out of our stooging round, he retracted the pod's optical panels and we dropped down to low level for a couple of minutes for my benefit. Then back to Dhahran for another night landing. An hour or so later we watched the fruits of our labours on one of the large video screens in the RIC. Both navigators seemed to have got the general idea of using Tiald, within the limitations of the day. It was interesting to see the images of Kuwait, but all of us were looking forward to seeing footage of Iraq on the screens.

As we signed in, Keith passed me a message. 'AJ rang – he will be at the Dammam Oberoi Hotel tonight and at Jeremy's house tomorrow,' it read. When I told AJ that I had been sentenced to six weeks in Dhahran, he had promised to come and visit me. I hadn't expected to see him that soon, though! After spending our flying training days and first tour on the Crusaders together, our careers had diverged. While I had always intended to have a full career in the RAF, AJ had kept an open mind. He had enjoyed a very successful tour with the Crusaders, during which he had been rather more skilled at the job than I had been, but the RAF had managed to mess him round once too often and he had decided to seek his fortune in the airlines. Now he was flying for British Airways.

The other name on the message was also a familiar one. Jeremy was another ex-Crusader from first tour days. Tall and sickeningly good looking, Jeremy was a navigator who was always a pleasure to fly with. Once he and I had dared to use the 'Gin and Tonic Trail', the low-flying area across Surrey and Kent – always guaranteed to get the telephones red hot with noise complaints! As we zoomed past Eastbourne, Jeremy pointed out the office block where he had once worked as a bank clerk. Just a few years earlier, in the midst of his mundane routine he had looked out of the window just as a fast jet went streaking past. 'I'd love to do that,' he had thought. And now he was able to savour that same view from the other perspective. It must have been a very satisfying moment indeed. As we sped on our way we both wondered if our flypast had managed to rescue another face at a window from a life of office-bound drudgery! Jeremy had also left the RAF for civil aviation, but a temporary medical problem had put that plan on hold for the moment. For the time being he was part of the large British Aerospace contingent at Dhahran. It would be fantastic to see them both again.

That evening, after ringing for instructions on how to get there, I took one of the cars and set off to find the Oberoi Hotel in Dammam. 'Very easy – you can't miss it,' said AJ. I could and I did. After a fruitless and frustrating two hours driving round and round Dammam, I gave up and went home. All in all it hadn't been a very satisfactory day.

The next morning I tried again, but another hour of cruising round Dammam also drew a blank. When I got back I discovered messages at the flat and ops desk; eventually we managed to make contact on the telephone and arranged to meet at Jeremy's house after my sortie.

A Tornado taxying out for a sortie from Dhahran. (Marcus Cook)

Platty and I were down to fly as Number Two, the 'shooter', following Al and CJ in the lead Tiald aircraft. The sortie brief for our first trip 'sausage side' was a bewildering experience, probably not helped by the fact that we had not been involved in the planning phase, so we went into the brief completely cold. First there was a pile of paperwork for each of us containing briefing sheets, route maps and detailed maps of the various Points of Interest that were to be filmed. Then came the briefing itself, which may as well have been in a foreign language. Domestic details, tanker plan, loser plan, route brief, detailed brief for each Point of Interest, tactics, code words, movements of all the other aircraft in the No Fly Zone, all came tumbling along one after the other. Al and CJ were aware how difficult we'd find our first 'real' trip in the new environment, having been through the same process themselves only four weeks earlier, and went through the brief very thoroughly for our benefit. Even so, after an hour of listening to them I'd picked up just enough to do my bit, and the rest went over my head. I was pleased we were only the shooter on this trip!

There was a very different feel about preparing for this sortie than for the Kuwait trainers. For a start it was very business-like – the feeling that we were about to do an important job. There was also the realization that it might be dangerous. And there was the usual uneasiness about the unfamiliar. Added to that was my own insecurity about tanking: today we would be refuelling from a Victor, a type I had never tanked from before. Given my lack of prowess in the past, I was more than a little concerned about how I might get on. At the end of the briefing I sat alone for a couple of minutes to try and prepare myself mentally for the sortie.

We dressed once again in our 'sanitized' flying suits, stuffed our pistols under our armpits, and donned our g-suits and survival vests. Then the minibus ride out to the aircraft. At check-in time we were ready to go. I was greatly relieved when my Havequick worked. It was only a short taxi out to the runway and we had just made it to the end of the runway when we received a call from operations. The mission was cancelled because of the weather over Iraq. I felt another deep sense of relief as we taxied back in. At least next time we'd start with a little more idea of what to expect. One less thing to worry about!

It was a good illustration of how critical the weather over Iraq was on every mission. Very obviously we had to have a clear view of the ground over each Point of Interest, or we would not be able to see it with the Tiald camera. We also had to be able to remain clear of cloud all the time we were over Iraq, either by flying around or over any cloud cover, so that we could see any missiles or gun fire which might be aimed at us. This was quite a limitation, and would become more relevant as winter wore on. In the meantime, today it meant that I could catch up on my friends earlier than I had anticipated.

In fact it was a reunion for four of us. As Gordon had been on the squadron at the same time as AJ, me and Jeremy, and he had his own car, I asked him along too. We drove across to Jeremy's bungalow on one of the compounds reserved for westerners, another strange oasis in this part of the desert! It was reassuring to be able to slip into the easy comfort of close friendship in this unfamiliar and alien

Four warriors at Dhahran: Kev, Larry and the two Dougies ready for a sortie over Iraq. (Dougie Roxburgh)

environment. Once again, I was reminded that the real strength of the RAF lay in its people and the strength of their relationship with each other. After a very pleasant evening of shared memories and gentle ribbing we headed back via Dammam to drop AJ at his hotel. I discovered that I'd been within fifty yards of it on each of my previous forays into Dammam!

The next day was an early start for our second attempt to fly over Iraq. As we made our way through the 'have-a-nice-days' towards the ops block, it looked none too promising. The sky was grey with ragged layers of stratus, spindrift sand danced ahead of the fresh south-easterly breeze and it was trying to drizzle. We trooped into the briefing room and grabbed our pile of paperwork without much optimism. Today the leaders were Kev and Larry, a couple of the junior boys on the squadron. Their brief, though, was both comprehensive and comprehensible. I think that the previous day's dry run had been invaluable in giving us at least a clue of what to expect.

A slightly surreal touch was introduced by Larry's choice of codewords for the reconnaissance points of interest. A great fan of the TV series *Blackadder*, Larry had us visiting 'Mrs Miggin's Pie Shop'. Quite what the Americans would make of this, I couldn't tell. However, I felt it went some way to make up for having to use the callsign 'Dundee' once again. The Americans had given themselves punchy callsigns like 'Killer' or 'Satan' or other such aggressively inspiring names, but for some reason we were given the name of a fruit cake. I wondered if they were trying to tell us something.

Once again we go through the ritual of dressing, getting out to the aircraft and starting up. Once again I am overjoyed and relieved when the Havequick works as advertised. We get to the runway, but the recall message we've all been expecting never comes. Kev gives me the wind-up signal, which I pass down the line, and give him a 'thumbs up'. A tap of the visor and an exaggerated head nod, I let the brakes off and push us into reheat. We move forward together. My head is now checking ahead to make sure we stay on our side of the runway and back at Kev, making sure that I keep his mainwheels in line. The rudder keeps us straight as small adjustments to the throttles moves my view of Kev's mainwheels forwards or back. His aircraft is my world: as far as I'm concerned it is stationary and everything else is moving past it. We thunder down the runway and I see his nosewheel lift. A twitch back on the stick and ours does too.

We're airborne. I raise the gear and see Kev's also retract. Now I'm looking along his wing, waiting for the flaps to move. Out of the corner of my eye I see Kev's head nod again, and then I see the flaps moving up. Eyes glued to his aircraft, I fumble for the flap lever outboard of the throttles, and jam it towards 'up'. Next a small plume of fuel from just under Kev's jetpipes tells me that he is cancelling reheat. I pull the throttles back to the detent and move slightly closer just as the clouds enfold us. As we climb through layers of cloud, Kev's aircraft alternately blurs into a dark silhouette in the fog, then returns to sharp focus when we lift above a cloudbank. As we get higher, the clouds gradually become lighter, until a hint of blue appears above us. Then we're out into glorious sunshine. Our shadows close together, ringed by a circular rainbow, race across the bright whiteness below. I relax now and drop back into a looser more comfortable position.

Below us the clouds are breaking up as we get further inland and soon we're cruising in an empty sky, with the desert floating past below. This view of the landscape is new to us; our previous trips have taken us up the Gulf coast, so this is the first time we have seen the Arabian Desert from on high. It is not as barren as I had imagined: colours range from mustard through khaki-green, greys and browns to damask, reflecting the diverse sand and rock formations. Dark shadows outline the courses of wadis or the ripples of dunes and here and there, surprisingly, are the dots of settlements. I wonder what people do, living so far out in the desert.

'Bulldog, Dundee as fragged,' calls Larry, confirming with the strike controller that the four aircraft of Dundee section are airborne as instructed in the Frag. The controller, in the Airborne Warning and Control System (AWACS) aircraft circling back near the safety of Riyadh, gives a curt reply and directs us to the tanker frequency. Once again we check in and all is silence. All the tanking is done silently, but the frequency gives a means of communication in the event of a problem.

A mixture of novelty, excitement and apprehension make the hour-long transit to the tanker tow lines pass quickly. Before I realize, Kev is taking us down to join 1,000ft below the tanker. The tanker marshal, also seated in the AWACS decides to give a helping hand and passes Kev and Larry a heading for the tanker. Kev adjusts his heading to the right a little and Platty confirms that he has the tanker on radar. Soon I see a large aircraft in the distance. Kev is heading to intercept it. But it doesn't look right. As we get closer we can make out some receivers already in company with it. I realize at the same time as Kev and Larry that it's the wrong tanker – a USAF KC-135 Stratotanker. Kev turns sharply left to keep well clear of it.

Larry and Platty start hunting in the radar for another likely blip. I can imagine Larry swearing at the tanker marshal for his meddling. Soon Larry finds another one and we head after it. This one is much more promising. As we get closer I make out its unique shape: it's the Victor. The Victor was designed in the 1950s as a nuclear bomber. Over thirty years later and relegated to the role of flying petrol station, the Victor still looks more like a futuristic spaceship than an aeroplane. It sails majestically through the sky, its sharp glazed nose, sweeping crescent wings and high V-shaped tailplane are the stuff of Dan Dare or Flash Gordon. The British really could make beautiful aircraft in those days. Kev takes us up into echelon on the tanker's right wing. Platty and I busy ourselves running through the pre-tanking checks, depressurising the fuel system and extending our probe: All this at the same time as flying a tidy formation on Kev and the tanker. It's hard work. A red flashing light under the Victor's belly clears us behind the refuelling baskets. Kev slides down and across to the left hose, while I move gently across to the right.

I stabilize four or five feet behind the basket, aware of a thumping heart, and look at the small set of traffic lights on the pod under the tanker's wing. The red light flicks off. I'm clear to join. Gripping the control column like a vice I feed on some power with my left hand. My whole concentration is focussed on the pod. I've lined up a small symbol in the HUD with part of the pod and keep it lined up as we move slowly forward; with every slight bump of air I make a minuscule correction to keep them aligned. I am so tense my body is almost locked in position. Suddenly there is a dull clunk. The aircraft pauses momentarily, and then carries on forward slowly. I see the hose reeling slowly back into the pod.

We're in! A feeling of jubilation fills me. But I can't relax yet. I still have to fly a precise formation behind the tanker's wing if we are to stay in contact. I push the hose back into the pod until the traffic light changes to green. I know that fuel is flowing. Out to our right, I'm aware that the other two members of the formation have arrived and are awaiting their turn. At last we're full and I reduce power ever so slightly. Slowly we back out from the basket and stabilize a few feet behind. I look across to the left and see Kev moving up to the pod under the tanker's left wing. I drop us down a little and slide underneath the Victor to join up on Kev's left wing. Then it's time for us to wheel away and head towards the border. As we leave the tanker I hold the stick in my left hand for a while and take off my right flying glove. I've been holding the stick so tightly behind the tanker that I've virtually cut off the blood supply to my middle finger. It's numb and a deathly white colour. I try to massage some feeling back into it. Even so I can't help feeling exceptionally pleased with myself. I found the Victor by far the easiest tanker I have refuelled from so far. It's a great relief.

Just south of the border, we go into a holding orbit, waiting for our push time. The idea is to get all the aircraft refuelled and ready to go in their correct positions. This ensures that all the fighters and defence suppressors are in position before we go in. It gives me a few more minutes to restore the blood supply to my finger. It also gives Platty and me time to carry out our checks before we go into hostile skies. I arm the guns and start cooling the missile seeker heads.

So obvious on the map, the Iraqi border is invisible on the ground. Identical desert stretches in all directions. For the first ten anti-climactic minutes or so we continue over the desert, which looks more rock than sand now. The sporadic 'paints' on the RWR tell us that Iraqi early-warning radars are looking at us. We pass over the airfield at Jalibah, which provides Platty and me with our first interest. This was one of the airfields attacked by Tornados during the Gulf War. It is a massive place, with three long parallel runways. But just like the two airfields in Kuwait, there is a large crater sitting in the middle of every taxiway intersection. Beyond the airfield, our track takes us across rows of the pipelines taking oil to Basrah.

A few minutes later the terrain changes abruptly. Desert gives way to marshland as we approach the Euphrates. Below us is a lush green, the sun occasionally glinting off of patches of open water. Now we can see roads and villages dotted along the riverbanks. We make for Qurna at the confluence of the Tigris and Euphrates. This was the fabled site of the Garden of Eden; certainly it was the cradle of civilization, for it was also the site of the ancient city of Sumer, capital of the thriving culture of Mesopotamia 3,500 years before Christ. I cannot help feeling sad as I cruise across the skies above it in a high-technology warplane that the only thing which separates us from those forbears in 5,500 years is that we have developed more ingenious methods of killing each other.

Near Qurna, with more to see on the ground, Platty thinks he'll have a go with the hand-held video camera. The only problem is that he cannot see much over the side, because of the large engine intakes on either side of his cockpit. The Tornado, of course, was designed to fly at low level, where the navigator would only want to look abeam or above the aircraft. Yet again aircrew initiative is required to overcome the designers' lack of foresight to get the job done. I start a series of gentle barrel rolls to give Platty a view of the ground through the canopy above him. This method seems to work quite well at first, but it is not long before Platty complains of feeling sick. I return to level flight the right way up.

From Qurna we pick up the Tigris heading north. Kev drops down to 10,000ft so that Larry can get on with filming. I drop down, too, but keep a bit of a height split, and sit back a little swept where Kev can see me if he glances over his shoulder. Larry's main task today is a 'line search' along the motorway which runs just to the west of the river. All our eyes are on the ground. That is where the threat is from, but it is also fascinating to be able just look at this unfamiliar country. Even from this height we can clearly see traffic moving along the road. Looking down on people going about their normal daily business feels uncomfortable and a little strange. It is like being a voyeur or an alien from a different planet. I am very aware that we haven't been invited into the country and that we are unwelcome. There can be little doubt that the locals know we are there, they must be able to hear our engines and they can probably even see us as small arrow-shaped specks arcing across the sky.

Patches of low cloud start obscuring our view of the ground. We're supposed to follow the road all the way up to Al-Amarah, but looking ahead it's obvious that we will not get that far. About halfway there we come across the airfield of Qal'At Salih. Once again there are the craters in the taxiways and holes in the shelters. This time, though, I can see a couple of bulldozers defiantly at work on the main runway. Qal'At Salih is as far as we get today. There is too much low cloud towards Al Amarah, so we wheel round to the left and head off to Larry's final Point of Interest (Mrs Miggin's Pie Shop), a nebulous point in the middle of the marshes. We have been asked to film this area, but have no idea what the photo-interpreters hope to see here. It is frustrating to work in the dark like this. It is all very well being told what someone wants, but if you are not told why they want it, it can be difficult to provide it. Down below I can see some evidence of damming and draining in the marshes. Perhaps that is what they want to see. Platty has another brave attempt to record it with the hand-held camera. Once again, though, we have great difficulty in actually using the thing.

Larry calls 'Bulldog' with the codeword that he is complete and that we're heading home. We turn south for the Saudi border and climb for the transit back to Dhahran. Happily the morning's rain clouds have moved off, leaving us with clear skies all the way home. As Kev starts the descent into Dhahran, I close up formation and tuck into his left wing. It is much easier to fly close formation now, without the distraction of cloud varying the visibility. Close formation can be hard work, but I find it very rewarding. I find the sight of two aircraft flying so closely together an inspiring one. Like all pilots, I watch with critical eyes. The Number Two should be there like a rock: any wobble is seen as lapse in professional standards! Inside the Number Two aircraft you have to work hard to achieve that apparent smoothness. Once again my attention is focussed entirely on Kev's aircraft. I am continuously making tiny smooth adjustments to throttles and stick, to stay in exactly the same position relative to him.

Platty and me walking in from a sortie at Dhahran

We head downwind at 2,000ft. I see Kev's hand move up to give me a 'flap' signal. Reaching across beyond the throttles I grab the flap lever and wait: an exaggerated nod of the head from Kev. Pause. Flap lever down and hand quickly back on the throttles. I see Kev's flaps moving on his wing just as I feel mine biting. This is a critical time from the point of view of not wobbling: as the flaps go down, you have to push the aircraft's nose down to stop ballooning because of all the extra lift generated by the flaps. I have to make sure that I push at the same time as Kev.

Happily wobble-free, I manage to stick with him. The speeds trickles back below 235kt and I see Kev's hand making a 'wheels' sign. Gear comes down. Eyes in the cockpit for a quick scan round to confirm I've done all the checks. Three green lights show me the gear is down and a pushbutton with a small green message reading 'low' tells me that the nosewheel steering is functioning properly. I rock the left throttle outboard to arm the lift dump. These are a line of spoilers which will pop out of the top of the wing when the aircraft senses it's on the runway, dumping all the lift from the wing and thus ensuring that we stay on the runway. Kev looks across to me and I raise a 'thumbs up', to show that I've done all my checks. The speed has stabilized at 210kt. A call from the radar controller turns us onto the final approach path. Full flap comes down without a wobble and we slide down the glideslope. With the airfield easily visible from some miles out, even in this haze, this seems a rather long-winded method of recovering.

Back at Brüggen we'd have smashed into the circuit in loose formation at 360kt, then, with a three second interval pulled into a decelerating descending circle onto the runway. Unfortunately this method doesn't lend itself to airliner flying, so, at an airfield with many civilian movements we have to do it their way. In the last 200ft, I widen the formation very slightly to land in the middle of my side of the runway. Kev aims for the middle of his side. My head is moving a lot now. Ahead to check the alignment on the runway, back to Kev to keep the same fore and aft position. Look back to the runway, then back to Kev. Then we're on the runway. I rock the other throttle outboard to get reverse thrust on the engines. The Tornado brakes are not too good, so we need to use the engines to slow down as much as possible.

It was the first time I'd taxied back to our flight line daylight, and on the previous two occasions I had parked on the first spot on the line. This time I had to taxi behind three other Tornados to get to my parking spot. I was rather concerned at the narrowness of the strip between the back of the aircraft and a large ISO container, which had been placed very close to the edge of the taxiway. I swept the wing backwards so that I could squeeze through and thought nothing more of it.

Back in the RIC, we watched the fruits of our morning's work. Larry had brought back some good footage of his Points of Interest, but our efforts with the hand-held video were almost unusable. Platty was very disappointed that he had been made to feel sick for nothing! The good news was that all the American canteens were closed at this hour of the day: instead we were entitled to have a free meal at the International Hotel, a five star hotel at the airport. A fine steak was the perfect end to an enjoyable and rewarding sortie.

Platty and I didn't have to wait long for the last sortie in our in-theatre work-up. After another early start, this time on a fine bright day, we were listening to the briefing from the Two Dougies. We were in the Number Three slot, the Tiald crew, with our own shooter as Number Four. The Two Dougies was an all-Scottish team and an excellent blend of two very different characters. Dougie the Pilot was a quiet type, whose modest nature belied tremendous strength of character and a very competent pair of hands. On the other hand, Dougie the Navigator was a flamboyant extravert guaranteed to light up any party, but who was surprisingly afflicted by a lack of professional self-confidence. They worked together very effectively as a team, the loudness of the one stimulating the other, who in turn provided the inner strength for both.

Today we would follow a similar route to the previous day. However, the tanker plan would require us to fill up twice before we crossed into Iraq. We would then head across the marshes to pick up the road to Al Amarah, then having reached Al-Amarah go back into the northern area of the marshes, then back to Al-Amarah to check out a barracks. We would then head west into the desert to search for the site of a SAM 3 battery and finally come south to An Nasiriyah to look for a troop concentration. In Harry's intelligence brief we learned that there was a lot of military activity beneath the No Fly Zone. The Iraqi army was on the ground in some force and we were to expect a step up in the intensity of operations against rebels hiding out in the marshes. It made us feel as if we were doing something useful over Iraq.

The transit to the tanker would have been unremarkable except that the Inertial Navigation System (INS) in our aircraft had somehow been misaligned. This meant

Myself and Platty are on our first Tiald sortie over Iraq. The Tiald is seen as a cigar-shaped pod under the aircraft.

that the aircraft's navigation kit started to wander with the induced errors. Platty had to work hard to keep updating it and try to remove the errors. A useful tool for this should have been a GPS system, which had been added to the aircraft as in-theatre modification. The problem here was two-fold. Firstly, the system was not connected to the aircraft's main computer, so had no direct input to the navigation system, and secondly and more fundamentally, the only place where the engineers could stow the GPS was in such a position that its aerials were nearly always blanked by other equipment in the bay. As a result, the system only worked very rarely, presumably only in the event of a peculiar juxtaposition of satellites. Needless to say the GPS was not working on this day.

Platty managed a litany of profanities all the way to the tanker as he wrestled with the kit. The two 'prods' on the tanker went reassuringly well and we crossed 'sausage side'. This time there was a thick haze layer over the marshes at around 2,000ft, making it very difficult to make out very much detail of the ground below. We then learned that the Two Dougies' pod had gone unserviceable: we would have to cover their targets as well as our own.

It was a very frustrating day. Platty struggled with the kit and was working extremely hard trying to film what he could with the Tiald video. I couldn't help him at all. The haze meant that I couldn't always tell how much error there was in the kit, and as I couldn't see directly beneath the aircraft, where he was looking, I couldn't use my eyes to 'talk' him on to any features that were outside the tiny field of view of the pod. We landed from a three hour twenty minute sortie with little to show for it except simmering frustration. Once again we squeezed between container and aircraft on the dispersal and headed back to the ops block. The debriefing in the

RIC was disappointing to say the least. However, one good thing to come from the day was that once again we had missed the American canteen and had to go for the slap-up hotel meal again!

A day off from the flying programme was an opportunity for Platty and I to enjoy the luxury of vegetating in our flat. Meanwhile, Taff and Chris were off on their last work-up sortie over Iraq. When they eventually returned, they seemed very depressed. They had managed to scrape their wingtip on the ISO container at the dispersal while taxying in after the sortie. As a punishment the DETCO had banned them from going to Bahrain for the near future. For their part, neither of them could understand how it could have happened, nor did they have any recollection of having done it. They had simply been taxying into the dispersal following the yellow centreline markings under the direction of a marshaller.

I decided to go and see the damage for myself and drove across to the flight line. The Senior Engineering Officer (SEngO) showed me round. He was also from the Crusaders, so he knew all of us well. The damage to the aircraft was limited to a cracked navigation light and a score on the wingtip about a millimetre deep. A very faint witness mark on the ISO container showed where Chris had just kissed the container as he swung off the taxiway onto the parking area. Sengo had measured it out and Chris could only have been a matter of inches off the taxiway centreline: the container had obviously been put far too close to the taxiway. The only reason that no one else had hit it was either because we had been plain lucky, or because we had been cautious and swept the wings back as we taxied through the gap. The SEngO agreed with me that the incident was down to bad luck more than anything else. He also said that he would get the container moved. In the meantime, I decided to talk to the DETCO about it the next day and suggest that he had been a little harsh on the boys. I was worried about the effect on their morale at being gated like schoolboys for something that was not really their fault. I didn't think that an operational detachment was the place to enforce pettiness at the expense of the welfare of crews operating over hostile territory. I came back to the flat and told Taff and Chris. Both were cheered a little by my promise to see what I could do.

In the evening I escaped to Jeremy's house, where he was holding a cocktail party for some of his British Aerospace friends. Once again it turned out to be a Crusader mini-reunion. This time it was a pleasure to see Terry, who was also working for British Aerospace in Dhahran. Terry and I had flown together on a number of occasions, and memories returned as we chatted about mutual friends from the 'good old days.'

The next day Chris and I were down for a night sortie, as the Number Three (the second Tiald aircraft). I took the late start as an opportunity to wander in to the squadron and visit the DETCO in his office

'Good morning, sir,' I ventured, 'I wonder if I could have a word.'

'Yes, come in, sit down. What is it,' he asked.

'It's about Chris and Taff, sir. I've been over and looked at the damage and I think they were just very unlucky rather than negligent. I don't think it's fair to make them scapegoats for what happened. The whole incident is as much a reflection on the rest of us as it is on them. I noticed that it was pretty tight round there but I never said anything, and that goes for everyone else here, too. We all knew that there was a problem, but none of us did anything about it. Even the engineers admit that it was a pretty stupid place to put the container. I agree that the two of them should be punished, sir, but I think that a hats-on rollicking would be appropriate in this case. Stopping them from going to Bahrain tomorrow is going to have a massive effect on their morale. Surely it's important on an operational detachment like this that we keep the crews well-motivated. Couldn't you give them a hats-on rollicking today and let then go to Bahrain with the rest of us? I think that would be the best way ahead.'

But my words fell on deaf ears. The DETCO's logic was that if an engineer made a mistake, he was always charged, therefore if aircrew made a mistake, they had to be punished, too, and in a way that was visible to the groundcrew. He did not accept my point that the engineers were not risking their necks over Iraq. The DETCO was slipping from the previous high esteem in which I had held him. It was not helped by his ruling on Marcus and Mal's incident with the fuel leak. We had all expected him to recommend the pair for a 'Good Show Award', recognition of a job well done. Instead he had criticized their handling of the emergency because when they got to Kuwait they were out of release to service limits for fuel imbalance. Instead of landing immediately as they did, the DETCO thought that they should have first carried out a low-speed handling check on the aircraft before attempting a landing. Technically he was absolutely right, but I felt he was being rather pedantic in this case. At least Marcus and Mal were vindicated a little later when an amendment to the release to service document arrived, which changed the fuel imbalance limits and put them well inside the new limits!

I saw more of the DETCO, in rather better form, that evening when he replaced CJ in the back of Al's aircraft as our shooter. We reached the tanker tow-line just as the sun was setting and met our Victor amid a spectacular scarlet and purple-coloured sky. Rather more confident in my abilities now, I was able to enjoy the view as we refuelled in the fading dusk. The Victor's callsign each day was 'Shark'. Now it was sporting a brand new shark's mouth painted under the nose, the jagged teeth gleaming white in the pale amber light. The effect was fantastic – the aircraft became a living thing, a huge predatory shark stalking the Iraqi border. As darkness fell, we left the tanker and headed towards Iraq.

A night-time sortie was very much a navigator's exercise. In daylight the pilot could give some help to the navigator, or could adjust the route, to follow the obvious line of a road for example. But at night I couldn't see anything of the reconnaissance targets, so my participation was limited to engaging the autopilot and monitoring the aircraft flying itself round the pre-planned route. With all his lights off, Al was also invisible in the darkness. He knew where I was on the track line, and knew my altitude. All he had to do was to avoid us in his own altitude block and scan the skies for missiles or gunfire. As we crossed the desert I was surprised at how many lights twinkled below us. With clear skies above as well as beneath us we seemed to be surrounded by stars. Approaching the Euphrates, the lights beneath us merged into a string of settlements along the riverbank. Ahead the dark area of marshes seemed relatively unpopulated, but another line of light beyond traced the line of the Tigris. The route was very similar to the previous two trips. We latched on to the motorway

Chris and Rick about to go flying at Dhahran. Rick managed to scrounge the occasional trip to escape from the planning room. (Chris Bearblock)

running up the west bank of the Tigris and followed it up past Qal'At Salih to Al-Amarah, then turned for home.

Once again, the results of our filming were rather disappointing. I was happy that Chris was progressing up a steep learning curve. I knew he found it frustrating that he seemed to be taking a long time to get to grips with Tiald, but this was only his third sortie with a pod. On the other two sorties he'd had to deal with weather or navigation kit problems, so really this was his first go with a pod in decent conditions. Even so, Chris came away from the debrief a little depressed and decided not to join me and Dougie the Pilot going to Bahrain.

Dougie and I headed off to the causeway linking Bahrain and Saudi on our own. The 'Causeway to Freedom' as we knew it was a remarkable feature. This was not because of the feat of engineering in building it across the ten-mile stretch of shallow water, amazing though that may have been. No, the thing which made it remarkable was the number of customs checkpoints on it: six in all! Dressed in uniform and driving our 'official' vehicle we were able to go straight to the head of the long queues at each of the checkpoints. We dutifully stopped and presented our paperwork six times. Surly customs guards waved us through. Although we had enjoyed a relatively hassle-free crossing, it had still taken us thirty minutes to travel the short distance.

When we got to the hotel we discovered that the team who had left Dhahran just before us fell at one of the hurdles and was sent back because they did not have the correct vehicle documents. Luckily they eventually managed to find a vehicle with the right paperwork and joined us later. As we sat in the bar enjoying a very welcome beer with some of the others who also had all the right documentation, we heard more stories of the customs posts on the causeway. Dougie the Navigator told us how he had returned from a foray in Bahrain having bought a new blank videotape. He had made the mistake of opening the cellophane wrapper to check the tape, before packing it in his bag. The customs immediately became suspicious when they saw this during the usual search of all baggage. Dougie spent the next two hours watching a completely blank video from start to finish as the customs men made sure that there was nothing illegal recorded on it.

Because of our late arrival after flying, it was not long before the hotel bar closed. We jumped into a taxi and headed off for the Gulf Hotel which boasted a twenty-four hour bar, aimed primarily at airline crews.

'Bloody hell, it's Mike the Knife,' shouted a bearded figure at the bar as I walked through the door. It was Baldy and another demonstration of how small the world of aviation can be. Now flying for British Airways, Baldy had been the squadron QWI when I arrived on the Crusaders first time round. Despite being one of the number of disillusioned middle-management on the squadron, Baldy had always done his very best for us first tourists. I had good reason to be grateful for numerous pearls of wisdom passed my way and it was good to enjoy a beer with him once more.

In Bahrain it was 2.30am in the morning, time to head back to our own hotel and bed. Dougie the Navigator assured Kev, Larry and me that it is 'only a fifteen minute walk' away. We set out along streets bedecked with flags flying from every lamppost. An hour later we reached our hotel, admittedly having had to slow down briefly to liberate a couple of flags. It was an entertaining sight watching Kev hobble down the road, flagpole down one leg of his trousers and the flag stuffed under his shirt like an overhanging beergut, trying desperately not to look suspicious.

I enjoyed the atmosphere in Bahrain. It was a pleasant blend of the more charming aspects of Arabian and western lifestyles. The Souk was fascinating to wander around; stalls heaped with exotic eastern spices jostled with others selling cheap plastic toys from Hong Kong, or others offering nuts and sweets. Shops selling expensive fabrics neighboured seedy looking establishments advertising pirated cassette tapes. Everywhere refinement and vulgarity mixed easily in the hustle and bustle. In some shops the shopkeepers sat idly or gossiped with their neighbours, while at the doors of other shops, vendors shouted out their bargains. I refused the many good-natured offers of fake watches, perfumes and alarm clocks. The gold souk was well worth a visit. Here the shops were laden with jewellery and metalwork. Surprisingly though, the prices reflected only the weight of the precious metal and no value was attributed to the artistry. In most cases this was hardly surprising: the emphasis was on brashness and garishness, with little or no place for finesse or subtlety. Surely artistic content is the most important feature of something intended to be a beautiful adornment?

That evening we returned to Dhahran and a night of torrential rain. It was still chucking it down as Chris and I made our way through the 'have a nice days' at

5.30am the next morning. We were both sure that we would be cancelled and were looking forward to returning to our dry and relatively warm flat. The thunderstorm had turned the area around the ops block into thick yellow mud, which migrated into the Portakabin. Here and there, buckets and plastic bins collected the rainwater as it dripped in through cracks and gaps in the ceiling. The whole place was miserable.

The briefing started to the accompaniment of the sound of rain drumming on the roof. We were to be Number Two to Al and CJ once more and the route would take us to the now-familiar area of marshes around Al Amarah and the Tigris. Harry gave us a comprehensive intelligence briefing about troop movements in Iraq. He told us that the campaign against the Marsh Arabs was continuing beneath the No Fly Zone. Fresh troops had recently been deployed around the perimeter of the marshes, which indicated a start to the increase in activity he had predicted a couple of days earlier. By the time we left the ops block with pistols under armpits, survival waistcoats on and maps strategically stuffed into pockets, the rain had abated. The expected recall never came. Thirty minutes or so later, I was on Al's wingtip climbing through thick cloud. At 24,000ft we burst out into the sunshine. Weaving round the occasional towering storm, we managed to stay clear of the cloud for the rest of the leg towards the tanker tow-lines.

Having been allocated the callsign 'Shark', our Handley Page Victor was decorated with a fine-looking shark's mouth. Platty and I, in the nearest Tornado, are waiting on the tanker's wing for our turn to refuel.

The air was clear over Iraq: the thunderstorms had swept away all traces of the haze which had masked the ground on our last daylight sortie. We were treated to the best view yet of the country. As the shooter we were free to manoeuvre as we wished, while Al and CJ were slaves to the Tiald route. I made the most of my freedom to have a good look round at the landscape below. Today there was much more water visible in the marsh areas, but it was much easier to see the extent of the drainage operation. The new floodwater was muddy brown as it surged along rivers and streams. Nearby, patches of still blue water stood behind dams and causeways. The biggest area of drainage was on the far side of the Tigris immediately east of Qurna. Here massive causeways divided the marshland into large squares, each of a different colour depending how much water remained.

Further north and east, close to the Iranian border, the marsh merged back into the desert. The ground was scattered with low mounds and breastworks, marking artillery emplacements from the long war with Iran. The ground below us had seen terrible fighting, more akin to the First World War than a modern conflict. Mass artillery bombardments, poison gas and human-wave tactics had been used by both sides over that ground. Today, though, it looked peaceful enough, with the numerous earthworks as the only reminder of the previous bloodshed.

Having seen my fill, I crossed over to the line of the Tigris. Here, too, there was evidence of major changes to the water's course. Along the river, azure-blue crescents lazily reflected the sunshine, while the turbulent grey followed a straighter line nearby. Whether these oxbow lakes were the result of artificial tinkering, or the force of nature I could not tell from high above. The bulldozers were still busy on the airfield at Qal'At Salih as we went past. It would have been great to be able to swoop down and buzz them; instead we stayed obediently above the day's minimum height. At Al Amarah we turned back over the marshes and intercepted the road running back towards An Nasiriyah. It looked newly built, probably a military road, to enable troops to move quickly round the outside of the marsh area. This was the very area where we might find Harry's troop concentrations. I scanned the ground with renewed interest – if we found the troops, we might also find their anti-aircraft defences. CJ filmed along the road with the Tiald video.

Once again I was grateful to be the shooter with the freedom to move about freely. The Tiald profile seemed rather tedious to me as well as being somewhat vulnerable because it was so predictable. It reminded me of a First World War reconnaissance aircraft droning up the frontline to photograph enemy trenches. Riyadh had tasked us with conducting a line search along the road, but I wondered at the tactical sense in flying down a line of communication that was probably well defended. Although we were not being shot at (as far as we could tell) I was sure it would only be a matter of time before the Iraqis tried something. Soon we came across a plume of smoke rising from the marshes, not far from the road. As we came closer, we could make out a large fire. Although it was difficult to make out fine detail from our height, we suspected that it was a village burning. Chris shot some footage on the hand-held video for good measure. I was overwhelmed with a sense of impotence. Murder was probably being committed below us, but we could do nothing about it. Troops on the ground would have been very aware of our presence, and probably aware, too, that we were powerless to stop them.

I wondered what we were actually achieving over Iraq. Unable to do anything but take film, we continued on towards An Nasiriyah. Just past Nasiriyah was the airfield at Tallil. Very close to the site of the ancient city of Ur, with its famous ziggurat, Tallil was an important Iraqi Air Force base during the Gulf War. Apparently the Iraqis had used this proximity to the ancient site to their advantage, by placing military equipment close to the ziggurat in the knowledge that Coalition forces would be unwilling to risk the bad publicity if they damaged the monument. Tallil was now unusable as an airfield, thanks to the usual strategically-placed bomb-craters, but we knew that the Iraqis were still using it as a sector headquarters for their air-defence system. Once again CJ's camera probed the area. I took the opportunity to see if I could locate the ziggurat, but saw nothing for my pains.

The weather had stayed cloudy and wet throughout the day in Dhahran. Those who hadn't had the dose of sunshine that we had enjoyed seemed thoroughly miserable. It stayed that way for the next few days. Chris and I led the Boss and Coulsy on a Kuwait trainer, but had to throw it away when the weather there was no better. Rainwater found its way through roofs and walls of buildings designed for dry weather. A feeling of frustration and depression took over the whole detachment. People moved dejectedly about. Even the shops and restaurants in Khobar were awash.

When Chris and I reported to the ops block, to read through the Frag and start planning the next day's mission we found two Sri Lankan workmen huddled in the coffee bar. Ever the gentleman, Harry had rescued them temporarily from the downpour outside. They had been sent to repair the leak in our roof, but in typical Saudi fashion they had not been supplied with any protective clothing. When Harry found them they were in the early stages of hypothermia. We had a lot of respect for the Sri Lankans: they did all the unpleasant jobs that no one else wanted to do, and had virtually nothing and no one to help them. They lived in the back of a truck trailer parked near the Khobar towers. Yet they were always cheerful, hard working and polite, with the dignity that comes with those virtues.

In the planning room we read through the Frag with dismay. Yet again we were tasked to patrol the marshes south of Al Amarah, an area which we had visited on every sortie over the past week and where we knew we would see nothing new. I phoned Riyadh, but the response was that I should get on and do as I was told. Without enthusiasm, we set about the task. At least there was a new target to visit first, Ad Diwaniyah, further west near the Euphrates. At lunchtime, Chris and I went over to 'The Warriors Den' a large tented canteen by the USAF flight line. It served the usual American 'gack', but at least it was convenient from the ops block. I had just got my plate of unappetizing grey-coloured burger when an American voice behind me spoke, 'Hey, Mike.' I turned round, but didn't recognize the smiling face in front of me. 'We flew together at Chivenor,' he reminded me. My eyes dropped to his nametag: Nick. Yes – suddenly I remembered the forty-five minutes of mayhem as we fought our way around South Wales in that four-versus-two some eighteen months previously! It was great to see him again.

The sky had cleared the next day. Chris and I were in early to check the final details before we briefed the rest of the formation. We were ready ahead of time, so I wandered outside into the dawn light, cup of coffee in hand. Looking eastwards into the distance I could see the grey silhouette of the motorway climbing a low bridge before it turned towards the causeway and Bahrain. The whole scene in front of me was washed in an inhospitable greyness. Then as I stood alone in the early chill, a miraculous thing happened. At first a glow, an aura, tinged the eastern horizon; then I became aware of the tip of a huge orange-glowing disc rising from the shimmering haze, apparently in front of the motorway bridge. It seemed as if the ground in front of me had opened up. I watched, awe-struck, on the desolate sand. Slowly the disc rose as if from the very earth in front of me, turning a blazing red as it revealed itself. The shadows shrunk away and colours returned as shafts of light and warmth embraced the world. I was now looking at a completely different scene: the disc, now golden bright, ascended majestically into the pale-blue sky. I was filled with an overwhelming sense of optimism.

'Napes are you ready, we need to get going.' The spell was broken. I flicked the dregs of my coffee onto the dust and went back inside.

Harry's intelligence brief was particularly interesting that morning. There was evidence of surface-to-air missile units being re-deployed beneath the No Fly

Plugged in – Platty and I take on fuel for a Tiald line search over Ad Dinawiyah and Al Amarah.

Zone (NFZ). As yet we did not know why. We also did not know why there had been increased activity at Al Jarra, the main Iraqi airbase north of the NFZ. A squadron of Russian-built MiG-25 Foxbat fighters were based there, and with the capability of flying at Mach 3, they could be a dangerous threat to us if they dashed towards us and took a shot. It was a worry for us on this day, as we would be running almost exactly along the 32nd Parallel, the northern boundary line of the NFZ. We hoped that we had a sharp team in the AWACS and the fighter escort for the day. In fact the intelligence opinion was that the threat to us was limited that day, but that there was a very real prospect of Iraqi operations against Coalition aircraft later over the Christmas period. Presumably Saddam reckoned that with Western politicians enjoying the Christmas holiday at home, he could strike against us with the real prospect that the whole thing would be forgotten about in the West before there could be any retaliation. Western politicians, slow to be recalled in mid-holiday would be reluctant to act. In the meantime, the media would have found other stories and public interest would be unlikely to support more action in the Gulf. But the Arabs would not forget a successful strike against Western aircraft.

We launched into blue skies. It was a real pleasure to be airborne once again, and away from the still dripping buildings. There was some novelty value to this trip. Instead of the usual tanker tow-line, we met the Victor and followed him up the border, along the line of the desert road past Rafha. With a pair of Tornados on each wing of the tanker, we took it in turns to fill up as we went. Chris and I began to realize that the aircraft's fuel tanks were not the only things to be filling up. That coffee before briefing was catching up with me. After our last 'prod' on the tanker, I knew that I was going to have to do something drastic. When I announced that I was going to have to use the emergency 'pee-bag', Chris said that he needed to go as well! The pee-bag was a small plastic bag with a long neck and a sponge in the bottom. One bag was stowed in each cockpit in case of emergency. Using it was easier said than done. First we had to unstrap. Chris and I put the safety pins back in our ejection seats – it wouldn't do to fire a seat accidentally and find oneself in mid-air over the desert with a pee-bag instead of a parachute! Then came a delicate manoeuvre in the very cramped confines of the cockpit to perch my buttocks on the edge of the ejection seat and fumble through layers of underwear, flying suit, g-suit. I was very relieved once I'd emptied my bladder, but to my horror I found that I hadn't managed to push myself high enough in the seat to ensure that there was no back-flow. I ended up sitting in a small puddle for the rest of the sortie! I gathered that Chris had been rather more successful.

With ejection seats re-activated, we carried out our fence checks and stepped over the border once more. Approaching the first target at Ad Diwaniyah, I double-checked that the missiles and guns were armed and took a greater than usual interest in the radar-warning display. From Diwaniyah we headed due east towards Al Amarah and the usual line search pausing halfway across the intervening desert to try and locate a SAM 3 site which had been reported by a US aircraft. We were feeling very vulnerable. A SAM 3 site should have shown up clearly with its distinctive 'four-in-a-fan' layout, especially if the old artillery emplacements southeast of Al Amarah were anything to go by. But despite overflying the exact co-ordinates we had been given we could find nothing. Perhaps it was well-camouflaged, perhaps it wasn't there, or perhaps we just missed it. The thought even crossed my cynical mind that the Americans might be using us as bait, to try and draw a Foxbat into the missile range of an Eagle. I didn't know which would be more dangerous to us – a Foxbat out to get us, or a trigger happy 'Yank'. It was a relief to reach the Tigris and head south back into relative safety. As we had suspected it would, the line search down the Tigris from Al Amarah provided nothing new.

In the evening, we headed to Bahrain, this time accompanied by Taff and Chris who had now served their penance. The occasion was a Christmas dinner kindly arranged for us by the British Club in Bahrain. We sat down en masse, aircrew, groundcrew and permanent staff and had a great time. There were silly hats, Christmas crackers, Turkey and all the ingredients of a traditional Christmas. By the time we got to the Christmas pudding we were all quite merry. Two of our engineers staggered over to where I was tucking in.

'Napes, you're coming with Dino and me after this,' announced Nick with a slight slur. I knew there could be no escape, and anyway I was flattered that the two NCOs should want to invite me to join them. I had a lot of respect for both of them. Nick was an avionics expert who could be relied on to sort out most problems we found for him. He also had a very amusing line in banter and took great delight in the verbal humiliation of any aircrew that came to debrief him on an aircraft snag. Dino's speciality was engines. He was a cheerful man, happily of fewer words than Nick. After the British Club, we made our way round various bars and refreshed ourselves in each. With his swarthy looks, Dino could easily passed himself off as a local and

I have vague memories of standing in the back of a local belly-dancing club after Dino's muttered negotiation with the manager.

'Right, it's time to go to the disco,' announced Dino. We squeezed into the back of a local taxi, and I realized with dismay that any chance of making a dash for home at a suitable time had disappeared for ever. Eventually we were turfed out of the taxi in front of a large nightclub on the outskirts of Manama. I could see the problem immediately: there was no way that the bouncers were going to let three drunken Brits in on their own.

'Look, mate, we're not going to get in. Let's jump in a taxi and go back into town,' I suggested to Dino.

'I'll sort it, trust me,' he replied unconvincingly and then came my second surreal experience of the day; as Dino stopped speaking, a taxi drew up and out got three British Airways stewardesses. He took the arm of one of them and headed through

The Crusader detachment at Dhahran on Christmas Day.

the doorway. Nick and I followed the other two and soon we were all inside. Then, just as quickly as they had appeared, the three girls melted away into the crowd. We never saw them again! Nick and I installed ourselves at the bar, while Dino went on the prowl. Eventually he rejoined us for another beer, and very happily for me, because the early start to the day was beginning to tell, he fell asleep in his beer. This was the moment I had been looking forward to! By taking an arm each, Nick and I managed to carry Dino out of the club and found a taxi to take us home.

After a day off in Bahrain, it was another early start at Dhahran. My alarm went at 4.30am, the earliest I'd ever been up on Christmas morning. I wished Platty a 'Merry Christmas' and received a seasonal grunt in return. Platty wasn't terribly chatty in the mornings. After a rushed breakfast we got into our car and, with Platty at the wheel we lurched off down the road. Whenever it was just the two of

Christmas at the operations desk: Keith, Dave our ops sergeant and Harry, plus festive decorations.

us, the unspoken agreement was that Platty always drove. I think it was a way of him getting his own back for me frightening him in the air. He certainly had me worried a few times!

The ops room was decorated with streamers and balloons. Unfortunately, the nearest we got to 'Santa' was Keith handing out the pistols. Out at the engineers' line hut, they were all in jovial mood. With lots of sniggering going on we realized that something was afoot, but didn't quite know what to expect. All became clear as we reached the aircraft. Each one had been adorned with a cartoon of 'Rudolph the Red-nosed Reindeer', with the message 'Merry Crimbo!' scrawled underneath.

We were airborne at 7.30am, flying Number Two to Al and the DETCO. The weather looked promising as we made our way up to the tanker. We topped up and set off 'sausage side'. The first port of call was As Samawah, a small town on the Euphrates some forty miles south of Ad Diwaniyah. We lingered for a while in a lazy orbit searching for military engineering equipment. From here we followed the Euphrates to An Nasiriyah before the inevitable line searches around Al Amarah. In the latter we were nothing if not predictable, which didn't please me greatly when I recalled the intelligence warnings of a couple of days before. It wouldn't take much on the Iraqi side to listen out for the 'Dundee fruitcakes' and know to expect them over Al Amarah sometime later. I was worried that we were becoming complacent in the routine over Iraq. The clouds began building after we passed An Nasiriyah. Al and the DETCO wove their way between them, their aircraft a dark silhouette against the dazzling-white cumulus. Again we could see columns of smoke rising from the marshes. Perhaps these were more settlements being burnt: Merry Christmas from the Iraqi army. I tried the barrel-roll technique once more for Chris to film these new pyres with the hand-held video. We had some success this time, but at the expense of Chris feeling unwell. I could look forward to an exciting drive home! After picking our way round the clouds all the way to Al Amarah and back we crossed the Shatt al Arab near Qurna whose biblical connections seemed particularly pertinent on this day.

Back at Dhahran we posed for a detachment photograph, then went to enjoy yet another Christmas dinner, this time in the US-forces messhall near the Khobar Towers. I decided to hang back and wait until everyone else was fed before I had my food. This was a fortuitous decision. All those who had elbowed their way to the front of the queue ended up with severe food poisoning a few hours later. Neil the Quack, the detachment doctor spent the afternoon rushing round making house calls to the afflicted. More than once he had to fit an intravenous drip to a patient who was still firmly rooted to the toilet. All in all it was a very unpleasant Christmas for the unlucky few.

For my part, I had enjoyed a very pleasant Christmas, made all the more so by a telephone call from my parents and the RAF's gift of a free call to my wife. The four of us in the flat, vegetated in front of the television – and our plastic Christmas tree of course – that evening. There was a knock at the door and a voice called out, 'How many of you in there.'

'Four,' we shouted back, whereupon four small boxes were lobbed in. Inside were assorted Christmas goodies and a penknife, and a card wishing us festive greetings from the Royal British Legion. I was amazed that someone had been thoughtful enough to put a small parcel together for every serviceman on duty over Christmas. It was such a kind thought and I was deeply touched. The penknife became a prized possession, not so much because of its obvious usefulness, but more because it was a token of someone else's anonymous and unselfish thoughtfulness.

With Christmas Day already in my logbook, I thought it would also be good to fly on Boxing Day. There was not much else to do if I was not on the flying programme, so working on these traditional holidays did not mean that I was missing anything. I rang the ops desk to find out if Chris and I were on the flying programme. Yes, we were down for a Kuwait trainer. I was quite happy with that, but as Chris was less than enthusiastic at the prospect, I suggested that Keith might like to come with me instead. Keith jumped at the chance, rather more as a result of having been on the ops desk more or less continuously for six weeks than enthusiasm at the opportunity of flying with me once more. Al and CJ were leading us and we still had the maps from our first trip to Kuwait with the Boss and Coulsy two weeks previously. That suited us well because Keith was keen to see the battlefield tour of Kuwait. After we had got him kitted out with Chris' survival vest and the rest of the clobber needed to fly in a Tornado we set off. The route was virtually an exact replay of that first trip two weeks earlier. Even the weather was hazy for the dash across Faylaka Island, so much so, in fact, that we nearly managed to collect a tall mast which loomed out of the mist at the last minute. Apart from that one heart-stopping moment, I think Keith enjoyed his tour of Kuwait and was amazed as we had been at the scenes of devastation. We flew past the redundant bridge to Bubiyan Island, the remains of the satellite tracking station, the squares of wreckage next to the Basrah road and the two airfields. We even managed another morale-raising visit to the US Army in mid-desert. I wondered how merry their Christmas had been. Harry had visited the camp when he had driven up to check out a bombing range in Kuwait a week or so before, and had reported that it was simmering with discontentment. Having been used to the high standards of the British Army, he had been shocked at the poor morale of the US troops. Perhaps our loud wake-up call on Boxing Day would bring a smile to someone's face down there. After we'd seen all the sights, we called up Kuwait International airport and asked for clearance to fly along the waterfront of Kuwait City. CJ, armed with his new camera (a bargain from Bahrain) wanted to get a photograph of a Tornado flying past the city's famous water towers. Three tall spires pierced enormous iridescent-blue spheres, looking as if they were made from peacock feathers which shimmered in the sunshine, stood close to the corniche. We slowed down to a more sedate pace and cruised past a couple of times, admiring the view while CJ snapped away. Then it was time to climb back up to high level for the return to Dhahran.

His Christmas treat over, Keith went straight back to the desk and I got on with some paperwork. The Boss had asked me to write out an order clarifying how we would move formations around the tanker aircraft if we ended up with four aircraft to refuel. With four small aircraft moving around a larger one, it was very important that everyone knew exactly what to do. Much like any formation manoeuvre, there was great scope to get it wrong and hit each other if you did not stick exactly to the brief. The problem was that the RAF procedure insisted that everyone should join on the tanker's right wing, then cycle through the hoses and go to the left wing. If the aircraft needed to tank again, all of them would have to move back across to the right wing, and then start again. We wanted to draw a line down the centre of the tanker and give one side to one pair and one to the other, which would make the whole process much simpler (and therefore safer). In fact it was what we were doing already, but Frank thought it would be useful if we wrote it down officially. I produced a draft order to put in our standard operating procedures folder – still a mercifully thin document – and showed it to Coulsy. He agreed that it all made sense, so I submitted it to the DETCO to check that he was happy. I thought that this would be a formality, since it was what another Wing Commander had decreed and it merely reflected what we were already doing. To my utter surprise he refused to allow me to publish the order, and could not be persuaded to change his mind. I think it was his way of reminding me that he was in charge, not Frank. I left his office feeling angry and disillusioned. Frank's helpful advice was 'Don't worry - he goes home in four days.' I went into Khobar with Platty, Chris and Taff and found solace in a hot curry at the Galaxy restaurant.

six

DOING IT FOR REAL

Sunday 27 December 1992 dawned in torrential rain. One glance out of the window at the chilly grey downpour was enough to persuade me to go back to bed. I hoped that it would abate before we were due to fly that evening. Over breakfast at a more civilized, but still grey, hour Platty, Taff, Chris and I thought back to O-level geography days. No one could recall heavy rain being a feature of the desert climate. Rain in these parts was particularly dispiriting because none of the infrastructure was designed to cope with being lashed with vast amounts of water. With most of the day left to kill, we drove into Khobar where we dodged brimming puddles and wandered aimlessly through dripping shopping arcades. It amused us for a couple of hours, then, once more, we were back in the flat, listless. Thoroughly bored, I rang the ops desk to find out what was happening with the weather. Were we still on the programme to fly? Instead of an updated forecast as I expected, Keith gave me a cryptic message that we ought to come in to work straight away with our tin helmets.

The whole ops block was awash with excitement. People were running around with their hair on fire, drawing maps, giving briefings, listening to briefings or answering the constantly ringing telephones. A USAF F-16 fighter had shot down an Iraqi Foxbat south of the 32nd Parallel. The morning op wave had been recalled from the tanker and our night sortie was now cancelled. We were on twenty-four hour manning to maintain two hours readiness to go somewhere and do something. No one knew quite what, though

Details of the engagement with the Iraqi aircraft slowly emerged. A cat-and-mouse game had been going on for a couple of days, though happily not while we had been in the No Fly Zone. Iraqi fighters would run towards the 32nd Parallel, and then peel off before they crossed. Each time, Coalition fighters had been directed to intercept them if they crossed the line. On one or two occasions, the Iraqis had even

More whale than shark – Platty and I fill up from a McDonnell-Douglas KC-10 Extender kindly provided by the USAF.

crossed the line while Coalition backs were turned, then scuttled out again as soon as fighters were vectored back towards them. One weakness in our fighter force was the French Mirage contingent. The pilots were great, and the aircraft an excellent one, except that it didn't carry much fuel. They were operating at maximum range close to the Parallel, so they had to run a continuous shuttle of aircraft to and from the tanker. Inevitably, sometimes there was a short gap in cover while one section had to leave for the tanker before the other section returned. It was this chink in the armour that the Iraqis had hoped to exploit. Unfortunately for them, in a rare flash of brilliance, the Americans had already thought of it. That day a formation of F-16s was on patrol using the French callsign. The Iraqis spent some fifty minutes rushing towards the 32nd Parallel and then turning away at the last minute. At that stage they must have been certain they had made the Coalition fighters use up all their spare fuel. When the 'Mirages' appeared to turn towards their tanker, the Iraqis dashed into the No Fly Zone. Unfortunately instead of seeing the rear end of Mirages, what they actually found was the front end of the F-16s. One Iraqi pilot got away with it, but the other collected an air-to-air missile.

After a couple of hours milling round the ops block, gas masks and helmets at the ready, common sense prevailed and we were all sent back to the Towers. My cynical view was that this was a storm in a teacup and we'd soon all be back to normal. On the way home, we noticed that security had increased markedly.

It was still raining on Monday. Luckily the previous day's panic had died down and we were allowed off the base. In the knowledge that we wouldn't be needed in the morning, the four of us in the flat left our gas masks and tin helmets behind and went to explore Dammam. Dammam was the next town along the road from Khobar. Where Khobar was frequented by ex-pats and was relatively cosmopolitan by Saudi standards, Dammam was a more authentic Arabian town. We parked the car in the centre and started the usual aimless wandering. The undoubted highlight of the visit was the gold souk, where it appeared that artistry was even less valued than in Bahrain. A whole street was lined on both sides by shops laden with the same hideous jewellery. We amused ourselves for thirty minutes or so looking in all the windows to see what tastelessness we could find. My favourite was a full-size gold crown lurking in one shop. The trouble with Saudi Arabia was that there were no street cafes or pubs where you could pass the hours just sitting and watching the girls go by. We used to spend hours doing that during weekends at Deci, but not alas here. As a result sightseeing visits downtown didn't last very long and the challenge to keep ourselves amused started all over again.

There is an old aircrew saying 'if in doubt – eat' so we repaired to the 'Desert Inn', another US-forces messhall for an early lunch. The Desert Inn was a recent find for the four of us, and one we kept quiet from the rest of the detachment. It was on the Saudi Air Force base, which occupied the north-western part of the airport, off the normal beaten track for the RAF. Outwardly it was the same as the other canteens and served the usual delicacies, like burgers and hot dogs. But we had discovered that the Sri Lankans who prepared the food there also cooked curries for their own meals. A bit of friendly banter was usually enough to obtain a very tasty plateful of curry. They all seemed to think this was very funny and all came trooping out of the kitchen to see the mad Brits who wanted their food instead of the delicious burgers. We sat down on a long table with a French crew who were looking down their noses at the burgers congealing on their plates. Yet again it seemed I couldn't go anywhere new without bumping into someone from the past. There amidst the Gallic throng I recognized Joel, the French exchange pilot at Chivenor while I'd been instructing there. We had all thought that Joel had left the French Air Force for the airlines when he left Chivenor, but obviously he had not, after all. The French rank insignia were something of a mystery, but from the vast amounts of gold braid on his flying suit I imagined that he must have been promoted. I went over to shake his hand. Joel was now flying the French Air Force KC-135 tanker, in support of the Mirages. He seemed happy with life.

At our flat in Dhahran, Platty and I were wondering how we were going to pass another wet afternoon. Another crossword, a game of Monopoly, or just vegetate in front of the Medusa television? A telephone call summoning us back to ops solved the problem. On the way across the airfield three unfamiliar shapes were on the approach: a pair of F–14 Tomcat fighters and a Hornet.

'Looks like the navy is in town,' observed Platty. Once we got nearer to the flight line we could see that it was full of Tomcats and Hornets. The US Navy was well and truly in town. Clearly things were hotting up over southern Iraq.

We had been called in to help the Boss and Coulsy plan the next day's sortie, but it soon became apparent that we were not so much helping as doing the whole thing. Frank and Coulsy were far too busy with furtive calls on the secure telephone to do any planning. In the end they scurried off and spent the rest of the day ferreting around in the background and being very secretive. We finished all the planning in the early evening and went to try out a newly discovered fish restaurant in Khobar to celebrate my first wedding anniversary. Platty, Taff and Chris were excellent company, but I would have preferred to have my wife there instead! We got back to the Towers at the same time as Frank and Coulsy. They were still being very secretive and we were sensible enough not to press them for details. All they would say was that the line-up for the next day's sortie had been changed and that Platty and I were to lead it. We nicknamed them the 'Secret Squirrels Club'.

Unsurprisingly it was still raining hard when we walked out to the aircraft. They had been standing in the rain for the past two days, so I was expecting problems. Modern electronics don't take well to being kept out in the cold and damp. I was not disappointed. Platty and I had to climb out of our first aircraft. As we were the lead Tiald aircraft, our pod had to come across to the new aircraft, too. Needless to say, it didn't work when it was plugged in. We decided to press onanyway. It would be good to get airborne and we might be able to help Larry in the Number Two aircraft to take some film over Iraq on the hand-held camera. We were not the only ones to have problems on start up: only two of us out of the planned fourship got airborne. We stayed in thick cloud all the way to the tow-line. I discovered that a pool of water had got into the combining glass of the HUD, so it was either completely obscured or too faint to be useable. A sensible man would have given up at that stage and handed the lead over to Kev and Larry, but I was too stupid and too proud to do that. Instead, I stuck with instrument flying on the head-down instruments, something we didn't practise very much and a skill that was easily lost without practice. All that I managed to do was overload myself and give Kev a hard time trying to stay on my wing.

The tow-lines were in thick cloud and once we got there we discovered that the tanker's datum position was ten miles away from ours. I tried to use the tanker marshal in the AWACS to help us find the tanker, but, like the last time he'd been involved, he proved to be useless. Platty and Larry both did their best to join us up and the radar navigator on the tanker tried his best, too, but to no avail. I think the closest we ever got was passing in opposite directions a 1,000ft apart, but we never saw them in the swirling cloud. After several frustrating minutes of blind man's buff we gave up and came home, having achieved nothing.

On the ground again we discovered that there were now four crews in the Secret Squirrels Club. Something of an 'us and them' attitude was dividing the detachment. I asked Frank if he could give me any indication of what was going on.

'I can't tell you anything at all, Mike,' he said, 'you can probably work it out yourself, but you're going to have to accept that Coulsy and I cannot tell you anything.' He was absolutely right, but it still made the rest of us feel like second-class citizens. That evening in the flat we speculated on what might be being planned. Some sort of airstrike, we thought, perhaps against Al Jarra to dissuade the Foxbats from bothering us again. The obvious problem with that would be that since Al Jarra was north of the 32nd Parallel, it would be outside the UN remit for enforcing the NFZ and would mark a major escalation on our part. Perhaps Tallil might be a more appropriate target.

Yet another rain soaked day followed. We were all called in for an intelligence update from Harry and his team. The map of southern Iraq was now filled with red circles showing the engagement zones around several new missile sites under the NFZ. Previously there had been only one, drawn around the SAM 3 site at Basrah. Now a number of mobile SAM 6 batteries were reported to have deployed. Although these were all relatively old Soviet-built missile systems, we were operating right in the heart of their engagement envelope, so they were still a very potent threat. Smaller circles marked newly plotted sites of Triple-A (anti-aircraft artillery). If we stayed outside all the red circles, we would not be able to fly north of the 31st Parallel. The good news was that the aircraft carrier USS *Kitty Hawk* and its attendant escorts were on station in the Gulf.

There was no flying for Platty and me. The Secret Squirrel Club went off for a training sortie over Kuwait, which merely underlined the fact that we would miss out on the fun. We all understood that someone would miss out and we also understood that the 'secret squirrels' couldn't let us in on what we didn't need to know, but none of that made it any easier to sit on the sidelines, and nor did it stop the consequent 'us and them' feeling. A low-profile op wave of just two aircraft launched in the afternoon, but both went unserviceable in the air. That didn't bode well for operations in anger. The good news was that the new DETCO, the Goldstars' new Boss, had arrived.

We had more luck on New Year's Eve. It was an early start. The rain clouds had gone and with them some of the chaos of the previous two days. Harry's map of Iraq seemed to have stabilized, albeit with a fair few red spots still spattering it. It was still pretty tense out there, though. This was reflected in the support package for us: we were only a pair, but four Hornets and two Tomcats would be our fighter escort and four Wild Weasels, and also two EF-111A Raven jamming aircraft, would be there to suppress the defences for us if needed. At least that gave us a cosy feeling. The plan was to refuel from the Victor tanker on the 'Orioles' trail up past Rafha, then push up towards the Euphrates. When we arrived for the briefing there was a message that it had all been changed. The Victor captain had injured himself playing squash, so there was no RAF tanker today. Instead we had been allocated a USAF KC-10 Extender tanker on the 'Giants' tow-line, just south of Kuwait. Kev and Larry disappeared into a corner to revamp their tanker plan; still wary of tanking despite my 100 percent record of success on the Victor, I went in search of someone who had tanked from a KC-10 before. In fact, I needed to look no further than Kev, who assured me that it was very straightforward.

We launch into clear skies and follow Kev in loose formation up towards the tanker. The KC-10 is a behemoth compared to our Victor: A large whale instead of a shark. The huge dark-coloured aircraft stands out well against the blue sky. Unlike our previous attempt to find a tanker, we see this one from miles away. The join up is easy and soon we're in tight echelon on the tanker's wing. The KC-10 has only a single basket trailing from the rear of the aircraft. Unlike the Victor with two hoses, one under each wing, we will have to take it in turns to top up. Kev goes first. I watch a little apprehensively as he prods successfully first time and then I have to wait for my go. Kev fills up then moves aside to the left wing ready for my go. At this stage the four Hornets also arrive on the tanker. It's reassuring to know that the fighter escort is here, but I could do without an audience right now.

I stabilize behind the basket. It's a chunky piece of metal, much heavier than that on the Victor, and it is remains rock solid in the airflow. It's now or never. With heart beating I push the throttles forward. The Tornado noses forward and nudges the probe straight into the basket with a reassuring clunk. Fuel flows! Once again I feel a mixture of pride and relief. In the background I can hear Larry on the radio. He has been called off to another frequency, but I'm far too busy concentrating on staying in the basket to be able to follow much detail. If it's important, he'll be sure to tell us later. Once I've filled to full, I slide out of the basket and move across outside Kev. The pair of us wheel off to the west, leaving the Hornets with the tanker to themselves.

It is a long transit from Kuwait up to Rafha. We follow Kev along the route, but it seems to be very quiet on the radio. Looking across I can see that Larry is very busily at work in the back seat. The occasional involuntary gesticulation from Kev shows that they're also having quite an animated conversation. Platty and I wonder what is going on. Eventually they call us up on the Havequick. There is a problem. The AWACS has gone unserviceable, leaving us only with the limited cover of ground-based radar. Back at headquarters they have decided, rather sensibly, that it would be best for us not to stray too far north. Instead we have been tasked to reconnoitre the newly-built airfield in the middle of the desert at Ghalaysan. I'm impressed with Kev and Larry as they rebrief us on the new mission. They have both done very well to sort this out. Like Platty sitting behind me, they are both on their first tour and have been dropped in at the deep end. I've flown with them quite a few times on this detachment and I have always been very impressed at the way they've done business.

The leg to Ghalaysan involves only a short dip into Iraq, but we are taking no chances. I push out into a wide battle formation and climb so there is a height split between our aircraft. The electronic warfare kit is up and running and the missiles are ready for use. As we cross into Iraqi airspace it is just like our first mission again, a mixture of excitement and nervousness. After a short time the airfield shows up easily in the distance: A single runway in the desert. Kev and Larry drop down to get the imagery. I decide to hang back a little and stay high, so I can get a good view under Kev's aircraft. That is where the missiles or Triple-A are going to come from. I manage to dip a wing so that Platty can do his bit with the hand-held camera. After one pass over the airfield Larry decides he's got enough film and we turn about to dash back into the safety of Saudi Arabia.

Although we had only nipped briefly into Iraq, it was a long sortie. Back at the ops desk, we logged three hours' flying time. After grabbing a can of coke, we all trooped into the briefing room for the usual debrief. At the end of it I called Chris and Taff to join us. Time for some 'hearts and minds' I thought.

'OK, guys, we all know about the secret squirrels. There is an A team and a B team and we're in the B team. I think it's very important for us to remember that we've *all* got a job to do over Iraq. The other guys are going through a busy time at the moment and they've got lots to do. But Operation *Jural* still goes on and now it's down to us to get on with the day-to-day recce missions, and not to whine. Please let's carry on doing that to the very best of our ability and support our

Platty and me on our way back to Dhahran after a sortie as shooter/escort for Kev and Larry.

buddies in the A team by doing our bit without any fuss. Remember that we might be the B team, but we have an important job to do, and we are not second-class citizens.' I hoped it sounded convincing.

Almost as soon as I finished speaking the door opened and Frank's head appeared round it.

'I want you and you,' he said pointing at Kev and Larry. They followed him out. The rest of us looked at each other.

'And then there were four,' I said, and we all bust out laughing.

Frank had also sensed the need for a 'hearts and minds' chat and called us all together. Although he couldn't say much for obvious reasons he indicated that a one-off attack was being planned against the Iraqi air-defence system. He also emphasized that no political go-ahead had been given yet. It was nice to have a bit more of an idea about what was going on, but I felt very disappointed not to be involved.

The first four crews from the Goldstars, who would be relieving our own first crews, arrived that afternoon. I went down to welcome them off the aircraft, and in the evening took them into Khobar for a meal. Platty was happy to have his squadron mates around him, though by now he had developed a loyalty to us as well. The newcomers were cheerful and excited about coming out to Dhahran at a time when trouble was brewing. My slight concern was that this new influx would split the detachment further.

New Year's Day 1993 was just another day in Saudi Arabia. My main duty for the day was to get the new arrivals through the groundschool. The first port of call was the intelligence section for an update. Overnight, Harry's map had sprouted yet more red circles. This time a number of SAM 3 missile sites were marked as active just below the 32nd Parallel – including the one we had searched for unsuccessfully just before Christmas. The SAM 3 was a long-range missile, so their circles covered lots of the map. These new sites might pose quite a threat to us during our operations north of the 31st Parallel. I could not understand how these new missile sites could appear so suddenly, because unlike the mobile SAM 6 batteries, SAM 3 was a static system, which required a prepared site.

I left the new boys reading through the books and discovered that I had appeared on the flying programme. One of the aircraft required an air check. It had a history of suffering from a cockpit warning of severe vibration in one of the engines. The engineers were certain that the problem was with the warning system rather than the engine. They had tinkered with various components and wanted a shake-down sortie to see if their efforts had worked. The navigator was to be Rick, as a small thank you for all the work he had put in as a mission planner. The first time we had flown together was also a thank you for his hard work almost exactly three years beforehand. Then he had been an enthusiastic young Pilot Officer holding with the Goldstars between navigation school courses. He hadn't lost any of his enthusiasm and was overjoyed to get back in the air again. We wondered what we should do to fill the hour's flying that the engineers had asked us to undertake. In Europe we would have flown a 'practice diversion': fly to another airfield, carry out an approach to land, but then fly back to base rather than landing. We thought it might be fun to try the same thing here and fly across to Riyadh to shoot an approach there before coming back to Dhahran. We filed our flight plan accordingly, but hadn't counted on the Saudi police state. Just as we were about to go out to the aircraft, the ops desk phone rang.

'Why do you want to go to Riyadh, are you landing there,' asked the Arab voice on the other end.

'No,' I politely explained, 'we just want to fly an approach there for practice then come back.'

'Do you have a mission in Riyadh,' the voice persisted, 'are you going to land there.'

'No, we're not going to land there. We just want to carry out a practice diversion, fly an approach and then come straight back here.'

'Yes,' replied the voice. From flying with Arab students at Chivenor, I knew this was Arabic for 'I have no idea what you are talking about, you infidel pig!' Thinking no more of it we went out to the aircraft.

As we taxied out, a heavy accent called us on the radio.

'Err, why you want to go to Riyadh,' he asked suspiciously. I explained once more. After a lengthy discussion all over again about whether we had business in Riyadh and whether we were going to land there, he concluded with another 'Yiss.' We got airborne and called the departure controller.

'Why do you want to go to Riyadh,' we started again. This time after I had explained the reply was; 'OK, you go to Al-Ahsa instead.' We never did get to Riyadh. Al-Ahsa was a small airstrip in the desert some sixty miles from Dhahran. I can only imagine from the enthusiasm that greeted our first call to the tower that they didn't get much business. We dutifully flew an ILS approach and whizzed past the tower at lots of knots but not many feet. The man in the tower loved that, too! So far the aircraft was behaving itself perfectly. I decided to try some aerobatics to see if g-loading made any difference. I lit the burners and pulled up into a loop. Sure enough, as the nose came up with a pull of about 4-g, the warning lights flashed and the 'VIB' caption illuminated on the warning panel.

'I always said your aerobatics were too rough,' commented Rick helpfully as we went home.

I spent the following morning on the ops desk to give Keith a break. In the periphery I was aware of Frank and the new DETCO scurrying around, with lots of use of the secure phone. After lunch I was called into the office. The planned attack had been delayed until further notice. Frank was due to return to Brüggen in a few days and could not afford to hold on in Dhahran 'just in case'. The decision had been made that I would lead any airstrike. I was now a 'secret squirrel' myself!

Frank and Coulsy briefed Platty and me on the plan so far. I had been right with my guess of the airfield at Al Jarra. We pored over the maps with great interest. Taking over someone else's plan is never ideal and I could see that Frank's approach was very different from the one that I would choose. As leader, Frank had chosen to fly the Tiald aircraft, seeing his role as the 'pathfinder' illuminating the target for the main force to bomb. This mode of operation fitted closely with the way we had been using Tiald/shooter tactics over Iraq up to now. My view was that the emphasis had now changed and if the mission was now bombing, then the leader should be the bomber, with the designator supporting him. I was also mindful that Platty lacked practice and confidence with the pod: we would both be much happier if we did not need to worry about that aspect of the operation. Luckily a signal amending the aiming points on the airfield arrived, which gave us an opportunity to change the plan without upsetting the other two!

Another change of plan followed, the next day. I was again sitting on the desk, ready to go along to a planning meeting in the American ops block if Gordon didn't make it there in time. I was surprised when one of the staff officers from Riyadh came in and suggested in strong terms that I should really go along to the meeting anyway. The reason became clear very soon after we got to the briefing. The US Navy was there in force to unveil another master plan. Instead of Al Jarra, they suggested, we should attack the adjacent air-defence centre at Al Kut. This idea struck me as rather more politically aware than the USAF's effort. The US Navy had done much of the initial planning overnight on the ship. Now they needed our expertise to do more detailed target area planning and work out how formations would deconflict from each other on the way to and from their targets. Once we had done that, there would be another briefing from the admiral in the afternoon. Platty and I returned to our own block and locked ourselves in the only totally secure place in the ops block, a large cupboard used to house communications equipment. We were beavering away when a Corporal from the tactical communications wing entered.

'You can't stay in here – all this equipment is secret,' he scolded us. Not for the first time on this detachment I had come across a pedant with a firm grasp of the non-essential. I explained that I wasn't the one who was going to leave. Having completed what we needed to do, I briefed the new DETCO on what we were doing. In contrast to his predecessor, he proved to be a delight to work for. As long as I kept him in the picture he was happy to give me free reign and his complete trust. I couldn't have asked for a better commander. I told him my line-up of crews for the mission. I would lead, with Chris and Taff as the second bomber. The Tiald crews would be Darren with Bamber, and Marcus with Mal. I regarded both these crews as exceptionally good. Darren was an excellent pilot whom I'd known for a long time. Both Bamber and Mal were superb navigators and accomplished Tiald operators. The new DETCO agreed that my proposed crewing made sense.

The afternoon briefing turned out to be a presentation of the plan to the top brass. There was a USAF three-star air General, a two-star US Navy Admiral and all their various acolytes. At the end the General stood up and gave us a rousing speech telling how wonderful the plan was. He didn't mention until the last sentence that there was still no political approval for offensive action yet. The more I thought about it the more I was sure that there would never be political approval from the Arabs for action north of the 32nd Parallel. The US military seemed curiously naïve as far as the political big picture was concerned. Their concept was of riding into town with a 'six-shooter' in hand: the subtleties of working with people from other cultures seemed to be completely lost on them. I found it both amazing and frightening that a global military force could be so ignorant of the world in which it operated. It seemed incredible that while they had embraced all the technological lessons from conflicts like Vietnam, they had learnt none of the human ones.

Grey skies and rain returned on 4 January. Harry's map had grown a new crop of red circles, all SAM 3 sites active below the No Fly Zone. They had all moved since the day before and were all supposedly up and running already. I was very sceptical about this intelligence. I could not believe that static SAM 3 batteries could move overnight and be set up in a new location overnight and be fully operational the next morning. I wondered as to the source of this information. Rain stopped Platty and me flying with Chris and Taff that night. We went for a curry instead.

The US Navy plan lasted all of two days before we were summoned for another briefing at the USAF ops block to be told it had all changed. We rubbed out our pencil lines and drew them towards Al Jarra again. The General stood up and gave us a rousing speech that *this* was actually the wonderful plan. However, this time at least there was some news on the political front. President George H.W. Bush would deliver an ultimatum to Saddam Hussein that day that he must remove all surface-to-air missile sites south of the 32nd Parallel within two days or military action would be taken. I didn't believe a word of it and was certain that there would be as many changes of plan in two days. Meanwhile, the BBC World Service became compulsory watching and newspapers from home provided light entertainment with their speculation about what we were doing. Most reported that we were sitting in the cockpits of bombed-up aircraft waiting to go.

By now morale on the RAF detachment was taking a dive. Part of the reason was the misery that comes with days of pouring rain and part that we hadn't flown for five days. Another was that unlike the new DETCO, the RAF headquartes at Riyadh were not prepared to trust my judgement or allow me free reign. The Group Captain had decreed that two crews from Marham would deploy to Dhahran and fly on any airstrike as the Tiald crews. None of us wanted that. I was absolutely certain that we did not need this input. I had every confidence with Bamber and Mal and I did not believe that crews from another squadron would bring any knowledge or ability that I did not already have in my team. More importantly I now had a close-knit team, each of whom I knew extremely well. I knew the strengths and weaknesses of every individual, and they knew mine. We had also flown together on many occasions and we knew what to expect from each other. Any newcomers would lack the intimate knowledge that we possessed and could only weaken the team. I resented the imposition of unknown crews on my team. I was not cheered up when for the second night on the trot our flying was cancelled because of the weather.

Third night lucky! The clouds had cleared and we got airborne with Chris and Taff on our wing to try our hands at refuelling from a USAF KC-135. It had been a bit of an uphill struggle. We were programmed exactly as on the preceding two nights for 'night currency', in other words, just get airborne and fly around for a bit in the dark. We all thought that was not the most efficient way of spending our time, so we tried to think of something more interesting to do. Taff had spotted this particular KC-135 in the Frag. It was tasked for the US Navy. This was a very important detail because the RAF and US Navy use the same 'probe-and-drogue' (basket) system. As ever, the USAF does things differently. Instead of a probe their aircraft have a receptacle; the tanker has the probe on the end of a long boom projecting from underneath. The receiver aircraft has to formate on the tanker, while a boom operator in the tanker flies the boom probe into the receptacle on the receiving aircraft. It is very complicated but means that less skill is required of the receiver pilot. Make what inferences you wish from that.

Our KC-135 would be fitted with the boom-probe adaptor: a very short hose and basket on the end of the boom. By now my lack of confidence about tanking was fast fading, and buoyed up by my successes so far I was beginning to get a bit cocky. This KC-135 sounded as if it would be much more fun than boring holes in the sky, so we checked to see if we were allowed to use it and if we could have some 'boom time' on it. The answer to both questions was yes. And here the problem started. The problem was in the form of one of the staff officers at Riyadh. The telephone in ops rang.

'Hello, what can I do for you,' I enquired.

'You do realize that you have booked a KC-135 tonight, don't you,' said a rather officious voice.

'Yes,' I replied very patiently.

'Why have you done that,' this was getting like the Saudi ATC.

'Because we wanted to do something better than droning around in circles and because we can use a KC-135,' I explained.

'I think you'll find that you can't,' Mr Officious informed me.

'I think you'll find that I can, according to the release to service,' I told him, referring to the huge and very boring tome, which set out exactly what we were allowed to do with a Tornado.

'Well yes, but there are lots of restrictions,' he countered.

'I know that – I have the release to service on my lap as we speak, would you like me to read it to you,' I was beginning to lose patience now.

'Well, you just be careful then,' he finished. I felt like saying 'Thanks for reminding me to be careful because I wasn't going to bother tonight.'

But now we are airborne on a beautiful moonlit night. We find the tanker easily enough and join up on the right wing. Out of the darkness a blinding searchlight shines straight at us.

'Switch that light off,' shouts an angry English voice – Platty or Chris, I don't know which. The searchlight is immediately extinguished. It is lucky the night is so bright, or we would be completely blind now. I slide across and under the tanker and stabilize behind the basket; I am dismayed to see that it is very small. The other difficulty is that it hangs so low from the tanker that there is nothing obvious to formate on as you close on the basket. After a couple of unsuccessful jabs, I discover that if I line up some of the symbology in the HUD with the leading edge of the tanker's wing, I can make a steady approach to the basket. Bingo – it works.

Now comes the next tricky bit. Most tankers have a 30ft hose which is rolled around a drum, like a garden hose. When you get into the basket, you push the hose back so that it rolls itself in a few feet. Once the hose is no longer taut, the fuel flows. But tonight the hose is only 9ft long and there is no drum. The technique is to move around 3ft forward, so that the hose has a kink in it. This is easier said than done, because the boom moves in the airflow as well as the hose, and only 9ft of hose wants to flap around much more violently than the languid swing of a 30ft hose. At this point I remember the sight of one of the French Mirages with a bent probe from being whipped about by Joel's KC-135. I grit my teeth and stay in there.

I manage about 500kg of fuel, which is all we want, really, but it feels like hanging onto a bucking bronco. The hose is now going round and round like a skipping rope and banging against the nose of the aircraft as it rotates. I realize that I have lost the will to stay in and relax almost infinitesimally. Immediately, the basket spits us out, and showers the windscreen with a dollop of fuel just to show who is boss. We slide out to the tanker's left wing for a ring side view of Chris' efforts.

'Christ that was sporting,' I confide to Platty.

'Yeah, I knew you'd get in OK,' Platty's reply takes me aback. I am touched at his complete faith in me. Then I realize that I've managed a 'bullseye' every time with the Victor, and I've never let him know about my insecurity about tanking. Meanwhile, Chris is having a fine time jousting with the basket, but he can't get in. I call up on the Havequick and tell him about the technique that worked for me. It works for him, too and he's soon plugged in. When he's taken his 500kg he disconnects, or perhaps he was thrown out, too, and joins me on the tanker's wing.

We drop out of the tow-line and gently accelerate away as we head for home.

Chris calls, 'Dundee lead from two.'

'Go'

'We're getting some quite marked airframe vibration – any ideas,' Chris reports. My first thought is the probe. Perhaps the tanker has given it a good yank and it has not been able to retract fully, or perhaps the basket has bashed the airframe as he disconnected.

'Is it coming from the probe,' I check.

'Don't think so,' replies Chris. In daylight, the next step would be for me to move into close formation to carry out a visual inspection of his jet – just as Joel had done for me in a Hawk when I'd hit the bird over south Shropshire. But at night it isn't that simple. Apart from the obvious fact that you wouldn't see much from a visual inspection in the dark and close formation at night is strictly forbidden. I knew that it was with good reason having witnessed a night mid-air all those years ago.

All this goes through my mind in an instant as I look back at Chris' aircraft, a 100yds away, slightly swept behind on my right. High in the sky, the moon is brilliant. Way beneath us, a luminescent sheet of altostratus reflects the moonlight back upwards. Everything is bathed in a soft light. There are no colours to the scene, but the aircraft stands out clearly like a sepia photograph as we cruise through the night. It is a beautiful sight.

Then an idea comes.

'Have you got a torch handy,' I ask Platty over the intercom. He affirms.

'I think there's enough moonlight here for me to formate on him, and we can give him a once over with the torch. Are you happy,' Platty says he is.

'OK, Two, you have the lead, I'll give you a visual inspection.' Chris pulls forward and I move into close formation. I know that this is strictly against the rules, but this is an emergency and I know I can do it safely. Crossing behind the gentle glow of Chris' jetpipes, I close slowly in to a tight line abreast on his right-hand side. So familiar in daylight, the Tornado looks different now in dull monochrome under the soft moonlight. I can see enough to formate quite happily, but there is no fine detail, only vague grey shapes offering the occasional hint of what might lie there. Shadows coyly hide the parts that the moon cannot reach. Taff and Chris are silhouetted in the green glow of their cockpit lights.

Platty trains his torch along the other aircraft. Even in the moonlight, the torch is a dazzling beam; a thin shaft of magic causing a small disc of colour and detail to play along the anonymous grey shape next to us. We inspect Chris' aircraft in minute detail. A close look around the refuelling probe, but that seems OK. Then a search around the nose for any signs of damage, but there's nothing obviously wrong. We can do no more, except keep out of their way while they take the aircraft back to the engineers at Dhahran.

'Can't see anything, mate. We'll follow you home.' I drop back into a loose formation and enjoy the wonderful view of Chris' wraith-like ship as he descends into the cloud.

I heard the news that Saddam Hussein announced that he would take back control of all Iraqi airspace below the 32nd Parallel with mixed feelings. It made the prospect of real action much more likely. I looked forward to the professional challenge, but on a personal level I hoped that I would not be found lacking. I knew that there was nothing worth dying for in Iraq. Meanwhile, the two-day cycle continued and the

A Tornado armed with laser-guided bombs sits forlornly in the rain. Apart from the red protective stops and bungs, note the masking tape which has been applied to the panel edges to keep out the rain. (Marcus Cook)

Al Jarra plan was consigned to the bin again. We were promised another plan in the near future. Meanwhile, I expressed my wish to retain my hand-picked team for the operation to the new DETCO and was delighted to hear his promise to support me.

A couple of days later, the two crews from RAF Marham arrived. I went to greet them, but it was difficult to hide my resentment, and my frame of mind was not improved by the onset of a head cold. I felt awful. Although I had not set out to make them feel unwelcome, I am sorry to say that I managed to do just that. It was not helped by the fact that I knew one of them fairly well: I had shared a house with Corky briefly a few years earlier. While he was very pleasant company socially, I felt that professionally he was an albatross who attracted bad luck like a magnet. There was no way that I was going to have him in my team.

The Group Captain chose the same day to visit the detachment for a quick morale-raising chat. It worked well. Vaughan enjoyed a lot of popularity and was able to fill us in on a bit more of the political background. Everyone felt buoyed-up by his visit. After he left, I was not surprised to be called into see the new DETCO. He explained to me that, despite his promise to me, he was now under pressure from above to use the Marham crews. I explained that there was no question of Corky being in the team. We compromised that I would use the other crew, Spiv and Ken. I was reassured that he had supported me as far as he could; the disappointment was the micro-management from higher authority who did not know the individuals involved. The next decision was who of my original team to send home. It was a difficult decision, because there was little to choose from them and I knew that whoever went home would be disappointed. After much thought, I elected to keep Marcus and Mal on the grounds that both were single and therefore slightly more expendable – and I thought they would welcome the chance to prove themselves again in public after the last DETCO's aspersions on their handling of their fuel leak.

I now had to take Ken and Spiv into my confidence. Unfortunately, I had no current plans to show them now that the Al Jarra plan had been shelved. Instead we looked through the pencil lines on that. It was quickly apparent that that both were fully up to speed on tactics for using laser-guided bombs. They had clearly done their homework. I was surprised to discover that Ken was a QWI: his quiet, unassuming and modest manner was at some variance to the usual 'glass-chewing' aggression of most graduates of the course. He was also a veteran of the Gulf War. I warmed to Ken immediately: he was happy to advise but was never pushy. His suggestions were invariably sensible and incisive. Spiv was much more extrovert and wasn't afraid to speak his mind readily. His inputs were also very useful and astute, but I felt that his enthusiasm might need to be reigned in a little. We dissected the Al Jarra plan and Platty and I listened with interest as Ken and Spiv identified possible weak points and suggested how to fix them. It was an invaluable chance to brainstorm our way through all the permutations and possibilities.

The value of this exercise proved itself when the next master plan was unveiled the next day. This time the US Navy had come up with a rather more appropriate and politically aware idea: in the Admiral's words, we would, 'poke out Saddam's eyes and ears below the 32nd Parallel'. There would be a simultaneous strike on the air-defence centres at Tallil, Al Amarah, An Najaf and As Samawah, and the SAM 3 sites at Tallil and Basrah. The first strikes would be made against the missile sites by USAF F-117 Nighthawk 'Stealth Fighters' operating from Khamis Mushayt. Then aircraft from Dhahran, including us, and those from USS *Kitty Hawk* would complete the attack. This plan looked like it would be a 'goer.'

We were tasked against Al Amarah, so the next meeting was with the package commander who was co-ordinating that particular part of the raid. With the other formation leaders, we decided who would go for which of the individual targets within the complex at Al Amarah. Avoiding some, which I thought might be too difficult for us in our untrained state, I opted for a headquarters building and a radar control bunker. I thought that we had a good chance of finding and hitting these targets with our equipment. The choice of weapon was easy, because we only had one: the 1,000lb laser-guided bomb. The F-15E Strike Eagle leader had much more choice, which gave him a real problem of making up his mind. He bored us all for about ten minutes as he spouted on about the benefits and disadvantages of the various weapons at his disposal. I was grateful to have had such an easy decision. We spent the day producing a rough plan which made sure that all the formations were deconflicted from each other during the attack. The final plan and minor detail would be completed once we were told that we would definitely be going.

I realized that I was losing my battle against a head cold. I went to see Neil the Quack, and got dosed-up with assorted drugs and took myself off to bed for the whole of the next day.

I prised myself out of bed on 11 January, still feeling awful, to say goodbye to Darren and Bamber. They were flying a Tornado back home. I spent the day sitting behind the ops desk, gradually feeling better. At 5.00pm, I retired to the flat only to be recalled thirty minutes later. The airstrike was 'on', and we were to fly it the following night. On the secure printer, a secret message spelled out our rules of engagement for the mission. It authorized the use of weapons, including our own pistols, only in certain very specific circumstances, which it then listed in precise detail. The operation, it told me, was to be called Operation *Ingleton*. When I had digested all the information, the new DETCO called me aside.

'Mike, are you fit enough for this,' he asked.

'Yes, sir; I'm fighting fit now,' I assured him. I felt much better. The plan took longer to finish than we had thought it would: our planning computer broke down halfway through the work, so we had to wait for an hour or two while the technician was found to fix it. I noticed that our callsign for the next day would be 'Bristol'. A slight improvement on the fruitcake, but I wondered what the Iraqis would make of our change of callsign. As we headed for bed at 2.00am in the morning the rain was already falling.

It rained all of the following day. We arose late and spent a restless and disquieted day in the flat. The usual easy banter was noticeable by its absence. Instead long brooding silences fell as we each thought about what the evening might bring. We went in to brief late that afternoon. The atmosphere was tense, the mood serious. We ran through the route, the tanker plan and the tactics we would use. Spiv noticed that one of the SAM 3 sites had been slightly mis-plotted, so we were 'grazing' just inside its engagement zone. We adjusted the turning points to keep us clear. Gordon came in and briefed us on the combat rescue teams and the procedure we would need if we got shot down. I finished the brief with the words: 'don't take any chances tonight: remember, there is nothing in Iraq worth dying for.' Then we shuffled over to the ops desk for a final 'out brief'. This time we took a little more interest than usual in our pistols when Keith issued them. We shook hands with him and the new DETCO, before heading for the aircraft.

The air of tenseness continued with the groundcrew. We didn't know how much they knew and we were very wary about passing on any information which might compromise the mission. The groundcrew for their part knew that something was up (bombs loaded to the aircraft were a fairly obvious clue!) but didn't want to ask any inappropriate questions. Instead they treated us with an unusual distant courtesy. We were all very awkward together. Out at the aircraft Platty and I set about checking the laser-guided bombs. This was the first time that either of us had seen one. I was amazed at the size of them: the seeker head and guidance mechanism on the front and the wings on the back made them twice the length of a normal 'dumb' bomb. We worked our way through the checklist ensuring that all the fixtures and fittings on each of the three bombs were as they should be. I was amused to read the graffiti, most of it rude, scrawled all over the bombs.

As we got to the cockpit, Dave our Ops Sergeant arrived breathless from the ops desk.

Platty and me with our fully-armed steed: three 1,000lb LGBs are loaded under the aircraft. This was the first time that either of us had seen one!

'You're cancelled tonight, sir,' he yells at me. The words hit me like a punch. I felt completely deflated.

Once again we spent an unplanned evening in the curry house.

It was not until the following morning that the significance of the date struck me. It was the Thirteenth of January. Needless to say, and despite it not being a Friday, there was lots of light-hearted banter about 'Friday the Thirteenth.' Aircrew are not particularly superstitious, but they do enjoy a line in cynical black humour.

Four years previously Alan and Smudger had been killed on that day and then two years later, almost exactly to the minute, Kieran and Norman had killed themselves by flying into the Arabian desert while working up for the Gulf war. That made four aircrew from the Crusaders killed on the Thirteenth of January over the past four years. Now I wondered why fate had delayed our mission until tonight. I knew the significance of the date would not be lost on Vaughan: as he had been commanding the Crusaders when both those unfortunate events occurred.

I tried to put such thoughts to the back of my mind, but with a whole day to kill they kept coming back. It became impossible to use the time to think through the mission: we had already done that too many times. Now thoughts of home intruded whenever I tried to think about the night's flight. Sitting quietly in our flat, I realized that an extra day of thinking time was taking its toll. At last 4.00pm came. We jumped into the cars and drove across to the USAF ops block for the mass brief.

After the dress rehearsal the day before, our own briefing was a much more relaxed affair. It all seemed familiar territory. Perhaps, too, we were encouraged that the weather was looking much more promising. There was even a 60kt tailwind on the last leg to speed us toward the target. We managed some idle banter as we out briefed, though Chris was still wearing a grave look. The new DETCO called me outside.

'I'm a bit worried about Chris. He doesn't seem very happy – is he OK,' he asked. I was taken aback. I knew that Chris was as solid as a rock, but like all of us he was in a serious frame of mind.

'He's absolutely fine. No worries at all. He's just focussed on tonight's mission at the moment,' I reassured him. What I did not know was that the new DETCO

The target: the headquarters of the Integrated Operations Centre (IOC) at Al Amarah. The administration building provides a distinctive landmark. (Crown Copyright/MoD)

had just given Chris a few paternal words of encouragement. Unfortunately he had chosen the wrong words and the wrong man, and Chris, who did not suffer fools, considered that he'd been patronizing rather than paternal, hence the apparently surly manner!

There was a much more informal air amongst the groundcrew when we got there. The distance between us was gone. We showed them the maps and told them what we were going to do. They appreciated knowing a bit more about what we were all as a detachment, trying to achieve. I had allocated myself 'Bravo Papa', the aircraft still painted in Crusader Squadron colours. As I walked out towards the aircraft, Dino stopped me.

'Can you bring me back a souvenir tonight,' he asked.

'Er, yeah, what do you want,' I replied suspiciously.

'Bring back Bravo Papa for me,' he laughed, and disappeared chuckling to himself into the night.

I was stopped again just before I reached the aircraft. It was Gilbert, the first student I had instructed during my time at Chivenor. He would be flying the airborne spare, ready to take the place of anyone who went unserviceable in the air.

'Good luck, Napes, give 'em rocks,' as he shook my hand.

'Thanks mate,' I was touched by this simple act of friendship.

My choice of Bravo Papa was not a good one. The radar warning gear was not working, and despite the best efforts of Nick's smiling face, it refused to do so. Decision time: We raced across for the spare, 'Delta Juliet' in Goldstar Squadron colours – a message there? We had just gone from having lots of time on our hands to barely enough. By now my nose was in full flow, too. Recalling that my handkerchief was in my other flying suit back in ops, I asked the engineer if he could get me a bit of cloth. He must have thought I wanted to clean the windscreen and was soon back polishing away with a clean rag. I managed to get it from him and wipe my nose, rather to his surprise!

Despite the aircraft change, Platty and I were ready on time and we taxied out behind a fourship of Strike Eagles.

Night flying has a unique dignity and sense of occasion. Tonight is no different. We move onto the runway, our taxi lights pushing their small pools of illumination ahead of us. The aircraft trembles against the brakes as I select reheat, and then we thunder down the dark runway, the lights streaming past on both sides like strings of pearls. Airborne; the undercarriage lights extinguish as the gear retracts and the darkness envelopes us. Fifteen second behind us, Spiv and Ken follow us into the night.

The lights of Dammam are sinking slowly behind us as we rise into the night sky and swing gently onto a north-westerly course. A small cluster of dull-red lights bobbing gently over my right shoulder is all that shows in the darkness of Spiv and Ken formating on us 300ft away. The aircraft are climbing slowly now, unaccustomed to the extra weight of the laser-guided bombs hanging under the fuselage. In the cockpit, I am busy concentrating on flying accurately, watching the altimeter needle winding slowly upwards, all the while trying to take my mind off the fact that tonight this is for real. In just under two hours' time, we will drop our bombs on a small complex just beyond the outskirts of Al Amarah, on the banks of the Tigris. The first hour will be fairly routine – a transit up to the Saudi border where we will top up from a waiting airborne fuel tanker, followed by a short wait while everyone gets into position. But then we will push into the unknown, over Iraq itself.

At last we reach our cruising altitude and as the aircraft slowly accelerates to a more comfortable speed, I engage the autopilot and feel I can relax slightly. By now, the second pair of Tornados will be airborne, following our route to the tanker. Although they are fifteen minutes behind us now, they will be following us all the way to Al Amarah and making their own attack just forty seconds after ours. As always in military flying, the timings for this flight have been worked out meticulously to the second, but for now, despite the nagging sweephand on my stopwatch, time is suspended as we fly onwards into the desert night. Above us the stars glitter brightly through the clear air, while beneath us the blackness of the desert floor is spangled with the 'constellations' of Bedouin campfires. Reality seems a million lightyears away and there's an overwhelming illusion of cruising amongst the stars in deep space. We travel on in silence, each alone with our own thoughts in the small world of our dimly lit cockpits. My mind wanders through thoughts of my wife and friends back home: none of them will be aware that at this moment we are airborne on the way to Iraq. With those thoughts comes a sense of loneliness: paradoxically in a service where I have always been surrounded by close friends, three strangers now accompany me on the very night that death might be lurking over the Iraqi border. Just six feet behind me sits Platty. We've been flying together for a month now and I have come to trust him and grown used to his sometimes languid style. I enjoy flying with him, but still there is some distance between us. Only 100yd away are Spiv and Ken, who I have known for just five days. Although I have warmed to them both professionally and socially, my ill-concealed resentment of the way they replaced my own choice of wingmen has rather stilted our relationship. This is the first time they have flown with me, and I know that they will be watching with critical eyes. And so, rather than flying to war, as I had always imagined, in a closely-knit and well-honed team, it is with a disparate group whose make-up has more to do with service politics than any thing else.

'Bulldog, this is Bristol one-one and one-two,' Platty breaks the silence, checking in with the controller whose radar eye is watching over us tonight. At his airborne post well to the south of us, the strike controller can place a tick next to the first two Tornados on his list.

'Roger,' booms an impressively deep bass voice in response. The voice sounds as if it has come from an intergalactic starship orbiting way above us, rather than an aircraft based on a 1950s airliner circling just north of Riyadh. But that single word brings with it a feeling of reassurance and security. One by one all the other formations check in on the frequency. We listen amongst the callsigns for the ones who will directly affect us: 'Stingray', the four USAF Strike Eagle fighter bombers which will be attacking Al-Amarah immediately before us, 'Mobil', our fighter escort and 'Pearl', the Wild Weasels whose job is to suppress any anti-aircraft guns or missiles before they get us. All told, there are about 100 aircraft involved in tonight's operation, including tankers, early-warning radar aircraft, and electronic jammers, as well as the strike aircraft and the fighter escort. Most are provided by the huge USAF detachments in Saudi Arabia and the aircraft carrier USS *Kitty Hawk* on station in the Persian Gulf, but the presence of our four bombers and eight French fighters make it a 'Coalition' force. Theoretically at least, this operation is in support of a United Nations resolution and our presence gives the force some legal credibility. However the niceties of the political big picture do not concern us at the moment. Our focus is simply on reaching and striking our target – and coming back in one piece.

As we approach the tanker tow-lines it is time to descend. Our tanker, a Victor, has taken off from Bahrain some ten minutes ahead of us and will be at the rendezvous at 18,000ft.

I take us down to 17,000ft. Platty starts looking into the radar scope to find our Victor, while I flick on the Tacan beacon which will give me a read-out of the range to the tanker. Fifty miles, forty-nine miles – the Tacan range starts clicking down as we and the Victor approach the rendezvous from opposite directions. If everything goes according to the plan, the Victor will get to the rendezvous point a couple of minutes before us, then do a U-turn to pass the rendezvous a second time fractionally ahead of us, but this time we are all going in the same direction. Then all we have to do is close up the last few hundred yards to join him. But it all hinges on him finding the rendezvous point successfully at exactly the right time with his rather basic navigation equipment. I look down at the Tacan and realize with dismay that the range is decreasing too quickly. It can only mean one thing: the tanker has made a small error in his timing and instead of us joining up behind him at the rendezvous we are going to meet him head on several miles short. We can no longer rely on precision navigation and timing to get us together properly. It is up to us to find the tanker ourselves using radar and our eyes and then manoeuvre into the right piece of sky.

'Contact – twenty miles and five degrees left of the nose,' barks Platty. I look but don't see anything but stars and campfires. But I know that I'll see something soon and swing right slightly to give me a little more turning space, all the while looking to where I expect the tanker's lights to materialize.

'Got him,' a cluster of dimly flashing lights appears just left of the canopy arch. A quick glance down to the Tacan: fifteen miles. The geometry is far from perfect, but with a closing speed of nearly 1,000kts I must turn now if there is going to be any chance of catching him. We turn left. Quite gently at first, then tightening, all the while very aware of my number two trying to hang on to our right wing as we manoeuvre. The tanker floats directly above us, its spot-lit underside like a ghostly spaceship amongst the desert stars. As we roll out a mile behind him, I feel quite pleased to have salvaged something from this shambles. Now we must observe the correct etiquette and move into formation on the tanker's right wing before we are allowed to go behind him to the refuelling hoses. Just as I am in the process of joining formation, the tanker turns away from us back towards the rendezvous. As the join-up has been done in the dark and in complete radio silence it's hardly surprising that the tanker crew are unaware that we are already hanging onto his coat-tails. Still convinced that they haven't yet overflown the rendezvous, they don't expect to see us for another minute or so. Instinctively I push the throttles up to full power to follow, but I cannot keep up. Instead I have to cut the corner and, with the bad manners born of necessity, I go straight for the left hose and leave Spiv to sort his own life out behind the right.

In daylight, the refuelling basket looks like a metal shuttlecock about 3ft across, on the end of a 20ft hose which snakes out of a pod under the tanker's wing. Tonight, though, it is just a circle of dull-white luminescent spots oscillating gently behind the faint silhouette of the pod. The basket's oscillations are made unpredictable by occasional bumps of turbulence, and as we get closer, the bow wave from my aircraft will try to push it away. I close behind the circle of lights, and then transfer my attention to the pod, aware all the time of the presence of the Victor's vastness just a few feet away in the darkness. I move gently forward, but it doesn't look right and I miss well below the basket. Try again slightly higher. I am supposed to formate on the tanker and ignore the basket, but I sneak a quick look. I am going to miss again, so I try to correct and end up making a wild lunge and missing anyway. An awful thought now strikes me – what if I am unable to get on the tanker tonight? I'll have to call in the spare and head for home, the laughing-stock of the air force. I realize that my professional reputation is on the line, and I realize, too, that Spiv and Ken, not to mention the crew of the Victor will be taking a close interest in my progress. I drop back and try to relax a little. A quick glance across shows that Number Two is already taking on fuel – at least he's OK. Count to five and then try again. Third time lucky, I hope. The third try is much better, but I still need a slight lunge to get in and a fist full of power to stay there. I jab the throttles into reheat, then slam them almost back to idle as they light, a tell-tale flash of flame from our jet-pipes advertising my ineptitude to the world. But we are in and a green light glowing on the tanker's pod shows me that fuel is flowing at last. I breathe a sigh of relief, ashamed of my performance at this relatively simple procedure, but find some excuse in the fact that I've hardly flown over the last couple of weeks. I realize that I have spent most of that time preparing for this mission in a cycle of planning, cancellation, re-planning and re-cancellation as our American allies have dithered about what to do. I am also still suffering from the after effects of the heavy cold, which laid me up in bed for a day. Perhaps, too, I hadn't appreciated how the extra weight and drag of the bombs would affect the aircraft.

As we fill up, I can feel the aircraft getting heavier and it needs more power to stay with the Victor. The gauges show that we are full, but we stay in contact a little longer – with a few more minutes to go before we have to leave, we might as well burn the tanker's fuel instead of our own. Soon, though, the time comes to depart, and we do so in rather better order than we joined, in smart echelon from the tanker's left wing just as the second pair arrive to refuel. Now we have another twenty minutes to kill before the 'push time' when we will cross the Iraqi border. Dropping down a couple of thousand feet we set up a race-track holding pattern in the marshalling area just south of the border and once again we are alone with our thoughts amongst the stars.

A busy mind doesn't have time to be frightened, but twenty minutes of enforced idleness is an unwelcome opportunity for fear and uncertainty to come bubbling into the consciousness. Although I don't think I'm superstitious, I have to admit that the omens are not good for tonight. The fact that my first aircraft became unserviceable on start-up and my performance on the tanker only seem to reinforce that view. Even the date is not an auspicious one for my own squadron and I shoot an involuntary glance up at the stars above us, hoping perhaps for some sign of a 'Guardian Angel'. But I find no reassurance in the familiar patterns of the constellations, just a stark reminder amongst the millions of stars of my own insignificance.

As we continue our orbit, fear is like a dull ache – a deep sense of unease at the unknown, tempered only by the knowledge that there's no way out. Nearly twenty years ago, I had travelled alone by train to my new school: in the rear carriage, facing backwards in the last row of seats, I had watched the track and passing landmarks receding from me as the train rumbled onwards towards its destination unseen in the distance behind me. It was a journey that I didn't want to end, but knew that it inevitably must: the same sense of unease had accompanied me then. Now, from the cockpit of a Tornado just south of the Iraqi border, the familiar landmarks of my life stretch into the distance along the track of passing years.

It had taken us fifty minutes to reach the tanker, then another ten minutes to fill up followed by a twenty-minute hold. By the time we are about to push over the border into Iraq, we have already been flying for 1½ hours. So far, in content at least, it has been like any other sortie from Dhahran: All that is about to change, though. As my mind grapples with a cocktail of emotions, of expectation, excitement and dread, I spare a thought for Gilbert. Our airborne spare is not needed tonight. He is waiting on the tanker's wing, full of fuel and loaded with bombs, for the call that will not come. I can imagine the disappointment – no less crushing because it was entirely expected – that he will feel as he turns back for Dhahran.

'OK that's the steering for alpha, and you can follow the timing,' from Platty. The clock's hand has moved on and fear is banished as my mind becomes busy again. The navigation displays now point me towards our push point on the border and the timing index in my HUD centres itself, showing that we are on time. Out to our left, our Number Two has moved off towards his own push point some five miles west of ours, trailing a sheet of blue flame from his reheat as he fine tunes his timing.

Platty and I quickly check the correct settings on our weapons controls, set up our electronic-warfare equipment and switch off all the kit that we do not need. Off go the aircraft lights and I look to the left just as Spiv and Ken douse their lights and they disappear into the black emptiness.

We head almost due north, pointing directly at Tallil. Hopefully this feint will distract the Iraqi defences. Hopefully, too, our altitude now will confuse them further. Any height finding radars looking at us will lead the defences further north to expect us at this lower level. Cruising onwards past the scattered lights below, the clear air gives an overwhelming illusion of being close to the desert floor, as if we are much lower than we really are. It is not a comfortable feeling. I push the throttles forward to full power, and the aircraft maintains a gradual climb up towards our height block. Once there, we will be deconflicted from the other formations and should be safely above the reach of Triple-A. There is no rush to get there. All the US aircraft are well above us, and the Iraqi gunners well ahead of us. In fact the Strike Eagle section, who are to attack Al Amarah immediately before us, are still behind us somewhere. Their higher cruising speed means that they will overtake us en route, well above us. That, too, should give the Iraqis something to think about.

Over enemy territory Platty and I are constantly checking and double-checking the aircraft systems. Ears listen for radio calls and eyes strain, searching the darkness for trouble. Ten minutes after crossing the border, the settlements along the Euphrates are a belt of densely packed lights. I scan the RWR more frequently now. Perhaps it will warn of activity from the SAM 3 site at Tallil, twenty miles west of us. Perhaps it will reveal a Triple-A site lying in wait for us amongst the townships below. Meanwhile, the stopwatch counts down to the first strike time.

As we reach the Euphrates and the sweep hand advances another second. Platty counts down to the Nighthawk's time on target.

'Three, two, one...' I look out to my left in time to see a brilliant flash on the ground. My ears imagine a dull 'Thump' accompanying it.

'That's Tallil,' says Platty, just as I catch a glimpse in my peripheral vision of another flash further away to the southeast; Basrah. Back out to the west a colourful line of fireworks arcs gracefully upwards. Anti-aircraft gunfire, and pretty big stuff too, judging by the size of the dashes of light. I know that we're safely out of range, but it still sends a shiver down my spine.

'That's the Triple-A starting up,' I reply, quickly looking ahead for any sign of gunfire from the direction of our own target. Al Amarah is still sixty miles away and I cannot see anything in the distance. Then strangely Tallil, too, falls quiet.

Five minutes to go to our attack. Fear returns. It's the same nervous heart-thumping that comes just before you stand up to talk to a gathering of strangers. But the feeling evaporates as suddenly as it came: Platty and I have to deal with another problem. The forecast 60kt tailwind has become a 40kt headwind instead! The USAF met man has got it wrong by a 100kt. I curse him roundly. Now the only way to make our time over the target is to use the reheat to accelerate us back to the correct groundspeed. I push the throttles through the gate and feel a gentle push as both 'burners' light. The glow from the reheat flames surrounds us. I can see the incandescent light in the mirrors, and it is dimly reflected from the wings and fuel tanks. With it comes an intense feeling of vulnerability. To any observer we must look like a bright comet blazing across the sky. I feel sure that we are going to attract attention. The groundspeed increases slowly and we almost reach our time-line.

Then all hell breaks loose. The RWR shrieks in my headset. The display lights up like a neon sign. We have been locked up by missile-guidance radar. Instinctively I cancel the reheat and recheck the screen to see what is happening. Already Platty is jabbing the button to shove out a bundle of radar-confusing chaff from one of our counter-measures pods.

'SAM two,' I shout. A bright green strobe on the RWR screen shows the radar is right behind us.

'Shit,' shouts Platty, sounding a bit rattled. I know that the Iraqis have perfected a tactic of launching their SAMs ballistically towards their target, then illuminating the target with the radar only in the last few seconds. My guess is that that is what has happened thanks to our dash with the reheat. I pitch the aircraft up slightly, rolling hard left and booting in the right rudder. I need to be able to see in that blind spot right underneath us. Is there a missile coming up after us? It's almost pointless looking – by now the rocket motor will have burnt out and a large unlit telegraph pole (or maybe a salvo of three) will be racing towards us at three times the speed of sound.

More than anything else my reaction is of stunned disbelief – I really cannot believe this is happening to me. Platty is still punching out the chaff. Now I'm rolling right, craning my neck round to see beneath us. Although I'm most unlikely to see the fiery trail of a rocket motor, at least my coarse control inputs have put the aircraft into a classic three-dimensional weave. That, plus Platty's cloud of chaff, and our countermeasures should confuse the missile enough to make us safe.

Decision time – do we punch the tanks and bombs off and run for home, or do we take our chances and press on? My mind races through all the missile sites on Harry's map. Surely none were round here. We can't be in range! The RWR is still 'trilling' away, but now cold logic takes over. We're well outside the range of all the known SAM 2 sites. The nearest must be miles away. Perhaps the Iraqi battery commander, working without his acquisition radar, fired on the lights of our reheat thinking they were nearer than they really were – an easy illusion on such a crystal-clear night. Or perhaps it was just a false alarm triggered by the myriad of radio transmitters out there. Still in disbelief, I go for the more comforting second option.

'Ignore it - it's got to be a false alarm. Let's press to the target,' I try to sound authoritative. Platty doesn't sound totally convinced, but he busies himself getting into the attack routine.

'We're running late,' he says. All the manoeuvring has slowed us down again and the only way to get back on our time line is to use the reheat again. I am very reluctant to do so after what happened last time and I certainly don't want to advertise our presence to any gunners searching the skies near Al Amarah. I decide to accept that we're going to be late. I also decide not to tell the others: it will be too late now for them to adjust their timings to suit us and a call will just add confusion. I know that Chris and Taff behind us certainly will not be early because of the headwind, so there is no chance of bumping into them. I also know that there is sufficient latitude in this particular attack to let us get away with a twenty-second timing error. It is a luxury of this particular attack profile. Normally the timing tolerance is plus or minus five seconds.

Platty selects the attack symbology and a green bar appears in the HUD showing me where the aircraft computer thinks the target is. With no lights showing, the target is invisible in the darkness and the target bar hovers over a black void. Suddenly there is a bright flash next to the target bar as the last Strike Eagle drops his bombs. At least I know that the computer position is pretty accurate. It is certainly accurate enough to drop a laser-guided bomb, but the rules of engagement say that we must identify the target positively ourselves before we can drop. Platty is working hard

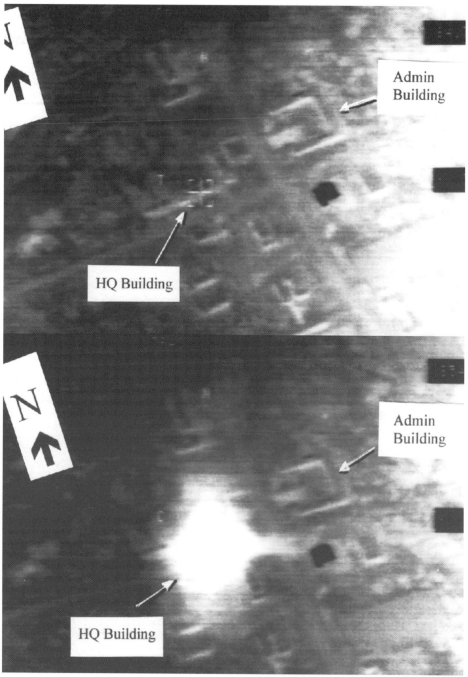

Still images from Ken's Tiald video of the attack on the IOC HQ building at Al Amarah. The administration building provides orientation. At top, Ken designates the building and at bottom, the bombs detonate on his mark. (Crown Copyright/MoD)

on the radar. He is trying to identify the offsets which we planned beforehand to help us find the target. The first is a road bridge in the marshes, but high floodwater after all the rain masks it on radar. The second offset also proves useless. The pressure is on. If Platty cannot find the third offset, we cannot drop. That really would make us a laughing stock.

'Got it,' Platty yells triumphantly as he finds our last offset, a bridge over the river two miles beyond the target.

Thirty seconds out. An exchange of codewords tells Ken that we're on our way, and he lets us know that he has found the target with the pod and is happy for us to drop. Platty and I run through our final checks and make sure that all the right switches have been made. As the time-to-go runs down in the HUD, my thumb is clamped on the attack commit button on the stick top. Thump, Thump, Thump! Just like driving fast over three large cobblestones. The bombs have come off.

I transmit, 'Stores away,' and then pull back on the stick and rolling right to barrel away from the bombs in case they explode below the aircraft as they arm. The aircraft is much lighter now and responds much more crisply as we wheel off to the southwest to clear the Triple-A sites along the Tigris. Behind us as we turn I am aware of the flash as the bombs explode.

Chris and Taff also run in to the strong headwind and like me they have to plug in the burners to get back on time. It only takes seven seconds for them to get back on time, but they are seven agonisingly long seconds. The same feeling of vulnerability, having hurled off the cloak of darkness, haunts them both. Two apprehensive pairs of eyes scan the RWR anxiously. Luckily they are spared the excitement that Platty and I enjoyed – they are back on the time and safely hidden once again in the folds of the night. In the Number Three aircraft, Mal finds the target easily – although it is a tiny building, the fan of roads nearby shows up clearly. I can hear the curt transmissions that tell me that Number Three and Four are running through their attack successfully. As they come off the target, the flash of their bombs detonating is accompanied by sporadic anti-aircraft fire. Taken off guard, the Iraqi gunners have finally got into position just as the attack is over.

We still have twenty minutes left over enemy territory as we run for home. Down below us, along the banks of the Tigris, occasional muzzle flashes show where small arms are being fired in impotent rage at the noise of our engines. We've obviously stirred them up, but having taken down their radars and control systems there is nothing they can do about it. Even so, Platty and I are still keyed up and alert for trouble. But none comes.

'Looked like good hits on your target, Mike,' replies Ken's reassuring voice.

'The second target looked good, too,' adds Mal. I double-click the microphone to acknowledge. The leg home goes on rails. A couple of fleeting paints appear on the RWR, but nothing else. There is a growing feeling of relief but also one of anti-climax. It certainly hasn't been as exciting as a *Red Flag* sortie! I feel a bit of a fraud – it was hardly what I had imagined. On the other hand we have reaped the benefits of an immaculately planned and successful surprise attack. The lights go back on as we cross back into Saudi airspace and we can relax a little. A couple of minutes later, the cluster of lights reappear at my right shoulder, announcing that Spiv and Ken have rejoined us for the recovery to Dhahran.

Once back on the ground, we taxied back past a battery of photo flashes from the groundcrew on the French Mirage line. Those not wielding cameras were frantically waving thumbs up at us. For a moment we felt like conquering heroes returning. Our own groundcrew gave us a warm reception, too. They were pleased to see us back and the aircraft in one piece. They were also delighted to see that we had delivered the bombs and the messages on them, to Saddam. In the corner of the line hut, the television announced great excitement in the CNN studios: 'Breaking news – Iraq under air attack from coalition aircraft once more.' The handshaking over, we had a quick technical debrief with them before retiring to the ops block. There we signed in from the sortie and returned our pistols, then debriefed the sortie amongst ourselves over a can of Coke. The tired crews lounging in tatty easy chairs were noticeably more relaxed than when I had briefed them over four hours previously! We strolled over to see the photo interpreters and watch the Tiald videos. The films confirmed that the attacks had gone as planned and we had scored direct hits on both targets. With great satisfaction, we knew that we could hold our heads up when we joined the rest of the crews at the mass debrief in the USAF ops block.

The USAF briefing room was full of sweaty aircrew, all chatting noisily, when we got there. I gave the package commander a still printout from the Tiald video showing our bombs exploding in the right place, which seemed to impress him suitably. We managed to squeeze in, and finding ourselves some vacant plastic chairs next to the Strike Eagle drivers, we added our voices to the throng. Suddenly the room fell silent to the scrape of chairs as everyone stood up for the arrival of the General. The first event, the roll call, told us the most important thing: that everyone is safely back. Then each formation ran through their results. Overall the attack was a great success, though some crews had been unlucky with technical hitches or had experienced problems finding their targets. The RAF team had done well. I felt that the taxpayers could be proud of us. We were a scratch team, most of whom had never even seen a laser-guided bomb before that evening, yet we had managed to drop six of them precisely on our targets. I am pleased to say that our achievement was not lost on the Americans.

The debriefing over, we retired to the International Hotel for a well-earned meal. We all felt immensely pleased with ourselves for a job well done. I think I had all expected to be met with a barrage of Triple-A, but in the event we had been unopposed. That made me feel more like a burglar than a brave aviator: if they had shot at us, at least I would have felt more honourable. I realized that I should be very satisfied that a well-planned raid had achieved complete surprise. However, we all had an overwhelming feeling of anti-climax. We retired to our flat at 2.30am in the morning, where Taff produced four miniature bottles of whisky which he had somehow managed to smuggle in; one each for Platty, me, Chris and one for himself.

'I've been waiting for a suitable moment,' he explained. We toasted our success and each other. The whisky tasted fantastic; all the better for our enforced abstinence during our stay in Saudi, and all the more enjoyable because it was illicit. It was

Daily Express

THURSDAY JANUARY 14 1993   WEATHER: WINDY   30p

ON THE ATTACK: British Tornados joined in the lightning raid

Saddam climbs down as Bush and Major issue warning: We will be back

BRITISH JETS BLITZ IRAQ

- Over 100 warplanes blast missile sites
- Tornado pilots safe after airfield raids

By CHRIS BUCKLAND and JOHN INGHAM in London
and MIKE PARRY and PHILIP FINN in New York

ALLIED warplanes last night launched lightning punishment attacks on Saddam Hussein's missile sites.

Waves of British, American and French jets delivered what Pentagon officials called a "spanking not a beating" for the Iraqi tyrant.

And after a successful mission with no western losses, he was warned: We will be back.

Saddam immediately caved in, promising to obey UN rulings from now on.

The allied force of more than 100 bombers and fighters pounded the weapons he had moved into Iraq's southern no-fly zone.

They also targeted airfields and command control centres.

The operation, spearheaded by U.S. Stealth fighters and RAF Tornado GRI bombers, met with some resistance.

American F14 Tomcats came under missile attack. But all the allied jets returned to their bases unscathed.

John Major, hailing the mission a success, said more strikes would follow without warning if Iraq further breached UN Gulf War sanctions. Saddam swiftly bowed to the pressure pledging to halt his

Page 2 Column 1

SO CONFIDENT: A happy Diana after returning to work yesterday

Smiling Diana rides out the storm

PRINCESS Diana and Prince Charles were in separate parts of the country yesterday as the row over the way their marriage breakdown was revealed raged on.

Diana vowed to carry on despite the pressure as she toured a hospice in Lancashire — her first public engagement since Christmas.

Charles broke a Norfolk shooting holiday to go to the Shetlands with Prince Philip.

Father and son brushed aside questions on the latest revelations.

A new row broke out when MI5 was accused of bugging the "Camillagate" phone call, said to be with Charles's friend Camilla Parker Bowles.

Media tycoon Rupert Murdoch moved to disassociate himself from the scandal after transcripts of the tape were published in Australia.

I'll never give up, says Diana: Page 3

Did MI5 bug royal phones? Pages 4 and 5

INSIDE: Weather 2, Opinion 8, Foreign News 10, Ross Benson 19, Crosswords & Target 33, TV 34 & 35, Radio & Millionaires' Club 36, Letters & Stars 37, Money 43- 45, Sport 46 - 52

We made it onto the front pages of most of the national newpapers on 14 January. This is how the Daily Express *reported our exploits.* (by kind permission of Express Newspapers)

then that I realized that the evening's events had brought the four of us much closer together. We had faced a challenge together, a shared experience which was unique to the four of us.

'We'll be doing this in Bosnia, next year,' I predicted.

We were not needed at work until 11.00pm the following night, so we enjoyed the luxury of another late start. The detachment was once again required to keep two crews at readiness, twenty-four hours a day. We were back in the same position we had been in after the original shoot-down over two weeks before. Tin helmets, crews at readiness, waiting. Meanwhile, the politicians were waiting to see what the Iraqis would do next. The Generals and Admirals were pondering their next move, too.

We reported to the ops desk to find out if there had been any developments overnight. Nothing new, but Keith pushed a signal over to me.

'You might be interested in this,' he said. The signal was from the C-in-C RAF Strike Command. 'My warm congratulations on a job well done to you and all your *Jural* detachment; especially tonight's aircrews. I have reported to the secretary of state and the chief of the defence staff. Both wished me to send on their personal congratulations and good wishes. Well done.' It was actually addressed to the Group Captain in Riyadh, but I felt that at least some of the congratulation and good wishes were meant for us.

Terry was holding a supper party at his house that evening, and he kindly invited me to bring the boys along as well. We all jumped at the chance to enjoy a 'normal' social life. Having hit the international news that day with our exploits the night before, we were minor celebrities. I was delighted to see Terry and Jeremy again and also Vic, my old flight commander from my first tour, who was there on good form. It was wonderful to share some time, so soon after seeing action, with friends from my closely-knit past. The presence of the 'Old Crusaders' went some way to counterbalancing the feeling of loneliness that had struck me en-route to the tanker. At 10.30pm we thanked our hosts and left for Dhahran and a night in sleeping bags on the floor of the operations planning room.

Hopes of a quiet night were quickly shattered. The new DETCO called me into the office.

'Mike, another strike has been planned for tomorrow – are you happy to lead it again,' he asked. I told him that of course I was.

'Well I want to change the line-up slightly. I'm still concerned at Chris. He didn't seem at all happy the other night, and I'd rather replace him than take any risks. I'm taking him and Taff off your team and replacing them with Stox and Jack.'

I was shocked. I still had total confidence in Chris and I did not relish the addition of newcomers to dilute my team still further. I knew that theoretically any Tornado crews should be able to operate effectively together; but I also believed strongly that we should fight like we trained, as closely-knit teams who flew together regularly. I also realized that the new DETCO was taking the opportunity to get his own squadron blooded. Stox and Jack were both from the Goldstars. In fact this was an entirely sensible move on his part: if he could trickle crews through the action he would always have a pool of experience as other crews, like us, returned home to Brüggen. At a more cynical level, there would be reflected glory for the Goldstars if they took an active role in these offensive operations. But I certainly could not complain at his choice of replacement crew. Jack, the navigator was a bright 'Geordie', a Gulf War veteran, a QWI and overall a very likeable and capable character. Stox was a very good and aggressive pilot, something of a 'loveable rogue.' He, too, would be good value. No, I could not complain about the new DETCO's choice, but I still felt as if I had betrayed Taff and Chris by agreeing. We had become close over the last few weeks and if ever there was a crew who had my complete confidence, it was them. I knew that they would be deeply disappointed by the decision; I also knew that they would realize that I had no choice in the matter.

I grabbed Platty and the two of us went along to yet another planning meeting with the Americans. Al Kut and Al Jarra were back on. The two plans of a week or so previously had been combined and resurrected. We would take part in a simultaneous attack on the air-defence centre and its neighbouring airfield. The first problem was our target: we were tasked against a large concrete bunker housing the ops set up for one of the squadrons based on the airfield. I wondered if our weapons would penetrate that much concrete. I discussed the matter with Ken and Jack, the two QWIs.

'I think that the only weapon that will damage that target is the American GBU twenty-four, two thousand pounder,' Ken advised.

'Can we get our hands on any, and can we carry them on a Tornado even if we can get hold of them,' I asked.

'Leave it with us and we'll find out,' replied Jack. The two of them went across to the flightline to speak with the armourers. I settled down with the file to read all about this new weapon. First of all it was a 2,000lb bomb, with a thick steel casing designed to penetrate concrete before exploding. There would be some difficulties in loading it onto a Tornado, but they didn't seem insurmountable. The biggest challenge would be in dropping the thing. The weapon's aerodynamics and guidance system were considerably more complex than our first generation laser bombs. Instead of riding the laser beam straight to the target as our 1,000lb bombs did, this one was dropped about twice the distance away and flew to overhead the target, then dived vertically into it. Delivery height and speed would be crucial and we would have to work out a profile for the designator to mark the target for twice the amount of time that we were used to with our present profile. Ken and Taff came back with the news that the armourers thought the weapon could be loaded on a Tornado and would get one from the Americans to try it out the next day. The Americans, for their part had helpfully agreed to let us have whatever bombs we needed. By 4.00am we had a plan sketched out and we had brainstormed our way through all the operational implications of dropping the weapons: so much for a quiet night.

We need not have bothered! By the time we were back in at lunchtime the whole plan had been binned once more. Yet another new plan was promised for that evening. With no more planning for a while, we took the opportunity to look at the post-strike reconnaissance photographs of our raid. It was very satisfying to see them showing that we had inflicted serious damage on both targets. Of all the formations which had participated in the raid, we were the only force to have achieved a 100 percent success rate. The rest of the afternoon was filled with a visit by Mochers, a long-established Tornado QWI, who was the weapons expert at the headquarters in Riyadh. He had been sent down to look at our plans to use the GBU 24. Mochers was a nice bloke, but he had an 'honours degree' in being miserable. He arrived with a long face and I think had expected to see a complete shambles. Instead he found that we had done all of our homework in the early hours of the morning. We had answers to all his questions and the engineers were able to show him how they were going to load the thing. At least the morning's work had not been wasted and we knew that if called on we could use the larger bomb. I think that Mochers went away impressed and pleasantly surprised.

When I returned from saying cheerio to Mochers, the new DETCO had news for me.

'You're back on tomorrow, Mike, with a time on target of noon local time. While you were away I sent Platty to the mass brief with Ken and Spiv. They've started the planning for you. Good luck.'

I returned to the planning room, to find my team assembled and waiting for me. The maps of the target area were neatly pinned up on the wall for us all to see. When I inspected the maps and I saw our target, I nearly went ballistic. It was at the air-defence centre just north of An Najaf. The target was north of the 32nd Parallel and rather too close for my comfort to the military airfields to the south of Baghdad. It was one thing to attack Al Jarra in the middle of a stream, but quite another to stick ourselves out on a limb, especially as we were the only coalition aircraft without a real capability to defend ourselves against fighters. All the USAF mud-movers were intrinsically manoeuvrable aircraft with effective air-to-air radars and radar-guided missiles. The Tornado was designed as a low-level bomber, a role for which it had been perfected at the expense of high-level performance. At medium-level, heavy with bombs and fuel, it would have all the agility of a pregnant hippopotamus. Furthermore, although the navigators could misuse the radar to find a slow moving and predictable tanker, it was designed for looking at the ground, and could not give us warning of incoming hostile fighters. Finally, the heat-seeking missiles we carried gave us only a limited air-to-air capability provided we saw the enemy first. Najaf struck me as being far too risky.

'Well, if you don't like it, go back and tell them,' said Spiv defensively. So I did. The package commander listened to my concerns and offered me a change of target. He explained that the new plan was to revisit the sites that we'd been to on the last airstrikes and finish off the targets that had been missed. If I didn't like An Najaf, I could go for some of the surviving radar aerials at Al Amarah. I looked at the available targets and realized with dismay that they were not really suitable for us, whereas the Americans had specific equipment to neutralize such targets. That led me back to An Najaf, where the radar control building had been missed by the US Navy during their attack on 13 January. It was almost identical to the one which we had hit at Al Amarah, so should be well within our capabilities.

Me in front of 'Delta Juliet,' the aircraft I flew on the first Operation Ingleton *sortie. The ground crew stencilled a LGB silhouette just above the 'Rettung' arrow to record a successful bombing mission 'sausage side.'*

'Well, I need to have assurance that our fighter escort will take out anything that looks like it might come near us,' I demanded. I was introduced to Jerry, a flight leader from the USAF Eagle fighter squadron. He assured me that if any Iraqi aircraft even as much as sniffed in our direction, his boys would shoot it down.

'We're mighty keen to get ourselves a MiG or two. You've got nothing to worry about – we'll shoot anything that moves.' Somewhat mollified, but still a bit suspicious that Jerry and his boys were using us as Foxbat bait again, I returned to our planning room, where Spiv shot me a 'told you so' look.

I decided that to minimize our risk from the air threat we should route directly to the target and attack it from the south, then scuttle back to the border by the shortest route. The problem here was that we would have to fly straight over a couple of Triple-A sites. I did not see that as a major problem. Light calibre Triple-A would not be a threat to us at our attack height, and in a way I relished the idea of challenging them head-on. In any case, I still thought that Iraqi fighter aircraft were a greater threat. The others went along with me, but there were some murmurings of dissent. We finished the detailed plans and retired to bed.

I was up early, at 6.00am, keyed up ready to go. At 6.05am a telephone call told me that we had been cancelled again. The rollercoaster of plan, re-plan, expectancy and cancellation was running again. It was emotionally draining. I sank back into my bed again.

In the afternoon we took four aircraft to Kuwait. It was a Tiald training sortie for the newest Goldstar crews whose work-up had been disrupted by our activities.

Tiald pod Rachel is joined by two 1,000lb laser-guided bombs underneath a Tornado.
(Marcus Cook)

We also took the opportunity to practise the GBU 24 profiles we had worked out for the Al Jarra plan. Choreographing an attack using these new weapons was a lot more complicated than the 1,000lb bombs which had become our bread-and-butter. It was hard work for both bomber and designator and our practice showed up a couple of problem areas we had not foreseen. I was very pleased we had been able to practise this attack over Kuwait in case we had to do it for real. Once we had ironed out all the teething problems, we left the Tiald crews to carry on practising while we dropped into low level. On the ground it was clear that the Kuwaitis were very worried about the recent developments. Army units were deployed across the desert. Here and there tanks were in position, artillery guns deployed, or platoons of infantrymen were digging positions in the sand. They seemed to be pleased to see us and we were greeted with waves as we sped past. We headed south, past the scattered hulks of Iraqi tanks abandoned in the sand after the last conflict, and pulled up for home.

Platty and I attended another mass planning meeting at midday on 17 January. We learnt that we would be flying that night against the same targets we planned for two nights earlier. This time a westerly wind was forecast, which put paid to my 'minimum exposure' plan with its northerly attack run. Our Triple-A site on the route was also reported to be trigger happy, so to the delight of the critics I agreed that we would re-plan the attack to run in from the west: That way we would at least avoid the Triple-A. Also we would be heading south back in the No Fly Zone when the bombs went off. I just hoped that Jerry and his merry band of cowboys in their Eagles could keep his side of the bargain. We had just finished replanning when the Americans changed their minds again. The mission was delayed until the next morning. What none of us realized at that point was that the US Navy was mounting a cruise-missile attack on Baghdad that night: The first we knew of this was when we came into work the following morning.

We awoke to a beautiful morning on 18 January. With clear skies and bright sunshine it was definitely a day to go flying. Platty and I came in early and spent thirty minutes before the mass brief at 7.00am checking through final details. Once more a set of rules of engagement were issued. I noticed that these were somewhat lengthier than those for Al Amarah. The reason was that we were expressly forbidden to do anything which might damage the nearby Shia holy site, the tomb of Mohammed's grandson Husayn. Not only would we have to identify the target independently before dropping weapons, but we would also have to establish that there was no risk to this site. We had not been aware of this constraint on the outskirts of the town when we had planned the attack. We double-checked our maps. Luckily the re-planned attack kept us well clear of the site. Somewhat relieved, we went over for the mass brief: More stirring stuff from the General, then back for our own briefing. This time, continuing our 'cities of Britain' theme, the Americans had decided we should be known as 'Norwich'. I ran through the plan once more, and stressed that we will take no chances. If we messed up the attack, then we would just bring the bombs back. With the US Navy close behind us, we did not have an option to re-attack.

The routine seemed quite familiar: pistols, survival kit, out to the aircraft, check the bombs. Once again I had chosen 'Bravo Papa' as my mount. Once again it let me down. This time I couldn't get the Havequick (HQ) to work. After a brief discussion, Platty and I decided that we could do without it, but the old superstitious doubts lingered in my mind. Had I opened Pandora's box? An even worse omen, it seemed that the non-HQ frequency was being jammed when we got airborne. There was a recording of English voices being played, calling out turns and speed changes like an early Jet Provost sortie. Were the Iraqis really clever enough to broadcast that sort of stuff on our frequency? I turned the volume down and managed to ignore it as we transited up to the tow-lines. It was a glorious day. All traces of the sullen grey rain clouds of the last few weeks had disappeared and the sun shone down on us. Down below the desert looked as fresh and exciting as it had done on my first sortie over 'sausage side'. I became brightly optimistic, putting all thoughts of HQ radios to the back of my mind.

The next surprise of the day was to find not one but two Victors on station. They had flown from Bahrain in formation and it was their voices which had been jamming our frequency. That, at least was one less worry! Lovely though it was to have two tankers it did complicate the issue, as our plan had been based on a single tanker. It was probably only a trivial detail to have more tankers than we needed, but in such circumstances you need as few changes to the plan as possible. The reason for the second tanker's presence was that it had been tasked to support the US Navy aircraft. The US Navy, we now discovered, had cancelled, perhaps sensibly after stirring up the hornets' nest with their cruise-missile attack the previous night. But it would have been nice to know about the extra tanker before we arrived.

I led Spiv to the front tanker and left the other free for Number Three and Four. With no need to leave our tanker for the back pair to use, we no longer needed to hold in an orbit before we pushed: we could now stay plugged in and burn the tanker's fuel instead of our own. As the push time approached, we left the hoses and, pausing briefly to give the tanker captain a cheery wave from alongside, we headed for the border. I must have been emotionally numbed by the previous two weeks of planning and cancelling and re-planning: I felt absolutely nothing this time as we crossed into hostile territory.

Once we were in Iraqi airspace I started a gentle weave in three dimensions. I didn't want to present any gunners on the ground with a predictable target. A couple of miles on my right I could see Spiv doing the same thing. The most important thing now was for me to keep a good look out under Spiv's aircraft so that I could warn him of gunfire or a missile launch. Apart from the occasional scan into the cockpit to check the instruments, my eyes were searching the desert ahead of him. Halfway along the leg up to the 32nd Parallel we passed the airfield at Ghalaysan, which we had visited with Kev and Larry on New Year's Eve. I thought that we might attract some attention from its defences. I shifted in my seat and tightened my grip on the throttles, ready to react instantly. But if anyone was at home, they were not shooting that day. We weaved our way past the airfield with a silent prayer of thanks and headed back out over desert. Ghalaysan was the only recognisable landmark in 300 miles of desert. We spent twenty anxious but thankfully uneventful minutes weaving our way up to the Parallel. As we crossed into this new piece of sky we carried out a slack cross-over turn, which put Spiv out very wide on our left and a few miles ahead of us. I lost sight of him in the brightness as Platty and I concentrated on getting sorted out for our attack. We were now heading due east exactly two miles north of the Parallel, with four minutes to run to the target. At least that was where we should have been. For a few heart stopping moments Platty told me he had problems with the navigation kit. With no features on the ground, I could not help him. Instead, I kept a good lookout to the north in case any Iraqi aircraft had managed to sneak past our fighters. After a manful struggle Platty announced that he had sorted the problem and we were OK.

A few last minute checks of the switches and then Platty goes into the attack symbology: The target bar appears in the HUD, but I still cannot identify anything on the ground. It is just a featureless vista of sand. Platty is confident, though, and is making encouraging noises as he works the radar. The time is running down to thirty seconds to go; I double check with Platty that he's happy. It's all going well. I transmit the codeword to Ken; silence. Time to go keeps running down. Platty is still happy. He's found all the offsets. The switches are made: just the commit button to go. My thumb hovers over it. Then Spiv shouts 'Stop, stop, stop.'

'Shit,' suddenly all the emotion that was absent for the last thirty minutes explodes into anger. We're going against an easy target on a perfect day. Today should be one of the highlights of my flying career: Now that idea has been blown out of the water. Why won't Spiv let us drop? The frustration of being over a target in Iraq with a full bomb load in perfect weather conditions is unbelievable and unbearable. I have not dropped on targets before because the weather was bad or they were late shows at low level, but at medium level on a beautiful clear day? I cannot believe it! I know that we briefed no re-attack, but that was only because the US Navy was supposed to be following us through. There is no navy. There is no Triple-A. Perhaps we can try again.

'Can you re-attack,' I ask curtly.

'Affirm,' comes the equally curt reply. We head back westwards. I don't know it, but Ken's pod is not giving him a good picture. The infra-red camera is no good in today's thermal conditions and the video camera is very grainy. The only way he is going to find the target is by recognizing the road layout inside the site.

Meanwhile, Mal's pod, built slightly differently, is much better and he has a clear video picture to work with. Even so, when Stox calls that he is twenty seconds from release, Mal still has not found the target. But he has found the site and he is confident that he can make out the radar control building. In fact he is still trying to find it when Stox calls that his bombs are on their way. Now the pressure is really on. Another twenty seconds before weapons impact. Mal finds the main gate of the site on the road from Baghdad, and then follows the road as it turns south then back west. Bingo – there's the building. Mal locks onto it with the laser. Seconds later Stox's three bombs are clearly visible on the video streaking towards the building, smashing into it in a towering cloud of dust and debris.

'Touchdown and the crowds go wild,' calls Mal – a little joke for our benefit, but he hits the wrong button and transmits it to everyone on the primary strike frequency. The second pair has made their attack successfully and are already homebound.

We're still heading eastwards to set up again for another attack. I still don't know why we have been unable to drop. Ken has not offered us any explanation, but he has said he was happy to re-attack, so I assume there's been some sort of 'Switch Pigs' in the other aircraft. With no secure radio to enquire what went wrong, I am reluctant to ask for more details. It does nothing for my dark mood. Unfortunately anger has clouded my judgement. Rather than finding out, I assume that Ken will be able to sort out the problem second time round. I assume that he will know what I want.

'Ten miles, OK,' I ask, rather ambiguously.

'Roger, ten miles,' from Ken. He thinks it is an instruction rather than a question. Each of us thinks the other is setting up this re-attack. Ken thinks I am because I'm the leader. I think Ken is because he is the only one who knows what went wrong. At cross-purposes, we swing back to the east and go through the motions again. In our aircraft it all goes like clockwork. Having seen them before, Platty finds the offsets easily and we are set up again to drop.

Again my code word is answered with silence: again just as we approach the drop point Spiv intervenes with 'Stop, stop, stop.' I have to accept that I will be taking the bombs back. It is time to go home and push our luck no further. Very reluctantly and with a deep sense of failure, I head back towards the safety of the Saudi border. Spiv reappears in formation and we weave our way southwards in stony silence. Three hundred miles of barren desert passes beneath us and as each passes my resentment grows. My anger simmers away for the next hour until we get to Dhahran.

This time it was thumbs down as we passed the French line. I was still angry.

'This had better be good,' I remarked pointedly to Ken and Spiv when they boarded the minibus back to the operations block.

'Well, how do you think we feel,' replied Spiv. He was absolutely right. I had not stopped to consider the disappointment and failure they must have both felt. At the debrief Ken explained that he just could not see the target at all on the Tiald screen. He was despondent. Both he and Spiv were unhappy about the way the re-attack had been handled and they were right. After specifically briefing that we would not do it I had changed my mind on the spur of the moment. I have no doubt that if Darren and Bamber had been there we would have been able to cobble together a re-attack which would have worked, or at least given the Tiald operator another fair chance. That was purely because we worked together often and knew exactly how each other operated. Spiv and Ken did not have the benefit of that experience. As it was, largely because in the ambiguities of my transmissions, Ken never got a decent go the second time round. On the plus side, the back pair were ecstatic about their success. And we were still the only force with a 100 percent record of hitting our targets. We went across to the RIC to see the Tiald video. On the large screen there, it was easy to see that Ken's marker came up right over the target, but he could not see it and moved his marker away, getting lost as he did so. The audiotape made us realize how hard he was working and what a nightmare he was having. Mal's tape showed a very different picture. It was much clearer. We checked and found out that the lenses in the two video cameras were different. The lighting conditions of the day favoured Mal's lens, whereas Ken's had been virtually useless on the tiny screen he had in the cockpit. He was onto a loser before we even started.

'I'm sorry, mate, you did your best,' I put a hand on his shoulder. He deserved an apology. I had been out of order.

The new DETCO had news for me when we returned to the operations desk.

'The group captain says do not worry about the no-drop. It is good PR because it shows that we are respecting the rules of engagement,' he told me. I could understand how important that was, given the American propensity to spray bombs and cruise missiles about. So that was a 100 percent record for hits on targets and obeying the Rules of Engagement. Even so it did not feel like a very satisfactory day.

I took the whole of the next day off. The news was that we could go home a week later, which at least was something to look forward too. It was difficult to envisage going back to reconnaissance patrols after our experiences of bombing. It would be difficult to keep the enthusiasm going for that. The new DETCO realized that, and was keen for us to move on as soon as we decently could. He suggested that it might be a good time to handover as detachment flight commander to Greg, who was the next in line. That would also mean handing over the lead of any potential future airstrikes. I need not have worried about missing out. The following day Bill Clinton was inaugurated as the 42nd President of the United States of America. Rather late in the day we wondered how much of the crisis had been engineered by the Americans so that George H.W. Bush could have a last crack at his enemy from the Gulf War. That might explain the stories of the rapidly moving static missile sites that suddenly completely disappeared overnight.

Mal's view of HMS Nottingham *– the Royal Navy's contribution to enforcing the No Fly Zone!* (Marcus Cook)

Or perhaps it had been engineered by Saddam to 'cock a snook' at Mr Bush and remind him that of all the major leaders involved in the Gulf War, only he, Saddam Hussein, was still in power. Whatever the real reasons for the crisis, one thing was clear: we had merely been pawns in a much bigger game.

It was fun reading through the newspaper reports of our activities. Some reports were well written while others were works of complete fiction. Our favourite was from the *Mail on Sunday* on the 17 January. It was an article by Sandy Gall, who had managed to fill two pages with his 'graphic front-line account on the RAF top guns who where the heroes of last week's strike on Iraq.' He had not even met any of us, but we were delighted that he still managed to be very complimentary! The RAF was being very protective about us and would not let the press have any direct contact. What amused us was that Sandy Gall had been staying at the International Hotel on the night of the first raid, and if he had come down to the restaurant in the early hours of the morning, he would have got himself a real scoop!

After catching up with all the newspapers, it took me a morning to hand over to Greg. There was a fair amount of 'niff-naff' that went with the flight commander job that all had to be explained. Then I took him through the planning routine and passed on what tips I could. I felt that the most important thing was for him not to have to learn everything from scratch as we had done. The last Al Jarra plan using the GBU 24 was still on ice. Platty and I went through it in minute detail so he would know why we had decided to do things the way we had. I knew that he would probably want to change things, just as we had done when we took over Frank's plan, but it was important that he appreciated the consequences of amending any detail. Although I was proud to be able to pass on a going concern, I was sad to hand over the leadership aspect of the operation. I would have liked the chance to have a third go: Third time lucky. Despite the great success of the two missions we had flown, I had not been able to produce a perfect performance. I was disappointed and it hurt my professional pride. Overall, though I had to admit that handing everything on was a weight from my shoulders. I was looking forward to going home.

In the afternoon it was great to sit as Number Four on a training sortie over the Gulf. The Royal Navy had sent HMS *Nottingham* to the area as a show of force. It was difficult to envisage quite how a naval destroyer was going to help out with enforcing the NFZ but it was a kind thought on the part of the Admiralty. Their practical help was to invite us to bomb their splash target. This was a small raft towed behind the ship so that it threw up a large splash of water a 100yd behind the ship. It made a pleasant change from the normal oil barrels in the sand, or rusting hulks in the Wash that we normally practised our bombing against. The navy was usually generous with scoring the bomb fall, too.

It was a lovely day for flying. The deep pellucid-blue waters of the Gulf were a welcome contrast to the yellow-brown desert or the blackness of night which had been our scenery for the last few weeks. Carrying practice bombs on the aircraft instead of the real thing also gave the sortie a recreational air. It was going to be fun and we were certainly going to enjoy it. We followed Spiv and Ken, who were leading the back pair, towards the ship's last known position. The Gulf was surprisingly busy with shipping, but we soon found our warship, grey and business-like in a clear area of sea. The splash target was streamed and we filled our boots bombing it. Once we were bombed out it was time to 'wire' the ship. It was the unwritten rule that the RN expected us to fly past the ship as low and as fast as we dared. We did our best, but I suspect they would have found our efforts pretty tame in comparison with flypasts from Fleet Air Arm hooligans they were used to! As we came off *Nottingham*, there was a large shape on the horizon: USS *Kitty Hawk*. Spiv called me into close formation and we called up the *Kitty Hawk* to ask if we could fly an approach to the deck. Aware that we were on display I made sure that we stuck to Spiv's wing like glue. I managed a couple of sneaky peeks at the ship as we went past though. As a ship it was absolutely enormous, easily dwarfing anything else I had seen. But as an airfield, particularly for operating fast jets, it was unbelievably small. I had a new respect for carrier pilots; fancy taking off from that knowing that you have to tank from a KC-135 then land back on the carrier at night. Not just one day, but every day. They were the boys!

Our original plan was to finish off with some low flying in Kuwait, but we had used up most of our fuel. Instead we flew around over the Gulf for a little longer. Ken gave us a firework display with his flares. The flares were coming up to the end of their life and he thought it would be better to use them than throw them away. It looked spectacular anyway. I wished that I'd given Platty my camera! We got back to Dhahran and after the swiftest of debriefs headed over the causeway for two much-needed days of complete relaxation in Bahrain.

Back from Bahrain, it was back to the old ways. We were flying reconnaissance trips again, as if nothing had happened, after a week in which there had been two airstrikes and a cruise-missile attack. I was beginning to wonder if I hadn't imagined the whole thing. It seemed as if a curtain had been drawn across the first three weeks of the year and we were starting again. Still, I was pleased to see that Platty's and my names were on the flying programme that day for an op sortie. This would be our first trip over Iraq without bombs on this year. We were to be Number Four again, another well-deserved relaxing 'back seat'. I was looking forward to flying again, especially as, with no pressure on me, I could enjoy it.

We were treated to another lovely day. I couldn't help wishing that the weather had been like this for the whole of the detachment. It certainly made a difference to everyone's frame of mind. The sunshine brought out the smiles and the can-do attitudes. It brought back the pleasure into flying, too. Taking off and landing in damp grey weather is bearable if in between you can punch up through the murk and into an azure-blue sky; if the whole sortie is spent working your way around the weather, it is very much more like work than pleasure. We seem to have had more than our fair share of dismal days since Christmas. And since most of that time had been spent on the ground, the effects had been more apparent. Platty and I were in cheerful mood as we sat at the back of the briefing with no responsibilities, except to follow our Tiald leader and keep an eye on him.

We found our Victor, just one this time, and I slipped in on the first prod. How much easier it was without the bombs on the aircraft. Then we pushed over the border. The landscape was instantly familiar, but it was difficult to reconcile the reality of bombs falling only a few days ago with the peaceful scenery below. The route took us up virtually overhead Tallil, where we had seen the Nighthawk's bombs detonating on our night raid. Tallil had been a strict no-go area for the last three weeks, but now we were free to roam as we wished in the overhead. Tallil's SAM 3 site no longer featured on the daily intelligence assessments and the engagement zone had been taken off Harry's map. And yet I had seen the US intelligence report after the first raid which stated that no damage had been inflicted there. Had it even existed, I wondered? I deviated round Tallil and dropped a wing so that Platty and I could both look down. I couldn't see any evidence of fresh damage, but I was looking at a massive area from a long way up, so it was not really surprising that I could not pick out any fine detail.

Then I remembered how concerned I had been before Christmas about our being complacent over Iraq. Just because we were not loaded with bombs anymore did not mean that the Iraqis might not want to surprise us with a missile or gunfire. I moved smartly away from Tallil and started to take my job more seriously again. Our first point of interest was the barracks at An Nasiriyah. I made sure that I stayed in immaculate formation and kept an alert eye on our man as he filmed the target. From there we flew along the Euphrates towards Qurna. Southern Iraq was enjoying a fine day; the marshes glistened in the afternoon sun and the visibility would have been perfect, but for two large fires burning south of the Euphrates, which served as a sharp reminder that a shooting war was still going on. We cruised past the plumes of smoke that spread out to form a haze underneath an inversion layer, and made for Ash Shanin at the head of the Shatt Al Arab. Here we were interested in a military engineering barracks. The Tiald navigator had some difficulty finding it, but I could see it clearly even from our height. I counted almost thirty Soviet-built GSP bridging vehicles as we circled overhead. I wished we had a decent pair of binoculars instead of the virtually useless hand-held video camera in the back seat. Our official task complete, we had one more job to do. The new DETCO had decreed that from now on every mission over Iraq was to include a practice Tiald attack. It was a good idea, to make sure that everyone on the detachment had experience flying the profiles that had been so new to us. At least if they were called on to do it for real, it would not be the first time they had flown an attack profile, as it had been for us.

I was sorely tempted by an invitation to visit the USS *Kitty Hawk*. I would have loved to see an aircraft carrier at close hand and talk to the aviators on board. Taff, Chris, Platty and Spiv jumped at the opportunity and were whisked off to the ship by helicopter. I decided to stay in Dhahran because the Chief of the Defence Staff was visiting on a morale-raising tour. I thought that as the leader of the RAF attack missions I should be there for his visit. Sir Peter was an impressive man, much taller than my own 6ft, and he spoke well in front of the assembled group of aircrew. He said that he was extremely pleased with our efforts over the past weeks and that view was also shared by the Prime Minister and the Cabinet. He added that he had also received kind words about us from the top at the Pentagon. I felt very proud to hear such comments and proud that I had led my team to spectacular success in front of the eyes of the world. We had completed all that we had been asked to do flawlessly. All this despite lack of equipment and training back home and the imposition of crews that threw strangers together. Spiv and Ken had made an absolutely invaluable contribution to the planning of the missions, but I remained convinced that when things started to go wrong in the air, as they had over An Najaf, an all-Crusader team could have done a better job sorting it out. In a service which gains such strength from the *esprit de corps* of flying squadrons, it seems foolish to deny that identity when it is most needed.

After Sir Peter had said his piece, Ken and I were introduced to him privately. I was rather hoping to be congratulated on the job well done, but instead we were treated to a short lecture on how well the Royal Navy was doing in Cambodia. The relevance of this information was rather lost on me. Perhaps he was telling me that 'England Expects Every Man to do His Duty' and there were no prizes for doing it. He was right of course – we had simply done the job we were paid to do. But even so, he could have said thank you. I was disappointed at the lack of recognition, especially as he had been so effusive in his public remarks. Also, we'd done so much for his credibility by our success. However, at least there was a word of thanks from Vaughan, who I'd cursed for meddling with the crew composition. That meant more to me than Sir Peter's ramblings.

When the boys returned full of enthusiasm from USS *Kitty Hawk*, I realized that I'd made a mistake not going. They had had the fascinating opportunity to see carrier

A Tiald-equipped Tornado seen from below.

operations at firsthand before being entertained at the Admiral's table as honoured guests. Seeing the carrier at work would have been much more interesting than staying in Dhahran as I had done; perhaps too, some kind words from the Admiral would have satisfied my egotistical sense of honour! I would also have liked the chance to meet some of the carrier crews we had been working with. I had always had a great respect for the US Navy fliers, and Platty, Taff and Chris all confirmed that the navy sense of professionalism, tinged with genuine modesty, was something that the USAF could learn from!

The next day was to be my last sortie in the Gulf. Keith had been hinting for some time that he would like to fly over Iraq. In the strictest of terms this was not possible, since it should only have been done by crews who were combat ready in theatre, or as part of their work up. Keith did not fit into either category, but I was sure that we could do it. I asked Platty if he would mind giving up his seat for Keith once again. He didn't mind at all: like me he was just looking forward to going back home. I then asked the new DETCO if he had any objections to Keith joining me 'sausage side' and was delighted when he said it sounded a great idea. Keith grasped the chance to escape from the ops desk and get airborne again. Obviously, I had not frightened him enough on our last sortie to Kuwait.

We were programmed at the back of the formation as shooter for the second Tiald aircraft. The route was a bit different from the well-worn path across the marshes: we were to visit two airfields in the western reaches, close to the border with Jordan. It was the first time I had seen either, which added to the interest factor.

We refuelled in good order and set off across the desert towards Wadi Al Khirr, another new airfield like Ghalaysan. In fact it looked identical. Presumably someone had a contract to build a job lot of airfields in this part of the desert. Further away and in a more remote area, we looked for Radif Al Khafi, a highway strip on the desert road. This was an interesting concept. I'd seen highway strips in Germany, stretches of dead straight autobahn with no grass in the central reservation. That was a sensible precaution in a crowded country to generate secret emergency landing strips in case the main airfields were put out of action. Here, where space was not a problem, it seemed strange not to build a purpose-built airfield, since the road strip would stand out anyway. I saw the Tiald aircraft start a slack turn overhead and projected where he would be in a couple of minutes. Meanwhile, Keith and I were far too absorbed with what was to be seen on the ground. As I had expected, the road was easily visible, but from our height I couldn't make out which bit of it was useable as a runway. What we could see was equipment and buildings in nearby compounds, which presumably contained the airfield infrastructure. I wondered if they also contained anti-aircraft gunners, squinting into the blueness to find us. We had a good look round, but we didn't want to hang about any longer than we had to. I rolled out in what I thought would be perfect battle formation heading for home, but when I looked across for the Tiald aircraft I could not find him at all. He had completely disappeared. Keith had lost him, too. It is unbelievable how quickly the sky can become empty; when it does it makes you realize how unlucky you'd have to be to collide with someone else. Having tried all the tricks of the trade, I thought we'd better come clean.

'Dundee three from four lost visual – range to golf.'

'Twenty miles,' was the reply.

'Roger,' I replied nonchalantly. Then to Keith more urgently, 'Christ they're fifteen miles ahead of us.'

How on earth could they have got that far away from us? Ever unflappable, Keith gave me a heading to fly and suggested that I had enough fuel to use the reheat for some time at least. With the throttles fully forward, and the wings fully back we hammered across the sky, reheats blazing at our tail. Keith started working out some minimum fuel figures for the route ahead. Provided we were above those figures, we could keep the 'burners' in. I could almost see the needles of the fuel gauges dropping as the reheats greedily emptied the tanks. Eventually we caught up with Keith's fuel figure and I cut the reheat. We started coasting back to a more sedate speed. By now our Tiald team were getting suspicious.

'Four, are you visual,' asked an inquisitive voice. Just then I caught a glimpse ahead.

'Affirm,' I answered truthfully. 'We're just a bit stretched at the moment. Jink starboard.' Our element leader did as we asked.

'Your three o'clock, about three miles,' I told him.

'Visual,' called the Tiald, engineering his turn to roll out with me back in formation and both of us headed the right way. Phew, got away with it!

More fun and games ensued. The AWACS called up and asked us to proceed to a position on the Saudi border to investigate something. It all got a bit confused at this stage because the AWACS controller wanted to talk to us on a secure radio that we did not have, and would not talk to us 'in clear'. We ended up milling around over the given position not really sure what we were supposed to be doing. The only thing I could see on the ground was what looked like a section of huge wide-bore pipe. Our element leader caught sight of a helicopter, but I never saw it and he lost contact very quickly. I wondered if the pipe had anything to do with it. The only way to get a close look was to swoop down beneath our base height. Should I break the rules to get the job done?

'Well, let's do it then,' Keith decided for me. And down we went, scorching past the pipe like a thunderbolt, then back up to the others. Unfortunately we were still none the wiser, but at least it probably frightened the helicopter pilot. With fuel now reaching the 'go home' level, we set off back towards Dhahran. It had been an entertaining end to my last trip.

More crews from the Goldstars had arrived in Dhahran, leaving Taff, Chris and me in a minority and giving Platty a crisis of loyalty. There were a few familiar faces among the newly arrived crews, amongst them Bertie, who had fired the missile with me three years beforehand. He was as friendly and scruffy as ever!

Meanwhile the political situation in the Middle East had calmed down. Saddam Hussein had withdrawn the errant SAM sites, which had provoked the three raids against Iraq, as a 'gesture of goodwill' towards the new US President. Things had calmed down noticeably and the sense of urgency of the past couple of weeks had all but evaporated. A sense of normality and routine returned to the detachment. I realized that Greg was not going to lead the team against Al Jarra. Rather selfishly I was quite pleased, as I knew I would have been disappointed to miss out. Having had the excitement of real action during our detachment, it was now an anti-climax to revert to the mundane 'marsh patrols'. It was a good job that there would be no more flying for any of us now. We were at the mercy of the RAF air movements people to get us home 'sometime'. In the meantime, we enjoyed a social life unfettered by the need to have to go to work.

AJ visited Dhahran again and I enjoyed a pleasant day with him and Jeremy. Their presence seemed an appropriate way to round off my stay in the Gulf. They had helped me find familiarity among the unfamiliar, and brought home to me the closeness of the RAF's flying community. Both had welcomed me there, now both were at hand to say farewell. Before I left the country, though, I found myself committing another heinous crime. I had already drunk a miniature bottle of whisky in this alcohol-free country thanks to Taff, now AJ and I perpetrated an even more serious offence. While Jeremy attended a medical appointment, AJ and I got in a car with his wife, Jane and drove into Khobar for a cup of tea. To do all this in the company of a woman who was neither married to nor related to either of us was a serious criminal offence. It really was time to get back to Germany!

Not surprisingly the RAF movers seemed unable to provide us with a trip home, so we decided to take matters into our own hands and approached the Americans instead. This scheming very nearly backfired on us. We found out the hard way that in the USAF people work in very small areas of responsibility. They are complete experts in their very specific field, but have absolutely no clue what goes on outside it. Nor do they have the faintest concept of who else might have a clue. If you ask exactly the right question phrased in exactly the right way, you can get a meaningful answer. If not, you get nowhere. It was like trying to operate an unfamiliar computer. At times like these, you realize how very different the two languages, American and English, really are. Somehow, after many frustrating hours of negotiations with various officials, each of whom gave a contradictory answer, we managed to get ourselves on a Starlifter transport aircraft going to Frankfurt. Even that had its moments. When we got to Frankfurt early in the morning, the engines stopped and then nothing happened. We waited and waited in expectant silence. After what seemed ages, the door opened and a USAF air-movements official peered in.

'Say, you guys, what are you all doing here,' he asked with genuine intrigue.

'We're the scheduled Starlifter that comes in here at this time every morning,' explained one of the crew.

'Gee, I never knew that.' We all suspected he had exactly the same conversation at the same time every morning.

seven

SNAPSHOTS FROM THE LAST CRUSADE

CJ was something of a legend. Rather older than the rest of us, he had flown his first tour on Gloster Javelins in Singapore before a distinguished career on the Buccaneer. He had then left the RAF for a while to run his own business, until the smell of Avtur [jet fuel] lured him back. A well-read and well-informed man of immaculate taste and the father of a large but close-knit family, CJ was the oracle who we all consulted for advice on how to navigate life's challenges. He was also the person who, every year, scrawled in the squadron operations diary page for the first of May 'Hurrah hurray, the First of May – outside shagging starts today!' One morning, soon after our return from Dhahran, he wandered casually into my office. There had been the usual flurry of postings from the squadron after we all got home and I was about to re-write the crew list.

'Ah, Napes,' muttered CJ in his avuncular manner, as he helped himself to the seat opposite my desk. 'I've been thinking about the crew list.' There was a pause. 'I think that you and I should fly together.'

And so it was that I found myself flying with CJ as the airborne spare for the massive flypast celebrating the 75th Anniversary of the RAF.

Apart from being ready to fill in if any of our Tornados dropped out through unserviceability our job was to act as 'whip' and check that the Brüggen formation; a 'Diamond Nine' was evenly spaced out. The best way to do this, we found, was to fly a big wingover across the tip of the formation, rolling inverted so that we could look up through our canopy and check what it looked like from above. It was great fun charging towards this ponderous great formation and then vaulting over it and rolling upside down as we arced over. We were certainly not disappointed to be

Myself and CJ at Gibraltar

relegated to the reserve bench for this event: more the opposite as we both rather cynically regarded the prospect of 170 aircraft in close proximity to each other as a recipe for a mid-air collision! After assembling at medium level over the North Sea, the drill was for the formation to descend to around a 1,000ft to fly in just south of Ipswich and then head north towards RAF Marham where, on the day, Her Majesty the Queen would admire the spectacle. The practice seemed to go well. The various other formations started out from different places but all came together just south of Marham to fly past in close order. Unfortunately, the great day itself was a day of low cloud and rain. We accompanied the 'Diamond Nine' as far as Ipswich, desperately hoping that no one would drop out, and then wished them luck as they disappeared into the dark-grey murk. Apparently over Marham the cloud was so low that by the time they had joined all the other formations, the rearmost aircraft were almost scraping their bellies on the grass!

It was a year later that we discovered that the risk of collision was not limited to those flying in the formation. We reprised our role as spare and whip for a more modest four-ship flypast at Brüggen, this time for the Air Officer Commanding's (AOC) annual inspection. Having got airborne from Brüggen, the formation flew a circular route which took it clockwise around the industrial urban sprawl of the Ruhrgebeit and back to Brüggen. The clear airspace to the east of Dortmund seemed like the ideal place for a quick practice and the fourship closed up into a tight box for us to inspect. Just as we had done previously, I charged towards the

This is the view that CJ and I were trying to get when we had a close encounter with a light aircraft. Actually this is an earlier formation, led by myself and Taff.

formation and pulled upwards, rolling briskly to keep them in view through the top of the canopy, whereupon, just as CJ muttered 'Hold on,' a small twin-engine aircraft flashed past my eyes. We had missed it by inches! We must have almost passed between its wing and tailplane, we were that close. When we landed we reported an 'Airmiss' but we never heard anything further: it seems that the pilot never saw us and never realized how close we had all come to calamity.

Flying with CJ was always good fun and we approached our sorties with the intention of enjoying ourselves as much as we could while we got the job done. CJ had seen, done and ticked off most things in life and he had nothing to prove as an aviator; for my part I felt that I had stepped off the steep learning curve of the previous years onto a plateau founded on a wealth of experience so that I, too, could take a more relaxed view. I was happy to let the 'thrusting' youngsters have a crack at leading formations and doing the hard work while CJ and I supervised from the back or acted as the bounce. We particularly enjoyed being the bounce as we could incorporate some constructive sightseeing between engagements, which added to our own enjoyment and interest.

With the German low-flying areas closed, the nearest easily-accessible area was in Northumbria to the north of Newcastle and this became our regular playground. One summer evening CJ had just disengaged from the first bounce.

'Did you see it,' enquired CJ, casually. I knew exactly what he meant. 'I think we ought to go back,' he added. So I turned around and retraced our steps.

When we had headed into the intercept I had caught a glimpse of huge expanse of lilac-coloured blossom as we sped past. It was a massive wall of rhododendrons in full bloom and that was what CJ wanted to see again! We spent the rest of the sortie dashing between the rhododendrons and the next engagement.

To save us spending long hours in transit between Brüggen and the LFAs in the UK, RAF Germany had established a turn-around facility at RAF Leuchars. Here, engineers loaned from Brüggen could refuel and re-arm us between sorties, so that instead of having two long transits with only about fifteen minutes of low-flying sandwiched between them, we could fly one transit followed by a good forty-five minutes or so of useful low-flying before landing at Leuchars. After a quick coffee and a sandwich we could then fly home using the reverse profile. Sometimes we took a couple of aircraft and simply decamped to Leuchars for a few days, frequenting the low-flying areas by day and the curry houses of St Andrews by night. An unexpected bonus in the revised arrangements for low-level flying was that we were allowed to do Operational Low Flying (OLF) regularly in order to maintain a decent level of skill. Previously OLF had only been authorized specifically for *Red Flag* exercises and the work-ups that preceded them. We would polish up our skills, then use them on the exercise – and then let them lapse. Now we were permitted to keep ourselves current, by flying an OLF sortie every so often. If we were starting from Leuchars, an early morning start could see us getting down to ultra-low level at the same time that most people were just getting out of bed.

After a short transit at medium level with the sun rising behind us, CJ and I drop to low level to the northwest of Inverness. We soon settle comfortably at 100ft, the Tornado cruising at an effortless 420kt. The plan is to fly southwards through the highlands and return to Leuchars. We are on our own today and we have the place to ourselves. I can't help but recall my first OLF sortie in Goose Bay six years previously. I have not had many moments of genuine fear in an aircraft, but that was one of them. It seemed downright dangerous to be flying so fast that close to the ground! So much of my brainpower was being used simply to ensure that I didn't hit the ground that I could only look straight ahead. And yet now, after several years' practice, I feel completely at home in the same environment. I move my head freely, looking all around us, pausing occasionally to drop my eyes into the cockpit to check the instruments.

A long, gentle left-hand turn takes us into a shallow glen and we streak low across its loch. Even from the air-conditioned cockpit, quiet but for a low background hum from the engines and faint whine of the electronics, we can feel the calm stillness of the early morning. The water is like a millpond, reflecting the pine forests on either side. Just ahead and to my right I am surprised to see a caravan parked on the sandy shore. The slight rise of the ground from the water puts it almost exactly at eye level. I watch it as we hurtle past, for in that instant a man opens the door and is looking straight at me, with barely 30yd between us. For a microsecond we look straight into each others eyes as he stares at me in jaw-dropped surprise: I suppose you don't expect to see a Tornado just outside your caravan door first thing in the morning! The caravan is soon far behind us and we continue rushing southwards, keeping to the low ground amongst the mountains.

In Goose Bay there is a feeling of isolation and loneliness in the low-flying areas because there is no trace of human activity: nor is there any evidence of animal life. The landscape there is completely untamed and devoid of civilization. Here it is different, for although the highlands are still virtually empty at this early hour, the carefully tended forests and fields, the occasional buildings and roads and bridges all remind and reassure us that we are amongst our own. And when I look across to the higher slopes as we breast a low ridgeline do I really see a stag standing there, magnificently silhouetted against the bright morning sky?

Even in the Cold War days before the continental low-flying system had closed for day flying, Northern England and the Scottish borders had always been our first choice for night flying. In the UK we could low fly at night freely using the TFR, whereas the continental night system had little tactical value and was very much a last resort. Thanks to the British climate much of the night flying was done under the usual thick cloud, but every now and then we would be blessed with a clear night. From the back of the formation, the sight of a fourship letting down to low level at night is a spectacular one.

I've taken my preferred slot as Number Four, and on this sortie I am crewed with The Iceman. The Iceman had struggled through his first few months on the squadron and I had thought him useless. But then we had both experienced something of a revelation. It was at Deci, during an air-to-air combat sortie that suddenly everything fell in place for him and in an instant he was transformed from useless baggage into a very competent navigator. I would not have believed that such an incredible step-change could happen, had I not seen it with my own eyes. I became a believer in The Iceman and now, from being once reluctant to share an aircraft with him, I'm quite pleased to be doing so.

We are at about 5,000ft in a gentle descent. The night is perfectly clear, the stars sparkle above us and the moon spreads its dull glow over the earth. Beneath us Harrogate and York merge into a broad fluorescent constellation that spreads around our left, extending on past Leeds and Bradford into the distance towards Manchester. We seem to float above it all as if on a magic carpet. With no way to judge distances, the whole scene beneath us seems three dimensional: it is like looking into the translucent entrails of some enormous somnolent beast. The orange streetlights of the dual carriageways trace its arteries, while the complex network of capillaries is picked out in the yellow lamps of smaller roads: And in between them all, the white glow emanating from houses and offices and shops hints at the skeleton that holds it all together. There is life moving through it: from all around, streams of headlights thread their way towards us, while red rear lights flow back in the opposite direction. Out to our right the lights fade away into a narrow thread of a tail, which stretches northwards until it meets the slumbering dragon of Teeside and Tyneside shining on the far horizon.

Ahead of us the dales lie hidden in a black emptiness. Against this dark background, the front pair show as two red beacons blinking under dull white tail lights. One is directly in front, while the other sits out to his right. Although they are five miles away from us, the clear air makes him seem much closer. Abeam of us on our right, our element leader is a cluster of red navigation lights.

Pookie and Pete seen at low level over the sea. (Crown Copyright/MoD)

The Iceman busies himself fixing the navigation kit and making sure that we are in good shape. I have selected the TFR and I quickly run through the checks to ensure that it is working as it should. On the screen just below the coaming, the E-scope paints its dull-green picture; in the HUD faint green symbols confirm that all is well. The track index is centred, so we're following the right route and the timing index is pegged in the centre at the planned 420kt. Looking through the HUD, just below the aircraft symbol, I can see the Number Two descending to low level. We are following his track exactly and we are precisely forty seconds behind him.

A night like this does not call for quite the same concentration on the systems inside the cockpit. I turn down the cockpit lighting, so that the instrument consoles around me glow in a dim red penumbra. Outside the pale moonlight paints the countryside with just enough of a ghostly lustre for me to monitor our progress by looking outside. Grey forests, shadowy hills and spectral farmsteads glide under us, punctuated only by the occasional flare of light from a car or a village. The HUD projects its symbols neatly in translucent jade onto the purse of the night sky ahead of us. The Tornado eases up over ridges and slides gently back into the valleys. And all the time the other three aircraft seem to stay in exactly the same positions. There is a powerful illusion that we are all perfectly stationary and that really the ground is rushing past us. It gives a tremendous impression that the four aircraft are locked together by some invisible bond. There is a feeling of pride, of belonging – and of invincibility, just as you feel when you march in step to a military band.

With most of the low-flying areas in Europe now closed to them, NATO's air forces had started looking further afield. The vast emptiness of Labrador held a particular attraction and even Goose Bay became almost appealing. In Goose itself, the Germans, the Dutch and ourselves started working together more, where previously we had done our own thing. Even the Canadians started sending their Hornets to Goose Bay to work with us. It was still a real challenge to find tactically realistic targets, but at least we could fill our boots with fighter affiliation. We were there in the early autumn, a season which was distinguishable from the summer by there being slightly more snow and slightly fewer black flies. Never a great fan of the place, I was even less than usually enthusiastic at the prospect of spending most of the detachment behind the duty authorizer's desk. So it really seemed that things had gone from very bad to even worse when one of our more zealous engineers discovered that there were cracks in many of the wing pylons, which carried the under-wing fuel tanks and electronic warfare pods. The aircraft were grounded while the engineers thought about the problem. Meanwhile the Boss thought about it too. By the next morning, after conferring with a few experts, he had decided that there was nothing in the books to stop us flying if we simply took the tanks and pods off – and that was what we would do. I was sceptical at first: it seemed very un-tactical. So I conferred with Stu, the squadron flying instructor who was our expert on the Release to Service document.

'Ah, yes,' he replied to my objections, with a twinkle in his eye, 'but look at this.' He held a page of the great tome open in front of him. I looked and then I realized why he was so enthusiastic about flying 'clean.' Instead of the usual 540kt peacetime limit, which took a bit of effort with the tanks and pods on, the speed limit would now be well over 650kt, something which a Tornado could easily sustain once freed from all the drag from tanks and pods. It was time to teach the Dutch something about tactics! The 'Cloggies' had become rather patronizing in their attitude towards us. They let us know that they thought that we were predictable 'easy meat.' This was certainly a bit of gamesmanship on their part, but it was hardly surprising really: to get the best training for ourselves we would design our routes to run through their CAPs – and do so at the 'standard' cruising speed of 420kt. Since they chose their CAP positions and they knew when we were coming, they held all the advantage.

That morning we planned as normal and met briefly with the Dutch to confirm the CAP positions and the Rules of Engagement. As far as they could see it was a perfectly predictable Tornado plan; all they would have to do was wait for us and shoot us!

Out in the northern low-flying area it's a good flying day. The visibility is almost infinite under a solid deck above at about 3,000ft, but the occasional outcrop of low scud on some of the hilltops and the relatively low cloud base will give the 'Cloggies' something to think about. Rick and I are Number Two, sitting as usual about 4km abeam our leader. The back pair are quite close behind, flying a very tight 'card' formation. At 600kt the pine trees and lakes of Labrador are motoring past at an impressive rate. We are cleared to fly as low as 100ft, but at this rather unaccustomed speed it seems more sensible to fly a bit higher. I feel comfortable at around 200ft and I am enjoying the ride. At this speed the Tornado takes on a new persona: with the wings slicked back all the way, it still slices

Tornado taxying out at Goose Bay. (Mike Lumb)

through any turbulence as if it wasn't there, but without any stores under the wings, the aircraft also feels very manoeuvrable. It is like flying a 'super-Hawk.' We check in on the tactical frequency and hear a very bored-sounding Dutchman reply, 'Roger.' I'm secretly impressed that anyone can pack such a mixture of smugness and contempt into just two syllables.

With no other radars in Labrador it is easy to see the direction of the F-16s on the RWR. Rick finds them on the radar, too, ten miles ahead and just left of the nose. 'Buster,' calls our leader and we push the speed up to 650kt – almost supersonic. A deep note like an organ pipe surrounds me as a shock wave forms on the forward canopy. I don't bother trying to follow the terrain too closely; I just make sure that I miss the ridges by 100ft, only dipping down to the valley floors if there is a long enough stretch before the next ridgeline. It is a gentle rolling switchback of a ride. The CAP is positioned over one of the larger lakes and in no time we're cresting the ridge, dropping down towards the surface. The calm waters are blue-grey reflecting the clouds above them, so for once they blend in nicely with our camouflage. We widen the formation to race along the shorelines on either side. I'm vaguely aware of a grey shape flashing past directly above me, but its soon apparent that the Dutch have rolled out heading south, expecting us to be five miles in front of them, when actually we're already well past them. I can almost imagine a large Dutch 'thinks bubble' as they try to work out how we can have completely disappeared from their radars!

We slow to a sedate 540kt for a simulated attack on some nebulous uninhabited islet, which today briefly becomes a 'simulated command bunker,' then its back southwards to see if the 'Cloggies' have got their act together yet. They haven't! Back at 650kt we bear down on them mercilessly. One minute they are setting up their CAP at a leisurely speed and height and the next they have been well and truly bounced. Lead and I take one each. I put the air-to-air sight onto mine and lock on the radar. The leader's target is foolish enough to try and turn, which just makes him a target for the back pair, too, while my Dutchman votes with his afterburner and disappears vertically upwards into the overcast. We blast past them and we're ten miles away before they can work out what has happened. Later, a rather subdued pair of F-16 pilots appears for the debriefing, 'Yezh – you did really got oozh there,' admits their leader, ruefully, before adding, 'boot of courshe, tomorrow is anudder day.' We laugh – we're all friends again, but I cannot help thinking as we head for a beer together that the balance of respect has been subtly restored.

The Crusaders were scheduled for another Exercise *Red Flag* in the New Year. It would be my fourth, but this time there was the added dimension that half of the sorties would be flown at night. Some of the tactical minds of the squadron were put to work trying to work out how we could evade fighters and ground threats at night while using the TFR to fly low, while others worked at how to solve the same conundrum if we flew at medium level. The problem was that if we could not see each other in the dark, we could not avoid each other while we manoeuvred. In our routine night flying everyone had their own tracks to fly and a strict 'timing contract' on the track, so that their formation mates knew exactly where they were. But what happened if one or all of the aircraft manoeuvred off their track and their timeline? How did everyone get back together without hitting each other?

We tried out various different tactics and techniques during our work-up at Leuchars. The resident fighter squadrons were only too pleased to help us experiment, so all of our sorties were flown against four Tornado F3s. Mostly we flew in fourships and we mixed low- and medium-level sorties, but there were just three of us when Davie and I flew our first work-up sortie. It was a busy couple of hours. We started in the daylight, climbing to medium level for affiliation with the fighters off the Northumbrian coast and a range detail at Cowden. Then we headed to a VC10 tanker, which was waiting for us to the east of Newcastle as dusk fell. After topping up to full once more, we dropped into low level for round two in the darkness. The weather was kind with fantastic visibility below scattered cloud. It was exhilarating flying, for it felt as if we were on the cutting edge of tactical flying. We fought our way through the ground threats at Spadeadam and onwards through the Scottish borders while the F3s harried us.

Later that evening, after a swift bite to eat in the Mess, Davie and I get airborne again as Number Two of a fourship. By now the clear skies of the afternoon have clouded over: an opaque sheet obscures the stars and the evening seems much darker now. The four of us have each taken off independently and we fly northwards alone, ploughing our way through the dense packs of cumulus that float across our route.

Then, just to the southwest of Aberdeen, the clouds part, leaving us in a black void. We start a lazy oval-shaped orbit to kill the time before we start the medium-level leg towards the fighter CAP. Below us the Grampians lie invisible in the darkness, while above us the stars begin to glow dimly through the cirrus. As my eyes become accustomed to the night, I notice a set of navigation lights just beneath us, tracing exactly the same path as us. It can only be our element leader. It occurs to me that rather than procedurally avoiding each other as we work our way onto our ingress tracks, it would be much easier if I join in tactical formation and simply follow the leader. Davie concurs. It looks pretty easy – all we have to do is descend 1,000ft and then close in the last 100yd. I'm supposed to get a read out from air-to-air Tacan and check the leader's speed before I join formation at night; but as we are already almost within touching distance, it doesn't seem necessary.

I call, 'Lead from two – joining in night Tac,' and receive a double click of the leader's transmit button in reply. I lock my eyes onto the leader's lights, push the nose gently down and trickle the throttles back to maintain the speed. We close in slowly. A quick check of the altimeter tells me that we are almost at the same altitude. I just need to slide in a bit closer. Then suddenly without warning the navigation lights expand rapidly outwards and I realize that we are closing very rapidly with the hard piece of metal in between them! I shove the stick hard forward and duck involuntarily. Davie manages a cry of 'Shee-yit,' as a large black Tornado-sized gap in the stars flashes across our canopy. A second later I look up and I can see that the aircraft is continuing its orbit a few hundred feet above us, its crew blissfully oblivious to the fact that we almost rammed them!

'Ready to join now, Lead,' I call ever so nonchalantly. 'Can you give us air-to-air tacan and confirm your speed.'

The Exercise *Red Flag* itself was as challenging and enjoyable as ever, but as one of the supervisors it was my lot to spend much of it on the ground. However, CJ and I still managed to fly three night sorties in the first week. After leading a low-level sortie we were Number Two for a medium-level sortie the following night.

CJ and I climb into our aircraft just before dusk. There are only two weather conditions in Las Vegas: either it is beautiful or it is awful. There is no in between. Today it is beautiful and we watch the sun setting majestically over Mount Charleston. The sky is deep indigo above us, fading seamlessly westwards through shades of cerulean to cornflower and then pale green to primrose. By the time it touches the horizon it is peach-pink and the dying sun washes the mountains to the east of us with a crimson hue. It is truly beautiful, but it fades away as we watch it, leaving us suddenly in darkness. Twenty minutes later we take off and soon find ourselves back in the twilight. The sun reluctantly reappears over the western horizon as we climb into the evening sky and then, as it dips back down again, CJ and I enjoy a replay of the stunning sunset painting the mountains around us. By the time the exercise starts it is pitch black once more. The route for our sortie is the now familiar push from 'Student Gap' towards our target at the western end of the area. Tonight we are tasked against some bunkers – but really they could be anything, for they will be invisible to me and only the radar offsets will appear as bright marks on CJ's radar scope.

We leave the marshalling area in a wide card formation, but you wouldn't know it: a plethora of stars and flashing lights surround us and there is no way to tell who is who, or even how far away the lights are. Each aircraft has its own sanctuary altitude which no one else can use – so at least we should not hit anyone! With so many aircraft in the package that means that we pretty much have to stay at our assigned level and manoeuvre if we need to in two dimensions. Pretty soon we need to manoeuvre. First we have to get past the fighters and then we run the gauntlet of ground threats. From being accustomed to scooting along at the very bottom of the engagement envelopes for most air-defence systems, we now find ourselves right in the heart of them. Apart from our own countermeasures, we are relying on a fleet of jamming aircraft and Wild Weasels to open a path through the defences. Even with their efforts, though, the RWR is alight with green strobes which reach out to ensnare us and our headsets are loud with almost continuous alarms. On the map, the route is a series neat straight lines between turning points, but reality is more of a continuous zig-zag, punctuated by 4-g turns. I need to use the burners to keep the speed up as CJ punches out chaff and flares. The sky is busy now with numerous lights racing past in different directions like shooting stars. Afterburner flames and incandescent streams of flares all make it seem like one hell of a fireworks display! The conditions are quite disorientating and I have to concentrate hard on the instruments to make sure that we don't drift out of our sanctuary height block. It is thirty minutes of mayhem: we have no idea where the rest of our formation is in relation to us, except that we all went through the target on our times in the right order. All that hard manoeuvring has split us to the four winds! It was so different from previous Exercise *Red Flag* sorties, but it was great fun and CJ and I are buoyed up on a high as we join the trail of aircraft jostling their way back towards the glittering lights of Las Vegas.

Meanwhile the RAF in Germany seemed to have lost its way: the sense of purpose provided by the Cold War had evaporated but even operations in the Gulf did not seem to replace it. The monthly no-notice exercises called in the small hours that had punctuated my first two tours were things of the past and even the dreaded Taceval turned out to be a pale shadow of its former 'glass-eating' self. We seemed to be wallowing, rudderless. Flying at Brüggen was also becoming pretty limited. With a sizeable number of the Wing's best aircraft away supporting the North American training programme and operations in the Gulf, there were not that many left in Germany for routine training. Added to this, a major cutback in spare parts was leaving us unable to repair broken aircraft. In fact this doubled the engineers' workload as the only way of sourcing spare parts was to take them from another broken aircraft. Soon we had a couple of HAS containing 'Christmas tree' aircraft that had been 'robbed' of most of their equipment to fix others, and engineers who were working all the hours God sent with little to show for their labours. It seemed a long way from the days of the Cold War when we seemed to have lots of aircraft to fly!

When we did manage to go aviating, though, there was often some good flying to be had. For example, Exercise *Mallet Blow* had evolved into Exercise *Brilliant Invader*, which followed most of its predecessor's structure, but introduced such

The Crusaders
at Brüggen – a
formal shot
of the whole
squadron. I'm on
the left-hand side
of the four flight
commanders
(third row back).

novelties as tanker support and weaponry at Luce Bay, near Stranraer. Somehow we managed to cobble together enough aircraft to mount fourships for the exercise and by using both the tanker and landing at Marham, we squeezed 1½ hours of high quality low-level flying into each sortie. It was just like the old days!

However, at the other end of the spectrum were sorties like a tedious medium-level night trip to Tain range near Inverness which I flew with Aussie Steve. After taking off from Brüggen we climbed up over Laarbruch and then set course northwestwards and plugged in the autopilot. Then we droned through the darkness in a straight line for the 1¾ hours to reach the range. Here, we had enough fuel for one bombing pass from medium level before it was time to turn back and retrace our steps on minimum fuel. Luckily the ejection seat was sufficiently uncomfortable to stop us nodding off on the long home leg.

Over the year since our return from Dhahran there had a big changeover of people on the squadron. I was particularly pleased to see three familiar faces joining us over the last twelve months: Loins my crew-mate from Goldstar days, Ken who had been with us in Dhahran and the ever-cheerful Cookie who joined me for a third tour together.

Most of our useful flying was at Deci or Goose Bay. Here at least we got priority for aircraft and spare parts, but I was beginning to grow tired of both places. The Americans had moved out of Deci, leaving it a quieter place, but Italian bureaucracy and petty rules seemed to hamstring our efforts on the ranges. At Goose Bay the chronic lack of realistic targets or a decent range detracted from the tactical value of each sortie and the limited facilities in the area made a week there seem like a much longer stretch!

But there was still some interesting flying at home. One dank grey morning, I came in to the squadron for the early met brief. It was a summer's day, but there was nothing summery about the weather at Brüggen that morning. Headless and I were down to be Number Two of a pair tasked for a strafe sortie against a splash target in the North Sea. At the appointed hour, the disembodied voice of the met man, emanating from his little round speaker next to the telephone, told us that the forecast everywhere else was pretty grim, too. I was ready to cancel the sortie and get the armourers to unload the guns, but Headless had other ideas: since he had written the flying programme he had a vested interest to make sure that it worked! He rang the captain of the splash boat at Great Yarmouth.

'He says the weather is fine there. I think that we should launch anyway,' reported Headless as he put the telephone down. 'Why not,' I thought, 'we might as well do something!' An hour or so later we take off from a rain-glistened runway and tighten into close formation on our leader's wing. We are soon enveloped in a damp grey fog as we climb towards Laarbruch for the transit across the Netherlands. It is hard work hanging on to the leader's wing through the thickening layers of cloud. Every few seconds the lead Tornado disappears from view completely, leaving just the faintest hint of the dim navigation light on his wingtip a few yards away in the mist, until he reappears a second or so later. Across Holland and out over the North Sea. We are still in cloud and I start to wonder if I should have let Headless persuade me: this looks like a classic busted flush.

Leading a pair recovering from Frasca Range back to Decimomannu.

Then, suddenly, the clouds part and we are in a large patch of blue sky. Behind us the continent is still shrouded and ahead we can see cloud building up inland, but a twenty-mile circle off the East Anglian coast is gin clear. Here, at least, it is a beautiful morning and the sun smiles on a tranquil dark-blue sea. Headless can't resist it: 'See I told you it would be OK,' he declares triumphantly, before delving into his radar scope to locate our target-towing launch. Between us we find it, motoring along twenty miles off Felixstowe. Once we have established contact, the launch streams the target, a deflector plate on a long cable, which produces a white plume of spray a few hundred yards behind the boat. The sun is shining here and still, clear air lies over a calm sea. We might be on a different planet from the rest of Europe! But the peace of the lovely morning in this small part of the North Sea is about to be shattered.

Our leader sets up an oval pattern, crossing the launch's track obliquely, so that we are aiming well behind the launch when we fire. As he pulls up from his first pass, I tip in and track the plume. It is moving at some 20kt, so I need to take some lead and I am also increasing the bank angle to keep the 'pipper' in the right place. Headless fires the radar ranger and I open up at longish range. The reason for opening early is that it will give me a chance to see the fall of shot. That is partly to help me check that I'm using enough deflection, but mainly because of a childish desire to see the shells explode! On land we use 'ball' ammunition, which is solid shot, like a large rifle bullet, but on the sea, because of the risk of ricochet, we get to fire high-explosive (HE) shells. Firing these is particularly gratifying because when they hit the sea they explode in a twinkling shower of flashes. So instead of pulling up as soon as I finish firing, I pause a little and see a pleasing little firework display just behind the splash. Pull up, turn downwind at 1,500ft and run through the checks.

As we are about to tip in again I notice that our pattern takes us right over a large passenger ferry, which is on a parallel course to the launch. The launch captain is the RSO and he is clearly not concerned, so I decide not to worry about it either. We tip in again and we are virtually overhead the ferry when we open fire. I cannot help wondering what the passengers are thinking as they have their breakfast: they see two Tornados circling noisily above them, taking it in turns to dive down and fire at the small vessel which is sailing along next to them! And so we spend the next fifteen minutes circling the North Sea ferry, swooping down and watching the twinkle of HE rounds churning up the sea.

One Friday morning a few months later Cookie and I set off to bounce a pair on a low-level evasion sortie over the Pennines.

'Tally – ten o'clock,' shouts Cookie. I see them at about the same time, a battle pair – two dark silhouettes followed by thin smoke trails, outlined as they crest the Pennines. Almost invisible to them against the backdrop of the valley, we are running in on the perfect intercept. What a good start to the bouncing, I think: a 'short, sharp shock' to sharpen up the lookout for the rest of the sortie! We have been limited to 'rear hemisphere' missiles today, so we have to get behind them to call a kill. No they haven't seen us; we arc upwards passing directly over the nearest Tornado, in a hard turn to engage the furthest one. The slight climb slows us just enough to let me squeeze the wings forward to get a better rate of turn. Once we are round the corner, I'll get the nose down, the wings sleeked back and with full reheat we will speed straight into the kill zone.

'Buster,' was the surprised shout from the pair. For some reason our Tornado is not turning at all well and they start to accelerate away from us. We seem to be wallowing in the sky in a way that makes the hairs on the back of my neck stand out. Instinctively, I roll us level and my left hand pushes the wing-sweep lever hard to check that it is fully forward. It is, but a quick glance outside tells me that the wings are not: they are still stuck at 45° sweep.

'Cookie, we've got a problem here, mate,' I inform him. With no way from the rear cockpit to tell the position of the wing-sweep lever, he had been unaware of this inconvenience.

'Hang on,' says Cookie, 'isn't this the jet that Mr Rusty was flying when he had the same snag a couple of weeks ago.' Then I remember that Mr Rusty had indeed had exactly the same problem in the exactly the same aircraft about two weeks previously. He was unlucky enough to discover the fault when he broke into the circuit at RAF Leeming at the end of a sortie on minimum fuel. Being a sharp bloke he had coped admirably well, but he had had to do some quick thinking. At least we have lots of fuel on board and therefore plenty of time to sort things out without rushing. Mindful that it is a Friday morning and that there is a squadron dining-in night that evening, my first idea is to fly back to Brüggen, but Cookie very sensibly vetoes that idea

'What if the wings aren't moving because there's a leak pissing hydraulic fluid everywhere,' he asks.

Cookie. (Mike Lumb)

'Good point,' I concede. And after a brief discussion we decide to dump our fuel to a sensible minimum and then land at Leeming. It is a beautiful day over the Yorkshire Dales and from 5,000ft we spend fifteen minutes admiring the scenery of rolling farmland and moorland as most of our fuel vents away in a long white plume behind us. Then it is time to land the beast. It starts off very easily: after nine years of QFI checks and instrument ratings I'm very used to flying swept-wing approaches. In fact I'm used to 67° swept-wing approaches, so a mere 45° of sweep seems like a walk in the park. The radar controller feeds us in for a PAR on Leeming's south-easterly runway and hands us over to 'Talkdown'. We complete our checks, drop the gear and I settle on the glideslope with the nose pointing upwards to maintain 15 units of Alpha. There is not much wind so the air is still; the Tornado sits obediently where it should, steadily following a 2½° degree glide-path towards the runway. The speed stabilizes at just over 200kt as we approach our decision height. There is no 'decision' to make today – we could see the runway from ten miles out – but 200ft marks the change from well-rehearsed script to hasty improvisation. For up until now every swept wing approach that I have flown has been a practice which has terminated by going around from decision height. I have never landed from such an approach, so I'm not sure what to expect.

There's just enough time to notice that instead of the runway being easily visible through windscreen, the touchdown point will be obscured by the raised nose, then the ground comes rushing up to meet us. Judging the landing flare is difficult and our first touchdown is a glancing skip. We settle onto the runway a few hundred yards further along and I push the nose wheel down, simultaneously rocking the throttles outboard to select reverse thrust, then shoving them all the way forwards. The first impression is the sheer speed at which everything is moving past: 200kt is frighteningly fast when your backside is only 8ft off the ground and you are rapidly running out of concrete! Reverse thrust does not seem to be making much difference and the end of the runway races towards us.

'Hook, hook,' shouts Cookie. I slam the throttles back and jab the circular green button on the left coaming. It glows brightly, telling me that the hook has dropped, but nothing else happens. Then there is a barely discernable bump as the main wheels cross the cable, followed by a smooth but firm deceleration which brings us to a halt on the 'piano keys' a few yards from the end of the runway. There is a quivering pause while the tension in the cable runs out and then it pulls us back slowly a few paces. I apply the parking brake and, with some relief, Cookie and I put the safety pins into our ejection seats. We open the canopy just as a fleet of fire engines, ambulances and duty vehicles screech to a halt around us, illuminating the scene with blue-flashing light.

We climb out of the aircraft, but the drama is not entirely over: we still have to get home for the dining-in night. RAF Leeming provides us with a staff car and a young Aircraftswoman driver, who is given the impossible-looking task of getting us to RAF Northolt, on the outskirts of London, in time for a flight in four hours' time. She rises to the challenge and after a journey which frequently reminds us of our dash down the runway that morning, she deposits us in front of an Andover, the personal transport of the Commander-in-Chief, British Army of the Rhine.

As we settle into the tatty seats behind the flight deck, the General saunters out from the well-appointed VIP cabin, to say hello. We thank him for waiting: 'Quite alright,' the great man assures us, 'it's given my wife time for a bit more shopping.' A few hours later Cookie and I, immaculately dressed in our mess kit, take our seats at the squadron dining-in night.

Summer approached and with it the end of my tour on the squadron – and the prospect of the dreaded ground tour. I began to realize that my flying days were numbered. It was strange to think that the focus and inspiration for my life to date was coming to an end, but equally I realized that it was probably best to quit while I was ahead. I had been to enough funerals of pilots who were much better than I could ever be, to understand the fickle nature of fate. I had also had enough close shaves of my own to understand that every time I flew, a ball with my name on it was bouncing around the roulette wheel of Fortune. In short, I had become very aware of my own mortality. I did not enjoy flying any less, but I became very fussy about what I did and with whom I flew. Other pilots crowded the operations desk to try to scrounge whatever flying they could, no matter its quality. I did not: I busied myself with the numerous tasks and duties that needed to be done on the ground unless there was a particularly high-quality sortie to fly. Perhaps it was a good time to finish.

I was never a great fan of the 'last trip' – it was frequently a recipe for disaster with too much temptation to bend the rules one last time. But I had enjoyed my own last trip at Chivenor and I wanted to mark my last ever Tornado flight with something suitable. My last week at work coincided with the visit of the Tornado Standardization Unit (TSU) and I was determined that I would not end my fast-jet flying with a check ride. I wanted to be able to savour it! After a rather tedious pairs sortie around Germany which ticked the standardization box in the morning, the Boss agreed that I could have an aircraft for one last flight in the afternoon. And of course there could be only one choice of navigator to accompany me: Cookie, my crewmate from my first tour who had followed me through Chivenor and back to the Crusaders.

We take off and climb up towards Laarbruch, before swinging westwards to follow the well-used path across the Netherlands to 'Mike Charlie Six'. It is a pleasant day with a benevolent sun brightening a powder-blue sky. We cross into UK airspace and let down to low level, dropping through a thin sheet of altostratus into the clear air beneath, to the coast near Southwold. England basks in a summer afternoon and once again I am struck – as I always am – by the utter beauty of our island. The lush greenness of England's landscape is unique and its lustrous tints are softer and more welcoming than the harsher shades of the Continent. We fly across East Anglia and I relish the sights that I will never see again from this perspective: the farms and villages of Suffolk, Norfolk and Cambridgeshire from just above rooftop height, tidy fields and neatly trimmed woodland in one continuous vista that is unimaginable from the ground.

Our first port of call is Sywell aerodrome, where I first learnt to fly long ago. I did not realize until I looked in my logbook at a much later date that this last Tornado flight is taking place exactly fourteen years and one day after my first solo flight at this airfield. I call Sywell tower and a slightly surprised voice clears me to join the circuit. At 360kt and 500ft I break into the circuit for the south-westerly runway. There is a light aircraft in the circuit, but I can't see him, so I keep us low as we rack round the turn onto downwind. We slide up to 800ft, some 200ft below the circuit height to keep us safe and then bend round onto a continuous base leg, wings forward, flaps and gear down. I wonder what any passers-by make of the sight of a Tornado preparing to land on a minute grass runway. Then power on, gear and flap up and by the time we streak past the tower we're back towards a more comfortable 420kt. Mentally, I salute the 17 year-old that I once was; who set himself to the task and never wavered, and made his dream a reality.

The grand tour continues as Cookie and I work our way northwards, through the rolling countryside of Northamptonshire and Leicestershire and onwards into the Peak District. We seem to have the place to ourselves and I am able to enjoy these selfishly private moments, soaking in the spectacular scenery. Cookie needs a height fix to update the navigation system, which is a good excuse to sweep across the Ladybower reservoir a bit higher but much, much faster than the 'Dambusters' managed in their practice runs fifty years previously. The Derwent valley leads us up onto the moors between Manchester and Huddersfield. We are squeezed between the no-fly areas of the urban north on either side of us and pressed in the small gap between the top of the moors and the base of the airways above us. It is not a route one would choose on a cloudy day, but today we are blessed. The high moor at Saddleworth marks the edge of the low-flying area to the west, while the tall mast at Dewsbury keeps us clear of the South Yorkshire conurbation on our right. We're passing through the land of dark satanic mills, but on a summer's afternoon the area still has a stark beauty of its own. Although we are only twenty minute's flying time away from Southwold, the scenery is dramatically different. On the far side, the low-flying area and the vertical airspace open out: time for a breather.

By now we are getting low on fuel: we have enough to get home at high level, but we have also booked a tanker, so Cookie and I pull up and head for the tow-line beyond Newcastle. Ten minutes later we find a VC10 flying majestic orbits amidst a swarm of Tornado F3s. With its high tailplane and swept wings, the VC10 is a truly beautiful aircraft. We wait patiently, watching our own fuel gauges slowly dipping towards the point where we will have to give up and go home. Then we are summoned. I push past the F3s and take up station behind one of the wing hoses. A green light glows on the tanker's wing pod and I ease in and fill to full. Tanking, which seemed so impossibly hard when I first tried it just a couple of years ago, has become second nature. Once full, we take our leave of the tanker and dive back towards low level, resuming our route near Skipton. Here among the Yorkshire Dales we visit some of the must-see sights for the last time. We dart past Settle and into Ribblesdale, the hillsides high around us and then we swing round the top of the valley to be greeted by the magnificent arches of the Ribblehead viaduct marching splendidly across the moorland ahead of us. It is an incredible privilege to see it from a 100ft or so above the tracks, travelling effortlessly at four or five times the speed of a locomotive. From one mode of earthbound transport to the next: we pick up the M6 motorway north of Lancaster and follow it northwards into the Lune Valley where the roadway climbs above the valley floor towards Shap. Keeping at 250ft above the river, we are offset just 100yd from the road exactly at eye-level to the vehicles coming towards us. It is a truly exhilarating experience to see the lorry drivers flashing their headlights at us as we sweep past them, banking steeply to match the curve of the valley. And as no final sortie would be complete without a visit to the Lake District we cut across to Haweswater, darting over the surface, following the line of the shore then reversing northwards into the main valley past Thirlmere and Keswick. Once again we enjoy spectacular scenery, which is at once both beautiful and quintessentially British.

Past Carlisle, I pick out the small chapel at Kirkandrews-on-Esk where, following my own footsteps, my son will be christened in just a few weeks. Now we are crossing the familiar border country, where I have spent so many hours flying over the last ten years. Its hills, glens, forests and moorlands have become familiar landmarks and I'm glad for the opportunity to wish them farewell from the cockpit of a fast jet.

From the border country we shoot through the 'Cumbernauld gap' between Glasgow and Edinburgh and soon we are winding our way between the mountains of the southern highlands. We fly a last leg along Loch Lomond and finish our low-level route on the west coast near Lochgilphead before climbing up for the long high-level transit home. It seems incredible to have flown almost the entire length of the country in just an hour and to have experienced such a richly varied landscape: it takes the privileged position of the cockpit of a fast jet to see it all firsthand and at close quarters in just one sitting. I realize that the last ten years has given me a fantastic appreciation of the geography of our country and an intimate knowledge of its terrain. I'm sure that it is an appreciation and knowledge that I share with every member of that elite 'Few' who have flown fast-jet aircraft in the RAF. We have all been granted a unique view of the facets of our beautiful island: its richly verdant hillsides and woodlands, its emerald-green pastures framed by hedgerows or stone walls and the hamlets and villages and towns and cities that nestle in its Lincoln-green folds. We have enjoyed a close intimacy with the landscape, from which comes the strong emotional bond with our homeland. And that, perhaps, is what inspired us all when we stood firm on the frontline of the Cold War.

We touch down at Brüggen 3½ hours after we took off. This time there are no crowds of aircrew waiting to greet me with the traditional bottle of 'fizz'; perhaps I had intentionally neglected to tell them that we had booked a tanker, so they were expecting us an hour ago. Now they have all gone home, leaving just the slightly irritated looking Boss, who would rather be in the bar. But I don't mind missing the crowds. It is an intensely personal moment when I climb out of a Tornado cockpit for the last time. I stand briefly at the foot of the aircraft ladder with Cookie and it seems entirely appropriate, as I am about to take my leave from a way of life that has forged the strongest friendships, that I should share this moment with one of my closest companions on the journey through the last ten years.

Glossary

ACMI   Air Combat Manoeuvring Instrumentation range – a range with telemetry pods that can be used to track aircraft throughout a flight so that the sortie can be fully debriefed afterwards.

ATC   Air Traffic Control

AWACS   Airborne Warning and Control System – a Boeing 707 with a large radar dish on the roof, used to direct tactical aircraft around the skies.

Bounce   An aircraft simulating being a fighter trying to intercept ground-attack aircraft.

Buster   Code word meaning 'full power.'

CAP   Combat Air Patrol – a race-track pattern flown by fighter aircraft while defending a particular area.

CFS   Central Flying School – where all RAF flying instructors are taught their trade.

Chop ride   A 'last chance' sortie during flying training: if you pass it you carry on, if you fail it you are 'chopped' from the course.

DH   Direct Hit – not a very common occurrence, but a particularly gratifying one when it happens!

EW   Electronic Warfare, a dark world of radio waves and radar beams.

Fox Two   Code word to warn that a heat-seeking missile has been fired.

FRA   First Run Attack – it was usual to carry out a 'dry pass' (i.e. a pass on which no weapons were dropped) at the start of a training detail on the range, but sometimes it was possible to carry out a FRA on the first run.

Frag   The part of the air-tasking order which gives detailed instructions to each formation of aircraft.

g   The force of gravity. 2g (i.e. twice the force of gravity) is needed to keep level in a 60° turn. In the Hawk we flew all formation turns at 4g.

Gizza   An aircrew term for any aide-memoir or bespoke planning equipment.

GLO   Ground Liaison Officer – an army officer on the squadron strength to liaise with army units and provide expertise on the military situation on the ground. It is also nearly an anagram of golf, which explains why people often said that there was no F-in GLO.

HAS — Hardened Aircraft Shelter – a concrete (allegedly) bomb-proof hangar for aircraft.

Havequick (HQ) — A secure radio network retro-fitted to the Tornado in a very awkward position in the front cockpit which could be a nightmare to programme.

HUD — Head Up Display – the prime flying instrument on the Tornado, the HUD was a collimating glass immediately in front of the windscreen, on which was projected most of the information needed to fly the aircraft and aim weapons.

IP — Initial Point – the starting point for a target run. The idea was to start at something big and unique (i.e. easily found) and then map read along a pre-planned track to find the (usually smaller and indistinct) target.

ILS — Instrument Landing System – equipment that allowed a crew to fly a precision approach onto a runway without any external input from ATC.

IMC — Instrument Meteorological Conditions – in other words 'inside a cloud.'

Kneecap — A manoeuvre to turn away from a pulsed-doppler radar to stop any forward motion towards the radar. A pulsed-doppler radar measures relative speed, so with no relative closing speed you disappear from the screen. At least that is the theory.

LFA — Low Flying Area – usually a geographic area in which crews could fly down to 250ft. There were eight LFAs in Cold War Germany as well as the Ardennes area of Belgium. The rest of the continental low-flying system was restricted to 500ft. In the UK we could low fly in most areas at 250ft and in some areas, with special authorization; we could go as low as 100ft.

Loft — (More accurately called Toss, but Loft was the Tornado term), a weapon delivery profile which involved lobbing the bomb off while pulling up. The bomb would fly forward for three to four miles. The Tornado weapon aiming system made this a surprisingly accurate method of attack.

MPC — Missile Practice Camp – an opportunity to fire nearly life-expired air-to-air missiles on the range in Cardigan Bay.

NATO — North Atlantic Treaty Organization.

Nav kit — Navigational equipment on board an aircraft.

Offset — If a target was not radar significant it was often possible to find it by locating something that was significant (the 'offset') and telling the weapon-aiming computer the exact range and bearing between offset and the target.

OLF — Operational Low Flying – flying down to within 100ft of the surface.

PAR   Precision Approach Radar – a running commentary (talk down) to the pilot enabling an approach to be flown accurately to a runway in poor weather conditions.

Playtex   To take off in close formation and widen-out almost immediately into battle formation. A term coined from the Playtex bra which claimed to 'lift and separate'.

QRA   Quick Reaction Alert – in Cold War days nuclear-armed Tornados were kept at fifteen minutes' readiness to launch from QRA.

QFI   Qualified Flying Instructor – a graduate of the CFS: only QFIs are allowed to teach flying skills in the RAF.

QWI   Qualified Weapons Instructor – QWIs were regarded as the top of the professional tree on a fast-jet squadron and were reputed to 'eat glass' and 'breathe fire'.

Rad Alt   Radar Altimeter – a device for measuring actual height above terrain very accurately (a barometric altimeter is less accurate and usually gives height above sea level).

SAM   Surface-to-Air Missile – Soviet systems were given numerical designations (e.g. SAM 3, SAM 6).

SAP   Simulated Attack Profile – at TWU this referred to the entire ground-attack sortie, but on front-line squadrons it simply referred to the part of the sortie between the IP and the target.

TFR   Terrain Following Radar – the heart of the Tornado night/poor weather low-level capability, the TFR looked ahead of the aircraft and gave instructions to the autopilot so that it could fly at a selectable height above the ground.

TACAN   Tactical Air Navigation – a radio-navigation beacon used by military aircraft.

Taceval   Tactical Evaluation, a particularly rigorous exercise and inspection of a flying station by NATO staff, designed to test every aspect of its ability to fight a war.

Tiald   Thermal Imaging and Laser Designator pod, which enabled the Tornado to drop laser-guided weapons.

Triple-A   Anti-Aircraft Artillery, formerly known as 'Archie' during the First World War and 'Ack-Ack' or 'Flak' during the Second World War.

TWCU   The Tornado Weapons Conversion Unit – a particularly harsh school which specialized in humiliating students as they learnt how to operate the Tornado.

TWU   The Tactical Weapons Unit – where students learnt the rudiments of tactical flying and weaponry.

Weedosphere   That part of the sky between 100ft and 300ft above the surface. It was the part of the sky that the Tornado loved best.

Wifferdingle   An aerobatic or air-combat manoeuvre so unbelievable that it defies accurate description.